# Rethinking the Presidency

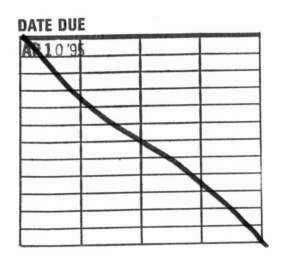

# Rethinking the Presidency

Thomas E. Cronin, editor

*Colorado College*

**Little, Brown and Company**

*Boston     Toronto*

Library of Congress Catalog Card No. 81-86023

ISBN 0-316-16151-9

9  8  7  6  5  4

ALP

Published simultaneously in Canada
by Little, Brown & Company (Canada) Limited

Printed in the United States of America

# Preface

The presidency has grown and expanded as the nation has grown and expanded. There is a certain plasticity in our basic conception of the presidency and its powers. Thus, whenever the country is in trouble we gradually expand a president's authority, allowing him more options and more flexibility to provide leadership. But when wars or depressions end and business returns to normal we rein in our presidents and worry about whether the office has become imperial. At such times we revitalize the checks and balances, sometimes even inventing new restraints.

The exact dimensions of presidential power are largely the consequence of an incumbent's character and energy, combined with the overarching societal needs of the day. About every third president has been a power maximizer, enlarging the office so he can better provide ecomonic, military, or other kinds of leadership. Plainly, an office that was only vaguely defined in the beginning has enlarged with accumulated traditions and with the cumulative legacy of brilliant achievements.

American presidents have extended the limits of executive powers throughout our history, but especially during the past fifty years. Now the presidency is the center of several major intellectual debates. Some argue that it is not powerful enough; some contend that our nominating process is inadequate; some warn us of the pitfalls of certain character types; others question the purposes or ends of presidential power; still others are puzzled about the roles presidents must now play in shaping national policies and responding to public opinion. These debates are treated in this book.

Rethinking the American presidency as we approach its two-hundredth anniversary is timely and necessary. The presidency has served us reasonably well — sometimes exceedingly well. Still, the presidency and presidential leadership are more fragile than most of us like to admit. We need to ask basic questions about how the presidency is doing and whether we could improve its effectiveness.

My own views on some of these topics are expressed in my book entitled *The State of the Presidency* (Little, Brown and Company, 1980). But the presidency is a much larger topic than can be covered in any one book, or even in a few books. This volume is designed around questions that were not adequately treated in the earlier book. I have reached out, wherever possible, and asked some of the brightest younger scholars in political science to treat major questions about the presidency. Most of the essays are fresh, current analyses. About half were expressly commissioned for this volume. I do not agree, nor will you, with all the views expressed in this book — but no one will read through it without gaining new insights and valuable perspectives that can help in reappraising this most central of American political institutions.

T. E. C.

# Contents

I. *Presidential Elections*                                          *1*

1. **The 1980 Presidential Election and Its Meaning**                **3**
   *Gerald M. Pomper*

2. **Selecting and Electing Presidents: 1936–1980**                 **29**
   *William R. Keech*


II. *Rethinking the Presidential Nominating Process*                *45*

3. **Reforming the Electoral Reforms**                              **47**
   *Cyrus R. Vance*

4. **Two Cheers for the National Primary**                          **55**
   *Michael Nelson*

5. **Two Cheers for the Presidential Primaries**                    **65**
   *William J. Crotty*


III. *Rethinking Presidential Character*                            *73*

6. **James David Barber and the Psychological Presidency**          **75**
   *Michael Nelson*

7. **On Presidential Character and Abraham Lincoln**                **87**
   *Jeffrey Tulis*

8. **The Eisenhower Revival**                                       **103**
   *Stephen E. Ambrose*

IV. *Presidential Power*      *115*

  9. **The President's Constitutional Position**      **117**

    *C. Herman Pritchett*

 10. **Presidential Power and the Crisis of Modernization**      **139**
    *Alan Wolfe*

V. *Rethinking the Separation of Powers Doctrine*      *153*

 11. **The Doctrine of Separated Powers**      **155**
    *Louis Fisher*

 12. **To Form a Government — On the Defects of Separation of Powers**      **162**
    *Lloyd N. Cutler*

 13. **In Defense of Separation of Powers I**      **176**
    *Thomas E. Mann and Norman J. Ornstein*

 14. **In Defense of Separation of Powers II**      **179**
    *James Q. Wilson*

VI. *Presidents and the Public*      *183*

 15. **Great Expectations: What People Want from Presidents**      **185**
    *Stephen J. Wayne*

 16. **Presidential Manipulation of Public Opinion**      **200**
    *George C. Edwards III*

 17. **Monopolizing the Public Space: The President as a Problem for Democratic Politics**      **218**
    *Bruce Miroff*

 18. **The Rise of the Rhetorical Presidency**      **233**
    *James Ceaser, Glen E. Thurow, Jeffrey Tulis, and Joseph M. Bessette*

VII. *Presidents as Politicians*                                      *253*

19. **Presidential Leadership of Congress**                           **255**
    *Reo M. Christenson*

20. **The President as Coalition Builder: Reagan's First Year**       **271**
    *Hedrick Smith*

21. **Presidents and Political Parties**                              **287**
    *Thomas E. Cronin*


VIII. *Rethinking the Presidential Advisory System*                  *303*

22. **Revitalizing the Executive Office of the President**            **305**
    *Don K. Price and Rocco C. Siciliano*

23. **Rethinking the Vice-Presidency**                               **324**
    *Thomas E. Cronin*


IX. *Presidents as Policymakers*                                     *349*

24. **Presidents as Domestic Policymakers**                          **351**
    *Paul C. Light*

25. **Presidents as Budget Policymakers**                            **371**
    *Donald H. Haider*

26. **Presidents as National Security Policymakers**                 **388**
    *James K. Oliver*

*Rethinking the Presidency*

# Presidential Elections

# I

**1. The 1980 Presidential Election and Its Meaning**

*Gerald M. Pomper*

**2. Selecting and Electing Presidents: 1936–1980**

*William R. Keech*

# 1. The 1980 Presidential Election and Its Meaning

## Gerald M. Pomper

The results were clear: Ronald Reagan was decisively elected president on November 4, 1980. Jimmy Carter was trounced in his attempt to win reelection. John Anderson and other independent candidates had little effect on the outcome of the election.

The meaning of the results was less obvious. Did Reagan's success constitute a personal mandate for the former California governor or a repudiation of the incumbent Democratic President? Did the election portend an enduring shift in American voting patterns or a more simple intention to "throw the rascals out"? Would the Republican party now be able to construct a new majority coalition, or would the trend toward party deterioration, evident in the presidential nominations, continue? The presidential election outcome was, I believe, predominantly a negative reaction to the leadership of Jimmy Carter, which yet provides an opportunity for building a Republican majority.

## The Results

### Geography

The Reagan victory was undoubted. He won 44 of the 50 states (he lost the District of Columbia), amassing 489 electoral votes of the national total of 538. He led in every area of the country including liberal Massachusetts, economically depressed Michigan, booming Texas, traditionalist Utah, and contemporary California. Of the 86 million Americans who cast their ballots, the Republican candidate won a clear majority, and he gained an even larger share of the vote for the two major parties, 55.3 percent.[1]

Still more impressive were the dimensions of Jimmy Carter's defeat. Only twice in the twentieth century had an elected incumbent president been denied a second term — William Howard Taft when his party split in 1912 and Herbert Hoover during the Great Depression in 1932. Carter rewrote this record. He received the lowest percentage of the popular vote of any incumbent Democratic president in American history and gained fewer electoral votes than any sitting chief executive except Taft, who lost most of his party to Theodore Roosevelt.

*Gerald Pomper teaches political science at Rutgers University and is the author of* Elections in America *and* Voter's Choice *and editor of* Party Renewal in America *and* The Election of 1980.

A striking feature of the electoral map of 1980 was the relative consistency of results across the country (Figure 1). Not only did Ronald Reagan win, but he won with fairly similar margins almost everywhere. A majority of states fell to the Californian by percentages that were within five points of his national average. The exceptions were essentially those states salvaged by Carter and those that gave three-fifths or more of their vote to Reagan. The similarity of results is an indication that the contest was determined by forces moving all of the nation in a Republican direction, not by influences that had contrary effects among different regions or voting groups.

In many ways, the 1980 electoral map is like that of the past presidential election (Table 1). The areas of relative Democratic and Republican strength are similar — but with the crucial difference that the absolute Republican strength was much higher, that of the Democrats lower. Thus, in 1980, the Democrats ran best in Georgia and received their lowest percentage in Utah, while Oregon stood in the exact middle of the ranking of the states by Democratic vote. In 1976, Georgia also had led the party to victory, Utah had provided the least support, and Oregon had stood 27th in the ranking of 51 areas (including the District of Columbia).[2]

Geographical vote patterns of this kind usually reflect a national response to current events, bringing victory to the incumbent party in a "maintaining" election (when voters are satisfied) or that party's defeat in a "deviating" election (when voters are discontented).[3] More basic changes in voter loyalties occur in "realigning" contests, when party loyalties shift to new dimensions. On a geographical basis, the overall 1980 results do not evidence fundamental shifts. The results show more variation than in 1976, however, possibly indicating some realignment.[4] While almost every state increased its Republican vote over the four years, this trend was particularly strong in the Mountain and Plains states. These areas, Republican in earlier elections, brought in astonishing margins for Reagan and may now have become virtually one-party states in presidential elections.

*Demography*

Divisions of the vote among groups of voters provide additional clues, summarized in Table 2. Since the 1930s, the Democrats had comprised a majority coalition based largely on social class rather than geography. The most significant elements were minority groups including blacks, Catholics, and Jews; those of lower income and in working-class occupations; residents of the larger cities; members of labor unions; and southerners, particularly those of lower status and in rural areas. The loyalties of these voters had been forged before and during the Great Depression and had been solidified by the social welfare programs of the New Deal. Even decades after these events, their political effects could still be seen in the common characterization of the Democrats as "the party of the people" and in the Democratic loyalty of 40 percent of the electorate. By comparison, only 23 percent of the voters were Republicans, and 37 percent were self-declared Independents.[5]

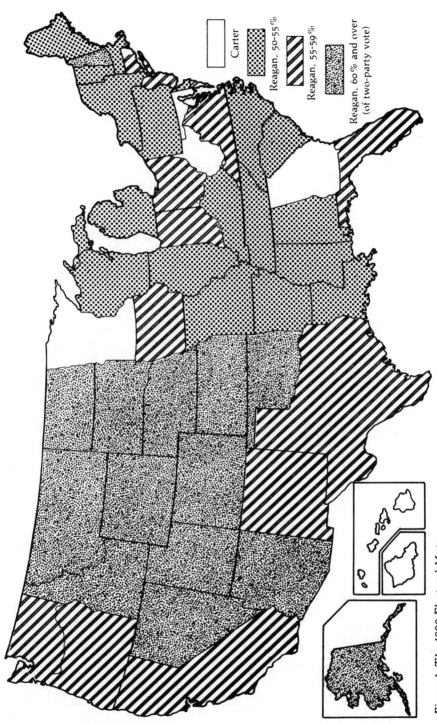

Figure 1. The 1980 Electoral Map

Table 1. The 1980 Presidential Vote

| State | Electoral vote | | Popular vote | | Percentage of three-candidate vote | | | Percentage of two-party vote | |
|---|---|---|---|---|---|---|---|---|---|
| | Carter | Reagan | Carter | Reagan | Carter | Reagan | Anderson | Carter | Reagan |
| Alabama | | 9 | 636,730 | 654,192 | 48.7 | 50.0 | 1.3 | 49.3 | 50.7 |
| Alaska* | | 3 | 41,842 | 86,112 | 26.5 | 54.7 | 18.8 | 32.7 | 67.3 |
| Arizona | | 6 | 246,843 | 529,688 | 28.9 | 62.1 | 9.0 | 31.8 | 68.2 |
| Arkansas | | 6 | 398,041 | 403,164 | 48.3 | 49.0 | 2.7 | 49.7 | 50.3 |
| California | | 45 | 3,083,652 | 4,524,835 | 36.9 | 54.2 | 8.9 | 40.5 | 59.5 |
| Colorado | | 7 | 368,009 | 652,264 | 32.0 | 56.7 | 11.3 | 36.1 | 63.9 |
| Connecticut | | 8 | 541,732 | 677,210 | 38.9 | 48.7 | 12.4 | 44.4 | 55.6 |
| Delaware | | 3 | 105,754 | 111,252 | 45.3 | 47.7 | 7.0 | 48.7 | 51.3 |
| District of Columbia | 3 | | 130,231 | 23,313 | 76.8 | 13.7 | 9.5 | 84.8 | 15.2 |
| Florida | | 17 | 1,419,475 | 2,046,951 | 38.9 | 55.9 | 5.2 | 41.0 | 59.0 |
| Georgia | 12 | | 890,955 | 654,168 | 56.4 | 41.4 | 2.2 | 57.6 | 42.4 |
| Hawaii | 4 | | 135,879 | 130,112 | 45.6 | 43.6 | 10.8 | 51.1 | 48.9 |
| Idaho | | 4 | 110,192 | 290,699 | 25.8 | 67.9 | 6.3 | 27.5 | 72.5 |
| Illinois | | 26 | 1,981,413 | 2,358,094 | 42.2 | 50.4 | 7.4 | 45.6 | 54.4 |
| Indiana | | 13 | 844,197 | 1,255,656 | 38.1 | 56.8 | 5.1 | 40.2 | 59.8 |
| Iowa | | 8 | 508,672 | 676,026 | 39.1 | 52.0 | 8.9 | 42.9 | 57.1 |
| Kansas | | 7 | 326,150 | 566,812 | 34.0 | 58.9 | 7.1 | 36.6 | 63.4 |
| Kentucky | | 9 | 617,417 | 635,274 | 48.1 | 49.5 | 2.4 | 49.3 | 50.7 |
| Louisiana | | 10 | 708,453 | 792,853 | 46.4 | 51.9 | 1.7 | 47.2 | 52.8 |
| Maine | | 4 | 220,974 | 238,522 | 43.1 | 46.5 | 10.4 | 48.1 | 51.9 |
| Maryland | 10 | | 726,161 | 680,606 | 47.5 | 44.6 | 7.9 | 51.6 | 48.4 |
| Massachusetts | | 14 | 1,053,800 | 1,056,223 | 42.2 | 42.4 | 15.4 | 49.9 | 50.1 |
| Michigan | | 21 | 1,661,532 | 1,915,225 | 43.2 | 49.7 | 7.1 | 46.4 | 53.6 |
| Minnesota | 10 | | 954,173 | 873,268 | 47.6 | 43.7 | 8.7 | 52.2 | 47.8 |
| Mississippi | | 7 | 429,281 | 441,089 | 48.6 | 50.0 | 1.4 | 49.3 | 50.7 |
| Missouri | | 12 | 931,182 | 1,074,181 | 44.7 | 51.6 | 3.7 | 46.4 | 53.6 |
| Montana | | 4 | 118,032 | 206,814 | 33.3 | 58.4 | 8.3 | 36.3 | 63.7 |

| State | Electoral vote | | Popular vote | | Percentage of three-candidate vote | | | Percentage of two-party vote | |
|---|---|---|---|---|---|---|---|---|---|
| | Carter | Reagan | Carter | Reagan | Carter | Reagan | Anderson | Carter | Reagan |
| Nebraska | | 5 | 166,424 | 419,214 | 26.4 | 66.5 | 7.1 | 28.4 | 71.6 |
| Nevada | | 3 | 66,666 | 155,017 | 27.9 | 64.8 | 7.3 | 30.1 | 69.9 |
| New Hampshire | | 4 | 108,864 | 221,705 | 28.7 | 58.3 | 13.0 | 33.0 | 67.0 |
| New Jersey | | 17 | 1,147,364 | 1,546,557 | 39.2 | 52.8 | 8.0 | 42.6 | 57.4 |
| New Mexico | | 4 | 167,826 | 250,779 | 37.4 | 56.0 | 6.6 | 40.1 | 59.9 |
| New York | | 41 | 2,728,372 | 2,893,831 | 44.8 | 47.6 | 7.6 | 48.5 | 51.5 |
| North Carolina | | 13 | 875,635 | 915,018 | 47.5 | 49.6 | 2.9 | 48.9 | 51.1 |
| North Dakota | | 3 | 79,189 | 193,695 | 26.8 | 65.3 | 7.9 | 29.1 | 70.9 |
| Ohio | | 25 | 1,752,414 | 2,206,545 | 41.6 | 52.4 | 6.0 | 44.3 | 55.7 |
| Oklahoma | | 8 | 402,026 | 695,570 | 35.4 | 61.2 | 3.4 | 36.6 | 63.4 |
| Oregon | | 6 | 456,890 | 571,044 | 40.1 | 50.1 | 9.8 | 44.5 | 55.5 |
| Pennsylvania | | 27 | 1,937,540 | 2,261,872 | 43.1 | 50.4 | 6.5 | 46.1 | 53.9 |
| Rhode Island | 4 | | 198,342 | 154,793 | 48.0 | 37.5 | 14.5 | 56.2 | 43.8 |
| South Carolina | | 8 | 430,385 | 441,841 | 48.6 | 49.8 | 1.6 | 49.4 | 50.6 |
| South Dakota | | 4 | 103,855 | 198,343 | 32.1 | 61.3 | 6.6 | 34.4 | 65.6 |
| Tennessee | | 10 | 783,051 | 787,761 | 48.8 | 49.0 | 2.2 | 49.8 | 50.2 |
| Texas | | 26 | 1,881,147 | 2,510,705 | 41.7 | 55.8 | 2.5 | 42.8 | 57.2 |
| Utah | | 4 | 124,266 | 439,687 | 20.9 | 74.0 | 5.1 | 22.0 | 78.0 |
| Vermont | | 3 | 81,952 | 94,628 | 39.3 | 45.4 | 15.3 | 46.4 | 53.6 |
| Virginia | | 12 | 752,174 | 989,609 | 40.9 | 53.9 | 5.2 | 43.2 | 56.8 |
| Washington | | 9 | 650,193 | 865,244 | 38.2 | 50.9 | 10.9 | 42.9 | 57.1 |
| West Virginia | 6 | | 367,462 | 334,206 | 50.1 | 45.6 | 4.3 | 52.4 | 47.6 |
| Wisconsin | | 11 | 981,584 | 1,088,845 | 44.0 | 48.8 | 7.2 | 47.4 | 52.6 |
| Wyoming | | 3 | 49,427 | 110,700 | 28.7 | 64.3 | 7.0 | 30.9 | 69.1 |
| *National Total* | 49 | 489 | 35,483,820 | 43,901,812 | 41.7 | 51.6 | 6.7 | 44.7 | 55.3 |

* Alaska third-party vote includes 18,479 votes for Ed Clark, Libertarian party, as well as 11,156 votes for Anderson.

*Table 2. Social Groups and the Presidential Vote, 1980 and 1976*

| | 1980 Carter | 1980 Reagan | 1980 Anderson | 1976 Carter | 1976 Ford |
|---|---|---|---|---|---|
| **Party*** | | | | | |
| Democrats (43%) | 66 | 26 | 6 | 77 | 22 |
| Independents (23%) | 30 | 54 | 12 | 43 | 54 |
| Republicans (28%) | 11 | 84 | 4 | 9 | 90 |
| **Ideology** | | | | | |
| Liberal (18%) | 57 | 27 | 11 | 70 | 26 |
| Moderates (51%) | 42 | 48 | 8 | 51 | 48 |
| Conservatives (31%) | 23 | 71 | 4 | 29 | 70 |
| **Race** | | | | | |
| Blacks (10%) | 82 | 14 | 3 | 82 | 16 |
| Hispanics (2%) | 54 | 36 | 7 | 75 | 24 |
| Whites (88%) | 36 | 55 | 8 | 47 | 52 |
| **Sex** | | | | | |
| Female (48%) | 45 | 46 | 7 | 50 | 48 |
| Male (52%) | 37 | 54 | 7 | 50 | 48 |
| **Religion** | | | | | |
| Protestant (46%) | 37 | 56 | 6 | 44 | 55 |
| White Protestant (41%) | 31 | 62 | 6 | 43 | 57 |
| Catholic (25%) | 40 | 51 | 7 | 54 | 44 |
| Jewish (5%) | 45 | 39 | 14 | 64 | 34 |
| **Family Income** | | | | | |
| Less than $10,000 (13%) | 50 | 41 | 6 | 58 | 40 |
| $10,000-$14,999 (15%) | 47 | 42 | 8 | 55 | 43 |
| $15,000-$24,999 (29%) | 38 | 53 | 7 | 48 | 50 |
| $25,000-$50,000 (24%) | 32 | 58 | 8 | 36 | 62 |
| Over $50,000 (5%) | 25 | 65 | 8 | — | — |
| **Occupation** | | | | | |
| Professional or manager (39%) | 33 | 56 | 9 | 41 | 57 |
| Clerical, sales, white collar (11%) | 42 | 48 | 8 | 46 | 53 |
| Blue-collar (17%) | 46 | 47 | 5 | 57 | 41 |
| Agriculture (3%) | 29 | 66 | 3 | — | — |
| Unemployed (3%) | 55 | 35 | 7 | 65 | 34 |

For some time, it has been evident that the position of the Democrats has been weakening. Personal memories of the New Deal are retained only by persons of retirement age so that loyalty to the Democrats is much weaker among younger generations. Some groups in the Democratic coalition have become smaller in number over the years as the population has moved from older cities into new suburbs, as some once-poor ethnic groups have risen into the middle class, and as membership has declined in industrial unions, once most supportive of the party. The South has been transformed by industrial development and the consequent movement of rural populations into metropolitan areas and the immigration of northerners and Republicans. These trends have produced an evident weakening of party loyalty on the presidential level. From the end of

*Table 2. (Continued)*

| | 1980 Carter | 1980 Reagan | 1980 Anderson | 1976 Carter | 1976 Ford |
|---|---|---|---|---|---|
| **Education** | | | | | |
| Less than high school (11%) | 50 | 45 | 3 | 58 | 41 |
| High school graduate (28%) | 43 | 51 | 4 | 54 | 46 |
| Some college (28%) | 35 | 55 | 8 | 51 | 49 |
| College graduate (27%) | 35 | 51 | 11 | 45 | 55 |
| **Union Membership** | | | | | |
| Labor union household (28%) | 47 | 44 | 7 | 59 | 39 |
| No member of household in union (62%) | 35 | 55 | 8 | 43 | 55 |
| **Age** | | | | | |
| 18-21 years old (6%) | 44 | 43 | 11 | 48 | 50 |
| 22-29 years old (17%) | 43 | 43 | 11 | 51 | 46 |
| 30-44 years old (31%) | 37 | 54 | 7 | 49 | 49 |
| 45-59 years old (23%) | 39 | 55 | 6 | 47 | 52 |
| 60 years or older (18%) | 40 | 54 | 4 | 47 | 52 |
| **Region** | | | | | |
| East (25%) | 42 | 47 | 9 | 51 | 47 |
| South (27%) | 44 | 51 | 3 | 54 | 45 |
| White South (22%) | 35 | 60 | 3 | 46 | 52 |
| Midwest (27%) | 40 | 51 | 7 | 48 | 50 |
| Far West (19%) | 35 | 53 | 9 | 46 | 51 |
| **Community Size** | | | | | |
| Cities over 250,000 (18%) | 54 | 35 | 8 | 60 | 40 |
| Suburbs-small cities (53%) | 37 | 53 | 8 | 53 | 47 |
| Rural and towns (29%) | 39 | 54 | 5 | 47 | 53 |

SOURCE: CBS News/*New York Times* interviews with 12,782 voters as they left the polls, as reported in the *New York Times,* 9 November 1980, p. 28, and in further analysis. The 1976 data are from CBS News interviews. For that year, the large-city vote is for communities over 500,000 population.
\* The figures in parentheses are the percentages of the 1980 voters belonging to each group. The table entries are percentages, which total approximately 100 percent in each row for 1980 or 1976. Missing data account for those categories that do not total 100 percent.

the Second World War, the Democrats have won only one convincing national election, in 1964; in eight other contests, the party has achieved three additional but narrow majorities and has lost five times.

As the party lost loyalists in some groups, it replaced them with others, but these new recruits only partially compensated for the defections. Young voters were more likely to be Democrats, but were largely independent of both major groups. Blacks and Hispanics increased both in numbers and voting turnout, stimulated by voting rights laws and registration campaigns, and became the most loyal Democratic partisans. These groups were not fully mobilized, however, and their voting rates lagged behind those of whites. The women's movement brought feminists into an active role in the party, but its liberal demands also aroused countervailing, more conservative attitudes among both sexes.

By 1980 voters were ready to abandon party loyalty in the voting booth. From their days in school to their nights before television sets, Americans were urged to "vote for the man or woman, not the party." Mass media presented elections as contests between individuals, not partisan teams. Candidates argued their own merits and largely ignored those who shared with them a line on the ballot or a philosophy of the party. Consequently, voters gave little thought to parties. Even those who did admit to being Democrats or Republicans were increasingly inclined to describe themselves as "weak" in loyalty. In assessing the reasons for their vote, relatively few voters mentioned the parties; in contrast to the past, a majority held negative evaluations of both major parties.[6]

The election of 1980 brought the culmination of these trends. Party loyalty failed Jimmy Carter. Having been first elected as an "outsider" successfully challenging the "establishment" within the Democratic party, having maintained his independence of the traditional coalition, and having argued against the orthodox party positions of Edward Kennedy in the nominating contest, he could not call upon traditional loyalties in his hour of need. A third of the self-identified Democrats rejected him, as did an even larger proportion of the self-identified liberals who comprised the ideological core of the party. Unable to hold this base, Carter was far less successful in gaining support from other segments in the political spectrum — Independents and Republicans, moderates and conservatives.

As Carter lost support, Reagan made gains that, significantly, were most evident in many demographic groups included in the traditional Democratic coalition. White Catholics gave Carter about the same proportion of the vote as the rest of the nation, instead of producing their past Democratic pluralities; Jews defected both to Reagan and to John Anderson; white southerners joined the majority groups in the population — Protestants, suburbanites, and non-union members — in strong support of Reagan.

The established Democratic coalition could be glimpsed only fleetingly among a few groups. Blacks provided strong support for Carter, as much support as in 1976, and they were joined by a majority within the small but growing ranks of Hispanics. Women showed more electoral support for Carter than did men, possibly reflecting feminist concerns, and younger voters were slightly more favorable to the incumbent. Union members and their families provided a bare plurality in favor of Carter, but gave him a lower vote than all other recent Democratic candidates except George McGovern. Even in these islands of relatively high ground for the Democrats, the waves of voter discontent caused considerable erosion.

With few exceptions, the most apparent feature of the vote was the wide degree of support won by Reagan. His majority was not fashioned from the coalescence of some groups in the population in opposition to others. Rather, that support was broadly distributed, at least among whites, throughout the electorate. This feature of the polling results indicates that there is not yet a distinctive coalition ready to endorse a new Republican direction in public policy. At the same time, the breadth of the voting support provides many opportunities for fashioning such a coalition.

## The Campaign

### Strategies

Discontent was the principal characteristic of the 1980 campaign. The voters did not see their options as happily selecting one of two (or more) acceptable candidates to be president. Instead, it was to be a forced choice of the "lesser of two (or more) evils," leading one wag to bewail "the evil of two lessers."

Voter dissatisfaction was shown by many indicators. Only a bare majority of the electorate was highly favorable to either candidate — the least enthusiasm displayed in three decades.[7] These critical attitudes were reflected by voter behavior. The proportion of undecided voters remained high throughout the fall. Almost a fourth of the nation did not reach a decision until the last week, and the actual voting turnout fell for the fifth straight election and came close to an historic ebb.

Voter hesitancy was shown in the pattern of opinion polls. As seen in Figure 2, the lead in the Gallup surveys changed five times in the course of the election year. A persistent Carter advantage became a decisive Reagan margin during the summer, only to be eliminated by the end of the Democratic convention and then partially restored during the month of October. A week before Election Day, on the eve of the only debate between the two major candidates, Carter seemed to have gained an edge, then lost it immediately after the televised confrontation. Until the end, no candidate was able to build a secure position, as if the voters were alternately repelled by whichever man seemed likely to be president.

In retrospect, these campaign trends evidence some logic. The basic political premise of the 1980 election was that Jimmy Carter was widely unpopular. On the basis of this unpopularity, a political scientist would have predicted that he would receive only 46 percent of the vote — nearly the exact proportion of the two-party vote he did achieve.[8] The question to be answered in the campaign was whether Ronald Reagan would be viewed as a satisfactory alternative to an unpopular president. Ultimately, the voters clearly answered yes.

As President, Carter had been the inevitable target of accumulated national discontents. The United States had seen itself as a strong, self-reliant, and prosperous country. Events of recent years had severely shaken confidence in this national image. Rather than achieve its will in international affairs, America was unable to gain the release of its hostages in Iran either through diplomatic or military means, and was forced to endure a year-long humiliation. Rather

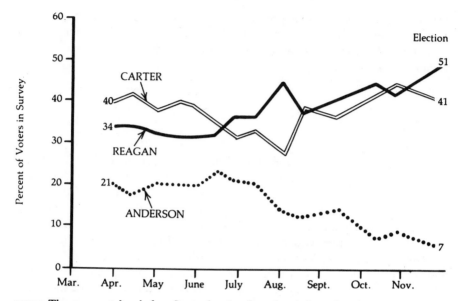

*Figure 2. The Presidential Race in 1980 Gallup Polls*

NOTE: The surveys taken before September 1 reflect the choices of registered voters. The surveys taken after September 1 reflect the choices of likely voters. Late October results based on partial survey taken before the October 28 debate.

than control its own affairs, America saw its life style, its economy, and its foreign policy subject to the unilateral decisions of Arab oil producers. Rather than improve its standard of living, America saw record levels of interest rates and inflation combined with rising unemployment and industrial decay. By 1980, the real income of the average American family, once wages were discounted by inflation and taxes, had fallen 5 percent below the level at the beginning of the Carter term. The electorate was prepared to shout, in imitation of the battle cry of the film *Network*, "I'm mad as hell and I'm not going to take this anymore!"

Jimmy Carter, of course, did not bear sole personal responsibility for these accumulated problems. The decline in national power abroad, the rise of OPEC, and the stagnant economy had been evident for some time, certainly before the Georgian's inauguration. Nevertheless, the public still found Carter wanting. The most persistent criticism of him related to his inability to seize control and point to solutions to national problems. Voters know whether they are satisfied or dissatisfied with an office-holder; they can only guess whether his opponent could have done better. This inevitable public emphasis on Carter's performance in office underlined his electoral vulnerability.

Inescapably running on his record, President Carter had three strategic options: to praise his accomplishments and promise future improvements (the most common technique, used by Lyndon Johnson in 1964 and Gerald Ford in 1976); to blame others for failures (as Harry Truman did in 1948); or to attempt to change the public's focus to the defects of the opposition. The Carter campaign, while mixing in the other options, relied primarily on the last strategy.

At the outset, the Carter emphasis had been on the President's positive accomplishments and his standing as a Democratic spokesman. As his campaign developed, however, a shift occurred toward an attack on Reagan, as well as John Anderson. The Carter campaign chairman, Robert Strauss, described the principal effort "to portray Reagan as 'simplistic' and 'not equipped to be President.' " A contrast would be drawn with Carter, who would be pictured as hard-working, aware of complexity, and knowledgeable about foreign affairs.[9] Little attention was given to Carter's future plans, and the President did not deliver a single major policy speech. Instead, dominant attention was given to Reagan's philosophy and personal qualities. The Carter forces no longer asked, as in 1976, "Why not the Best?" Instead, they argued, "It could be worse."

Aside from its unorthodoxy, this strategy had its dangers. It implied a considerable change from the 1976 characterization of Carter as a competent manager of government. The strategy was also open to counterattack. If Reagan could present himself and his programs decently, he could ride to victory on public discontent with the undefended Carter record. Still, despite its problems, the Carter strategy appeared to be succeeding — until Election Day.

The Reagan strategy was more conventional. In keeping with the expected stance of the challenger, Reagan emphasized the alleged failings of the Carter administration. The thrust of the Republican campaign was summarized in two slogans — the party national convention's theme, "Together, A New Beginning," and its televised advertising phrase, "For a Change." These slogans were empty of any substantive comment; they only promised something different. Reagan himself articulated the challenge at the conclusions of the televised debate and his preelection address. He asked the voters:

> Are you better off than you were four years ago? Is it easier for you to go and buy things in the stores than it was four years ago? Is there more or less unemployment in the country than there was four years ago? Is America as respected throughout the world as it was? Do you feel that our security is as safe, that we're as strong as we were four years ago? [10]

The attack on the Carter record was specified in much detail, such as charges of high taxes, prices, and unemployment; inadequate defense spending and foreign policy failures; excessive government regulation; and general national demoralization. While Republicans also suggested solutions to the problems they found, and the party platform was the longest in its history, the emphasis in the campaign itself was on Carter deficiencies. Reagan offered a general conservative philosophy and a vague vision of better times, while emphasizing that "this country doesn't have to be in the shape that it is in."

Reagan also defended himself against Carter attacks. The most frequent Republican television advertisement presented details of Reagan's record as governor of California, to emphasize his governmental experience and competence. An exhausting campaign itinerary served to refute any suspicions about his health. Days were spent in preparation for each of two televised debates so that Reagan would be seen as knowledgeable and reasonable. The premise of these efforts, according to Republican National Chairman Bill Brock, was that "the undecided voters really weren't undecided about President Carter. They were undecided about Governor Reagan because they didn't know him." [11] Through the campaign, they came to know him and, if not to love him, to accept him.

The courtship of the electorate involved considerable alteration and explanation of policy positions. Reagan had come to political prominence, and had won the Republican nomination, because of his championing of conservative causes. The philosophy he espoused had been written into the party platform, but it received little emphasis in the campaign. Instead, Reagan sought to assure various groups that his election would not represent a threat to their vital interests.

Reversing positions he had held at one time or another, Reagan endorsed the farm-parity system, federal aid to New York City and automobile manufacturers, occupational health and safety regulations, prevailing wage laws, and union exemption from antitrust acts. His opposition to the Equal Rights Amendment was replaced by endorsement of statutory enactment of the same principle, and his endorsement of a constitutional amendment to ban abortion was replaced by silence. Downplaying his past antipathy toward communist regimes, he supported recognition of the People's Republic of China and nuclear arms negotiations with the Soviet Union. Reagan presented himself as a moderate, rather than as an ideological conservative. Barry Goldwater, in 1964 the last conservative Republican candidate, would "rather be right than President." Reagan preferred to be elected.

*Events*

From the end of the Democratic convention in mid-August, the campaign went through four overlapping phases, each leading to an apparent change in the race. The first of these periods was one of Reagan's decline. Though he emerged from his own party convention with a large lead in the polls and a united Republican organization, the Californian was soon lagging. The exciting contest and ultimate reconciliation at the Democratic conclave brought many of that party's voters back into the fold. At the same time, Reagan appeared to be confirming many of the worst fears about himself. In the early weeks of the campaign he rekindled old antagonisms about the Vietnam war by calling American intervention there "a noble cause"; he appeared to oppose the theory of evolution; he inaccurately and ineptly criticized Carter for attending a rally at "the birthplace of the Ku Klux Klan," while he himself visited a Mississippi county fair favored by segregationists; and he suggested renegotiating the agreement that had led to diplomatic relations with China. These actions led to embarrassing explanations, apologies, and even a transoceanic argument between Reagan and his running mate, George Bush. The errors were easily used by the Democrats to argue that Reagan was both unknowledgeable and reactionary.

For their part, the Carter forces used the powers of presidential incumbency, as they had during the nominating contest. Reagan's assertions on foreign policy were refuted by the ambassador to China and by Secretary of State Edmund Muskie. Vindicating the administration's military record, Secretary of Defense Brown confirmed a leak that the United States was developing a bomber that would be virtually invulnerable to Soviet radar — while downplaying the fact that the airplane would be unavailable for many years. Refurbishing his image as Middle East peacemaker, Carter announced that Israeli Prime Minister Menachem Begin and Egyptian President Anwar Sadat would join him in a postelection summit conference.

Throughout the fall, the administration employed its executive authority to court crucial votes. Vice-President Walter Mondale announced that large naval repairs would be done in Philadelphia, providing jobs in the closely contested states of Pennsylvania and New Jersey rather than in Virginia, which was considered lost to Reagan. Seeking the vital electoral bloc of a New York burdened by welfare costs, Carter endorsed a federal takeover of Medicaid payments, although he had previously opposed the action. In the Midwest, he suggested restrictions on imported steel and automobiles as possible means to relieve the region's unemployment. Wherever possible, federal grants were announced during campaign trips, with $50 million provided for Michigan alone during one week and $20 million to the Cleveland area in a single day.

The second phase of the campaign, extending roughly through the latter part of September and the first week of October, saw a Reagan revival. His campaign speeches were reviewed more carefully, new advisers accompanied him on the campaign plane, and he eliminated most news conferences or appearances before right-wing groups. These steps were taken, as his former campaign chairman foresaw, to avoid Reagan's need for "explaining every day why you're not an idiot." [12] Most importantly, Reagan gained a national television audience of 50 million voters by appearing in a debate with John Anderson.

The debate was the first of four planned by the League of Women Voters. As a private organization, the League could invite whichever candidates it chose. Unlike the television networks, it was not required to include minor aspirants. Once the League decision was made, the networks were free to cover the debate as a news event, unrestricted by legal guarantees of "equal time" to other candidates.

The League's own tradition was one of open access to all serious candidates. Moreover, John Anderson had great personal support among members of the organization, who responded to his intellectual ability and his strong feminist position. In issuing its invitation, the League created a new standard — it would include any candidate who, because of a 15 percent rating in public opinion polls (and official placement on state ballots), had a significant chance of winning the Presidency. When Anderson barely met this standard early in September, he was invited to a debate on September 21, along with Carter and Reagan. The Carter campaign refused. Seeing Anderson as a direct competitor for the liberal votes they sought, they hoped that Carter's absence would deprive Anderson of attention and would make the debate unimportant.

The Carter strategy did succeed in reducing the television audience — aided by ABC's counterprogramming of a motion picture. Reagan still used the occasion for his own benefit. While he did not change any of his positions drastically, he presented his arguments moderately and thereby served to dispel some doubts about his candidacy while undercutting Anderson's appeal to Republicans. Although few viewers said their preferences had been changed by the debate itself, the opinion polls showed that Reagan converted a 4 percent deficit into a 5 percent lead over Carter and that most voters were now convinced — contrary to their earlier views — that Reagan "understood the complicated problems a President has to deal with." [13]

The Democrats were now fully engaged in attacking Reagan as dangerous, as untrustworthy with control of nuclear weapons, and as a threat to the social welfare benefits of the aged, poor, and minorities. Carter himself pressed these points, depicting the election as a "choice between peace and war," hinting that Reagan promoted racism, and suggesting, "if I lose this election, Americans might be separate, black from white, Jew from Gentile, North from South, rural from urban." [14]

Reagan's response to these attacks was largely cool, such as his depiction of the President as subject to "fits of childish pique," but occasionally sharp, as in his characterization of Carter as "the greatest deceiver ever to occupy the White House." [15] The press found Carter's rhetoric "mean" and "vindictive" and one liberal columnist complained that "all along the President has acted as if a successful 1980 campaign could consist of nothing more than horror stories about Ronald Reagan." [16] The public, too, reacted; a near-majority now believed that Carter "says too many things carelessly, without considering the consequences." [17]

No candidate could benefit from these characterizations, but they were especially serious as criticisms of Carter. He had been attempting to focus the campaign on Reagan's personal deficiencies, but now found he was the target. Moreover, Carter's greatest personal assets were threatened — his past reputation as a moral and decent individual, and the esteem of the presidential office he held. His vitriolic attacks on Reagan diminished his standing and demeaned his office. Carter, realizing the error of his ways, offered a semiapology in a television interview, initiating the third phase of the campaign.

In this period, President Carter rallied the traditional Democratic coalition. Buoyed by the endorsements of most major unions, he emphasized the social welfare programs of the Democratic party. Carter conducted a series of televised "town meetings" around the nation, in which he responded to easy questions from citizen audiences and demonstrated his command of the government and his personal involvement in particular problems. Through visits to black churches, union halls, and senior citizen centers, he sought to spur these groups to revived party loyalty. Hopeful signs of economic recovery began to appear and were emphasized by the administration.

There also were signs that foreign policy questions were beginning to have an impact. The public's greatest concern about Reagan continued to be his ability and moderation as a possible commander-in-chief. This shift in attention was accelerated by events abroad. Iran, still holding the American hostages, was invaded by the neighboring country of Iraq, and it soon became evident that Iran could not repel the invasion but would need outside assistance. Thus, the Iran-Iraq war might lead to a release of the hostages in exchange for the release of Iranian assets impounded in the United States. It was widely believed that, if this deal were made, Carter would be seen as a national hero and would be triumphantly reelected. Fearing this result, the Reagan camp attempted to discount its impact in advance, warning that Carter planned this "October surprise" and complaining about the "cynical manipulation" of the public by the administration.

As the campaigners neared the finish line, the race became extremely close, with Carter apparently moving toward a narrow victory. The Reagan camp, which had hoped simply to hold its early lead, now saw the need for more dramatic action and revived discussion of a second televised debate. Previously, the Republican campaigners had acted cautiously, fearing a spontaneous error by their candidate. They had insisted that Anderson be included in any confrontation, knowing that Carter would not agree to this condition. With news about Iran blanketing the press, however, they feared that their own messages would be lost, and began to call anew for a debate.

President Carter had left the door open by saying that he would engage Reagan alone. The League of Women Voters, noting Anderson's decline in the polls, reversed its past policy that the congressman would be included in all debates. Instead, it accepted Carter's condition, and Reagan promptly agreed to a two-man event. While Carter advisers, by this point, had "all pretty well reached the conclusion that a debate could only hurt us," [18] Carter himself eagerly accepted the challenge. The ninety-minute confrontation was scheduled for one week before the election.

The debate itself probably contributed considerably to public awareness and decision. Over 100 million persons watched as each candidate argued his basic campaign themes. Carter stressed the benefits of his programs to specific constituencies, placed himself in "the mainstream of the Democratic party" and emphasized his experience in office (mentioning the President's "Oval Office" ten times). He attacked Reagan's statements on such policies as Medicare, and even — at his own initiative — cited his teen-age daughter as a source for his concern over the spread of nuclear weapons. Reagan had prepared for three days for the debate. He offered detailed and moderate answers, cited his record as governor of California several times, and was ready to respond to all criticisms, leavening his factual rebuttals with deprecating humor. The difference in the candidates' tones can be seen in this exchange regarding the strategic arms limitation treaty:

> CARTER: This [Reagan's] attitude is extremely dangerous and belligerent in its tone, although it's said with a quiet voice.

> REAGAN: I know the President's supposed to be replying to me, but sometimes I have a hard time in connecting what he's saying with what I have said or what my positions are.[19]

Many newspaper comments and public opinion polls were devoted to the question of who "won" the debate. As is common with such events,[20] relatively few voters actually changed their preference as a direct result, although these few did favor Reagan. The more important effect of the debate was to reinforce previous commitments and again center the election on the basic question: Was Reagan an acceptable alternative to Carter? Because Reagan showed himself as competent, because he made no errors, and because he appeared pleasant and reasonable, he was able to settle any doubts raised during the campaign. By not losing, he won; the polls now showed him in the lead.

This lead was transformed into a Reagan sweep on Election Day. Events in Iran contributed to the shift. The Iranian government seemed ready to release the American hostages, but then established four prior conditions for the freedom of the captives. President Carter flew back to Washington to direct preparation of an American response, but he could take no quick, dramatic action to resolve the situation. Instead, the nation would suffer another disappointment on the very anniversary of the takeover of the Teheran embassy. There was no "October surprise," feared by the Republicans, but only a "November frustration" for Carter and the nation.

While these events did not cause the late changes in and of themselves, they served as "metaphor" and "catalyst" for the expression of long-standing antipathies toward the Carter administration.[21] Again, the United States was shown dependent on the whims of another nation's leaders. Again, presidential desires had been frustrated by legislative delay — and this time not by an American Congress but by a body with strange customs and unknown members. Again, President Carter had seemed to promise a happy result, only to act indecisively and unsuccessfully. Discontent had been the keynote of the election year; on November 4, the keynote swelled to a chorused disapproval.

## Results and Implications

### The Anderson Difference

Congressman John Anderson received considerable acclaim from the press and from some groups in the electorate for his intelligence, persistence, and willingness to take specific and unpopular policy positions. He faced difficult odds, beginning his independent candidacy late, supported by no formal party organization, and bereft of secure financing. In these circumstances, he did relatively well. A bipartisan national ticket was established, with former Wisconsin Governor Patrick Lucey the running mate in Anderson's "National Unity Coalition." The ticket secured a place on the ballot of all fifty states, despite formidable legal and political hurdles. The campaign raised almost $12 million, largely through direct-mail contributions.

The Anderson campaign failed in its ostensible objective: presidential victory. Organizational difficulties, advertising and money shortages, the diversion of time and money into the struggle to win legal access to the ballot, and the remaining strength of the two major parties explained part of this failure. Furthermore, Anderson himself never won widespread popular enthusiasm. At no point did he gain a plurality of favorable comments from the electorate.

The independent candidate never developed a strong electoral base. His appeal remained largely restricted to the "young, liberal, well-educated, white and affluent" voters and extended little into the broader ranks of the middle and working classes. Moreover, Anderson's support was inherently soft, concentrated among younger persons, who vote infrequently, and among persons who were least certain of their own preferences. Most importantly, there was no distinctive ideological character to this vote. Anderson ran as a middle-of-the-road candidate in a race in which his opponents also claimed the same place on the political highway. Unlike most protest candidates, his dissent lacked a strong emotional issue.

In the final results, Anderson's efforts were not decisive. Even if all the Anderson voters had chosen Carter instead, Carter still might have been defeated, although the race would have been considerably closer. Anderson won most of his votes from Independents, rather than committed partisans, and of the remaining support he received almost as much from Republicans as Democrats (see Table 2). Those who remained with Anderson to the end actually preferred Reagan to Carter; and eliminating Anderson from the ballot actually might have further swollen the Reagan majority.[22]

While not affecting the final results, Anderson certainly affected the campaign, particularly the Democratic effort. Concern about Anderson dominated and warped many of Carter's strategic decisions. His forces spent much time and money in a futile effort to deny Anderson access to the ballot — in the process arousing Anderson's ire and determination to remain in contention, even if Reagan were elected. Because Anderson won the important endorsement of the Liberal party in New York, a traditional backer of Democrats, the Carter campaign devoted exceptional efforts to that state. With funds running low, the opportunity to campaign elsewhere was lost.[23] Carter's evasion of the first debate, and his attacks on the Anderson candidacy, contributed to the deterioration of his own reputation. Furthermore, by delaying the debate with Reagan in order to exclude Anderson, that single confrontation gained exceptional importance.

With no time for a second meeting with Reagan, President Carter was proven vulnerable. By contrast, Reagan, also accepting the premise that Anderson would take votes from Carter, was free to appear magnanimous toward the independent candidate.

The ultimate decline of the Anderson effort is a testament to the institutional strength of the two-party system in the United States. As a new and independent candidate, Anderson had to devote weeks and thousands of dollars to earning a place on state ballots. The major candidates had automatic access and were free to devote themselves to addressing the voters. While Republicans and Democrats each had $29.4 million in federal funds for their campaigns (and their parties could raise an additional $4.6 million), Anderson had to raise all his money privately. By winning over 5 percent of the national vote, he did receive, retroactively, partial federal financing, but he could not secure advance bank loans on this uncertain collateral — and the Carter administration pressured banks to deny him such loans.

The Anderson decline was basically due to the realities of two-party power in the nation, the ultimate fact that the elected president would be either a Democrat or a Republican. While he received over 20 percent of polled preferences during the summer, Anderson finally held only a third of his potential support. Even if unhappy with the choice, most voters still wanted to make a president, not merely to make a protest. With the race perceived as close, the value of each vote increased, and the luxury of an Anderson ballot became too costly.

### The Election Mandate

The extensive Reagan victory raised basic questions of its ideological meaning and its impact on the relative future strength of the two major parties. Can the Republican triumph be seen as a victory for the conservative ideology? Can the victory then be understood as a realignment of American politics around a "new Republican majority," comparable to the critical elections of 1928–36, which created the Democratic New Deal majority? [24]

Certainly, voter discontent was apparent in the congressional as well as presidential results. In the Senate, Democratic liberals were almost entirely the targets of this discontent, while House races brought the defeat of major leaders of the congressional party and its left-wing. These results had a decided partisan character, with the voters choosing not only a Republican president but a Republican and conservative-to-moderate government. Party, however, is more important than ideology in explaining these outcomes. Particularly in the presidential race, the weight of the evidence is that the 1980 election was a negative landslide based on dissatisfaction with Carter and his record rather than a direct endorsement of conservative philosophy.

Elections that involve upheavals in the party coalitions have certain hallmarks, such as popular enthusiasm and diverse voting shifts. These indicators are largely lacking in 1980. Turnout actually fell, instead of showing the increase that would be expected in the enthusiasm of a rising cause. The victorious candidate, Reagan, lacks the personal popularity we would expect of the leader of a mass crusade.

Analysis of the effect of ideology and partisanship on the vote provides further evidence. There is a striking similarity in the voting patterns of 1976 and 1980. If the Reagan victory marked a major partisan change based on conservative philosophy, we would expect to find that the Republican vote had become distinctly more conservative, while the Democrats were reduced to a predominantly liberal party. But analysis shows there is a continuity between these two years.

Two points are clear: (1) the vote was affected more by party loyalty than by ideology in both contests; and (2) particularly relevant to this discussion, Carter lost support among all groups in 1980, and lost more among liberals and Democrats. The President's change in fortunes was not the result of conservatives rallying around the Republican cause; Carter's defeat was the effect of a widespread desertion from his own ranks.[25]

Another way of looking at the results is to determine the ideological character of the candidates' coalitions (i.e., to see whether their constituencies lean toward the liberal or conservative direction). Table 3 presents these figures for 1976 and 1980. A striking feature of the table is the lack of any change in the parties' ideological constituencies over the two elections. Carter in 1976 won the bulk of his vote from moderates, while tilting in a liberal direction. His 1980 coalition was essentially identical, but he received fewer votes from every group across the philosophical spectrum. The two Republican candidates were virtually carbon copies of each other. Both Reagan and Ford got their votes principally from moderates, with a considerable proportion of conservatives and a noticeable sprinkling of liberals. In sum, Reagan's victory came from getting more voters, from every group, not from the arousal of a conservative mandate.

The cause of the shift to Reagan was primarily economic. His greatest strength was among those who believed their economic position had worsened in the past year, and among those who considered inflation the primary problem facing the nation. Over three-fifths of these groups voted for the Republican. Those who felt their financial condition to be improving, and even those who worried most about unemployment, remained with Carter. This Republican support from persons concerned with inflation is not new, but the pervasiveness of the concern meant that the party's candidate would win millions of votes previ-

*Table 3. Ideological Composition of Candidate Coalitions*

|  | Carter 1976 | Carter 1980 | Ford 1976 | Reagan 1980 |
|---|---|---|---|---|
| Liberals | 28% | 27% | 10% | 10% |
| Moderates | 54 | 55 | 47 | 48 |
| Conservatives | 18 | 18 | 43 | 42 |
| Total | 100% | 100% | 100% | 100% |

*Table 4. The Carter Vote and Economic Satisfaction\**

|  | Improved economic position | Worsened economic position |
|---|---|---|
| Democrats | 77 | 47 |
| Independents | 45 | 21 |
| Republicans | 18 | 6 |
| Liberals | 65 | 44 |
| Moderates | 59 | 26 |
| Conservatives | 33 | 16 |
| Protestants | 51 | 24 |
| Catholics | 53 | 28 |
| Jews | 52 | 30 |
| Union households | 65 | 34 |
| Nonunion households | 48 | 22 |
| Total | 53 | 25 |

\* Each entry in the table is the percentage of the designated group voting for Carter, e.g., Carter received 77 percent of the votes of Democrats who believed their family finances had improved in the past year.

ously in the Democratic column. Those who saw their financial condition worsening completely reversed their 1976 ballots: three-fourths of them had endorsed Carter in 1976; now, three-fourths voted against him.

Economic grievances were at the heart of the Reagan vote. Economic dissatisfaction was the most direct influence on the 1980 vote, and it had a greater impact than any other issue. Despite their philosophy, those liberals who felt worse off financially opposed Carter. Despite their partisanship, those Democrats suffering economically defected to Reagan and Anderson. Traditional supporters of the party, such as Catholics and unionists, remained loyal — but only when their pocketbooks remained full. More widespread economic satisfaction would have brought the president reelection, by a two-party margin over Reagan of at least 53–47. Jimmy Carter was not defeated in the marketplace of ideas; he was trounced in the marketplace of food and gasoline and mortgages.

### The Republican Opportunity
If the election provides no mandate for conservatism, it does provide the opportunity for Republicans to develop an electoral majority that will consistently support a conservative direction in public policy. The Reagan administration has a chance similar to that of Franklin Roosevelt in 1932. That President, too, was elected in a time of economic distress, when the voters dismissed an incumbent chief executive (who also happened to be an engineer). Those who turned to the Democrats that year were not advocates of a New Deal program that had not yet been created, but they and their children became its loyal supporters when that program improved their lives. A Reagan Presidency — supported by

a Republican majority in the Senate and a conservative, if Democratic, House — may have similar effects.

A major change in American politics did not occur in 1980 — but it may be coming. "Every American election," wrote Theodore White, "summons the individual voter to weigh the past against the future." [26] In 1980, neither Carter nor Reagan facilitated this process. Rather, as James Reston complained early in the fall, the contest was "a phony campaign of pretense, with Carter and Reagan savaging each other and blowing off about the past in order to avoid the hard questions of the future." [27]

The failure to address these questions was particularly marked for the Democrats, who prided themselves on being the party of innovation. President Carter had rejected some elements of traditional Democratic liberalism in his nominating campaign against Senator Kennedy, but he presented no alternative ideology. Ultimately he returned to the older ideas. Unconvincing in this late philosophical rebirth, he lost substantial support from liberals without making compensating gains among other groups. Essentially, on the presidential level, no modernized liberal ideology was presented. Its appeal, therefore, was not rejected; it was simply untested.

Carter persistently discussed past errors, or present difficulties, not future possibilities. This had been his focus in 1976 when he stressed the deficiencies of Gerald Ford. In 1980 he turned toward the past again — the old statements of Reagan, not his own intentions and directions. The lack of attention to the future was Carter's major philosophical problem.

Reagan, for his part, also provided little specific direction for the future. His program was criticized for offering nothing more than a nostalgic and impossible return to the 1950s or, as Garry Trudeau satirized it in his *Doonesbury* cartoons, for replacing clear forward-looking vision with rose-colored hindsight. The Reagan campaign, too, came to stress the past — both its reputedly glorious years before Carter and its failings under the incumbent administration.

Nevertheless, the Reagan candidacy did present a more hopeful stance toward the future, despite the lack of novelty in its policy proposals. His vision was vague, but it was still more inspiring than Carter's condemnation of American "malaise." By calls to patriotism, the recitation of established homilies, and the re-creation of the national past, Reagan was able to invoke the concept of American exceptionalism, of the United States as "a city on a hill," providing world leadership.

The Iranian revolution had shown the power of appeals to traditional morality and nationalistic purpose. Combining these romantic images with pocketbook complaints of economic distress, Reagan received public recognition as "a strong leader" who "offers a vision of where he wants to lead the country." [28] As Thomas Cronin had forecast earlier in the year, "the 1980s will be shaped by people and presidents who have confidence in themselves and can radiate confidence in the nation. . . . Today, the bully pulpit — amplified as it is by the remarkable electronic opportunities of the age — beckons once again." [29]

There is an opportunity for Reagan, building on the public's desire for leadership, to develop a dominant coalition. Such opportunities are not always taken, and they can be lost through circumstances. Lyndon Johnson after 1964 was unable to develop his Great Society because of Vietnam, and earlier Republican prospects were subverted after 1972 by Nixon's Watergate corruption. Reagan and the Republicans now have a second chance. The election of 1980 was not an endorsement of their programs, but successful programs can lead to future and persistent electoral endorsement.

In the effort to develop a new majority among the electorate, Reagan will have the benefit of two political assets. Population changes and movements, the first asset, are tending in directions that largely favor the Republicans. The 1980 election was conducted on the basis of the outdated population figures of 1970; future contests will be based on the just-completed census of 1980. This census will necessitate a decided shift of congressional representation and presidential electoral votes away from the Northeast and Midwest — areas of relative Democratic strength — and toward the Far West and the sunbelt states such as Florida and Texas — areas of relatively high Republican strength. States that gave Reagan above-average support will gain sixteen electoral votes.

Reagan's most important political asset is the Republican party. Although the GOP is still a distinct minority in the electorate, it has become an ideologically coherent and organizationally efficient party. The most significant aspect of the Republicans' victory in 1980, in the long run, may be precisely that it was a Republican victory rather than the triumph of particular individuals. While Reagan won his nomination as an individual factional leader, he did represent the core of the party. While Reagan won the election as an individual challenger to a particular incumbent, he did campaign as a Republican spokesman, unlike Eisenhower and Nixon. For the first time in fifty years, a president has been elected who admits that he is a Republican.

The Reagan campaign was a party effort, closely coordinated with a year-long national effort to rally support for Republican candidates for the Senate and House. The coordination of these campaigns was dramatized by a joint appearance of Reagan and most Republican congressional candidates on the steps of the Capitol during the fall. Announcing a "solemn covenant with the American people," the party leaders subscribed to a series of pledges to cut taxes, reduce the federal budget, increase military weaponry, and promote business investment. This program approximated the ideal of party government, in which parties "bring forth programs to which they commit themselves" and "possess sufficient cohesion to carry out these programs." [30]

Promoting this unity is the remarkable organizational revival of the national party. Unlike the Democrats, who have attempted reform through broadened mass participation, the Republicans have devoted their efforts to increased electoral efficiency. Fund raising has been extended through direct-mail programs and administratively centralized in the national committee. Under the leadership of Chairman Bill Brock, the party has sought to revitalize its basic leadership by active recruiting of candidates for public office from the state legislatures to Congress. The national party provided low-budget surveys of public opinion, conducting 250 local polls. It dispatched organizational experts to congressional constituencies, conducted 100 training sessions on the use of the mass media and other electioneering techniques, and ran a regular series of workshops for campaign managers, culminating in the graduation of 160 persons from a "campaign management college." Computerized data analysis and policy research were coordinated, a permanent headquarters was established, and a party journal of opinion, *Commonsense,* was published regularly. Finances were integrated so that the contributions from state parties were pooled with national resources. Further, the central party provided $3 million for state legislative candidates (in contrast to the national Democrats' total neglect of these races).

The most hopeful sign for the party is that their candidate won a presidential election on economic issues. For five decades, these issues have been the major advantage of the Democrats. Having won popular support on these basic questions, the Republicans have successfully attacked their opponents at their strongest point. If they can deal with the problems of inflation, endemic unemployment, energy, and industrial decay, the Republican party will be well along in the construction of a new and persistent majority coalition. If the economic problems of the United States are too deep-rooted for political solution, the Republican victory will prove shallow and short-lived.

## The Democratic Opposition

The Republican triumph also provides opportunities for the Democratic party. Defeat also has its uses, even if they are less enjoyable than the possibilities created by victory. The Democrats can exploit weaknesses evident in the Reagan electoral coalition, while they use the time out of power to regroup.

The most disturbing aspect of the Reagan victory is the exclusion from the winning majority of almost all blacks and the majority of Hispanics. Republican programs will not succeed if they lack concern for these groups. Politically as well, the Republican coalition will be vulnerable if it ignores the claims of groups that represent an increasing proportion of the population. Morally, a purely white majority would violate basic human and American values of equality and opportunity. The Democrats can still prosper as the party demanding empathy for minority groups.

There also are prospects for the Democrats among the near-majority of the population that did not vote in 1980. Turnout has always been greater among persons of high social status, particularly those with the most education. Until 1980, this difference did not affect the electoral outcome greatly.[31] In the last contest, however, there was a marked contrast between voters and nonvoters. Reagan's forces were more likely to register and actually to come to the polls. While four out of five Reagan backers registered, the proportions fell to three of four Carter supporters and to two of three Anderson enthusiasts. If all adults had voted, Reagan still would have won the election, but his lead would have been cut in half, to only a 5 percent margin over Carter. The large number of unregistered and nonparticipating citizens offers the Democrats a possibility for political mobilization.[32]

To exploit the possibility, Democratic rebuilding is necessary. The party emerges from the election of 1980 still predominant in the loyalties of the voters, and still in control of most of the state legislatures and governorships and of the U.S. House of Representatives. Inevitably it will return to national power. Restoring its long-term dominance, however, will require more than awaiting the swing of the electoral pendulum. The organization is weak and, despite four years in the White House, the national party is still heavily in debt. The core of its leadership has been eliminated through deaths and electoral defeats. Party reform has preoccupied the Democrats for a dozen years, but has not contributed substantially to the basic goal of any political party — winning office. Democratic resurgence will require much attention, beginning with such mundane activities as compiling lists of contributors and preparing attractive television spots. But technical expertise will not renew the party. The fundamental need of the Democrats is for ideas that are meaningful and convincing. Party loyalty and old ideas are no longer sufficient.

SOURCE: Gerald M. Pomper, "The Presidential Election," chap. 3. Gerald M. Pomper with colleagues, *The Election of 1980: Reports and Interpretations* (Chatham, N.J.: Chatham House Publishers, Inc., 1981), pp. 65–94. Copyright © 1981 by Chatham House Publishers, Inc. Reprinted by permission of the author and publishers.

## Notes

1. The voting results are from *Congressional Quarterly Weekly Report* 39 (17 January 1981): 138. Of minor party candidates, Ed Clark of the Libertarian party received 921,188 votes and Barry Commoner of the Citizens party received 234,279.

2. The rank-order correlation of states (Spearman's rho) in 1976 and 1980 is an impressively high .88. The linear correlation is also high historically, at .84, for the two-party vote.

3. See Walter Dean Burnham, *Critical Elections and the Mainsprings of American Politics* (New York: Norton, 1970).

4. In 1980, 24 states differed considerably (by more than five points) from the national Republican percentage. This is a noticeable increase from 1976, when only 18 states showed such variation.

5. These data, from the studies of the University of Michigan's Center for Political Studies, are presented in John Kessel, *Presidential Campaign Politics* (Homewood, Ill.: Dorsey, 1980), p. 224.

6. Norman Nie et al., *The Changing American Voter* (Cambridge, Mass.: Harvard University Press, 1976), p. 59.

7. E. J. Dionne, in the *New York Times,* 2 November 1980, p. 37. By contrast, in 1956, 92 percent of the voters were highly favorable to Eisenhower and/or Stevenson.

8. The percentage would be received by a President with only a 30 percent popularity rating in the Gallup poll — Carter's standing before the election. See Lee Sigelman, "Presidential Popularity and Presidential Elections," *Public Opinion Quarterly* 43 (Winter 1979) : 534.

9. *Time* 116 (15 September 1980) : 11. The shifts in television advertising are reported in the *New York Times,* 17 September 1980, p. 33; 26 September, p. A18; and 1 October 1980, p. B7.

10. *Congressional Quarterly Weekly Report* 38 (1 November 1980) : 3289.

11. *New York Times,* 9 November 1980, sect. 4: E1.

12. John Sears, quoted in *The New York Times,* 27 August 1980, p. A17.

13. CBS News/*New York Times* poll, 19–25 September 1980.

14. *New York Times,* 26 September 1980, p. A18; and 7 October, p. D21. The "war and peace theme was cited so often that the President's plane was nicknamed 'Tolstoy' " — *Newsweek* 96 (3 November 1980) : 34.

15. Howell Raines in *The New York Times,* 12 October 1980, p. 32.

16. Anthony Lewis, "Carter Against Himself," *New York Times,* 16 October 1980, p. A31.

17. CBS News/*New York Times* poll, 16–20 October 1980.

18. *New York Times,* 9 November 1980, p. 1.

19. The text of the debate can be found in *Congressional Quarterly Weekly Report* 38 (1 November 1980) : 3279–89, the quotation on 3285.

20. See Sidney Kraus, ed., *The Great Debates* (Bloomington: Indiana University Press, 1962, 1979).

21. George Will, "Rebuke to a Party," *Manchester Guardian Weekly* 123 (16 November 1980) : 17.

22. The final CBS News/*New York Times* poll before the election showed 38 percent of the Anderson supporters preferred Carter as a second choice, 42 percent preferred Reagan, and 13 percent would not vote in a two-man race. The survey of voters on Election Day found that of those actually casting Anderson ballots, 33 percent preferred Carter to Reagan, 29 percent were more favorable to Reagan than Carter, and 33 percent would have abstained in a two-man race.

23. See *New York Times,* 15 August 1980, p. A1; and 15 October, p. A26.

24. On the Democratic coalition, see Kristi Andersen, *The Creation of a Democratic Majority* (Chicago: University of Chicago Press, 1979); and Everett C. Ladd and Charles D. Hadley, *Transformations of the American Party System* (New York: Norton, 1975). On recent prospects, see Kevin Phillips, *The Emerging Republican Majority* (New Rochelle, N.Y.: Arlington House, 1969); Richard Scammon and Ben Wattenberg, *The Real Majority* (New York: Coward-McCann, 1970); and James Sundquist, *Dynamics of the Party System* (Washington, D.C.: Brookings Institution, 1973). The original concept is found in V. O. Key, "A Theory of Critical Elections," *Journal of Politics* 17 (February 1955) : 3–18.

25. The data are from the Election Day CBS News/*New York Times* exit poll. The pro-Carter change of liberal Republicans is an intriguing exception but involves only a tiny, 2 percent share of the total electorate.

26. *The Making of the President, 1960* (New York: Atheneum, 1961), p. 254.

27. "The Political Traps," *New York Times,* 3 September 1980, p. A19.

28. In the CBS News/*New York Times* poll of 16–20 October 1980, 62 percent

and 67 percent, respectively, agreed with each of these characterizations of Reagan.

29. "Looking for Leadership," *Public Opinion* 3 (February/March 1980): 19–20.
30. "Toward a More Responsible Two-Party System," *American Political Science Review* 44 (September 1950): 1, supplement.
31. Raymond Wolfinger and Steven Rosenstone, *Who Votes?* (New Haven, Conn.: Yale University Press, 1980), esp. chap. 6.
32. See E. J. Dionne, in the *New York Times,* 5 November 1980, p. A23; and Adam Clymer's analysis of the CBS News/*New York Times* exit poll in the *New York Times,* 16 November 1980, p. 1.

# 2. Selecting and Electing Presidents: 1936-1980

## William R. Keech

Americans have perhaps the most popularly based methods of selecting chief executives of any nation in the world. Not only is the final choice highly responsive to popular preferences; the means of defining the final alternatives are highly responsive to them as well. Most democratic chief executives are not chosen by the mass publics but by legislators who are, in turn, selected by the people. The United States is fairly unusual in basing the final choice as directly on popular votes as it does, and it is quite unusual in the lengths to which it goes to ensure that the nominations are also popularly based.

Whatever the limitations of the American presidential selection processes, they are second to few, if any, in the degree to which the people make the important choices. This does not mean our system is perfect or even the best. Any inferiorities of the system, however, are not due to insufficient democracy.

### Securing the Republican or Democratic Nomination

There are two basic steps to the Presidency. The election stage is the final decision, and in that sense is the most important, but the most crucial step toward reaching the Presidency is achieving nomination by the Republican or Democratic Party. Those two parties have controlled access to the White House since 1860. Only once since then did someone other than the Republican or Democratic nominee rise as high as second place. That was in 1912, when Theodore Roosevelt, a former Republican President, ran as a Progressive and polled more votes than President William H. Taft.

While the election chooses between two serious candidates, the nominating stage does far more to narrow down the alternatives. When the Republicans and Democrats choose their presidential nominees, more individuals are ruled out than at the general election. This stage also determines how meaningful and how desirable the final alternatives will be. The 1972 election is a good example of a case in which the alternatives were sufficiently flawed that for many voters there was no desirable choice. The Republicans renominated a president who would only narrowly escape impeachment and would become the first president

*William R. Keech teaches political science at the University of North Carolina and is the author of several books, including* The Impact of Negro Voting *and* The Party's Choice.

to be forced to resign from office. The Democrats chose a candidate who was deeply controversial in his own party and who would receive a smaller proportion of the votes from his fellow Democrats than any nominee since before Franklin Roosevelt's presidency.

Even when the candidates are not flawed as they were in 1972, some observers feel that the kinds of choices made by the Republican and Democratic parties narrow the range of policy alternatives to an undesirable degree. George Wallace has proclaimed loudly in recent years that there is not a "dime's worth of difference" between Republicans and Democrats, and in 1976 former Senator Eugene McCarthy, speaking from a different political perspective, said that Republican and Democratic candidates were so similar that he would not care if his candidacy drained away enough votes from the Democrats to cost his former party the election victory.

The differences between a Carter and a Reagan in 1980 seemed vital or trivial depending on the observer. Some recent efforts to increase the distinctions between the parties have been associated with shattering defeat in general elections. Barry Goldwater sought in 1964 to give the voters "a choice, not an echo" but was overwhelmingly defeated at the polls. George McGovern's candidacy was about as distinctively leftist as Goldwater's had been rightist, and he too was demolished at the polls. Yet Ronald Reagan has long been a spokesman for the conservative wing of his party, and he won decisively.

Before Reagan's victory, the defeats of Goldwater and McGovern had often been taken as indicative of what happens to candidates who deviate from the centrist mainstream of American politics. But even then it was apparent that both Goldwater and McGovern had unusually poor ratings from the voters as candidates, and that they both ran against powerful incumbents who many observers thought were unbeatable. Reagan, in contrast, was viewed more positively by the voters than Goldwater and McGovern had been. Further, his opponent had lower popularity ratings than any president seeking reelection since polls have measured such things.

Thus, Reagan's victory indicates that presidential politics are not so limited to the political center as previous experience had suggested. While the prospects for ideologically distinctive candidates' winning election are better than Goldwater's or McGovern's fortunes suggest, these prospects seem closely tied to the voters' evaluation of the incumbent administration as well as to their evaluation of the ideologically distinctive challenger. In any case, it is the nominating process that determines the nature of the choices to be offered the voters, and whether the options are sharply distinct, as in 1964 and 1972, or only moderately different, as in 1960 and 1968.

## The Nominating Process in the In-Party

The nominating process in the party controlling the White House is dominated by the incumbent president and usually results in the renomination of that incumbent. Only three times among the twelve nominations since 1936 was that not the case. One of these exceptions occurred in 1960, when President Dwight D. Eisenhower was completing his second full term at age sixty-nine. Even if Eisenhower had wished to run again, he would have been ineligible by virtue of the Twenty-second amendment to the Constitution, which limits presidents to two terms. Eisenhower's Vice-President, Richard M. Nixon, became the early favorite for the nomination, and in spite of extensive preliminary activity in late 1959 by New York's Governor Nelson Rockefeller, Nixon was never seriously challenged.

The other two cases in which incumbents were not renominated were more complicated. In 1952 and 1968, Presidents Truman and Johnson had completed one full term in their own right after having been elevated from the vice-presidency on the deaths of Presidents Roosevelt and Kennedy, respectively. Both were presiding over unpopular wars in Asia, and both had become sufficiently controversial and unpopular that it was doubtful that they could win reelection. Nevertheless, it was widely assumed that each would run for renomination, since neither had withdrawn as the primaries began in March.

Both Truman and Johnson were challenged in the early primaries by candidates who were not thought to have much hope of success. Senator Estes Kefauver, who challenged Truman in the 1952 New Hampshire primary, and Senator Eugene McCarthy, who challenged Johnson there in 1968, were lightly regarded and not viewed as serious threats to the President. Nevertheless, Kefauver actually defeated Truman in the New Hampshire primary, and McCarthy did so much better than expected (41.9 percent to Johnson's 49.6 percent) that the result was considered a moral victory. Both Truman and Johnson withdrew from candidacy soon afterward.

It is tempting to conclude that these presidents withdrew because of their misfortunes in the primaries, but this would be a mistake. Truman had decided earlier that he did not want to run again, and he had sought unsuccessfully to persuade Chief Justice Fred Vinson and Governor Adlai Stevenson of Illinois to run. It was only because he did not have a candidate to back as his successor that he had not withdrawn already. Senator Kefauver, who defeated him in New Hampshire, was not acceptable to him or to most of the leaders of the Democratic party, largely because of the way the senator had handled some highly publicized investigations into organized crime. There is little doubt that President Truman could have won renomination if he had sought it.

President Lyndon B. Johnson also claimed he had intended all along to withdraw, though there is less independent evidence of this, and he had not made any efforts to choose a successor. It was apparent that he did not favor Senators McCarthy and Robert Kennedy, and though he doubtless preferred Vice-President Hubert H. Humphrey to them, he took no active steps to support Humphrey's candidacy. As in Truman's case, there is little reason to believe that Johnson would have been defeated for renomination had he sought it. But in

*Table 1. Major Party Nominees and Election Victors, 1936–80*

| Year | Preprimary front-runner | Leader of final poll of party rank and file | Nominee | Election outcome |
|------|------------------------|----------------------------------------------|---------|------------------|
| | | A. Party Controlling Presidency | | |
| 1936 | Roosevelt | Roosevelt | Roosevelt | won |
| 1940 | Roosevelt | Roosevelt | Roosevelt | won |
| 1944 | Roosevelt | Roosevelt | Roosevelt | won |
| 1948 | Truman | Truman | Truman | won |
| 1952 | Truman | Kefauver | Stevenson | lost |
| 1956 | Eisenhower | Eisenhower | Eisenhower | won |
| 1960 | Nixon | Nixon | Nixon | lost |
| 1964 | Johnson | Johnson | Johnson | won |
| 1968 | Johnson | Humphrey | Humphrey | lost |
| 1972 | Nixon | Nixon | Nixon | won |
| 1976 | Ford | Ford | Ford | lost |
| 1980 | Carter | Carter | Carter | lost |
| | | B. Party Out of Power | | |
| 1936 | Landon | Landon | Landon | lost |
| 1940 | ? | Willkie | Willkie | lost |
| 1944 | Dewey | Dewey | Dewey | lost |
| 1948 | Dewey-Taft | Dewey | Dewey | lost |
| 1952 | Eisenhower-Taft | Eisenhower | Eisenhower | won |
| 1956 | Stevenson | Stevenson | Stevenson | lost |
| 1960 | Kennedy | Kennedy | Kennedy | won |
| 1964 | ? | Goldwater-Nixon tie | Goldwater | lost |
| 1968 | Nixon | Nixon | Nixon | won |
| 1972 | Muskie | McGovern | McGovern | lost |
| 1976 | ? | Carter | Carter | won |
| 1980 | Reagan | Reagan | Reagan | won |

both cases renomination would have come only after a divisive battle that would have damaged the president's prestige and would have further reduced his already limited prospect of reelection.

Thus it would be a mistake to conclude that the New Hampshire primaries of 1952 and 1968 defeated these presidents or forced their withdrawal. More accurately, they increased the price of renomination at the same time that they reduced its value for the incumbent. Surely these primary setbacks reinforced any previous inclination the presidents had had to retire.

In all the remaining cases from 1936 on, the incumbent president was renominated. In fact, no incumbent was defeated for renomination since that happened to President Chester A. Arthur in 1884. This does not mean that incumbents since then were not vulnerable. The third-term issue made President Franklin D. Roosevelt vulnerable in 1940, but there was no very credible alternative to him. Truman's prestige was so low in 1948 that numerous prominent Democratic leaders sought to persuade General Eisenhower to run as a Democrat. The general declined, and again there was no credible alternative.

The nomination that best illustrates the power of the incumbency is that of Gerald R. Ford in 1976. Because of the unique way he had become president, on Nixon's resignation and without ever having been nominated for office by a national party convention, Ford had the weakest electoral claim to the office of any president ever. This unusual vulnerability was aggravated by the fact that he was challenged by the strongest opponent any incumbent had faced since President Taft was challenged by former President Roosevelt in 1912. Ronald Reagan was the most popular alternative Ford might have faced, and a far more formidable threat to the incumbent than Senators Kefauver and McCarthy had been. Still President Ford won the nomination.

President Carter's popular support had sunk to record lows in 1979, which, along with his weak ties to party organization, made him unusually vulnerable. And he was challenged by Senator Edward Kennedy, the most formidable alternative to Carter in the Democratic party. Yet while Kennedy seemed a major threat as a potential candidate, he was ineffectual as an active one, and Carter (with the "help" of the Iranian hostage crisis) turned aside Kennedy's challenge.

What happens when the incumbent president is not a candidate? There are too few recent examples to draw any meaningful generalizations, but being vice-president helps. Vice-President Nixon was nominated with ease in 1960 when Eisenhower was ineligible. Vice-President Humphrey was much advantaged by the office when he won in 1968. This is especially apparent when we compare his weakness when he ran for president as a senator in 1960.

Popularity with the party rank and file also helps (and being vice-president is a good way to become popular). Vice-Presidents Nixon and Humphrey led the polls of their parties' rank and file when they were nominated. In 1952, Senator Kefauver led the polls, but was unable to overcome the opposition of party leaders.

None of the three incumbents who were not candidates actively promoted his successor, for a variety of reasons, including the likelihood that such an effort would backfire. No one who was unacceptable to the president was chosen, and in Kefauver's case, the opposition of the president and party leaders was the central factor in his defeat. (However, with recent rules changes and reforms, it will be more difficult for party leaders to deny a popular candidate the nomination.)

*The Nominating Process in the Out-Party*

Nominations in the party out of power are not structured by the presence of a dominant figure such as an incumbent president. Accordingly, they are much more likely to involve open competition and division about who should be the nominee. Until recently, many out-party nominations were rather similar to in-party nominations in that they were dominated by a single candidate from start to finish. Specifically, in five of the nine nominations from 1936 through 1968, a single candidate was identified as the front-runner before the first primaries began. Each of these five survived the primary season with his advantages and support intact and won the nomination. This is how the nomination was won by Governor Landon in 1936, Governor Dewey in 1944, Governor Stevenson in 1956, Senator Kennedy in 1960, and former Vice-President Nixon in 1968. In most of these cases the primaries did not play a significant part in the selection process. These men won because they were the most popular candidates in the party, and because, as centrists, they were reasonably acceptable to most segments of the party. These advantages were apparent before the formal process began, and though some received more serious challenge than others, all survived the obstacles and achieved nomination on the first ballot.

Two other out-party nominations were somewhat similar in that the competition was highly structured from start to finish. In both 1948 and 1952 the Republicans had close races between two candidates with rather even chances to win, which were at the same time battles between the moderate and conservative wings of the party. Both times, Senator Taft was the candidate of the conservative wing, whereas in 1948 Governor Dewey represented the liberal or moderate wing and General Eisenhower did so in 1952. Both contests were hard-fought struggles from beginning to end, and both were won by the moderates, who were the candidates with the greatest support among rank-and-file Republicans, though not from all strata of party leaders. Each contest was close: Dewey won on the third ballot, and Eisenhower was able to win on the first ballot only after Minnesota shifted its votes from Stassen to the General.

In spite of a reputation for importance in nominating politics, presidential primaries had little to do with any of these nominations. In fact, during this period between 1936 and 1968, the primaries did not eliminate any candidate who was otherwise likely to win, nor were they instrumental in the victories of any candidate who was otherwise likely to lose. In 1940 and 1964, the contests were far less structured, but the first of these was won by Wendell Wilkie, who had entered no primaries at all, and the second was won by Barry Goldwater, whose performance in the primaries was very mixed.

Beginning in 1972, however, the primaries have become central to out-party nominating politics. In 1972, Senator Edmund S. Muskie was the preprimary front-runner, but his candidacy was so badly battered after he lost four of the first six primaries that he withdrew from active contention. Senator George S. McGovern, on the other hand, was seen before the primaries as an also-ran, but he used the primaries to develop a popular following and to amass a body of delegate votes that brought him the nomination. Senator McGovern certainly could not have won the 1972 nomination without the system of presidential primaries, and it is highly probable that Senator Muskie would have won it without them.

Again in 1976, the primaries were central. There was no preprimary front-runner like Muskie for the primaries to eliminate. Jimmy Carter was one of about a dozen candidates, and while he had shown some promise, the same could be said of several others. Before the first primary in New Hampshire, he had scarcely registered in the polls, but he was to win in New Hampshire and in all but three others of the first fourteen primaries.

These primaries established Carter as the man to beat and gave him a substantial lead in the ultimate currency of nominating politics — delegate votes. No resource is worth more in nominating politics than the number of delegate votes it can be translated into, and Jimmy Carter was far ahead in these. His performance in the remaining primaries was indifferent, bringing him only seven victories in the fifteen others he contested, but he managed to maintain enough momentum to win the endorsement of several important party leaders. These successes broadened his appeal and brought him enough delegate votes to assure the nomination.

The 1980 nomination marked a return to the earlier pattern in which pre-primary front-runners go on to win. Ronald Reagan was the candidate to beat before the primaries, and while he was briefly set back by George Bush's superior showing in the February Iowa caucuses, Reagan swept most of the remaining primaries, and won the nomination with ease.

*Some General Observations on the Nominating Process*
Since their deeply divided convention in 1968, the Democrats have gone through two cycles of effort to reform procedures for nominating candidates for President. These efforts have led to numerous changes in party rules and many state-law changes that have also affected the Republicans. The most obvious and notable result has been the proliferation of presidential primaries, which have doubled in number to over thirty-five, and which now control the selection of at least three-quarters of the delegates.

Plainly, these election reforms have changed a lot of things. The belief that nominations are now more open and democratic seems to have attracted more candidates into contests for the out-party nomination, and the delegate votes are much more directly tied to popular preferences than before. These changes are surely also related to the increased importance of the primaries in defining the range of alternatives. Several times in the past, the primaries transformed previous unknowns in presidential politics into serious contenders, most notably Senator Kefauver in 1952 and Senator McCarthy in 1968. But before 1972, no person who owed his seriousness as a candidate to the primaries ever won the nomination. Since then, however, the primaries were central to the campaigns of both McGovern and Carter.

Yet it is easy to overestimate the importance of these changes. This is most apparent when we assess how democratic previous choices had been by the most relevant available standard: the polls of the party rank and file. Most nominees of both parties stood at the top of the final polls of their party's rank and file since the polls were first taken in 1936. (See the table on page 32.) This was as true before the reforms as after. There were several close cases, but only one in which a clear leader in the polls was denied the nomination. This was the 1952

Democratic nomination, when Senator Kefauver was turned back in spite of having far more popular support than any other candidate.

Under the reformed rules, it would be far more difficult now for party leaders to veto a candidate who had run successfully in most primaries as Kefauver did, but there are few other nominations that would obviously have turned out differently under different rules. The new rules may help ensure that the people's voice will be heard in nominating politics, but the evidence suggests that that voice has long been heard and heeded. Party leaders may have been more influential in past nominations, but they seldom supported unpopular candidates. Leaders like to win elections, and it is easier to do so with popular candidates.

This is not to say that the leaders always prefer the candidate who is most popular with the rank and file. They obviously did not in the Democratic party in 1952, and there are other examples. But the leaders do not always prevail over the rank and file when there are disagreements. Thus George McGovern was chosen in spite of the opposition of most party leaders, but with the help of the rules changes. The most interesting example before the reforms was in the Republican party in 1952: Taft was the choice of the lower echelon of party leaders such as the county chairmen, but Eisenhower was the choice of the rank and file and of the top echelon of leaders such as the party's governors. Eisenhower, of course, won.

Another kind of division within parties has received considerable attention in recent years. It has been repeatedly observed that the people who supported Goldwater for the Republican nomination in 1964 and those who supported McGovern for the Democratic nomination in 1972 were not representative of their parties' voters. Specifically, Goldwater's supporters were said to be more conservative than most Republicans and McGovern's supporters were said to be more liberal than most Democrats. Because partisans of relatively extreme views prevailed in these nominations, it is said, their parties could not appeal effectively for the votes of independents and partisans of the opposition, as is necessary in order to win elections.

There is much truth in these assessments, but it would be a mistake to conclude that this is the common pathology of nominating politics. Plainly, such activists of relatively extreme views are rarely so much in evidence as they were at these times, though some similarities are to be found among the supporters of Senator Eugene McCarthy in 1968 and in 1980. But Goldwater and McGovern were able to prevail not only because of their superior organizations of activist supporters but also because of the division in the remainder of their parties.

The reforms have weakened the influence of party leaders and professionals and have enhanced somewhat the influence of amateur candidate enthusiasts. They have added to the directness of the influence of the party rank and file, but these party voters were indirectly influential before the reforms. Probably the more persistent characteristic of recent nominees before and after the reforms is that they usually have a better claim than any of their opponents to the support of their parties' voters.

In this respect, little change is needed (though the system could surely use simplifying and streamlining). A major innovation such as a national primary would usually lead to the same result as has otherwise occurred (except in the Democratic nominations of 1972 and 1976). But the present system has one feature that a national primary would not have. The series of state primaries that begins with a few smaller states gives unknown challengers a chance to make themselves known and to develop a following. Only two such persons have won the presidential nomination (McGovern and Carter), but the possibility is a healthy one that is almost unique to our system.[1]

## Election

Once the Republican and Democratic parties have chosen their nominees, the choice is up to the voters, whose preferences are filtered through the Electoral College for the final decision. Most of the time, this involves a simple choice between two candidates wherein the winner of the largest number of popular votes is elected, but it is possible for the result to turn out otherwise. Because all the electoral votes of a given state go to the candidate who wins more votes there than any other candidate, a narrow victory in a large state like California can bring more than forty electoral votes, while an overwhelming victory in neighboring Nevada can bring only three. This phenomenon is likely to lead to electoral-vote totals that distort popular margins, and it is possible for the Electoral College to award the presidency to someone who did not win the largest number of popular votes. This has not happened since 1888, however, when President Grover Cleveland received more popular votes than Benjamin Harrison but "wasted" many of them in big margins in the states he had already won while Harrison's votes were more evenly dispersed. Every president since Harrison has won a plurality of the popular vote as well as a majority in the Electoral College, but there is no guarantee that no popular vote winner will lose the presidency in the Electoral College sometime in the future. Indeed, a small shift of votes in Ohio and Hawaii in 1976 could have cost Jimmy Carter the presidency without denying him his popular vote majority.

Even though all presidents for more than a century have been nominees of the Republican or Democratic party, a minor-party candidate can have an impact on either the popular or the Electoral College outcome, or both. The 1980 contest between Reagan and Carter was too one-sided to be affected by John Anderson's respectable showing, but the 1968 and 1948 elections show clearly the potential effects of minor party candidates. Governor George Wallace ran in 1968 as an "American Independent" and received 13.5 percent of the vote. Because the contest between Nixon and Humphrey was so close (43.4 percent to 42.7 percent), these Wallace votes could have changed the popular-vote outcome.

Twenty years previously, in 1948, minor-party candidates also came close to denying a popular-vote victory to the likely winner of a two-man race. In 1948 there were two minor parties. Former Vice-President Henry A. Wallace was the Progressive candidate for president, and Governor Strom Thurmond of South Carolina (now a Republican senator from that state) ran as a Dixiecrat. While Wallace was to the left of President Truman and Thurmond was to the right, both were former Democrats, and most of their supporters were likely to be people who would otherwise have voted for Truman. To the surprise of most observers, however, the President won in spite of the votes he lost to Wallace and Thurmond.

Third-party candidates usually do not care very much what they do to popular-vote totals, which are not decisive in presidential elections. Some hope to concentrate their votes enough to win several states and deny victory to the major-party candidates in the Electoral College, where an absolute majority is required. This would throw the election into the House of Representatives, where each state would vote as a unit. This has not happened since 1824, but Governor Wallace was hoping to bring it about in 1968. Had Wallace been first instead of a respectable second in North Carolina, South Carolina, and Tennessee, Nixon would have won by only 1 of the 538 electoral votes. Of course, nobody knows what would have happened if the election had been thrown into the House of Representatives.

These peculiar possibilities in the Electoral College have led many people to favor a change to a direct popular vote for president and abolition of the Electoral College. This might well be a step forward; but as indicated, there is no guarantee that the most preferred candidate would win even under direct popular vote. This is because a third candidate might drain away enough votes from the most popular individual to deny him the popular majority. Accordingly, most proposals for direct popular elections provide for a runoff between the top two candidates if no one receives 40 percent of the vote. Thus the possibility that the "wrong" candidate may win is inherent when there are more than two candidates, and is not a peculiarity of either the Electoral College or the direct popular vote.[2]

## How Popular Votes Are Determined

Presidential elections have, overall, been quite competitive in recent years. Three times since World War II, the popular winner has received less than 50 percent of the vote (because of third-party candidates). And even though some of the other elections have been landslides, neither party has held the White House for more than eight years since 1953. This is true in spite of the fact that Democrats outnumber Republicans by a three-to-two margin among the voters. Even though Republicans failed to win control of either house of Congress between 1954 and 1980, they have been at least competitive in all presidential elections in this period except that of 1964. Although independents outnumber Republicans, independents have favored Republican candidates in six of the last seven elections, and Democrats themselves regularly defect to Republican candidates in large numbers, as was notably the case in 1980.

Even though voters' party identifications may be the most important single factor in presidential elections, these party loyalties are declining in two ways. Fewer people identify with a party, and those who do are less likely to support its candidates. Short-term forces associated with a given election are more decisive than before. The issues, the candidates, and the campaign decisively influence election outcomes.

In recent years, Republicans have regularly chosen presidential candidates more preferred by the voters than Democratic candidates. Among the years 1952–1980, only in 1964, when President Johnson ran against Senator Goldwater, was the Democratic candidate more favorably viewed by the voters than the Republican. Only in that year did public perceptions of both candidates together help the Democrats more than the Republicans. This observation is based on the unsurprising facts that Eisenhower was viewed more favorably than Stevenson and that Nixon was seen more favorably than McGovern. It is based also on the somewhat more surprising fact that Nixon was more of an asset to the Republicans in 1960 than Kennedy was to the Democrats. In spite of the decline in his reputation, and the controversial image that followed him throughout his political career, Nixon was a distinct asset to the Republicans each of the three times he ran for President.

Many commentators have deplored the facts that candidate image and candidate personality are so important in electoral politics and that issues do not count for more. Actually, candidate personality is a perfectly legitimate and proper subject for voters to evaluate and weigh. Presidents do far more than respond to the issue preferences of the voters. They have enormous discretionary power, and their personalities can importantly affect the way they handle issues and decide public policy.

Thus, James David Barber argues that presidential personality has been responsible for some major policy misfortunes.[3] He says personality was responsible for Woodrow Wilson's tenacious refusal to compromise his version of the League of Nations treaty. This, in turn, led to the failure of the United States to join the League, which crippled that body's capacity to maintain peace. Barber also says personality was responsible for Herbert Hoover's refusal to provide direct relief for the needy during the Depression, and for Lyndon Johnson's commitment to the Vietnam War long after it became apparent that our goals would not be achieved at reasonable cost. Barber finds similar unfortunate personality characteristics to have been exhibited by President Nixon well before the Watergate affair ensured his demise.

While one may or may not agree with all of Barber's interpretation, personality doubtless can affect the way a president will behave in office. If personality can lead to tragedy, as Barber suggests, perhaps it should weigh more heavily and more systematically in public deliberations rather than less.

Apparently it is not easy for voters to make such judgments, however. Barber finds Johnson and Nixon to have had the most dangerous personalities among presidents since Hoover; yet as we have seen, both were regarded more favorably by the voters than their opponents. Both were reelected as incumbents with landslide margins, only to be subsequently hounded from office.

*Issues in Electoral Politics*

Issues play a more complicated role in electoral politics than candidate personality. This is because issues are only indirectly involved in elections. Voters directly decide issues only in referenda, which do not occur in American national politics. Only the names of candidates and their parties are on the ballot in our national elections. Issues are important or are resolved only insofar as they become involved in the differences between the candidates, and there are many ambiguities in the ways that candidates and issues become associated.

Even when only a single issue is involved in an election, it may be ambiguously involved because the candidates may not clearly differentiate themselves with regard to it. Even if they do, the distinctions may not be clearly seen by the voters, or may not be decisive in many voters' choices. When many issues are involved in an election, as is typical, the complications are multiplied. Different issues may be salient to different voters, and candidates may find that they can gain more votes by appealing to minorities that care very much about an issue than by appealing to majorities that do not. Naturally, candidates who want to maximize their chances of victory will emphasize issues where they are advantaged and de-emphasize issues where they are not. This of course detracts from the clarity of the distinctions and contributes to the ambiguity with which elections handle issues. In addition, candidates sometimes mislead the people, deliberately or otherwise.

Involvement in a foreign war has been an issue in numerous elections, and has presented examples of several ways in which elections do not provide for precise popular control over the disposition of issues. Three times in this century, Democratic presidents have campaigned as peace candidates and subsequently involved us in war. In 1916, a key slogan of President Wilson's campaign was "He kept us out of war," but by 1917 America was involved in World War I. President Roosevelt promised in 1940 that "your boys are not going to be sent into any foreign wars" shortly before we became involved in World War II. Our entry into the Korean conflict did not follow any discussion of that issue in a campaign, but the sharpest escalation of our involvement in the war in Vietnam followed the 1964 presidential campaign, in which Goldwater seemed to be the hawk and Johnson the peace candidate who would not send American boys to fight an Asian war. We know that President Johnson's advantage over Goldwater in that election was enhanced by the fact that the President was seen as better able to handle foreign affairs.

How to get out of a war has been an important issue in modern campaigns, though again elections have not offered very precise control to the voters. In 1952, the Korean conflict was a great liability to the Democrats, and the Republicans were helped importantly by General Eisenhower's pledge to end the war. The general did not say much about how he would do it, but his personal prestige as a war hero and the fact that he was not identified with the incumbent administration lent credibility to his pledge. Whether or not it would have done so without his election, the war did end soon thereafter, leaving one of the better apparent examples of popular control of policy through the electoral process.

How to end the war in Vietnam was a central issue in the 1968 elections, but ironically, it had very little impact on the distribution of votes between the Republican and Democratic candidates.[4] This was because both Humphrey and Nixon were seen by the voters as close to each other near the center of a hawk-dove continuum, and as close to where most of the voters were. This did not provide the voters with much of a choice between the two candidates on this issue, but in one sense the voters could not lose: No matter which candidate won, the victor would be identified with a position that was close to that of most of the voters. If the candidates had distinguished themselves from each other more clearly, the voters might have had more of a choice, and perhaps some better options, but if we want publics to control policy, we cannot really complain when candidates identify with the voters' most preferred positions.

Vietnam was still an issue in the 1972 election, which provided a much clearer choice between an incumbent identified with an "honorable end to the war" and a challenger advocating an immediate end to the war, more or less regardless of the consequences in South Vietnam. President Nixon won decisively, and his handling of foreign affairs was a major factor in drawing votes to him. However, in spite of the electoral victory for him and his policies, in just over two years South Vietnam was taken over by the Communists, which was presumably not a result many people had in mind when they considered an "honorable end to the war." The Vietnam issue thus illustrates several great ironies about the role of issues in electoral politics.

Race is an issue in which elections have not always been constructive, though considerable strides have been made recently. After the end of Reconstruction, neither party did much to advance civil rights and racial equality. The blacks who could vote generally supported Republicans, apparently because Democrats were identified with white supremacy in the South and because the Republicans were identified with Lincoln, emancipation, and Reconstruction. After the Great Depression began, however, most blacks shifted to the support of the Democratic Party, not because it had embraced the cause of civil rights but, apparently, because it had become identified with economic underdogs, which included most blacks.

Harry Truman was the first twentieth-century president to make a sustained and direct appeal to black voters on civil-rights grounds. His proposal of civil-rights legislation and his executive orders to establish fair employment practices and to eliminate discrimination in the armed forces served to identify Truman as more favorable to civil rights. Several of these moves were designed to help him win black votes. These events suggest how efforts to appeal for votes can lead to constructive policy changes — though, of course, this is not always the case.

In the 1950s, the parties returned to a more ambiguous stance and to vaguer differences on civil rights. Neither Dwight D. Eisenhower nor Adlai Stevenson was clearly identified with a stance for or against civil rights. Both were considered moderates on the issue. Stevenson was the Northern candidate for the Democratic nomination who was most acceptable to the South, while Eisenhower was, on the one hand, distinctly cool to the *Brown v. Board of Education* school-desegregation decision and, on the other hand, the president who sent troops to Little Rock to enforce the law regarding school desegregation. Under the circumstances, many voters found it understandably hard in the 1950s to identify the party most likely to advance the cause of civil rights.

It was in the context of this ambiguity that the 1960 election took place. The differences between the candidates were marginal. John F. Kennedy had identified himself as slightly more pro civil rights by an important symbolic gesture, a telephone call to Mrs. Martin Luther King, Jr., when her husband was in jail. Kennedy also criticized the Eisenhower Administration for not making a "stroke of the pen" to sign an executive order that would outlaw discrimination in public housing.

These things helped solidify black support behind Kennedy, but once he had been elected, he seemingly gave civil rights a low priority. He proposed no civil-rights legislation until 1963, after the Birmingham riots, and he himself did not make the stroke of the pen regarding public housing for almost two years after he took office.

The Civil Rights Act of 1964, the most important piece of legislation in this area since Reconstruction, was passed after Kennedy's death. President Lyndon B. Johnson thoroughly identified himself with the law and campaigned in 1964 as an advocate of civil rights. During his subsequent administration, other important civil-rights acts were passed.

From time to time presidents, once elected, violate expectations based on their previous careers or on what they have said in campaigns. This is, of course, sometimes to be deplored, but not always. In retrospect, it seems that President Johnson violated the promises he made in the 1964 election, with disastrous results. Few would now applaud his Asian policies, though soon after the election public support for his escalation of American involvement in Vietnam was high. In the short run, what turned people against Johnson was less that he involved them in a war after leading them to expect otherwise than that his policy was a failure. The cost in men, money, and time was far greater than anyone had expected, and the desired result was still not forthcoming.

President Richard Nixon did several things that were divergent from policies he had been identified with, and at least some were viewed positively. Although he had been viewed as a conservative in economic affairs, his policies included several things we might have expected Nixon himself to have criticized the

Democrats for as being too liberal. The dollar was devalued in relation to foreign currency, and, though Nixon had long been a critic of government control over prices, he instituted a wage-and-price freeze with subsequent government regulation of increases. Nixon's Family Assistance Plan, which would have provided a guaranteed income to working poor families, was perhaps the most daring proposal for innovation in income-support policy since the Social Security Act of 1935 and in many ways he outflanked the Democrats with a proposal they might have feared was too liberal to propose.

The most widely applauded of Nixon's policy innovations was surely his move to open and normalize official diplomatic contact with the People's Republic of China. Nixon had been associated with no policy more clearly than with a vigorous anti-Communism. He had been a strong defender of our association with Nationalist China, and veteran Nixon-watchers might have expected him to be the first to criticize a president who would normalize relations with the Communist Chinese. Surely it was easier for conservatives to accept this innovation from Nixon than it would have been for them to accept it from a Democrat.

Sometimes these turnabouts from previous expectations are applauded, as in the case of Nixon's China policy, and sometimes they are vilified, as in the case of Johnson's war policy. In either case, they are illustrations of the limitations of elections as instruments of popular control of public policy. Once elected, public officials have considerable freedom to create new policies that may be quite divergent from the expressed preferences of their supporters. Although there are times when this is to be deplored, there are others in which this seems to leave possibilities for creative leadership and innovation that would be far less likely to occur if the officials had to have the approval of voters in advance of their decisions.

In general, then, elections are a blunt instrument of popular control. V. O. Key, Jr., once said the voters' vocabulary is limited to two words, "yes" and "no." Insofar as this is true, one cannot expect voters to be able to provide precise direction of the affairs of government. Still, American presidential nominations and elections are, to a large extent, popularly based. Most of the limitations of popular control over presidential politics are more directly rooted in the inherent limitations of representative government than in the limitations of our own unique electoral institutions.

SOURCE: An earlier version of this essay appeared in Thomas E. Cronin and Rexford G. Tugwell, eds., *The Presidency Reappraised* (New York: Praeger, 1977).

## Notes

1. For more detailed analysis of these nominations and all others between 1936 and 1972, see William R. Keech and Donald R. Matthews, *The Party's Choice* (Washington, D.C.: Brookings Institution, 1976).

2. For a more detailed analysis of American voting behavior, see Herbert Asher, *Presidential Elections and American Politics: Voters, Candidates and Campaigns Since 1952* 2nd edition. (Homewood, Ill.: Dorsey Press, 1980), and Norman H. Nie, Sidney Verba, and John R. Petrocik, *The Changing American Voter* (Cambridge, Mass.: Harvard University Press, 1976).
3. James David Barber, *The Presidential Character* rev. ed. (Englewood Cliffs, N.J.: Prentice-Hall, 1977).
4. For a detailed analysis, see Benjamin I. Page and Richard A. Brody, "Policy Voting and the Electoral Process: The Vietnam War Issue," *American Political Science Review*, vol. 66 (September 1972), pp. 979–95.

# Rethinking the Presidential Nominating Process

# II

**3. Reforming the Electoral Reforms**

*Cyrus R. Vance*

**4. Two Cheers for the National Primary**

*Michael Nelson*

**5. Two Cheers for the Presidential Primaries**

*William J. Crotty*

# 3. Reforming the Electoral Reforms

## Cyrus R. Vance

In 1980, more than a dozen candidates in 37 primaries spent more than $100 million campaigning for the privilege of being nominated for the presidency. The experience has produced, among politicians and voters, the growing conviction that we must change the manner in which we choose our presidential candidates. In fact, the problems are so acute that action is required now, before the imminent start of the 1984 campaign. In a world of rapid change, we can no longer afford an electoral system that tends to hobble the governmental decision-making process for months. This not only harms us at home, but concerns and alarms our friends and allies, and tempts our adversaries.

Presidential candidates are currently nominated in the quadrennial rite of the national party conventions, which are preceded by months of state conventions, primaries and caucuses in which delegates to the national conventions are chosen. The process suffers from a number of problems. First, it takes too long. The state primaries and caucuses stretch from January to June of the election year. A successful campaign requires months of preparation before the first primary to organize supporters and raise money. The successes of George McGovern in 1972 and Jimmy Carter in 1976 have shown the value of early grass-roots organization in primary and caucus states. Senator McGovern announced his candidacy in January 1971, 18 months before the Democratic convention, and President Carter announced his candidacy in December 1974, 19 months before the convention. Both, in fact, had spent many months testing the political waters before making their formal announcements. In addition, the federal election law of 1974 gives a financial incentive to an aspiring candidate to begin his campaign early. The law requires a candidate, in order to qualify for public financing, to raise $5,000 in at least 20 states through contributions of $250 or less.

The upshot is that the race for the nomination has become at least an 18- to 24-month endurance test which provides an advantage to candidates who can devote a substantial amount of time to campaigning. In the last two elections, two former governors — both free of any official public office long before they were nominated — have won their party's nomination and gone on to be elected president. Two of Governor Reagan's principal opponents in the 1980 Republican primaries, George Bush and John Connally, were also free of the demands of public office when they ran as candidates.

*Cyrus R. Vance, a New York attorney, has held a number of important governmental positions including Secretary of State in the Carter administration.*

In short, the nominating process has become a marathon in which many highly qualified potential candidates, unable to leave private jobs or public responsibilities to devote many months to campaigning, cannot compete. Senator Howard Baker, who started his primary campaign late because of his duties as Senate minority leader, learned this lesson well in 1980.

A second, related and very serious problem is the effect that a long primary campaign has on the ability of the executive branch to make policy decisions. An incumbent president who must campaign for his own party's nomination must begin running for reelection as early as the third year of his four-year term of office. The long period of highly charged electioneering results in the shelving of some policy decisions until after the campaign. Other decisions may be influenced by the politics of reelection, or at least invite charges that the president's office is being used for political purposes — a result which hurts both the country and the president.

President Carter, for example, was compelled to wage a long and fruitless battle with Senator Edward M. Kennedy over a national health program beginning with the Democratic midterm convention in December 1978 and continuing through the 1980 primaries. The politics of campaigning forced the President to invest considerable time and energy in formulating and defending an alternative program to Senator Kennedy's and prevented him from negotiating a compromise plan. And some critics accused the President of using the crisis in Iran for his own political advantage during the primaries — for example, his announcement on the morning of the Wisconsin primary that he had made some progress in efforts to secure the release of the hostages. As President Lyndon Johnson said in his book, "The Vantage Point," "The old belief that a President can carry out the responsibilities of his office and at the same time undergo the rigors of campaigning is, in my opinion, no longer valid."

While the prospect of a second term has always affected presidential decisions to some degree, this condition has been aggravated by the fact that incumbent presidents are now more likely to have to campaign for renomination. Traditionally, the power of incumbency was sufficient to assure that a president would be renominated without challenge. A serious challenge from inside the party ranks to an incumbent president — a rare event prior to the 1960s — was tantamount to a party's admission that his nomination in the first instance was a mistake. The present primary system, with public campaign financing and an emphasis on grass-roots support, encourages challenges to a president's renomination. President Ford narrowly defeated a bid by Governor Reagan in 1976, and President Carter came from behind in the polls to defeat Senator Kennedy in 1980.

Third, the present primary system isolates the candidate from party and congressional leaders. In the past, a candidate usually rose through party ranks in a system that was not always democratic; party bosses often chose candidates in smoke-filled rooms. But the parties tended to produce candidates accustomed to working with diverse groups and to forging a consensus among the competing factions within the party. Over the years, the system produced good presidents like Franklin D. Roosevelt, Harry S. Truman, and Dwight D. Eisenhower, and undistinguished ones like Warren G. Harding. The rules have changed, however, and now a candidate can win his party's nomination by appealing directly to primary voters and bypassing party leaders.

In 1980, more than 75 percent of the delegates at both national conventions were selected by voters in primaries. This process has the virtue of giving an "outsider" a chance to win the nomination, as seen in the case of Senator Mc-Govern in 1972 and President Carter in 1976. But this process places a premium on stamina, grass-roots organization, fund raising and amassing delegates. It does not insure that a successful candidate will have the experience, acumen and political skills needed for leadership. Nor does it insure that a candidate will have the support of political leaders whose alliance may be essential in enacting legislation. Such a candidate may find it impossible to transform an electoral victory into a governing coalition.

The isolation of candidates from party leaders has also contributed to the weakening of the party system. Over the years, the importance of political parties has been diminished by the growth of single-interest groups, the appeal to voters through television and direct mail, and the wide use of polls. The present trend of increased use of primaries, however, may prove to be the death knell of the parties by eliminating the role of party leaders in the nominating process. There were, for example, only eight senators and 37 House members among the 3,331 delegates to the 1980 Democratic National Convention. The Republicans fared little better, with 26 senators and 64 House members among the 1,994 delegates to their convention.

Moreover, in the past decade, the news organizations have replaced the parties in designating the crucial testing grounds, determining which candidates are to be taken seriously and interpreting the votes of the electorate. The small, seemingly insignificant New Hampshire primary has been elevated by the media into a major contest that can affect the outcome of an entire campaign. A candidate does not even have to win the New Hampshire primary to be successful; he merely has to win more votes than the press and television have predicted he will win.

The 1972 New Hampshire Democratic primary is a case in point. Senator Edmund Muskie defeated Senator McGovern by nearly 10 percent of the vote, but the media crowned McGovern the winner because they had predicted that Muskie would win by a greater margin. Senator McGovern then went on to win the Democratic nomination.

Success in the early primaries results in media exposure and other benefits for a candidate far in excess of that warranted by events. This phenomenon is commonly called "momentum." To gain momentum, candidates spend heavily on advertising in the early primaries with the hope of gaining free media coverage as a result of a stronger-than-expected showing.

Finally, the present system prevents convention delegates from exercising independent judgment in casting their votes at the national party conventions. Under party and state rules, the vast majority of delegates are committed on the first ballot to vote for a particular candidate according to the results of primaries and caucuses. As a result, delegates merely ratify the results of the primaries. During the months between the state primaries and caucuses and the national conventions, public opinion may shift significantly or events may transform the political scene. Nevertheless, with only a few exceptions, the delegates must vote for the candidate to whom they are committed. Given this fact, and the fact that every Democratic and Republican presidential candidate after 1952 has been elected on the first ballot, it is doubtful that conventions as presently run now serve any useful purpose.

How did we arrive at this system of nominating presidential candidates? The system is largely the product of 12 years of reforms, which have had some unintended and undesirable effects.

Beginning in 1968, the parties initiated reforms to change the presidential nominating process. At the turbulent 1968 Democratic National Convention and during the years that followed, opposing views of how the president should be nominated clashed within the Democratic party. On the one hand was the view, which had prevailed in practice up to that time, that delegates, and eventually a candidate, should be chosen by established party leaders. On the other hand was the view, held by the reformers, that delegates should be democratically selected by the party members. This second view prevailed, significantly reducing the role of the party leaders in the selection process and increasing the reliance on a direct selection of candidates by the party members.

Between 1968 and 1976, the Democratic party, led by liberal members, revised the party's method of selecting delegates by extensive and often controversial changes of rules. Among the more significant changes were (1) the abolition of the old unit rule (under which a state could decide to vote at the convention in one solid bloc) in favor of a rule requiring state delegations to reflect the portion of the vote each candidate received in that state's primary or caucus; (2) the provision for representation of party and elected officials totaling 10 percent of each state's delegates, and (3) the imposition of quotas to encourage participation by and representation of women and minorities.

Republican reforms have been more cautious than those of the Democrats. The Republicans created a panel to make recommendations for more open delegate selection, but few substantive proposals were accepted by the Republican national party leadership.

In response to party reforms, many states changed the manner in which they selected delegates to the national conventions, with the result that by 1976 delegates in both parties were selected through either a presidential primary or a reformed caucus-convention system. The increase in the number of delegates chosen through presidential primaries has been the most dramatic change. In 1968, the Democrats selected 40 percent of their convention delegates in 17 state primaries. In 1976, they selected 75 percent of their delegates in 30 state primaries. In 1980, they selected 80 percent of their convention delegates in 34 state primaries. This trend has been paralleled in the Republican party. By 1976, the G.O.P. selected 66 percent of its delegates in 28 state primaries. In 1980, the G.O.P. selected 76 percent of its delegates in 35 state primaries.

Other significant election reforms were initiated by the federal government, principally in response to Watergate. Federal legislation was enacted to regulate, monitor and subsidize primary and election campaigns. Before 1974, there were few rules governing how candidates could raise and spend money in primaries. There was no limit on the amount that an individual could contribute to a candidate, and there was no limit on the amount that a candidate could spend in his campaign.

The federal election law of 1974, and subsequent interpretations of that statute by the Supreme Court, dramatically changed campaign financing. Candidates now may either qualify for public financing and accept the spending limits that go with it, or forgo public financing and spend without limit any funds they can raise privately. If a candidate qualifies for public financing, he may spend no more than $10 million (plus a cost-of-living adjustment) in the primaries, with the allowable addition of up to 20 percent of that amount to raise money. However, the candidate who qualifies has to raise only part of the $10 million; the balance comes from the federal treasury.

The party rule changes and the federal campaign-financing legislation have profoundly changed the strategy for candidates in the primaries: Assisted by federal campaign funds and no longer required to court party leaders, candidates in larger numbers begin earlier campaigns.

Every candidate for the presidential nomination, even one who does not qualify for public financing, is limited with respect to the size of contributions he may accept. An individual may not contribute more than $1,000 to any one candidate in the primaries, while most political action committees (P.A.C.s) may contribute up to $5,000 to a candidate.

These provisions encourage special interests to become more involved in politics, since they can now receive contributions that in the past went directly to the candidates. The P.A.C.s have become the vehicles of single-interest groups which are able to collect and spend large amounts of money to help a particular candidate, as long as the P.A.C. does not coordinate its efforts with the candidate's campaign. There were only 700 P.A.C.s in 1975. There are now more than 2,500. The proliferation of P.A.C.s has further weakened the national parties. Indeed, the single-interest focus of a P.A.C. is the antithesis of a political party, which is a coalition of voters with numerous interests.

During the 1970s, the merits of the nominating-process reforms made since 1968 were debated constantly. Many political analysts and politicians now appear to believe that the present nominating system should be changed, and numerous proposals to alter the system have been put forth. A review of the proposals must begin with consideration of the objectives the system should serve.

First, the selection procedure must be legitimate; the public must have confidence in the system. The process must be perceived by the public as being consonant with democratic principles and general notions of fairness. A system not perceived in this way will lead to disrespect and confusion on the part of the electorate and a focus on issues not germane to the election. Democrats learned at the bitter and acrimonious Democratic convention of 1968 that an unruly and divided convention can forfeit a subsequent election.

Second, the selection process must be rational and efficient; it should not be an endurance contest discouraging participation by qualified potential candidates. Nor should it be so long that it adversely affects the decision-making process of an incumbent president.

Third, the selection procedure should insure that a successful election coalition will be transformed into a governing coalition. The nominating process should embrace both the democracy of the direct primaries and the judgment of political leaders. To insure that a candidate has the support of party, state, and congressional leaders, the system should include the participation of the political parties. But the role of political peers should not be such that it discourages participation by "outsiders."

With these objectives in mind, I would like to discuss several of the more promising proposals to change the nominating process. Unfortunately, there is no one change that will solve all of our problems or meet all of the objectives. A number or combination of changes will be required. It is also clear that the effort will require the federal government, the states, and the political parties to work closely together to develop a rational and coordinated package of reforms.

One proposal, which I favor, is simply to shorten the period of primary elections. The primary campaign could be compressed into two months rather than six months, and there is no need for the long delay from the last primary to the national conventions. The primaries could be held within a required period of time: for example, from June 1 to July 31. The national conventions could then be scheduled for the last two weeks of August. Seventy-five years ago, when transportation and communications were slower, it may have been prudent to set aside a month between the end of the primaries and the holding of a convention. That is no longer necessary.

A second proposal would group the numerous state primaries into several regional primaries. The party conventions would remain intact, but five or six primaries scheduled several weeks or a month apart could be held in different regions of the country. If a state within one region held a primary election, it would be required to schedule it on the same day as the other states within the region. Such a plan would prevent the results of one state, such as New Hampshire, from being exaggerated by media coverage.

A second proposal, a variation of the regional-primary plan, has been proposed by Senator Robert Packwood, Republican of Oregon. Under this proposal, five regional primaries would be held, and the states in each region would have to hold their primaries on the same day. The order of regional primaries would be determined by lottery by a federal elections commission. The date of each regional primary would be revealed only 70 days before the event. Candidates would not know the order of the primaries and, therefore, would not be able to concentrate their campaigning in one area at the expense of another. Although the regional-primary proposal would reduce the number of primaries, there is the risk that the first round would become the equivalent of New Hampshire with all of its excesses.

A third proposal is for a national primary. This system would replace the current state primaries and conventions with a nationwide vote. The attractiveness of this proposal is its simplicity. However, a national primary would be a grand media event, preceded by a blitz of television spots, slogans and barnstorming, and might unfairly favor those with existing name recognition. Such a plan would eliminate local issues and encourage campaigns that focus not on issues but on personalities. It would also, in my view, mark the final demise of the role of the political parties in the selection of a candidate.

A fourth proposal — which could be used with either of the first two proposals mentioned above, and which I believe has considerable merit — would attempt to restore a balance between direct selection of a candidate by voters in primaries and selection by party and congressional leaders. There are numerous variations of this proposal, but the common element is that each would reserve a bloc of seats at the convention (from a third to a half of the total) for delegates designated by party officials and office-holders in each state. These delegates would remain uncommitted until the first convention ballot. This uncommitted bloc would give the seasoned party leaders a greater voice in the nomination. It would also return the convention to the role of a nominating institution and revive the possibility that a candidate could enter the race late and still emerge with the nomination.

Other proposals have been offered which do not call for reform of the primary system but which would significantly change the manner in which a presidential candidate is nominated. One key proposal — which I support — would limit a president to one term of six years. The idea of a single, limited presidential term is not new. It was proposed, debated and initially adopted by the Committee of the Whole at the Constitutional Convention in 1787. The issue was later revived by Andrew Jackson, and many presidents since him have publicly subscribed to the belief that the national interest would be better served by presidents who are not intent on being reelected. The virtues of a single, six-year term are that a president could devote his full attention to national needs, rather than spending much of his energy on trying to win reelection; the paralysis in decision-making that grips the executive branch during the long primary campaign could be eliminated, and a single-term president would be less inclined to use his office for the purpose of courting voters to win reelection. A similar proposal would limit the service of senators to two six-year terms and the service of representatives to four three-year terms.

Critics of a single-term presidency contend that forcing a president to run for reelection keeps him accountable to the voters and acts as a check on the abuse of power. In addition, it is argued that six years might not be long enough for a president to formulate and carry out his programs, while six years is too long for a president who loses the support of the voters during his term of office.

Finally, it is clear that the campaign-finance laws should be reexamined in the light of our experience with primary campaigns since 1974. For example, the present requirement of raising $5,000 in donations of $250 or less in each of 20 states to be eligible for federal matching funds should be modified or eliminated so that a candidate is not compelled by financial necessity to start a primary campaign early. In addition, and most importantly, the contribution limits that encourage the formation of single-issue P.A.C.s should be reconsidered.

The problems arising out of our present system are by and large the unforeseen results of well-intended efforts to reform the primary system. It is widely recognized that another round of reforms is needed to reform the reforms. Determining how to effect new reforms may be even more difficult than deciding on a course of action. Any solution can be accomplished only by cooperation among congressional leaders, governors, and national and state party leaders, with the governors playing a central role.

Before we embark on a new round of reforms, however, it is important to debate the full range of options available to us. This process must begin now, before the primary candidates of 1984 begin to crisscross the plains of Iowa and the fields and mountains of New Hampshire in their campaign for the presidency.

SOURCE: *The New York Times Magazine,* February 22, 1981, © 1981 by The New York Times Company. Reprinted by permission.

# 4. Two Cheers for the National Primary

## Michael Nelson

We need a clearer, simpler, and more democratic presidential nominating system, one that would grow from the adoption of two or perhaps three measures: one of them old, one of them new, one of them borrowed.

The old idea — 70 or more years old now — is for a national primary method of nominating party candidates for president. Since 1911 and shortly after, when Representative Richard Hobson of Alabama introduced the first piece of national primary legislation and Woodrow Wilson endorsed the concept, some 125 such bills have been offered in Congress. Most have been close kin to the one introduced by Republican U.S. Senator Lowell Weicker, which would work like this:

Each major party's supporters, along with interested independents, would choose their nominee for president directly, with their votes.[1] To get on the primary ballot, a candidate would have until June 30 to round up valid signatures equal in number to one percent of the turnout in the most recent presidential election (around 800,000 in 1980) — a high enough standard to screen out frivolous candidacies, but not "outsider" ones. Ballots would be cast on the first Tuesday in August. If no candidate in a party got 50 percent, there would be a runoff between the top two finishers three weeks later.[2]

By definition, a national primary would be a simpler system than the present one, or any other that has been proposed: the candidate who received a majority of votes would win. It offers the clearest connection between popular votes and outcome as well.

It was characteristic of the political theories of the framers that the electoral role of the citizen in the complex political process was to be clear, if not direct, and comprehensive to him and to those who represent him. First among those principles of constitutional government that the framers subscribed to, writes Clinton Rossiter, was that "government must be plain, simple, and intelligible. The common sense of a reasonably educated man should be able to comprehend its structure and functioning." [3] Henry Mayo notes in his *Introduction to Democratic Theory* that simplicity and clarity are hallmarks of all representative electoral processes:

> If [the] purpose of the election is to be carried out — to enable the voter to share in political power — the voter's job must not be made difficult and

*Michael Nelson teaches political science at Vanderbilt University and is a former editor of* Washington Monthly. *He is the author of* How the Government Works: The Case of CETA *and coeditor of* The Culture of Bureaucracy.

confusing for him. It ought, on the contrary, to be made as simple as the electoral machinery can be devised to make it.[4]

It may be argued that the framers of the Constitution did not have candidate nominations in mind, that their notion of where citizens fit into the governing process was much more constricted. That is true, but beside the point. The framers also did not envision direct election of United States senators or universal adult suffrage. But, by allowing for amendments and for state discretion, their Constitution left open the possibility that the boundaries of popular political participation might expand. What remained constant was the principle that whatever doors of influence were opened to citizens, it should be clear to them how they could walk through.

Democratic theory, in mandating simplicity and clarity in citizen participation, treats elections as a *process*. But, especially to the extent that electoral rules become subjects of political controversy and government regulation, that process also should be thought of as *public policy*. (Certainly elections have been treated that way in the history of nominating politics.) It is useful, then, to consult the literature of policy analysis as well as that of democratic theory for guidance.

Again, one finds simplicity and clarity valued, this time as essential ingredients to sound implementation. In this case the policy is that some public officials be chosen democratically; the selection system is the method of implementation. "[A]n appreciation of the length and unpredictability of necessary decision sequences in implementation should lead the designers of policy to consider more direct means for accomplishing their desired ends," wrote Jeffrey Pressman and Aaron Wildavsky. They add that

> simplicity in policies is much to be desired. The fewer the steps involved in carrying out the program, the fewer the opportunities for a disaster to overtake it. The more directly the policy aims at its target, the fewer the decisions involved in its ultimate realization.[5]

But what other consequences might we reasonably expect of a national primary?

1. *Voter participation in the nominating process would rise substantially.*[6] In part this is almost tautologically true. In 1976, for example, 28.9 million people voted in 30 state primaries, a turnout rate of 28.2 percent of the voting age population in those states. If all the other states had held primaries, and if voters in those states also had turned out at a rate of 28.2 percent, some 38.5 million people would have participated in the process, an additional 9.6 million.[7]

Actually, it seems likely that the turnout *rate* would rise in a national primary as well. Austin Ranney has found that voters in states whose primary results are binding on delegates — where there is, in short, a direct causal relationship between votes and outcomes — turn out at a higher rate than voters in states whose primaries are advisory.[8] In a national primary, cause and effect not only would be direct, but obvious: there would be no delegates or other intermediaries between voters and candidates. Presumably, voter turnout would reflect this.

In addition, the replacement of state primaries with a national primary would mean that there no longer would be any such thing as an early or late primary, with the corrosive effects that order has on electoral participation. Specifically, all the candidates would be on the ballots of all the voters (no one's choice would be circumscribed by anyone else's) and no candidate would be prematurely declared the winner (no voter would feel that his or her vote was coming after the fact). Interestingly, in 1980 voter turnout rose substantially from 1976 levels in the early primaries, when the nomination contests still were up in the air (51 percent in 1980 v. 48 percent in 1976 in New Hampshire; 35 percent v. 25 percent in Vermont; 43 percent v. 33 percent in Massachusetts),[9] but fell precipitously after that. Richard Stearns of the Edward Kennedy campaign reported that:

> According to the polling we've done, a large part of the explanation for the declining rate of participation after the early primaries has been a growing assumption among voters that the races effectively had been decided. Television and newspaper reporters told them, in effect, that their votes no longer had any particular value.[10]

2. *Participants would be more representative of ordinary party identifiers.* In nomination politics, it seems, there is a direct linear relationship between the volume of participation and its representativeness. Caucus participants are substantially more affluent, educated, and ideological than their fellow partisans. Similarly, Ranney found, "each party's [state] primary voters are unrepresentative of its rank-and-file identifiers in the same ways as the caucus-convention activists but not to the same degree." [11] The effect in some cases is that candidates for a party's nomination must make ideological or special-interest appeals that will harm them in the general election campaign. Having a larger, more representative national primary electorate would reduce this dysfunction.

Other consequences probably would follow from adoption of a national primary, some of which also would stimulate turnout.

3. *Votes would count equally.* The advantage, or disadvantage, of living in a particular state or voting on a particular date vanishes when everyone votes at the same time. The present violations — in spirit if not in letter — of the "one person, one vote" standard no longer would exist under a national primary.

Not everyone sees the elimination of bias as an advantage. Jeane Kirkpatrick, citing arguments by opponents of direct election of the president to the effect that minority groups receive advantages under the electoral college system, maintains that the present nominating process has an identical bias that would, in the same way, be vitiated by a national primary. But other scholars question her very premise, arguing that the electoral college actually places disadvantages on blacks and some other minorities.[12]

4. *Campaigns would change.* It is too much to say, as some advocates do, that a millennium of rational debate on national issues would follow adoption of a national primary.[13] But it does seem likely that candidates would place less emphasis on local issues that are disproportionately important to crucial early states, such as gun control in New Hampshire and old-age benefits in Florida. And if, as is proposed and predicted below, nationally televised debates become an institutional feature of presidential nominating politics, voters would have a greater opportunity to hear and assess directly candidates' stands on national issues.

The campaign period also presumably would shorten. Strenuous campaigning that now begins a year before the Iowa caucus in January might start seven months later if the only voting day was in August. It might begin even later: local publicity in key early states can be obtained as a reward for campaigning in the pre-election year; publicity in the national media, the most valuable kind for a national primary, would not be so easy to come by that far ahead of the election. Candidates still would have to have the physical endurance of athletes to survive their campaigns, but perhaps not of marathon runners.

5. *The strategic position of the incumbent would change.* The shift from local arenas of conflict to a national one would, on the one hand, make it difficult for the challenger to a sitting president to concentrate his or her efforts and other resources in a small state like New Hampshire in order to gain credibility for other challenges elsewhere, as McCarthy did in the 1968 New Hampshire primary. On the other hand, the president's ability to gain an advantage by redistributing federal grant and contract monies to key states would disappear if there were no key states.[14]

6. *The press's influence in the nominating process would diminish.* Not disappear; diminish. Clearly the press still would have to decide which candidates it is going to take more seriously than others; its resources for campaign coverage are not unlimited. Clearly, too, reporters would continue to write and talk about who is ahead and who is behind. But a national primary offers its own scoreboard, which the present system does not. Polls provide relatively objective measures of how the candidates are faring prior to voting day. So the existing need for reporters to decide, as well as report, the shape of the race no longer would be present.

## The Opponent's Perspective

Historically, opposition to the national primary has come from those who feel that it would have another, less desirable consequence. According to Ranney:

National primaries would be the final nail in the coffin of the party system. What they would do is eliminate any possibility that the parties might come back. National parties have never been tremendously strong in this country, but at least there was an event every four years — the nominating convention — that brought together party leaders from around the country who would meet in private and wheel and deal and decide who the nominee would be and maybe even who the Cabinet would be.[15]

One can concede and even endorse the argument that the parties should not willfully be destroyed without accepting the corollary that a national primary would do so. Richard Scammon, for example, argues that with the parties already comatose, a national primary could only help them, "especially from the standpoint of reducing divisiveness. A series of bitterly fought state primaries and caucuses is like a series of wounds; it usually inflicts greater damage than one wound. And as the examples of the states and cities that choose their local candidates by primary show, a single primary settles things. It's clear; it's public; it's open. The verdict is accepted. You don't have people arguing about caucuses being packed or conventions being rigged." [16] Scammon's argument directs our attention to a related point, which is that direct primary nomination of candidates, far from being a bizarre, untested idea whose consequences are beyond anticipation, is the practice for virtually all other elected offices at all other levels of government in all states and regions of the United States. "Many of the strongest party machines in the country thrived in primary systems — Boss Crump in Memphis, Harry Byrd in Virginia, and Dick Daley in Chicago, among others." [17]

Would national party conventions become extinct if candidates for president were not chosen there? Not necessarily; there still would be the need to nominate vice-presidential candidates, make party rules, and, potentially most important, write the platforms. F. Christopher Arterton suggests that these latter activities, so central to the health of the party as an enduring organization, are not performed well in present-day "candidate-centered conventions":

[I]n a candidate-centered convention, platform writing and party governance issues will naturally and inextricably become linked to the nomination question. Although the platform and rule issues do provide real and symbolic prizes, useful for unifying the party around the nomination outcome, we need to consider the consequences of having all party business determined by the nomination struggle. Such a system is tantamount to parties being no more than arenas for candidate competition.[18]

If, as James David Barber has suggested, "Purpose comes first, then party — . . . themes of unity so compelling that they will attract allies whose allegiance might survive the selection" of this year's candidate, then divorcing conventions from the nominating process well might free them to become idea and theme-setting forums whose products the parties now seem to need.[19]

Another oft-predicted consequence of a national primary system is that it would limit the field of contenders to the already-famous and close out the possibility of a less well-known candidate ever gaining the resources to mount an effective campaign. Bruce Adams, issues director of Common Cause, asks: "How could Jimmy Carter have convinced the press and the financial contributors that he was a serious candidate in 1976 if he hadn't had a chance to prove himself in a couple of small states first?" [20]

Adams's objection is a strong one. Just as the present system seems biased toward out-of-office politicians with unlimited time to campaign, the prereform system leaned too heavily toward Washington politicians, and a national primary system might swing the pendulum back too far in their favor. An ideal system would not place handicaps on any reasonable candidate. To help approach this ideal, we need to add a borrowed idea to our old one: debates before the primary among all candidates who qualify for the ballot. Debates already are close to being a routine practice in the present nominating system — the Democrats held several in 1976 and the Republicans did in 1980 — and their track record of bringing outsider candidates before the public on equal footing with their opponents is well-established. John Anderson, for example, rose to public prominence largely on the strength of his performances in a pre-Iowa caucus debate, where he alone endorsed a tax on gasoline, and a pre-New Hampshire primary debate, in which he spoke out for gun control. He did so even though neither of these debates was nationally televised, as they almost certainly would be if a national primary were in operation. At the same time, the presidential candidacies of incumbent officeholders who can spare time for debates but not for daily campaigning would not be at a disadvantage.

A further objection to the national primary proposal generates our third, more tentative proposal, this one for something new. A primary, writes Ranney, "has no way of identifying, let alone aggregating, [voters'] second and third choices so as to discover the candidate with the broadest — as well as the most intense — support." [21] Thus, a candidate of the left and a candidate of the right, even though opposed by a majority of voters in a party, might end up facing each other in the runoff because each has the ardent support of a faction of zealous ideologues. This is not a truly serious problem — few have found cause to complain about it at the state or local level, where all candidates are nominated by primary — but it would be nice to solve it.

Interestingly, Australia has come up with a novel and time-tested solution in its legislative elections. Since 1918, voters there have been called upon to number their candidate preferences on the election ballot — first choice, second choice, and so on. If no candidate receives a majority of first-choice votes, the lowest ranking candidate is dropped, and voters' second and if need be third and fourth choices are divvied up until someone has a total of 50 percent or more. Thus, the extreme candidate who leads on the first count because he has the support of an intense but relatively small minority, but who gets few second choice votes, will not be elected; a candidate with more broadly based support will. No runoff at all is needed. Leon Epstein notes that the Australian "preferential voting" system "has proved to be entirely compatible with stable, majority-party control of the House of Representatives" in that nation.[22] Nor is it wholly foreign to the United States. Cambridge, Massachusetts, for example, has used a ranked-vote system to choose its city council since 1940. Some years ago, Cleveland tried preferential voting in its mayoral election, and Ann Arbor, Michigan, did so in 1975. Both cities rapidly abandoned the system when it resulted in seemingly anomalous outcomes.[23]

Steven Brams advocates a variation on the Australian method that he calls "approval voting." [24] Brams's proposal would allow primary participants to vote for as many candidates as they liked in a given field, though not more than once for each candidate. Brams, who campaigned strenuously but unsuccessfully to persuade the New Hampshire legislature to adopt his system for the 1980 primary, argues that approval voting has all the purported advantages of the Australian system, yet is more likely to result in the choice of the candidate acceptable to most voters than either it or the runoff system. Brams offers the following hypothetical example:

> It is entirely possible in a three-candidate plurality race in which A wins 25 percent of the vote, B 35 percent and C 40 percent that the loser, A, is the strongest candidate who would beat B in a separate two-way contest (because C supporters would vote for A), and would beat C in a separate two-way contest (because B supporters would vote for A). Even a runoff election between the two top vote-getters (B and C) would not show up this fact. On the other hand, approval voting in all likelihood would reveal A to be the strongest candidate because some B and C supporters — who liked A as much or almost as much — would cast second approval votes for A, who would thereby become the winner....
> [The Australian system] has a major drawback: it may eliminate the candidate acceptable to the most voters.... [Candidate] A would have been eliminated at the outset.[25]

Approval voting also has the advantage over the Australian system of being easily comprehended by voters. They do not have to express a preference — even a fourth-place preference — for a candidate they despise. And the candidate with the most votes wins. Part of the problem in the Cleveland and Ann Arbor elections was that second-place finishers ended up being elected, a result that, though "logical," runs against grain of experience with voting.

## Prospects for Change

Approval voting, however imaginative a proposal it may be, is an idea whose time admittedly has not yet come — the more achievable task is to get a national primary law enacted, one that not only will simplify and clarify the nominating process for voters but make it more responsive to them as well. Distressingly, a major short-run obstacle seems to be the lack of seriousness of the proposal's present sponsor in Congress. To wit: When I called Senator Weicker's office in March 1980 to ask for an interview with the senator about his national primary bill, his press secretary's honest response was: "Do we have a national primary bill?" And when I sat down with Weicker in his office the following week, he told me that he did not know if his bill had attracted any cosponsors, did not know if there were comparable bills being looked at in the House of Representatives, and was not sure whether hearings had been scheduled on it in the Senate or not. He thought there might be hearings in 1981. (Hearings were to be held by the Senate Committee on Rules and Administration on September 10, 1980.) [26]

Nonetheless, the national primary has the kind of popular support among voters that may eventually win it serious consideration in Congress. The Gallup Poll, which has been asking people what they think of the idea every election year since 1952, has discovered bipartisan support ranging from 2 to 1 to almost 6 to 1; its January, 1980 survey found 66 percent supporting the national primary — 62 percent of all Republicans, 65 percent of Democrats, and 72 percent of the Independents — and only 24 percent opposed. The level of support also was almost uniform across educational, regional, sexual, occupational, and religious lines, as well as those of age, income, and place of residence. George Gallup included the national primary in a *Reader's Digest* article he authored on the "Six Political Reforms Americans Want Most." [27] With even doubters like Austin Ranney conceding that a national primary "certainly would be better than what we have now," they someday may get it.

But the American political system still is best conceived as being invested with all the qualities of Newton's First Law of Motion. When it comes to existing programs and policies, American government tends to stay in motion; almost nothing is undone, even in conservative periods. But in treating new proposals for action, American government tends to stay at rest, except in times of crisis. Thus, there is any number of ideas kicking around Washington that, although an overwhelming majority of the public favors them and has for some time, show little sign of becoming law. Sometimes the reason is that of the many people who favor these ideas, only a small number have a strong enough personal commitment to them to push fervently for their enactment. As a result, the few who are ardently opposed triumph, taking advantage of the built-in inertia of our checked and balanced, separated-powers constitutional system. At other times, strong advocates of change, because they disagree on what the nature or method of change should be, "hang separately." One thinks of gun control, national health insurance, direct election of the president — and the national primary.

A reasonable forecast, then, is for more of the same; the counterreformationists have as little reason for hope as national primary advocates. This will remain the case unless and until some significant segment of the presently apathetic, pro-national primary majority becomes active on behalf of its cause. Given the history of nominating politics in the United States, this seems most likely to occur as an outgrowth of some decisive intraparty factional clash resembling those that have preceded and produced our previous nominating systems.

SOURCE: Adapted and updated from a longer paper presented by the author at the second annual meeting of the Association for Public Policy Analysis and Management, Boston, Mass., October 24–25, 1980.

## Notes

1. Minor parties, that is, those that received less than five percent of the popular vote in the most recent presidential election, would not be covered by the national primary requirement.
2. Other recent versions of the national primary proposal, such as those offered by Senators Mike Mansfield (Democrat, Montana) and George Aiken (Republican, Vermont) in 1972, and by Representative Albert Quie (Republican, Minnesota) in 1977 differed from Weicker's in that they would not have allowed independent voters to participate. The Mansfield-Aiken bill also would have defined 40 percent as sufficient for victory in the first primary.
3. Clinton Rossiter, 1787: *The Grand Convention* (London: MacGibbon and Kee, 1968), p. 63.
4. (New York: Oxford University Press, 1960), p. 73. Among the definitional characteristics of "polyarchal democracy," as Robert Dahl defines it, are these: "In tabulating . . . votes, the weight assigned to the choice of each individual is identical." "The alternative with the greatest number of votes is declared the winner." *A Preface to Democratic Theory* (University of Chicago Press, 1956), p. 67. As is argued above, the present nominating system fails to meet the first standard, and, on occasion, could fail to meet the second as well.
5. *Implementation* (Berkeley, Ca.: University of California Press, 1973), pp. 143, 147.
6. High levels of political participation, though only among those considered eligible to vote and in those governing processes to which citizens were invited to participate, also was desired by the framers, as evidenced in their concepts of "Republican Virtue." See Robert Salisbury, "Republican Virtue and Affirmative Citizenship." (Paper presented at the Foundation of Political Theory Meeting, held in conjunction with the 76th annual meeting of the American Political Science Association, Washington, D.C., August 28–31, 1980.)
7. Austin Ranney, *Participation in American Presidential Nominations, 1976* (Washington, D.C.: American Enterprise Institute, p. 20).
8. *Ibid.*, pp. 27–28.
9. "The Voters Turn Out," *Newsweek* (March 17, 1980), p. 36.
10. "Primaries '80." According to journalist Rhodes Cook, "Generally the turnouts increased in states that received heavy attention from candidates and media." "Carter, Reagan Exhibit Similar Approach in Preference Primaries," *CQ Weekly Report* (July 5, 1980), p. 1875.
11. Austin Ranney, *The Federalization of Presidential Primaries* (Washington, D.C.: American Enterprise Institute, 1978), p. 16. Also see Ranney, "Turnout and Representation in Presidential Primary Elections," *American Political Science Review* (March, 1972), pp. 21–37.

12. Jeane Kirkpatrick, *Dismantling the Parties* (Washington, D.C.: American Enterprise Institute, 1978), pp. 24–27. Cf. Lawrence Longley, "Minorities and the 1980 Electoral College" (paper presented at the 76th annual meeting of the American Political Science Association, Washington, D.C., August 28–31, 1980).

13. See, for example, the remarks of Representative Lee Hamilton, *Congressional Record* (February 9, 1977), pp. H1026–27.

14. Cf. Peter Goldman, "See Jimmy Run — in Place," *Newsweek* (February 18, 1980), p. 45: "One obstacle in [Kennedy's] pursuit is Carter's lock on the vast resources of the Presidency — not just the call of patriotism but the power of the Federal purse. 'He's got $87 billion a year to give out,' says a House Democratic elder, and this President, like most, has been giving where and when it counts. More than $1 billion in Treasury largesse showered on Florida before a party straw vote there last fall; Carter won. A similar flow found its way to Maine in advance of this week's Democratic caucuses — a $75 million gush of grants in a single month, the sudden reversal of a decision to phase out Loring Air Force Base, enough new Navy contracts to keep a faltering shipyard afloat. In New Hampshire, where the primary season opens on Feb. 26, Mayor Maurice Arel of Nashua was leaning to Teddy until Carter phoned his best wishes for a local housing project then trammeled in red tape. The mayor switched to Carter, the red tape quickly unwound and $500,000 headed north to Nashua."

15. Interview with the author, March 7, 1980. Also see Kirkpatrick, *Dismantling the Parties,* pp. 27–28.

16. Interview with the author, March 6, 1980.

17. *Ibid.*

18. "Strategies and Tactics of Candidate Organizations," *Political Science Quarterly* (Winter, 1977–78), p. 671.

19. James D. Barber, *Pulse of Politics: The Rhythm of Presidential Elections in the Twentieth Century.* (New York: Norton), 1980.

20. Interview with the author, March 7, 1980.

21. Austin Ranney, *Federalization of Primaries,* p. 20.

22. "The Australian Political System," in Howard Penniman, ed., *Australia at the Polls* (Washington, D.C.: American Enterprise Institute, 1977), p. 33.

23. Malcolm Browne, "Can Voting Become Safer for Democracy?" *New York Times* (June 1, 1980); George N. Hallett, "Reply to Approval Voting," *National Civic Review* (January 1980), p. 10.

24. Steven J. Brams, *The Presidential Election Game* (New Haven, Conn.: Yale University Press, 1978).

25. Drawing from an ABC News poll of New Hampshire primary voters that asked them which candidates were acceptable to them, Brams deduced that under an approval voting system, Reagan would have risen 8 percentage points, from 50 percent to 58 percent; Bush 16 points, from 23 to 39; and Baker 28 points, from 13 to 41 — and second place. "Baker Could Have Survived N.H.," *Concord Monitor* (March 8, 1980). For an even more speculative treatment of the 1976 contest, see John Kellett and Kenneth Mott, "Presidential Primaries: Measuring Popular Choice," *Polity* (Summer, 1977), pp. 528–37.

26. Looking back to the Senate statement Weicker made when he introduced the bill on January 15, I found that he inaccurately said the run-off would come two weeks after the primary, not, as his own bill specifies, three. *Congressional Record.* (January 15, 1980), p. S116.

27. *Reader's Digest* (August 1978), pp. 59–62.

# 5. Two Cheers for the Presidential Primaries

## William J. Crotty

Former Secretary of State Cyrus Vance, former North Carolina governor Terry Sanford, and Congressman Morris Udall, along with a host of other officials and political scientists, say the current system of choosing or presidential nominees is too long, too difficult, too expensive, and maybe even too democratic. The nominating system, they say, emphasizes the wrong kinds of skills, and often encourages the wrong kind of choices.[1]

Strong words. They indicate an intense dissatisfaction with our present methods of selecting presidential nominees and the consequences that arise from it.

The dissatisfaction appears to be both pervasive and long-running. The problem has been studied and studied and studied again. And, in 1982, we again have national commissions — both party and private — studying the nominating process.

One of the principal points of debate in the controversy is the role, or proper "mix," between caucus and primary systems at the state level in selecting presidential delegates and, therefore, presidential nominees. The *caucus system* refers to meetings of local and state party members and leaders to choose the delegates to the national convention. The *primary system* provides for a much larger number of party members participating in the presidential nomination process by means of voting for their preferred candidates in an election held prior to the national conventions.

Critics of the primaries say the caucus system allows for a greater role for party leaders. We need, they say, to reintroduce an element of screening by party leaders. It is also said that the party activists who participate in the county and state caucus and conventions are treated to a political education that the simple act of voting, as in a primary, cannot begin to match.

Defenders of the primaries say our system at present is more democratic, more open, and permits more citizens to participate in the selection of their leaders than is the case in any other democracy. Moreover, primaries seem well suited to permitting various party coalitions to make their individual cases in a wide variety of places before a wide variety of groups.[2]

Much of the criticism of primaries seems to come from people who are frankly upset that the choice of presidential candidates is being made by ordinary people — the American voters. It is as if they think that somewhere there should be a

*William J. Crotty teaches political science at Northwestern University and is the author of several books, including* Political Reform and the American Experiment *and coauthor of* American Parties in Decline.

controlling group of elders that is better than the people — party bosses, highly educated folks, or long-time party regulars.

I want especially to treat this clash of values between the pro-caucus and pro-primary schools.

First, a little background on my own position. I believe a strong and vital party system is extremely important to orderly democratic government. I also feel that to be strong, relevant, and responsive to people's needs and interests, the party system must include within its deliberations the people it hopes to represent. And a responsible, accountable party system representing citizens' needs is what I see the party reform movement as being all about.[3]

Where does the primary/caucus debate fit into this overall picture? As primaries have grown in influence and number over the last decade, critics have taken to blaming them for the problems faced by the party and, to an extent, a nation in search of leadership capable of dealing with the profound social and technological crises the country now faces. The questions are asked:

1. Couldn't a better way of picking a president be found that would result in better candidates better able to handle the problems confronting the nation?
2. In this regard, wouldn't a better way of selecting a president place less reliance on primaries and more on caucuses?
3. And wouldn't an increased reliance on the caucus system in presidential nominations help build a stronger party system?

I cannot answer these questions. At least, not directly. I am not sure whether an institutional change of this nature will bring about the ends sought, and in fact I rather doubt it. I do think there are differences in values and emphases between caucuses and primary systems. There are problems and advantages associated with both, and the two forms do serve somewhat different ends.

In this context, I will treat some of the issues and problems of concern in evaluating the growth of primaries and some of the factors that should be considered before we discourage primaries or move to some other system for nominating presidential candidates.

## Points to Be Considered in the Primary/Caucus Controversy

1. Primaries developed — or, at least, became popular — just after the turn of the century. They were intended to increase participation in party affairs and, not incidentally, decrease the control of the political boss.

The boss survived. He learned to manipulate the primary electorates and to master the mechanics of party elections. Reformers became disillusioned with the results and with the costs involved in primary elections — for the first time, incidentally, reliable figures on party election costs had become available — and the inability of primaries to change significantly the nature of party nominations. By 1916, primaries were on the wane; they became a minor appendage to the way in which presidential nominees were selected.

Between 1916 and 1968, this remained pretty much the case.

2. Since 1968, primaries have been back in vogue. In the Democratic Party, there has been an increase from 17 in 1968 to 23 in 1972, 30 in 1976, and 36 in 1980. Primaries now dominate presidential nominating politics, and they threaten to completely replace caucus nominations at the state level. Why ?

3. Critics blame the party reform movement for forcing a move towards the primary. *But there is nothing explicit in the reforms that requires a state party to adopt a primary.* The reforms do require open and fair procedures, and they do encourage participation by the greatest number of party members. Many state parties felt that a primary was the best way to meet these requirements, which says something about the nature of primaries and perhaps, inferentially, about the nature of caucuses as well.

Moreover, many state parties wanted to attract the media exposure and public attention that are associated with primaries. Whatever the reasons, once the movement towards adoption of primaries began, it snowballed.

Today, 75 percent of the delegates to the national conventions in both parties are selected through primaries. For better or worse, primaries play a more significant role in presidential nominations now than ever before. The threat is that primary elections will completely replace the state party convention and caucus processes. We are almost at that point now.

4. Even the severest critic would concede, I believe, that the use of primaries has not been all bad. First, if you favor increased participation in party decision-making by the rank and file, the primary is a good means of achieving such a goal.

If you believe that in a time of a dwindling party base and a weakened party voice in general elections and national affairs, it is absolutely essential that a major party in the 1980s reach out and include as many people as possible in its processes, then primaries may be your best bet. *They do increase participation.*

Between 1968 and 1980, involvement in both parties' presidential selection processes has increased from 13 million to 32 million, with the overwhelming balance of the change (97 percent) being accounted for by the primaries.

It is extremely difficult to get an accurate fix on this, but some analysts estimate that primaries draw about one-half (55 percent) of the party-registered eligible voters and caucuses about one-twentieth (5–6 percent). Primaries outdrew caucuses in voter turnout in both 1972 and 1976 by a ratio of almost 10 to 1.

In 1980, in the Democratic Party, the primaries drew an average of over half a million voters (532,727), and the 18 caucuses an average of 29,944 apiece, a ratio of about 18 to 1. If you like participation, you'll love primaries. (Once the party voter is attracted to the primary, shouldn't it be the party's job to attract him or her into other party activities?)

5. Parallel to the rise in primaries has been an increase in "minority" group representation in presidential nominations and national party conventions. Women's participation is up from 13 percent in 1968 to 49 percent in 1980; that of blacks from 7 to 14 percent; and that of youth from 4 to 11 percent. These are significant gains. I see no reason why primaries should represent the sole, or even major, way of insuring adequate minority-group representation. Yet the growth in one has been associated with a growth in the other. I do feel that if any changes are made, care should be exercised that the *meaningful* (as against symbolic) gains in minority group representation, having been made, are not lost. Protecting these in some states may prove more difficult in a caucus-dominant system (though it is far from impossible).

6. A more sensitive issue has been the decline in the role of party and elected officials in presidential nominations. These officials, along with interest group representatives, controlled presidential nominations in the pre-reform era. To-day, their influence has been seriously undercut.

The decline is illustrated in a comparison of the pre-reform and post-reform presidential nominating systems in relation to the composition of national conventions (see Table 1).

Some political observers see a turn to a caucus nominating system as a way to return party and elected officials to a role of prominence in the selection of presidential nominees. This is an issue with broad ramifications — ones that go beyond the primary/caucus debate — but it is probably true that a caucus system would increase party and elected officials' influence over *all* stages of the nominating system. Is this desirable? What are the costs involved in such a change? These are questions that should be addressed before any modifications are implemented.

7. The presidential system cannot be returned to the pre-reform days. The old system failed. A party attempting to increase its relevance and prolong its useful life by reshaping and modernizing its nominating structures would be ill-advised to contemplate anything approaching a return to the closed decision-

*Table 1. Elected Official Participation in National Conventions*

| Delegates to national conventions (Democrats) | Pre-reform, % (1956–1968) | Post-reform, % (1972–1976) | 1980 |
|---|---|---|---|
| U.S. Representatives | 41 | 15 | 14 |
| U.S. Senators | 75 | 27 | 14 |
| Governors | 82 | 64 | 74 |

making of the caucus/state convention nominating system of earlier days. The reform initiatives that were taken did not resolve all the difficulties associated with a party system in trouble and, not surprisingly, they did manage to raise new ones.

Some foresee a return to an approximation of the system of the 1950s and the 1960s through a forced return to a caucus/state convention nominating system. If this is the objective, it is to be guarded against. Alternatively, however, a caucus system that included safeguards protecting open, participant-oriented and procedurally fair caucuses may not involve the repudiation, which many reformers fear, of reform objectives *and achievements.*

We should realize, however, that we had a caucus/state convention system before and it became outdated.

8. It has become fashionable in recent years to talk of "party cohesion" and "governance" and then to seek ways to assure such ends through structural changes in party institutions. This was one concern (although not the only one) of the Democratic Party's Winograd Commission of 1978.

I am not at all sure it can be done. I fail to see how structural change — whether it be a turn toward a caucus system or not — is going to increase party cohesion. The party's, and the country's, problems are far too complex to yield so easily to such an elusive goal.

Meanwhile, I would argue that a great deal of harm could be done in a search for "consensus" that forces major, and poorly considered, structural changes. The Michigan experience may exemplify the problem.

The Michigan Democratic Party responded to the Winograd Commission seriously. In the search for a party-building consensus, the Michigan party closed its nominating system substantially. By implication, if not in actuality, it appeared to require a financial contribution as a precondition for party membership and some formal, party-inspired acknowledgment of membership as a condition for participation in its caucus-centered presidential nominating system. The caucus system of 1980 replaced the primary system in effect in 1976.

The results: 704,149 Michigan Democrats participated in that state's presidential nominating process in 1976. In 1980, only 40,635 managed to qualify to participate in the presidential nominating caucuses and only 16,048 actually did participate.

What happened to the "lost" 688,101 Democrats? Who knows?

Does such a change promote party vitality? Or party consensus-building? Or party anything? It is hard to believe that it does.

Further, the Michigan party then held a "beauty contest" primary in conjunction with the Republican primary about 6 weeks after its delegate-selection caucuses. Sixty-five thousand Democrats participated. Neither Carter's nor Kennedy's name appeared on the ballot and the results had no influence on the state party's national convention delegation. The delegates had already been selected. Shades of pre-reform days.

It can be argued that the Michigan experience in 1980 was experimental, which is true. It can also be argued that there were foul-ups and misunderstandings, which is also likely and, in fact, which any changes to a more restricted system are likely to entail.

What was gained? I don't know. On the most immediate level, however, the lesson may be to exercise extreme caution in instituting any changes likely to have so profound an immediate impact.

9. Finally, there is the question of representation: which system better represents the party voter and the party's coalition — primaries or caucuses? This is an old question. More academic research attention has been given to it than to any other associated with primaries and it can still generate controversy. The presumption has been that there is a major difference between the types of people participating in caucus as against primary systems and that, consequently, they afford a different quality and type of representation.

More recent studies cast doubt on these assumptions. After examining *demographic* variables, such as age, sex, race, ethnic status, occupation, union membership, education, religion, political background, and experience, and *attitudinal* indicators relating to ideology (liberal or conservative), policy views on domestic and foreign issues, views on party reform, and attitudes towards party welfare, the authors of these studies conclude there may be *less* difference between the systems in these areas than previously expected and that *few* significant differences may in fact exist.

If true, then this finding could be used to argue either that (a) the present mix with its heavy emphasis on primaries is adequate, or (b) a change to a more heavily weighted caucus emphasis would produce few if any changes of consequence in the quality of representation.

Presumably, again if these studies are correct, primaries afford *more* of the same types of people the opportunity to participate directly in the process of selecting a presidential nominee than do caucus systems. This is not an inconsequential inference.

## Conclusion

Where does all of this leave us? Change is coming. That much is certain. The Democratic Party has yet another reform commission (headed by Governor James Hunt of North Carolina), and several committees of the Congress have indicated an interest in reassessing presidential selection practices. Countless academic and civic conferences are being held on the subject. The proposals for change being advanced are numerous and range from ones that would drastically alter present practices — with profound but somewhat unpredictable consequences — to ones that would result in relatively minor incremental changes in present operations.

Among the alternatives being considered are:

a national primary
regional primaries, or regional or chronological groupings of primary and
    caucuses on selected dates, and
a national election commission to coordinate and simplify state party rules
    and requirements.

If the national parties want to retain their direct control over their own nomination processes, they are going to have to act fast and present convincing evidence that they have seriously considered and responded to the major criticisms directed against their operations.

They will also have to satisfy their own party members that whatever they decide upon best promotes the ends of an open, representative and vital party. This will not be easy.

Where does this leave the controversy over the caucus and primary systems? It may well be that any shift, mandated by the national party in some form as yet unforeseen, towards a caucus system will accomplish much less than its proponents expect. The problems with which the American party system must contend are profound. Change may well be needed, but the dissatisfaction with the present nominating practices may be rooted in conditions upon which a caucus/primary choice can have little effect.

SOURCE: Much of this essay was prepared as a speech presented in January 1981 at a conference on the presidential selection process sponsored by Americans for Democratic Action in Washington, D.C.

## Notes

1. A recent example of this view is found in Terry Sanford, *A Danger of Democracy: The Presidential Nominating Process* (Boulder, Colo.: Westview, 1981). *See also* Cyrus R. Vance, "Reforming the Electoral Reforms" earlier in this text.
2. This is a view presented in John Kessel, *Presidential Campaign Politics: Coalition Strategies and Citizen Response* (Homewood, Ill.: Dorsey, 1980).
3. On the party reform movement see William Crotty, *Decisions for the Democrats* (Baltimore, Md.: Johns Hopkins Press, 1978); *Political Reform and The American Experiment* (New York: Crowell, 1977); and Gerald M. Pomper, ed., *Party Renewal in America* (New York: Praeger, 1980).

# Rethinking Presidential Character

# III

**6. James David Barber and the
Psychological Presidency**

*Michael Nelson*

**7. On Presidential Character and
Abraham Lincoln**

*Jeffrey Tulis*

**8. The Eisenhower Revival**

*Stephen E. Ambrose*

# 6. James David Barber and the Psychological Presidency

## Michael Nelson

The United States elects its president every four years, which makes it unique among democratic nations. *Time* magazine runs a story about James David Barber every presidential election year, which makes him *unique* among political scientists. The two quadrennial oddities are not unrelated.

Barber was 42 years old and chairman of the political science department at Duke University when the first *Time* article appeared in 1972. It was about a book he had just published called *The Presidential Character*. The book argued that presidents could be divided into four psychological types, which Barber called "active-positive," "active-negative," "passive-positive," and "passive-negative." What's more, according to Barber via *Time,* with "a hard look at men before they reach the White House" voters could tell in advance what candidates would be like if elected: healthily "ambitious out of exuberance" like the active-positives; or pathologically "ambitious out of anxiety," "compliant and other-directed," or "dutiful and self-denying" like the three other, lesser types, respectively. In the 1972 election, Barber told *Time,* the choice was between an active-positive, George McGovern, and a psychologically defective active-negative, Richard Nixon.

Nixon won the election, but Barber's early insights into Nixon's personality won him and his theory certain notoriety, especially in the wake of Watergate. So prominent had Barber become by 1976, in fact, that Hugh Sidey used his entire *Time* "Presidency" column for October 4 just to tell readers that Barber was refusing to "type" candidates Gerald Ford and Jimmy Carter this time around. "Barber is deep into an academic study of this election and its participants, and he is pledged to restraint until it is over," Sidey reported solemnly. (Actually, Barber had told interviewers from *U.S. News and World Report* more than a year before that he considered Ford an active-positive. Carter, who read Barber's book twice when it came out, was left to tell *The Washington Post* that active-positive is "what I would like to be. That's what I hope I prove to be." And so Carter would, wrote Barber in a special postelection column — for *Time*.

The 1980 election campaign witnessed the appearance of another Barber book, *The Pulse of Politics,* and in honor of the occasion, two *Time* articles.

*Michael Nelson teaches political science at Vanderbilt University and is a former editor of* Washington Monthly. *He is the author of* How the Government Works: The Case of CETA *and coeditor of* The Culture of Bureaucracy.

This is all to the good, because the first, a Sidey column in March, offered more gush than information. ("The first words encountered in the new book by Duke's Professor James David Barber are stunning: 'A revolution in presidential politics is underway. . . . Barber has made political history before.'") It wasn't until May 19 that a "Nation" section article revealed anything at all of what the new book was about, namely, Barber's cycle theory of twentieth-century presidential elections. The theory holds, readers learned, that steady four-year "beats" in the public mood, or "pulse," have caused a recurring alternation among elections of what Barber calls "conflict," "conscience," and "conciliation" ever since 1900. *Time* went on to stress, though not explain, Barber's view of the importance of the mass media both as a reinforcer of this cycle and a potential mechanism for helping to break us out of it.

The kind of fame that *Time*'s infatuation with Barber has brought him comes rarely to scholars, more rarely still to political scientists. For Barber, it has come at some cost. Though his ideas now have a currency they otherwise might not have, the versions of those ideas that have circulated most widely are so cursory as to make them seem superficial or even foolish — instantly appealing to the naïve, instantly odious to the thoughtful. Partly because of this, Barber's reputation in the intellectual community as *un homme sérieux* has suffered. In the backrooms and corridors of scholarly gatherings, one hears "popularizer," the ultimate academic epithet, muttered along with his name.

This situation is in need of remedy. Barber's theories may be seriously flawed, but they are serious theories. For all their limitations — some of them self-confessed — they offer one of the more significant contributions a scholar can make: an unfamiliar but useful way of looking at a familiar thing that we no longer see very clearly. In Barber's case, the familiar thing is the American presidency, and the unfamiliar way of looking at it is through lenses of psychology.

## II

A sophisticated psychological perspective on the presidency was long overdue when Barber began offering one in the late 1960s. Political scholars long had taken as axiomatic that the American presidency, because executive power is vested in one person and only vaguely defined in its limits, is an institution shaped largely by the personalities of individual presidents. But rarely had the literature of personality *theory*, even in its more familiar forms, been brought to bear. As Erwin Hargrove reflected in post-Vietnam, mid-Watergate 1974, this failure was the source of some startling deficiencies in our understanding of the office. "We had assumed," he wrote in *The Power of the Modern Presidency*, "that ideological purpose was sufficient to purify the drive for power, but we forgot the importance of character." Richard Neustadt's influential *Presidential Power*, published in 1960, was typical in this regard; it simply took for granted that "a President's success in maximizing power for himself serves objectives far beyond his own. . . . [W]hat is good for the country is good for the President, and *vice versa*."

Scholars also had recognized for some time that the attitudes Americans hold toward the presidency are psychologically as well as politically rooted. Studies of schoolchildren had found that they first come to political awareness by learning of, and feeling fondly toward, the president. There was also a sense that popular nationalistic emotions that in constitutional monarchies are directed toward the king are deflected in American society onto the presidency. Again, however, this awareness manifested itself more in casual observation (Dwight Eisenhower was a "father figure"; the "public mood" is fickle) than in systematic thought.

The presidencies of John Kennedy, Lyndon Johnson, and Nixon changed all that. Surveys taken shortly after the Kennedy assassination recorded the startling depth of the feelings that citizens have about the office. A large share of the population experienced symptoms classically associated with grief over the death of a loved one: they cried; were tired, dazed, nervous; had trouble eating and sleeping. A quick scan through history found similar public responses to the deaths of all sitting presidents, popular or not, by murder or natural causes. If Kennedy's death illustrated the deep psychological ties of the public to the presidency, the experiences of his successors showed even more clearly the importance of psychology in understanding the connection between president and presidency. Johnson, the peace candidate who rigidly pursued a self-defeating policy of war, and Nixon, who promised "lower voices" only angrily to turn political disagreements into personal crises, projected their personalities onto policy in ways that were both obvious and destructive. The events of this period brought students of the presidency up short. As they paused to consider the nature of what I will call the "psychological presidency," they found Barber standing at the ready with the foundation and first floor of a full-blown theory.

Barber's theory offers a model of the presidency as an institution shaped largely by the psychological mix between the personalities of individual presidents and the public's deep feelings about the office. Beyond that, it proposes methods of predicting what those personalities and feelings are likely to be in given instances. These considerations govern *The Presidential Character* and *The Pulse of Politics*, books that we shall examine in turn. The problem of what is to be done on the basis of all this knowledge — of how we can become masters of our own and of the presidency's psychological fates — also is treated in these books, but receives its fullest exposition in other works by Barber.

III

The primary danger of the Nixon administration will be that the President will grasp some line of policy or method of operation and pursue it in spite of its failure. . . . How will Nixon respond to challenges to the morality of his regime, to charges of scandal and/or corruption? First such charges strike a raw nerve, not only from the Checkers business, but also from deep within

the personality in which the demands of the superego are so harsh and hard.
... The first impulse will be to hush it up, to conceal it, bring down the
blinds. If it breaks open and Nixon cannot avoid commenting on it, there is a
real setup here for another crisis.

James David Barber is more than a little proud of that passage, primarily
because he wrote it on January 19, 1969, the eve of Richard Nixon's first inauguration. It was among the first in a series of speeches, papers, and articles
whose purpose was to explain his theory of presidential personality and how to
predict it, always with his forecast for Nixon's future prominently, and thus
riskily, displayed. The theory received its fullest statement in *The Presidential
Character.*

"Character," in Barber's usage, is not quite a synonym for personality, but he
clearly thinks it "the most important thing to know about a President or candidate." As he defines the term, "character is the way the President orients himself toward life — not for the moment, but enduringly." It is forged in childhood, "grow[ing] out of the child's experiments in relating to parents, brothers
and sisters, and peers at play and in school, as well as to his own body and the
objects around it." Through these experiences, the child — and thus the man to
be — arrives subconsciously at a deep and private determination of what he is
fundamentally worth. Some emerge from all this with high self-esteem, the vital
ingredient for psychological health and political productiveness; the rest face
the further problem of searching out an external, and no more than partially
compensating, substitute. Depending on the source and nature of their limited
self-esteem, Barber suggests, they will concentrate their search in one of three
areas: the affection from others that compliant and agreeable behavior brings;
the sense of usefulness that comes from performing a widely respected duty; or
the deference attendant with dominance and control over people. Because politics is a vocation rich in opportunities to find all three of these things — affection from cheering crowds and backslapping colleagues, usefulness from public
service in a civic cause, dominance through official power — it is not surprising
that some less than secure people find a political career rather attractive.

This makes for a problem, Barber argues: if public officials, especially presidents, use their office to compensate for private doubts and demons, it follows
that they will not always use it for public purposes. Affection-seekers will be so
concerned with preserving the good will of those around them that they rarely
will challenge the status quo or otherwise rock the boat. The duty-doers will
be similarly inert, though in their case, it will be the feeling that to be "useful"
they must be diligent guardians of time-honored practices and procedures that
will account for this. The danger posed by the power-driven, of course, is the
greatest. They will seek their psychological compensation not in inaction, but
action. Since such action will be motivated by the desire to maintain or extend
their personal sense of domination and control through public channels, it is
almost bound to take destructive form: rigid defensiveness, aggression against

opponents, or the like. Only those with high self-esteem are secure enough to lead as democratic political leaders must lead, with persuasion and flexibility as well as action and initiative. And Barber recognizes that even they sometimes will fail us, psychological health being a necessary but not a sufficient condition for successful political leadership.

All this — the theoretical element in Barber's character analysis — is fairly straightforward and plausible. Moving to the predictive realm is more problematic. How in the heat and haste of a presidential campaign, with candidates notably unwilling to bare their souls publicly for psychoanalytic inspection, are we to find out what they are really like?

Easy enough, argues Barber: to answer the difficult question of what motivates a political man, just answer the simpler ones in its stead: Is he "active" or "passive"? ("How much energy does the man invest in his presidency?"); and is he "positive" or "negative"? ("Relatively speaking, does he seem to experience his political life as happy or sad, enjoyable or discouraging, positive or negative in its main effect?") According to Barber, the four possible combinations of answers to these questions turn out to be almost synonymous with the four psychological strategies people use to enhance self-esteem. The "active-positive" is the healthy one in the group. His high sense of self-worth enables him to work hard at politics, have fun at what he does, and thus be fairly good at it. Among twentieth-century presidents, Barber places Franklin Roosevelt, Harry Truman, Kennedy, Ford, and Carter in this group. The "passive-positive" (William Howard Taft, Warren Harding) is the affection-seeker; though not especially hard-working in office, he enjoys it. The "passive-negative" neither works nor plays. As with Calvin Coolidge and Eisenhower, it is duty, not pleasure or zeal, that gets him into politics. Finally, there is the power-seeking "active-negative," who compulsively throws himself into his presidential chores even though the effort does not satisfy him. In Barber's view, active-negative Presidents Woodrow Wilson, Herbert Hoover, Johnson, and Nixon all shared one important personality-rooted presidential quality: they persisted in disastrous courses of action (Wilson's League of Nations battle, Hoover's depression policy, Johnson's Vietnam, Nixon's Watergate) because to have conceded that they were wrong would have been to cede their sense of control, something their psychological constitutions could not allow.

*The Presidential Character* caused quite a stir when it came out in 1972. Not surprisingly, it generated some vigorous criticism as well. Many argued that Barber's theory is too simple: his four types do not begin to cover the range of human complexity. At one level, this criticism is as trivial as it is true. In spelling out his theory, Barber states very clearly that "we are talking about tendencies, broad directions; no individual man exactly fits a category." His typology is offered as a method for sizing up potential presidents, not for diagnosing and treating them. Given the nature of election campaigning, a reasonably accurate shorthand device is about all we can hope for. The real question, then, is whether Barber's shorthand device is reasonably accurate.

Barber's intellectual defense of his typology's soundness, quoted here in full, is not altogether comforting:

> Why might we expect these two simple dimensions [active-passive, positive-negative] to outline the main character types? Because they stand for two central features of anyone's orientation toward life. In nearly every study of personality, some form of the active-passive contrast is critical; the general tendency to act or be acted upon is evident in such concepts as dominance-submission, extraversion-introversion, aggression-timidity, attack-defense, fight-flight, engagement-withdrawal, approach-avoidance. In everyday life we sense quickly the general energy output of the people we deal with. Similarly we catch on fairly quickly to the affect dimension — whether the person seems to be optimistic or pessimistic, hopeful or skeptical, happy or sad. The two base-lines are clear and they are also independent of one another: all of us know people who are very active but seem discouraged, others who are quite passive but seem happy, and so forth. The activity baseline refers to what one does, the affect baseline to how one feels about what he does.
>
> Both are crude clues to character. They are leads into four basic character patterns long familiar in psychological research.

In the library copy of *The Presidential Character* from which I copied this passage, there is a handwritten note in the margin: "Footnote, man!" But there is no footnote to the psychological literature, here or anywhere else in the book. The casual reader might take this to mean that none is necessary, and he would be right if Barber's types really were "long familiar in psychological research" and "appeared in nearly every study of personality." But they aren't, and they don't; as Alexander George has pointed out, personality theory itself is a "quagmire" in which "the term 'character' in practice is applied loosely and means many different things." Barber's real defense of his theory — that it works; witness Nixon — is not to be dismissed, but one wishes he had explained better why he thinks it works.

Interestingly, other critics have taken Barber's typology to task for being not simple enough, at least not for the purpose of accurate preelection application. Where, exactly, is one to look to decide if down deep Candidate Schuengel is the energetic, buoyant fellow his image-makers say he is? Barber is quite right in warning analysts away from their usual hunting ground, the candidate's recent performances in other high offices. These "are all much more restrictive than the Presidency is, much more set by institutional requirements," and thus much less fertile cultures for psychopathologies to grow in. (This is Barber's only real mention of what well might be considered a third, coequal component of the psychological presidency: the rarefied, court-like atmosphere — so well described in George Reedy's *The Twilight of the Presidency* — that surrounds presidents and which allows those whose psychological constitutions so move them to seal themselves off from harsh political realities.) But Barber's alternative — a study of the candidate's "first independent political success," or "fips," in which he found his personal formula for success in politics — is not all that helpful either. How, for example, is one to tell which "fips" was first? In Barber's appropriately broad definition of "political," Johnson's first success was not his election to Congress, but his work as a student assistant to his college president. Hoover's was his incumbency as student body treasurer at Stanford. Sorting through someone's life with the thoroughness necessary to arrive at such a determination may or may not be an essential task. But clearly it is not a straightforward one.

These theoretical and practical criticisms are important ones, and they do not exhaust the list. (Observer bias, for example. Since Barber provides no clear checklist of criteria by which one is to type candidates, subjectivity is absolutely inherent.) But they should not blind us to Barber's major contributions in *The Presidential Character*: a concentration on the importance of presidential personality in explaining presidential behavior; a sensitivity to its nature as a variable (power does not always corrupt; nor does the office always make the man); and a boldness in approaching the problems voters face in predicting what candidates will be like if elected.

## IV

The other side of the psychological presidency — the public's side — is Barber's concern in *The Pulse of Politics*, which was published midway through the 1980 primary season. The book focuses on elections, those occasions when because citizens are filling the presidential office, they presumably feel (presidential deaths aside) their emotional attachments to it most deeply. Again, Barber presents us with a typology; the public's election moods come in three varieties: "conflict," "conscience," and "conciliation," and this time the types appear in recurring order as well, over 12-year cycles. Again, the question he raises — what is the nature of "the swirl of emotions" with which Americans surround the presidency? — is important and original.

But again, too, the reasoning that underlies Barber's answer is as puzzling as it is provocative. Although his theory applies only to American presidential elections in this century, he seems to feel that the psychological "pulse" of conflict, conscience, and conciliation has beaten deeply, if softly, in all humankind for all time. Barber finds it in the "old sagas" of early man, and in "the psychological paradigm that dominates our age's thinking: the ego, instrument for coping with the struggles of the external world [conflict]; the superego, warning against harmful violations [conscience]; the id, longing after the thrill and ease of sexual satisfaction [conciliation]." He finds it firmly reinforced in American history: conflict in our emphasis on the war story ("In isolated America, the war-makers repeatedly confronted the special problem of arousing the martial spirit against distant enemies. . . . Thus our history vibrates with *talk* about war") ; conscience in America's sense of itself as an instrument of divine providence ("our conscience has never been satisfied by government as a mere practical arrangement") ; conciliation in our efforts to live with each other in a heterogeneous "nation of nationalities." In the twentieth century, Barber argues, these themes became the controlling force in the political psychology of the American electorate, so controlling that every election since the conflict of 1900 has fit its place within the cycle (conscience in 1904, conciliation in 1908, conflict again in 1912, and so on). What caused the pulse to start beating this strongly, he feels, was the rise of the national mass media.

The modern newspaper came first, just before the turn of the century. "In a remarkable historical conjunction," writes Barber, "the sudden surge into mass popularity of the American daily newspaper coincided with the Spanish-American War." Since war stories sold papers, daily journalists wrote about "politics as war," or conflict, too. In the early 1900s, national mass circulation magazines arrived on the scene, taking their cues from the Progressive reformers who dominated that period. "The 'muckrakers' — actually positive thinkers out to build America, not destroy reputations" wrote of "politics as a moral enterprise," an enterprise of conscience. Then came the broadcast media, radio in the 1920s and television in the 1950s. What set them apart was their commercial need to reach not just a wide audience, but the widest possible audience. "Broadcasting aimed to please, wrapping politics in fun and games . . . conveying with unmatched reach and power its core message of conciliation." As for the cyclic pulse, the recurring appearance of these public moods in the same precise order, Barber suggests that there the dynamic is internal: each type of public mood generates the next. After a conflict election ("a battle for power . . . a rousing call to arms"), "reaction sets in. Uplift is called for — the cleansing of the temple of democracy" — in short, conscience. But "the troubles do not go away," and four years later "the public yearns for solace," conciliation. "Give that four years to settle in and the time for a fight will come around again," and so on.

In *The Pulse of Politics,* unlike *The Presidential Character,* the difficulties arise not in the predictive gloss (a calendar will do; if it's 1980, this must be a conciliating election), but in the theory itself. If anything, an even more secure intellectual foundation is needed here than with the character theory, for this time there is an assertion not only of types, but of an order of occurrence among them as well. Once again, however, there are no footnotes; if Barber is grounding his theory in external sources, it is impossible to tell — and hard to imagine — what they are. Nor does the theory stand up sturdily under its own weight: if, for example, radio and television are agents of conciliation, why did we not have fewer conciliating elections before they became our dominant political media and more since? Perhaps that is why some of the retrospective predictions Barber's theory leads to are as questionable as they are easy to make: Coolidge-Davis in 1924 a conflict election?; Eisenhower-Stevenson in 1952 conscience?; Nixon-Humphrey-Wallace in 1968 conciliating?

The most interesting criticism pertinent to Barber's pulse theory, however, was made eight years before it appeared by a political scientist who, also concerned with the public's presidential psychology, wrote of it in terms of a "climate of expectations" that "shifts and changes. Wars, depressions, and other national events contribute to that change, but there is also a rough cycle, from an emphasis on action (which begins to look too 'political') to an emphasis on legitimacy (the moral uplift of which creates its own strains) to an emphasis on reassurance and rest (which comes to seem like drift) and back to action again. One need not be astrological about it." (A year earlier this scholar had written that although "the mystic could see the series . . . marching in fateful repetition beginning in 1900 . . . the pattern is too astrological to be convincing.") Careful readers will recognize the identity between the cycles of action-legitimacy-reassurance and conflict-conscience-conciliation. Clever ones will realize that the passage above was written by James David Barber in *The Presidential Character.*

## V

There is, in fact, a good deal about the public's political psychology sprinkled here and there in *The Presidential Character,* and the more of it one discovers, the curiouser and curiouser things get. Most significant is the brief concluding chapter on "Presidential Character and the Moods of the Eighth Decade" (reprinted unchanged in the 1977 Second Edition), which contains Barber's bold suggestion of a close fit between the two sides of his model. For each type of public psychological climate, Barber posits, there is a "resonant" type of presidential personality. This seems a central point in his theory of the presidency: "Much of what [a president] is remembered for," he argues, "will depend on the fit between the dominant forces in his character and the dominant feelings in his constituency." Further, "the dangers of discord in that resonance are great."

What is the precise nature of this fit? When the public cry is for action (conflict), "[i]t comes through loudest to the active-negative type, whose inner struggle between aggression and control resonates with the popular plea for toughness. . . . [The active-negative's] temptation to stand and fight receives wide support from the culture." In the public's reassurance (conciliation) mood, "they want a friend," a passive-positive. As for the "appeal for a moral cleansing of the Presidency," or legitimacy (conscience), that mood "resonates with the passive-negative character in its emphasis on *not doing* certain things." This leaves the active-positive, Barber's president for all seasons. Blessed with a "character firmly rooted in self-recognition and self-love, [t]he active-positive can not only *perform* lovingly or aggressively or with detachment, he can *feel* those ways."

What Barber first offered in *The Presidential Character,* then, was the foundation of a model of the psychological presidency that was not only two-sided, but integrated as well, one in which the "tuning, the resonance — or lack of it" between the public's "climate of expectations" and the president's personality "sets in motion the dynamic of his Presidency." He concentrated on the personality half of his model in *The Presidential Character,* then firmed up (after "de-astrologizing" it) and filled in the other half — the public's — in *The Pulse of Politics.* And here is where things get so curious. Most authors, when they complete a multivolume opus, trumpet that fact. Barber does not. In fact, one finds in *The Pulse of Politics* no mention at all of presidential character, of public climates of expectations, or of "the resonance — or lack of it" between them.

At first blush, this seems doubly strange, because there is a strong surface fit between the separate halves of Barber's model. In the 18 elections that have been held since Taft's in 1908 (Barber did not type twentieth-century presidents farther back than Taft), presidential character and public mood resonated 12 times. The six exceptions — active-negative Wilson's election in the conscience year of 1916, passive-negative Coolidge's in conflictual 1924, active-negative Hoover's and passive-negative Eisenhower's in the conciliating elections of 1928 and 1956, active-negative Johnson's in conscience-oriented 1964, and active-negative Nixon's in conciliating 1968 — perhaps could be explained in terms of successful campaign image-management by the winners, an argument that also would support Barber's general point about the power of the media in presidential politics. In that case, a test of Barber's model would be: did these "inappropriate" presidents come to grief when the public found out what they really were like after the election? In every instance but Eisenhower's and Coolidge's, the answer would have been yes.

But on closer inspection it also turns out that in every instance but these two, the presidents who came to grief were active-negatives, whom Barber tells us will do so for reasons that have nothing to do with the public mood. As for the overall 12 for 18 success rate for Barber's model, it includes seven elections won by active-positives, whom he says resonate with every public mood. A good hand in straight poker is not necessarily a good hand in wild-card; Barber's success rate in the elections not won by active-positives is only five of 11. In the case of conscience elections, only once did a representative of the resonant type — passive-negative — win, while purportedly less suitable active-negatives won three times. A final problem is born of Barber's assertion, made in the face of his prediction that Ronald Reagan would be a passive-positive president, that in the post-New Deal era of big government at home and active government abroad, the demands of the presidency — and of seeking it in the modern campaign mode — effectively will screen out passive types as would-be presidents. (In the period from 1929 to the present, the only passive president has been Eisenhower, and Barber admits that "his case is a mixed one.") Since two of his three moods — conscience and conciliation — are said to resonate with passive presidents, their elimination from contention rather trivializes the question of fit as Barber has posed it.

## VI

I leave it to Barber to explain his failure to claim credit for what he has done, namely, offered and elaborated a suggestive and relatively complete model of the psychological presidency. Perhaps he feared that the lack of fit between his mood and personality types — the public and presidential components — would have distracted critics from his larger points.

In any event, the theoretical and predictive elements of Barber's theory of the presidency are sufficiently provocative to consider carefully his prescriptions for change. Barber's primary goal for the psychological presidency, it should be noted, is that it be "de-psychopathologized." He wants to keep active-negatives out and put healthy active-positives in. He wants the public to become the master of its own political fate, breaking out of its electoral mood cycle, which is essentially a cycle of psychological dependency. With presidency and public freed of their inner chains, Barber feels, they will be able to join to forge a "creative politics" or "politics of persuasion," as he has variously dubbed it. It is not clear just what this kind of politics would be, but apparently it would involve a great deal more open and honest sensitivity on the part of both presidents and citizens to the ideas of the other.

It will not surprise readers to learn that, by and large, Barber dismisses constitutional reform as a method for achieving his goals: if the presidency is as shaped by psychological forces as he says it is, then institutional tinkering will be, almost by definition, beside the point. Change, to be effective, will have to come in the thoughts and feelings of people: in the information they get about politics, the way they think about it, and the way they feel about what they think. Because of this, Barber believes, the central agent of change will have to be the most pervasive, media journalism; its central channel, the coverage of presidential elections.

It is here, in his prescriptive writings, that Barber is on most solid ground, here that his answers are as good as his questions. Unlike many media critics, he does not assume imperiously that the sole purpose of newspapers, magazines, and television is to elevate the masses. Barber recognizes that the media are made up of commercial enterprises that also have to sell papers and attract viewers. He recognizes, too, that the basic format of news coverage is the story, not the scholarly treatise. His singular contribution is his argument that the media can improve the way it does all of these things at the same time, that better election stories will attract bigger audiences in more enlightening ways.

The first key to better stories, Barber argues, is greater attention to the character of the candidates. Election coverage that ignores the motivations and developmental histories of its protagonists is as lifeless as dramas or novels that did so would be. It also is uninformative — elections are, after all, choices among people, and as Barber has shown, the kinds of people candidates are has a lot to do with the kinds of presidents they would be. Good journalism, Barber argues in a 1978 Prentice-Hall book called *Race for the Presidency,* would "focus on the person as embodying his historical development, playing out a character born and bred in another place, connecting an old identity with a new persona — the stuff of intriguing drama from Joseph in Egypt on down. That can be done explicitly in biographical stories." Barber is commendably diffident here — he does not expect reporters to master and apply his own character typology. But he does want them to search the candidates' lives for recurring patterns of behavior, particularly the rigidity that is characteristic of his active-negatives. (Of all behavior patterns, he feels rigidity "is probably the easiest one to spot and the most dangerous one to elect.") With public interest ever high in "people" stories and psychology, Barber probably is right in thinking that this kind of reporting not only would inform readers, but engage their interest as well.

This goal — engaging readers' interest — is Barber's second key to better journalism. He finds reporters and editors notably, sometimes belligerently, ignorant of their audiences. "I really don't know and I'm not interested," quotes Richard Salant of CBS News. "Our job is to give people not what they want, but what we decide they ought to have." Barber suggests that what often is lost in such a stance is an awareness of what voters need, namely, information that will help them decide whom to vote for. He cites a study of network evening news coverage of the 1972 election campaign which found that almost as much time was devoted to the polls, strategies, rallies, and other "horse-race" elements of the election as to the candidate's personal qualifications and issue stands combined. As Barber notes, "The viewer tuning in for facts to guide his choice would, therefore, have to pick his political nuggets from a great gravel pile of political irrelevancy." He adds that "Television news which moved beyond telling citizens what momentary collective preferences are as the next primary approaches, to telling them what they need to know — precisely on the issue of presidential choosing — might yet enlist intellectual apparatus." Critics who doubt the public's interest in long, fleshed-out stories about what candidates think, what they are like, and what great problems they would face as president would do well to check the ratings of CBS's "60 Minutes."

Barber's strong belief, then, is that an electorate whose latent but powerful interest in politics is engaged by the media will become an informed electorate, and that this will effect its liberation from the pathological aspects of the psychological presidency. On the one hand, as citizens learn more of what they need to learn about the character of presidential candidates, they will be less likely to elect defective ones. On the other hand, this process of political learning also will equip them better to act "rationally" in politics, freed from their cycle of emotional dependency on the presidency. So sensible a statement of the problem is this, and so attractive a vision of its solution, that one can forgive Barber for cluttering it up with types and terminologies.

SOURCE: From *The Virginia Quarterly* (Autumn 1980). Reprinted with permission. The author wishes to thank Thomas Tillman, who helped with the research for this essay.

# 7. On Presidential Character and Abraham Lincoln

## Jeffrey Tulis

Our everyday understanding of "character" may be changing, due in large measure to a book which first appeared the year of the Eagleton incident — James David Barber's *The Presidential Character*. After Barber, many Americans may no longer be concerned primarily with presidential judgment as such, but rather with personality "types" that lie behind the judgments. To be more precise, many commentators now see "judgment" as a reflection of a psychological variable rather than as an independent cause. Barber's study is not the first study of political personality, or even of presidential personality, but it is the most important because it may be shaping the way citizens evaluate their presidents and presidential candidates. One may consider the examination of the meaning of Barber's enterprise to be a matter of public policy, since Barber has employed his studies in efforts to support candidates in the last two elections.[1]

In addition to the practical concern, there is a scholarly impetus to seriously examine the Barber study. Barber appears to have avoided several of the significant flaws attributed to earlier studies of political personality. The model typological analysis before Barber was Harold Lasswell's *Psychopathology and Politics*.[2] Lasswell constructed a typology based upon data collected in interviews with men who had held political positions, but who, in most cases, subsequently became mental patients. Most of the political positions that these men had held were as low-level functionaries. Lasswell assumed that all were "political men," each embodying a mix of three types: the agitator, the administrator, and the theorist. He sought to discern these types by employing an avowedly Freudian analysis. Thus, Lasswell attempted to fathom the meaning of a political personality from a vantage point that appeared far removed from politics: the men he examined were not significant politicians; he did not focus upon politicians *within* particular political roles; he employed the psychological approach which probes most deeply into the private aspects of his subject's minds. This brief sketch of noteworthy characteristics certainly does not do justice to the Lasswell study. These characteristics are noteworthy, however, because none of them is present in *The Presidential Character*. To be sure, many of the often praised aspects of Lasswell's work have found their way into the Barber study, and these are noted by some of Barber's reviewers.[3] But one should also note

*Jeffrey Tulis teaches political science at Princeton University and is coeditor of* The Presidency in the Constitutional Order.

that Barber, building upon his previous work examining state legislators, looks at important politicians in their political settings and he eschews strictly Freudian theory. Barber prefers an eclectic approach which, remaining closer to the surface, takes more seriously the actors' own perceptions.

> The psychological approach is simple; some will find it too simple. With a few quite minor exceptions, included for their wider interest, psychoanalytic interpretations at the symbolic level are avoided.... My approach to understanding Presidents is much closer to the psychology of adaptation, stressing the ways interpersonal experience shapes the person's self-image, his worldview, and his political style, and how, in turn these internalized lessons of experience are turned back to shape interpersonal experience.[4]

Barber's study also represents a departure from previous studies of presidential personality, because it is the first attempt to construct a generalized predictive theory of the presidency. A well-known earlier study, *Woodrow Wilson and Colonel House,* by Alexander and Julliette George, utilized a more sophisticated psychological approach, but its restriction to one case precluded the development of a political theory.[5]

Barber does not limit himself to prediction. As Alexander George noted in his review of *The Presidential Character,* "Barber's study emerges as the first systematic effort to apply personality theory to the task of *assessing* candidates for the Presidency." [6] Barber attempts to link specific kinds of character to specific kinds of policy making. In the final and most important step of the study Barber hierarchically orders the kinds of policy making in an effort to encourage selection of a particular kind of man.

*The Presidential Character* is significant not only because it culminates in conscious prescription, but also because the prescription is rhetorical rather than institutional. In other words, Barber suggests criteria to guide citizen deliberation about candidates, rather than laws to affect either the selection process or the conduct of the presidential office. Because the presidency is "so highly personalized" Barber suggests that the office has little to do with presidential behavior. "You can organize [the] office in many different ways, but the person who inhabits the office is going to use those instrumentalities for his own purposes." Barber's key to improving the presidency is not to change the office, but rather to help the citizenry select the right man. "If you can't really control the president effectively by law, if you can't really control him effectively during his term of office by a skeptical attitude of public opinion, then basically what you're left with is the thought that you'd better control him at the time you're picking him." [7]

## *The Presidential Character in Brief*
Barber's objective is fourfold. He attempts to describe the bearing of presidential character upon presidential performance in the twentieth century. He at-

tempts to predict presidential behavior in two ways. On the basis of fundamental characteristics which constitute a particular type of personality, Barber attempts to predict associated characteristics of men of that type. On the basis of study of early life, Barber attempts to predict behavior in later life. Finally, he attempts to assess which kind of personalities become the best (and worst) presidents.

There are four basic types of presidential personality generated from the combination of two "baseline" variables. All men are more or less active in their lives' endeavors and all men more or less enjoy those activities. On the basis of data culled from biographies of presidents, Barber classifies each as predominantly active or passive, and predominantly positive or negative with respect to enjoyment. This produces four cells arrayed below and filled in with respective presidents (Table 1).

Barber reconfirms his initial categorization with the aid of five major concepts: style, world view, character, power relations, and climate of expectations. The latter two concepts, "power relations" and "climate of expectations," represent Barber's attempt to depict the historical scene that surrounds each president. Barber finds that the "resonance" (or lack thereof) between man and circumstance illuminates personality.

Given depiction of the constellations of power and climate of expectations, "the burden of this book is [to show] that the crucial differences can be anticipated by an understanding of a potential president's character, world view, and his style." These three major concepts are utilized to discern the "integrated pattern" that constitutes each president's personality.[8] The concepts are delineated as follows:

Character is the way the President orients himself toward life. ... Character is the person's stance as he confronts experience.

World view consists of [a president's] primary, politically relevant beliefs,

*Table 1*

|          | *Active*  | *Passive*  |
|----------|-----------|------------|
| *Positive* | Jefferson | Madison    |
|          | FDR       | Taft       |
|          | Truman    | Harding    |
|          | Kennedy   | Reagan     |
|          | Ford      |            |
|          | Carter    |            |
| *Negative* | John Adams | Washington |
|          | Wilson    | Coolidge   |
|          | Hoover    | Eisenhower |
|          | Johnson   |            |
|          | Nixon     |            |

particularly his conceptions of social causality, human nature, and the central conflicts of the time.

Style is the president's habitual way of performing his three political roles: rhetoric, personal relations, and homework.[9]

Style is the most salient indicator of presidential personality, and Barber spends most of his analysis describing the disposition of presidents in their three political roles. However, Barber concludes that character is the most important factor within personality.

For purposes of prediction, Barber notes that "in general character has its main development in childhood, world view in adolescence, style in early adulthood." The three themes coalesce, and are expressed by style. The appearance of style is somewhat peculiar. Barber maintains that presidential style is most clearly visible at the point at which a youngster moves from home into a wider public, similar to the period labeled by others as the time of "identity crisis." Barber labels this period, "the first independent political success," although it involves running for office in only a few of the cases. According to Barber, the style surrounding the first independent political success *reappears* (having been somewhat dormant) upon election to the presidency. Barber does not know why this happens. "Something in him remembers this earlier victory." [10]

Barber's attempt to predict adult character on the basis of adolescent personality rests on the adequacy of the concept "first independent political success." However, it is Barber's other sort of prediction, the attempt to assess the probable texture and direction of policy making in the White House on the basis of the president's adult personality, that is our main concern here. This kind of prediction rests crucially upon the accuracy of the general description of the several basic presidential personality types. The following summary indicates the prevailing tendencies that Barber discovered in each:

> The "active-positive" character is "adaptive." He displays a congruence between much of his activity and his enjoyment of it, thereby "indicating relatively high self-esteem and relative success in relating to the environment." He shows "an orientation toward productiveness as a value and an ability to use styles flexibly, adaptively.... He sees himself as developing over time relatively well defined goals," and emphasizes "rational mastery."
>
> The "active-negative" character is "compulsive." He experiences a "contradiction ... between relatively intense effort and relatively low emotional reward for that effort." His activity has a "compulsive," compensatory character; "he seems ambitious, striving upward, power-seeking.... He has a persistent problem in managing his aggressive feelings. His self-image is vague and discontinuous."
>
> The "passive-positive" character is "compliant." He is "receptive" and "other-directed," a personality "whose life is a search for affection as a reward for being agreeable and cooperative rather than personally assertive." He experiences a contradiction ... between low self-esteem (on grounds of being unlovable, unattractive) and a superficial optimism.
>
> The "passive-negative" character is "withdrawn." He is oriented "toward doing dutiful service; this compensates for low self-esteem based on a sense of

uselessness." His tendency is "to withdraw, to escape from the conflict and uncertainty of politics by emphasizing vague principles (especially prohibitions) and procedural arrangements." [11]

Barber suggests that the best policy and leadership for the nation comes from an active-positive president. His personality leads him to be flexible, and to avoid irrational decisions, to be open to criticism and advice. "This may get him into trouble; he may fail to take account of the irrational in politics," but on the whole the country is safest if its president is an active-positive type.

The worst kind of president for Barber is the active-negative. The active-negative tends to pursue a tragic "rigidification" of policy which is impervious to criticism, public opinion, or the surrounding power situation. Johnson's escalation of the Vietnam War, Nixon's continuance of the war and his behavior in the Watergate affair, Wilson's self-defeating League of Nations campaign, and Hoover's economic policies are all cited as examples of such rigidification. These policies are all considered "disastrous" or near-disastrous.[12]

Passive-positive and passive-negative presidents may in certain times provide the country with reassurance, and respite from previous tumult. But there is a danger that with a passive president the country may "drift," or be lulled into a false sense of security "which diverts popular attention from the hard realities of politics." "What passive presidents ignore active presidents inherit." [13]

All of the analysis and predictions in the first edition of *The Presidential Character* were retrospective, except one: the Nixon "tragedy." In the second edition Barber predicted the presidential characters of Ford and Carter, but due to the short tenure of each, Barber's pre-Watergate predictions of Nixon's second term remain "so far this scheme's main test." [14] Nearly one quarter of Barber's book is devoted to analysis of active-negative Richard Nixon. Of course Barber's study did not, and was not intended to, predict historical events like Watergate. Rather, Barber claims to have been successful in predicting Nixon's manner of dealing with Watergate, and more importantly, he predicted that Nixon would probably seize upon and pursue *some* line of policy in the manner of Watergate.[15] Barber's Nixon prediction has been contested by Alexander George, who suggests that Nixon did not "rigidify" his behavior as did other active-negative presidents, most notably Woodrow Wilson. George calls upon Barber to give greater weight to the differences between presidents within each of Barber's types, and less attention to similar tendencies. He suggests that Barber expand the number of cells, adding "mixed types" to the four original categories.[16] It is important to recognize that this kind of criticism is not fundamental. That is to say, whether correct or not, it remains within an horizon of agreement with Barber regarding the theoretical possibility of his enterprise. Thus, the issue between Barber and his critics appears to be over the adequacy of Barber's individual interpretations and over the relative merits of a simple versus a complex typology, not over the limits inherent to a typological understanding per se.

## Replicating the Barber Study

What follows is another "test" of Barber's theory, one which is intended to raise questions about the nature and consequences of his endeavor as a whole. Barber's theory will be partially replicated by applying it to Abraham Lincoln. Lincoln is a crucial case because his administration and political qualities have been well studied and are so well known. Lincoln is widely regarded as America's greatest president, possessed of qualities so admirable that it is common for scholars, citizens, and pundits to yearn for his uncommon kind of leadership. It is reasonable to expect that a prescriptive thesis like Barber's would square with the considered judgment of Lincoln, or at least not run directly counter to the widely accepted view without explanation. But as will be indicated below, Lincoln does not fare well by Barber's criteria. He appears to have been an active-negative, the worst type of president for Barber.

It should be emphasized that this brief case study is intended to be a faithful replication of the Barber mode of analysis. While interpretations of the sort Barber employs cannot be replicated with the automatic ease of other political studies such as those employing survey techniques, it should not be assumed that no standards or guidelines are available. Barber has been helpful to scholars by making accessible background instructions he gave to his research assistants as well as by publishing an article that reconstructs the logic and method of his inquiry. To be sure, in *The Presidential Character* itself Barber does not devote much space to his methodology, preferring instead to get right to the business of actual interpretation.[17]

### Abraham Lincoln

Throughout his political career Lincoln worked incessantly. He campaigned for many candidates, rarely missed legislative sessions, and undertook his own research and clerical work. Biographer Benjamin P. Thomas gives this account: "Lincoln was diligent in the routine work of the House. He rarely missed a roll call and performed his full share of labor on his two committees — that of the Post Office and Post Roads, and the Committee on Expenditures in the War Department. *Few first term members have been more active,* yet his colleagues generally appraised him as a droll westerner of average talents." [18]

When Lincoln ran against Douglas in the now-famous senatorial battle (which Lincoln lost), he arranged the debates, preparing seven long speeches. The rigorous and long debates, however, represented only a small part of the campaign activity of both men. Thomas reports that "between the debates each man spoke almost everyday for four months to large crowds in the open air, and travelled incessantly between engagements, by railroad, steamboat, or horse and buggy, putting up with the scanty comforts and poor food of country inns and never, so far as the record shows, missing a single engagement." [19]

In the White House, Lincoln pursued the same frenetic pace. He started work early; by breakfast at 8 A.M. he had been at work for an hour. In the early days of the presidency he refused to limit visiting hours. (Later he was convinced to do so by his aides.) In addition to the usual policy preparation, Lincoln personally signed every officer's commission and promotion. He wrote his own speeches, state papers, and wrote many letters, often making copies for his files. Eating little, he would read the newspapers at lunch, visit hospitals at about tea time every day, work through the evening until about midnight. Before he went to bed he would visit the War Department telegraph office for the latest cables from the battlefields. He usually read before sleeping (often *Macbeth* or the *Merry Wives of Windsor*), and would finally doze off, sleeping "light and fitful." Once per week the White House would hold an open house reception; Lincoln's hand was reportedly swollen several times from greeting thousands of visitors each week. (It is claimed by Lincoln himself that such handshaking was the cause of his wavering signature on the Emancipation Proclamation.) The volume of Lincoln's writings is also a measure of his overall activity. It has been tallied that his published words "numbered 1,078,365 in comparison with 1,025,000 for the complete works of Shakespeare, and 926,877 for the entire Bible." [20]

It is clear enough that Lincoln had an active, rather than passive, personality, but where would he fall on the "positive-negative" spectrum? This broad dimension is intended to encompass the president's attitude toward his myriad activities and toward himself. In depicting Lincoln's subjective state, it will be helpful to delineate three predominate themes: his rhetorical style and skills, his world view revealed by his objects of interest (his singleness of purpose), and his character exhibited through expressions of inadequacy and mental torment.

Consistent with the styles of several "negative" presidents (Wilson and Coolidge) speechmaking served as a release, a burst of exuberance, a surge of good feeling, for Lincoln. He wrote his own speeches, injecting literary allusions and polishing his style. There was a marked contrast between the excitement of his speeches and the ordinary character of his normal discourse. J. C. Randall comments that "no one could call his speeches crude; on the contrary they sometimes rose to the height of literary mastery, though in familiar conversation and in informal utterance he lapsed into colloquialisms." Another scholar notes the difference between Lincoln's prepared and unprepared remarks. "His best ideas and finest phrases did not occur in impromptu speeches. In public he seldom was ready with words." [21]

Lincoln's voice would change as audiences responded to his rhetoric. Beginning in a high pitched "squeaking" voice, Lincoln would gain confidence and mellow a bit in the midst of many of his speeches. When his public speeches were carefully prepared, they served as one of his most effective tools of leadership. "Mastery of language may have been that ultimate factor without which he would have failed." [22]

In his personal relations Lincoln was often reserved; he liked to draw out information without revealing his own thoughts and feelings. He was protective of himself, while inquisitive of others. The blatant contrast between the "prepared" public and the private Lincoln reminds one of Calvin Coolidge's "impenetrable silences."

Lincoln's rhetorical style cannot be completely depicted without mention of the place of humor in his speech. Humor served Lincoln several functions. He used "stories" to avoid discussion of sensitive topics, he told jokes to cheer himself up in times of stress, and he veiled some of his bitterest criticism in cloaks of sarcasm. Sarcasm, carefully planned, replaced a good fight for Lincoln. One Lincoln scholar labeled his humor "merciless satire," but pointed out that Lincoln the president matured to the extent that he suppressed the bite of some of his attacks. (Examples of the early *ad hominem* attacks include Lincoln referring to Douglas as a great man, "a lion in fact, a caged and toothless lion." ("A living dog though is better than a dead lion," he said.) Earlier Lincoln wrote to a friend that his party's strategy would be to ignore Douglas. "Isn't that the best way to treat so small a matter?" [23]

The personal attacking function became more and more suppressed as Lincoln grew into the presidency, but the other functions became more pronounced. At times, Lincoln would engineer his speeches around a joke. For example, Lincoln declared that "the Dred Scott decision made popular sovereignty as thin as homeopathic soup made by boiling the shadow of a pigeon that had starved to death." [24]

Lincoln's ability to joke in times of stress can be cited as a "positive" strand in his personality. As will be apparent later, however, his laughter was not enough to compensate for his feelings of inadequacy, and often his laughter itself might have been a kind of not-so-frivolous self-criticism.

A second "negative" theme is revealed in Lincoln's rhetoric. Two modes of justification were characteristic of Lincoln. One was an emphasis upon duty; the other a constant recourse to the will of God. Both of these justificatory devices remind one of style traits of active-negative Woodrow Wilson. Taken together, these devices reveal a tendency to appeal inflexibly to "principle."

As Lincoln emerged from obscurity and retirement, when the Kansas-Nebraska bill was passed, he affirmed that he was embarking upon a "moral challenge." The Kansas-Nebraska bill repealed the Missouri Compromise, thus allowing determination of the legality of slavery in new states to be left to "popular will." "The news aroused him, 'as he had never been before.' Three months later we shall find him back in politics. But he will emerge as a different Lincoln from the ambitious politician whose hopes were seemingly blighted in 1849. His ambition, reawakened, will become as compelling as before, but it will be restrained by devotion to a cause." [25]

Lincoln often justified his actions by referring to his duty to perform them. Shortly before his second presidential election, for example, Lincoln stashed a note in his desk which promised his opponent cooperation to save the Union between election and inauguration should Lincoln lose the election. After victory, Lincoln read the promise to his cabinet, prompting question as to what he would have done if he had lost the election and if his opponent McClellan had refused to cooperate. Lincoln replied, "At least I should have done my duty and stood clear before my conscience." [26]

Consistent with this adherence to duty was a tendency of Lincoln to "stick to" his decisions. "Those closest to the President had learned that while he came to his decisions slowly, once made he seldom reversed them." [27]

An often discussed set of incidents which reveals Lincoln's duty-bound inflexibility occurred between his first election and inauguration. At that time Lincoln remained silent on major issues, sticking by his previous statements. He was besieged by newspaper editors for his "latest" views. Lincoln refused to budge.

> I could say nothing which I have not already said, and which is in print and accessible to the public. . . . Please pardon me for suggesting that if the papers like yours which have heretofore persistently garbled, and misrepresented what I save said, will now fully and fairly place it before their readers, there can be no further misunderstanding. I beg you to believe me sincere, when . . . I urge it as the true cure for the uneasiness in the country. . . . The Republican newspapers now, and for some time past, are and have been republishing copious extracts from many published speeches, which would at once reach the whole public if your class of papers would also publish them. I am not at liberty to shift my ground. That is out of the question.[28]

The death of Lincoln's son Willie affected him tremendously. It bolstered his duty-bound notions with a recourse to God. "More and more his official utterances and state papers breathed dependence on a Higher Power, whose existence he may have doubted in his callow years." [29]

Lincoln used the notion of God to justify singleness of purpose in his own mind. If there is a clear difference of opinion, both opinions could not be right, because God would not will a contradiction.[30] Lincoln's notion of duty and increasing recourse to God bolstered his belief that his specific policies were the right ones. Consonant with other active-negatives, Lincoln was often "inflexible." Rhetoric, humor, and other justificatory resources (duty and God) are all ways in which Lincoln made sense of his deeper feelings. That is, he attempted to obliterate, manipulate, or camouflage his feelings with the devices I have discussed. These all are devices that other active-negative presidents have employed.

More fundamentally, Lincoln had negative feelings toward himself. He was self-critical, and often doubted his ability to be president. Lincoln did not harbor bitter feelings over political defeat (as had Richard Nixon, for example). Losing his Senate battle against Douglas, Lincoln recalled thinking at the time that "it's a slip and not a fall." Nevertheless, Lincoln did not have positive feelings toward becoming president. Early in 1860, Lincoln remarked to a newspaper editor, "I must, in candor, say I do not think I am fit for the Presidency." This may have been a political tactic. However, subsequent statements seem to reinforce the sincerity of the claim. When he was "in the running" Lincoln sent an autobiographical sketch to John Fell (to serve as the basis for a campaign biography) with the following note appended. "There is not much of it, for the reason, I suppose, that there is not much of me." [31]

Shortly after the nomination, two fellow Republicans, celebrating with Lincoln in Springfield, noted his reaction to the event.

> Lincoln looked much moved, and rather sad . . . feeling the heavy responsibility thrown upon him.[32]

> Lincoln's response had been modest and brief, yet not colorless: he almost wished the "high honor" had fallen to another.[33]

Just before his train departure from Springfield which would, after many victory stops, carry Lincoln to Washington, he said goodbye to his law partner Billy Herndon: "The two men parted with a firm clasp of hands, 'I am sick of office holding already,' Lincoln said, 'and I shudder to think of the tasks ahead.' " [34] Along the train route to Washington, Lincoln delivered thirty-seven "greetings" in five days. "Often Lincoln struck the note of self-depreciation. He referred to himself as an old man; once he had a passage read by 'younger eyes,' at times he confessed he had not the 'voice' nor 'strength' for longer speaking. . . . He declared that 'without a reason why . . . [he] should have a name,' there had fallen upon him, 'a task such as did not rest even upon the Father of our country.' " [35]

During the middle of his first term Lincoln was under a constant barrage of abolitionist criticism for not emancipating slaves. Lincoln, thinking that the time was not right for a proclamation, also felt the tremendous pressure of his delay: "I know very well that many others might . . . do better than I can; and if I were satisfied that the public confidence was more fully possessed by any one of them than by me, and knew of any Constitutional way in which he could be put in my place, he should have it. I would gladly yield it to him." [36]

Three months later, Lincoln was subjected to yet another shelling of criticism, this time concerning his cabinet. One of the cabinet members recorded Lincoln's statements at the time in his diary: " 'They (a Senatorial Committee) wish to get rid of me, and I am sometimes half disposed to gratify them. . . . We are now on the brink of destruction . . . I can hardly see any ray of hope. . . . The Committee is to be up to see me at 7 o'clock. Since I heard last night of the proceedings of the caucus, I have been more distressed than by any event of my life.' " [37]

Lincoln looked forward to a second term (which was contrary to the current presidential practice) but he did not look forward with any semblance of joy: "A second term would be a great honor and a great labor, which together, perhaps I would not decline if tendered." Clearly it was a sense of duty (not of enjoyment) that propelled Lincoln. "The President showed no elation at his renomination." [38]

Lincoln's self-criticism and self-doubt manifested itself in physical forms. Much evidence suggests that Lincoln was "worn," "tired," and suffered from periodic depression. Herndon observed that "melancholy dripped from him as he walked." Another friend, W. H. L. Wallace, observed in 1860 before Lincoln had been inaugurated (although after the election), "I have seen Mr. Lincoln two or three times since I have been here, but only for a moment and he is continuously surrounded by a crowd of people. He has a world of responsibility and seems to feel it and to be oppressed by it. He looks more careworn and haggard and stooped than I ever saw him." [39]

Lincoln's haggard look increased throughout the presidency as indicated by successive photographs. Although Mary Lincoln also suffered increasing depression throughout her later life, her basic demeanor contrasted with her husband's. "Her qualities were complementary to those of her husband. She was to be a stimulus to him, even if at times that stimulus was somewhat of an irritant. His friends unanimously testify to his sadness, his periods of absent thought when he saw nothing around him." Mary Lincoln's fits of depression led her into irascible states; Abraham's depression manifested itself in melancholic silence — perhaps a response to the pressure of his wife's behavior. [40]

A distinctive development — a note of maturity — in Lincoln's later life, was his increasing ability to control his outward emotions. "So long as I have been here [in the presidency], I have not willingly planted a thorn in any man's bosom," he wrote. [41] Yet his outward control could not obliterate his inner torment. It cannot be said that Lincoln enjoyed being president.

Few of the presidents in *The Presidential Character* fit unambiguously into one of the four cells. Most reveal characteristics of several types, although one emerges as the dominant one. Such is the character of Abraham Lincoln. While his ability to joke reveals an active-positive strain, and his melancholy silence reminds one of the passive-negatives, overall Lincoln was an active-negative president — ambitious, an incessant worker who didn't enjoy his work, but doggedly unwavering in pursuit of objectives he considered to be "right."

## On Presidential Character

If the electorate in 1860 had been guided by Barber's theory, they would have rejected Abraham Lincoln, who as an "active-negative" had the worst type of personality, in favor of Stephen Douglas, whose "active-positive" personality is the type most highly recommended by Barber. [42] Although it is impossible to know how successful a Douglas presidency might have been, the historical judgment of Lincoln's administration, both its sober praise and sometime adulation, contrasts markedly with the dire conclusion reached by applying Barber's theory. Why is there such a disparity between the common assessment of Lincoln's presidency and the "active-negative" conclusion generated by Barber's theory? Perhaps the answer lies in the difference between the starting point of the political understanding of citizens and politicians from that of theoretical perspectives like Barber's. For Lincoln, Douglas, and their contemporary public, issue differences were at the heart of the political crisis. Barber, on the other hand, begins his study by assuming that the content of political issues is of little importance in assessing presidential behavior. Instead of looking through the eyes of the politician under study, Barber encourages his readers to look through the lens of a conceptual apparatus different from that common to political life itself.

By beginning with the assumption that political differences as understood by politicians are unimportant, Barber's theory rules out a myriad of hypotheses which might best explain the Lincoln presidency. Because Barber is attempting to construct a theory, and not simply a set of detailed descriptions of various administrations, he is forced by this theoretical objective to create categories which are formal enough to transcend the exigencies of this or that time, or the infinite variety of political opinions and issues. As a theory, Barber's project requires concepts like "rigidity" and "flexibility" because these are generally applicable, while issues and opinions are not.

Barber is quite aware of the nature of his, or any, typological theory. "What is de-emphasized in this scheme?" he asks. "Everything which does not lend itself to the production of potentially testable generalizations about presidential behavior. Thus we shall be less concerned with the substance or content of particular political issues." Barber is not unconcerned with the content of political issues, but his concern is different from that of the politician. For Barber, political debate covers or partially hides more fundamental aspects of the participants' personalities.

> By moving a step up the ladder of abstraction, from particular issue stands and standardized ideological expressions to the leader's worldview we begin to get at themes at once more persistent and more significant in shaping action. A close review of what he has said over the years may reveal a fairly consistent set of assumptions — about how history works, what people are like, what the main purposes of politics are (to use the three I have found most useful). The product is a cognitive operational code of sorts, a set of politically relevant perceptual habits, *hardly ever put together in a systematic way by the leader himself* but derivable from his many comments as he experiences practical problems.[43]

The locus of thought relevant to personality is "worldview." The advantage of this concept to the theory builder is that one can focus upon static or at least enduring attachments. Thus, thought is transposed for the purposes of this kind of research into "belief-systems" which are visible to the investigator but not to the investigated.

To be fair, Barber did not adopt this kind of analysis simply because that was what "theory" inherently required. Rather, he turned to constructing a theory because he found issue positions and "ideology" of little help in describing what presidents did.

> The straight-out analysis of the content of the reasons the actor offers for his actions is of limited utility. Variations in the actual responses of political leaders to roughly the same circumstances warn against relying too much on the leader's plain spoken explanations. . . . Nor are his expressed intentions much help. . . . Nor have presidents' ideologies — left or right — helped much in explaining what they did.[44]

Barber's first study of presidential personality was devoted to the political styles of Calvin Coolidge and Herbert Hoover. Barber does not indicate why Hoover's or Coolidge's reasoning can't account for their behavior, but he goes on to make an even more startling claim — that if his theory works with these presidents, it can work with all presidents.

> The dull Presidents are a trial for the political analyst, particularly for the student of personality and political leadership. . . . They . . . provide "hard case" tests for the supposition that personality helps shape a President's politics. If a personality approach can work with Coolidge and Hoover, it can work with any chief executive.[45]

It may be necessary to simplify the "variables," including thought, that impinge upon a weak or common president in order to discern the determinants of presidential behavior. If this proves true, Barber's kind of approach might be the most fruitful way to study most presidents. However, Barber is wrong to suggest that his theory "can work with any chief executive." A theory that explains the behavior of mediocre presidents cannot be assumed prior to investigation to explain the actions of great presidents.

Like the view that political issues and political judgment matter, the notion that some presidents are great in terms of political skill and perspicacity is one common to the citizen perspective. Scholars frequently denigrate the appellation "great" because it often betrays unreflective hero-worship rather than sober analysis, but it is hard to deny that some of our political leaders have had uncommon abilities. Barber might respond that he does not mean to deny that some presidents are greater than others, but rather to identify a clearer and more adequate basis for evaluation. Yet Barber's theory precludes one of the important traditional qualities of greatness — uncommon perspicacity. If one takes seriously the possibility that a politician may be great in this sense, one must begin by assuming that the politician may have been able to see and understand things which, without his assistance, remain inaccessible to the inquiring scholar. In short, one must begin by assuming that one may learn something *from* a president before, or at least while, one attempts to learn *about* a president. This procedure by no means prevents one from reaching the conclusion that a particular president had nothing to teach, but proceeding as Barber does in assuming that he is capable of knowing Lincoln's most important thoughts better than Lincoln precludes the scholar from discovering that he is mistaken. The "great" presidents pose special difficulties because they are supposed to have had minds incapable of description according to criteria simple and formal enough to be applied to most men.

Among Barber's own case studies, one can find some evidence that this problem plagued Barber. Noteworthy is his admitted difficulty in describing Franklin Roosevelt. Barber considered FDR "the most remarkable of all modern Presidents." Not surprisingly, he also proved to be for Barber, "the least self-revealing president." Although FDR held the longest presidential tenure in history,

Barber devotes relatively few pages to discussion of FDR's White House years. In fact, he devotes twice as much space to the discussion of each of the Truman and Kennedy presidencies. Barber spends most of the brief FDR discussion explaining away two incidents that appear to reveal active-negative tendencies. While obviously "active" and obviously "positive," FDR (like Lincoln and the active-negatives) does not unambiguously resemble other presidents of his type, when one proceeds beyond the "baseline" variables.

Does the possibility that presidential understanding molds behavior mean that "thought" is a completely independent variable, attaching itself to the things presidents see? It is not quite plausible, as a personality theorist might argue, that presidents don't see everything around them, but rather have selective perception, seeing and discussing some things and not others? Certainly this must be true, but the fact that presidents like everyone (even personality theorists) have selective perception should not propel one to the immediate conclusion that the spectacles through which presidents view the world are unknown to them. One of the most striking facts about pre-Civil War politics is the degree to which Lincoln and Douglas chose to view the issues of their day through a constitutional lens. Without going into the merits of their respective arguments — one beginning from the principle of equality, the other from popular sovereignty — it must be emphasized that the agenda of issues that constituted their dispute and framed their arguments was set by the Constitution. The character of the political dispute just prior to the Civil War derived from a widespread deference to "issues." And in this case constitutional issues were the crucial political consideration.[46]

What is the practical consequence of the theoretical deprecation of issues? In considering this question, we move from the adequacy of Barber's theory as explanation to reflection upon the worth of his theory as a pedagogy. Barber is quite explicit in offering his teaching as a guide to the citizenry's selection of future presidents. Implicitly, Barber's theory is also a pedagogy for presidents themselves, because presidents will try to appear to be what their electorate expects. V. O. Key noticed this same political consequence when he criticized the denial of issue voting in seminal studies of voting behavior.

> If leaders believe the route to victory is by projection of images and cultivation of styles rather than by advocacy of policies to cope with the problems of the country, they will project images and cultivate styles to the neglect of the substance of politics. They will abdicate their prime function in a democratic system, which amounts, in essence, to the assumption of the risk of trying to persuade us to lift ourselves by our bootstraps.[47]

To the extent that Barber's vocabulary enters the realm of politics itself, politicians may come to believe that success depends primarily upon appearing to have the right character. This poses difficulty for Barber's future empirical work, because statements which were formerly uttered naïvely by politicians unaware of the use to which they would be put (statements like "I enjoy my work") may now be uttered with the conscious purpose of projecting the right character.

The main problem, however, is not the future adequacy of Barber's empirical studies, now that his theory is public, but rather the relative merits of a constitutional pedagogy versus the new personality teaching for the actual conduct of the presidency. Certainly no personality theory, even one wholeheartedly embraced by a president and his public, could obliterate the president's day-to-day concern with issues or with constitutional matters in times of crisis — that is not the danger. Presidents will continue to fashion policies and defend them before Congress and the public. But how sound will these policies be, and how capable will the public be to judge them? Isn't it probable that presidential policy will be better formulated and presidential rhetoric more intelligent if presidents function under the auspices of a public opinion informed by a theory emphasizing policy and reason than by a theory that places a premium on character and style?

SOURCE: Adapted from Jeffrey Tulis, "On Presidential Character," in Joseph M. Bessette and Jeffrey Tulis, eds., *The President in the Constitutional Order* (Baton Rouge, La.: Louisiana State University Press, 1981). Reprinted by permission.

## Notes

1. James David Barber, *The Presidential Character*, 2nd ed. Englewood, N.J.: Prentice-Hall, 1977; orig. pub. 1972). *See also,* "The President after Watergate," *World,* July 13, 1973; "Tone-Deaf in the Oval Office," *Saturday Review/World,* Jan. 12, 1974; "Active-Positive Character," *Time,* Jan. 3, 1977; "The Question of Presidential Character," *Saturday Review,* Oct. 1972.
2. Harold Lasswell, *Psychopathology and Politics,* rev. ed. (New York: Viking Press, 1969).
3. Alexander George in "Assessing Presidential Character," *World Politics,* 27 (January 1974), 246; James H. Qualls, Barber's Typological Analysis of Political Leaders," *American Political Science Review,* 71 (March, 1977), 185; Erwin Hargrove, "Presidential Personality and Revisionist Views of the Presidency," *American Journal of Political Science,* 42 (November 1973), 4.
4. Barber, *Presidential Character,* vi.
5. Alexander George and Juliette George, *Woodrow Wilson and Colonel House* (New York: Dover, 1964). There have been many other important single-actor studies (for example Erik Erikson's *Young Man Luther*), but except for George and George, the best of these do not examine American presidents.
6. George, "Assessing Presidential Character," 278 (Author's emphasis).
7. "The State of the Presidency" (interview) Chicago *Sunday Sun-Times,* Sept. 23, 1973, Sec. 1A, p. 2.
8. Barber, *Presidential Character,* 5.
9. *Ibid.,* 7–8.
10. *Ibid.,* 10.

11. This summary of remarks by Barber was compiled by Alexander George. See George, "Assessing Presidential Character," 248–49, and Barber *Presidential Character,* 12–13.
12. Barber, *Presidential Character,* 446–48, 458, 460.
13. *Ibid.,* 145.
14. But see *ibid.,* 445.
15. *Ibid.,* 470.
16. George, "Assessing Presidential Character," 273–75.
17. James David Barber, "Strategies for Understanding Politicians," *American Journal of Political Science* (May 1974), and "Coding Scheme for Presidential Biographies," mimeo. (January 1960), 39 pp.; cited in Barber, "Strategies."
18. Benjamin P. Thomas, *Abraham Lincoln* (New York: Knopf, 1952), 121.
19. *Ibid.,* 184.
20. *Ibid.,* 456; J. G. Randall, *Lincoln the President,* 2 vols. (New York: Dodd Mead, 1945), II, 165; Richard N. Current, *Lincoln Nobody Knows* (New York: Farrar, Straus, 1958).
21. Randall, *Lincoln,* I, 49; Current, *Lincoln Nobody Knows,* 12.
22. Thomas, *Abraham Lincoln,* 500.
23. Thomas, *Abraham Lincoln,* 70; 181; 93.
24. *Ibid.,* 173.
25. *Ibid.,* 143.
26. *Ibid.,* 454.
27. *Ibid.,* 358.
28. Thomas, *Abraham Lincoln,* 226.
29. *Ibid.,* 303.
30. *Ibid.,* 339.
31. *Ibid.,* 195; 200.
32. Randall, *Lincoln,* I, 279.
33. *Ibid.,* II, 243.
34. Thomas, *Abraham Lincoln,* 239.
35. Randall, *Lincoln,* I, 279.
36. *Ibid.,* II, 160.
37. *Ibid.,* 243.
38. Thomas, *Abraham Lincoln,* 409; 425.
39. *Ibid.,* 135; 231.
40. *Ibid.,* 267; Randall, *Lincoln,* I, 63.
41. Thomas, *Abraham Lincoln,* 21.
42. A case analysis of Stephen Douglas suggesting he would be classified as an "active-positive" can be found in Jeffrey Tulis, "On Presidential Character," in Joseph M. Bessette and Jeffrey Tulis, eds., *The President in the Constitutional Order* (Baton Rouge, La.: Louisiana State University Press, 1981), pp. 301–305.
43. Barber, "Coding Scheme," p. 3; and "Strategies for Understanding," 464 (Author's emphasis).
44. *Ibid.,* 463.
45. Barber, *Presidential Character,* 211.
46. See Harry Jaffa, *Crisis of the House Divided,* 2nd ed. (Seattle, Washington: University of Washington, 1971). For a discussion of Lincoln's character in light of his understanding of the political issues, see Lord Charnwood, *Abraham Lincoln* (New York: Henry Holt, 1916).
47. V. O. Key, Jr., *The Responsible Electorate* (New York: Vintage Books, 1966), 6.

# 8. The Eisenhower Revival

## Stephen E. Ambrose

> For all the jokes about golf playing, he did a far, far better job of handling
> that office than anyone realized.
>
> — Ronald Reagan on
> Dwight D. Eisenhower

Since Andrew Jackson left the White House in 1837, 33 men have served as
president of the United States. Of that number, only four have managed to serve
eight consecutive years in the office — Ulysses Grant, Woodrow Wilson, Franklin Roosevelt, and Dwight Eisenhower. Of these four, only two were also world
figures in a field outside politics — Grant and Eisenhower — and only two had
a higher reputation and broader popularity when they left office than when they
entered — Roosevelt and Eisenhower.

Given this record of success, and the relative failure of Ike's successors, it is
no wonder that there is an Eisenhower revival going on, or that President Reagan and his staff are attempting to present themselves as the Eisenhower administration resurrected. Another major reason for the current Eisenhower boom is
nostalgia for the 1950s — a decade of peace with prosperity, a 1.5 percent annual
inflation rate, self-sufficiency in oil and other precious goods, balanced budgets,
and domestic tranquillity. Eisenhower "revisionism," now proceeding at full
speed, gives Ike himself much of the credit for these accomplishments.

The reassessment of Eisenhower is based on a multitude of new sources, as
well as new perspectives, which have become available only in the past few
years. The most important of these is Ike's private diary, which he kept on a
haphazard basis from the late 1930s to his death in 1969. Other sources include
his extensive private correspondence with his old military and new big business
friends, his telephone conversations (which he had taped or summarized by his
secretary, who listened in surreptitiously), minutes of meetings of the cabinet
and of the National Security Council, and the extensive diary of his press secretary, the late James Hagerty. Study of these documents has changed the predominant scholarly view of Eisenhower from, in the words of the leading revisionist, political scientist Fred Greenstein of Princeton, one of "an aging hero
who reigned more than he ruled and who lacked the energy, motivation, and
political skill to have a significant impact on events," to a view of Ike as "politically astute and informed, actively engaged in putting his personal stamp on

*Stephen Ambrose teaches history at the University of New Orleans and is the author
of several books including* Rise to Globalism *and* The Supreme Commander.

public policy, [who] applied a carefully thought-out conception of leadership to the conduct of his presidency."

The revisionist portrait of Ike contains many new features. Far from being a "part-time" president who preferred the golf course to the Oval Office, he worked an exhausting schedule, reading more and carrying on a wider correspondence than appeared at the time. Instead of the "captive hero" who was a tool of the millionaires in his cabinet, Ike made a major effort to convince the Republican right wing to accept the New Deal reforms, an internationalist foreign policy, and the need to modernize and liberalize the Republican party. Rather than ducking the controversial issue of Joseph McCarthy, Eisenhower strove to discredit the senator. Ike's failure to issue a public endorsement of *Brown v. Topeka* was not based on any fundamental disagreement with the Warren Court's ruling, but rather on his understanding of the separation, the balance, of powers in the U.S. government — he agreed with the decision, it turns out, and was a Warren supporter. Nor was Ike a tongue-tied general of terrible syntax; he was a careful speaker and an excellent writer who confused his audiences only when he wanted to do so.

Most of all, the revisionists give Eisenhower high marks for ending the Korean War, staying out of Vietnam, and keeping the peace elsewhere. They argue that these achievements were neither accidental nor lucky, but rather the result of carefully conceived policies and firm leadership at the top. The revisionists also praise Ike for holding down defense costs, a key factor in restraining inflation while maintaining prosperity.

Altogether, the "new" Ike is an appealing figure, not only for his famous grin and winning personality, but also because he wisely guided us through perilous times.

"The bland leading the bland." So the nightclub comics characterized the Eisenhower administration. Much of the blandness came from Ike's refusal to say, in public, anything negative about his fellow politicians. His lifelong rule was to refuse to discuss personalities. But in the privacy of his diary, parts of which have just been published with an excellent introduction by Robert H. Ferrell (*The Eisenhower Diaries*, W. W. Norton), he could be sarcastic, slashing, and bitter.

In 1953, when Ike was president and his old colleague from the war, Winston Churchill, was prime minister, the two met in Bermuda. Churchill, according to Ike,

> has developed an almost childlike faith that all of the answers to world problems are to be found merely in British-American partnership. . . . He is trying to relive the days of World War II. In those days he had the enjoyable feeling that he and our president were sitting on some rather Olympian platform . . . and directing world affairs. Even if this picture were an accurate one of those days, it would have no application to the present. But it was only partially true, even then, as many of us who . . . had to work out the solutions for nasty local problems are well aware.

That realistic sense of the importance of any one individual, even a Churchill or a Roosevelt, was basic to Eisenhower's thought. Back in 1942, with reference to MacArthur, Ike scribbled in his diary that in modern war, "no one person can be a Napoleon or a Caesar." What was required was teamwork and coopera- tion.

Although Lyndon Johnson, John F. Kennedy, Hubert Humphrey, and other Democratic senators of the 1950s catch hell from time to time in Ike's diary, he reserved his most heartfelt blasts for the Republicans (he never expected much from the Democrats anyway). Thus, Ike wrote of Senator William Knowland of California, "In his case there seems to be no final answer to the question 'How stupid can you get?' " In *Eisenhower the President* (Prentice-Hall), Wil- liam Bragg Ewald Jr., a former Eisenhower speechwriter, records that when Republicans urged Ike to convince Nelson Rockefeller to take the second place on a 1960 ticket with Richard Nixon, Ike did so, rather halfheartedly, and then reported on Rockefeller: "He is no philosophical genius. It is pretty hard to get him in and tell him something of his duty. He has a personal ambition that is overwhelming." Eisenhower told Nixon that the only way to persuade Rocke- feller to run for the vice presidency was for Nixon to promise to step aside in Rockefeller's favor in 1964.

Ike didn't like "politics," and he positively disliked "politicians." The behind- the-scenes compromises, the swapping of votes for pork-barrel purposes, the will- ingness to abandon conviction in order to be on the popular side all nearly drove him to distraction. His favorite constitutional reform was to limit congressional terms to two for the Senate and three or four for the House, in order to elimi- nate the professional politician from American life.

Nor did Ike much like the press. "The members of this group," he wrote in his diary, "are far from being as important as they themselves consider," but he did recognize that "they have a sufficient importance . . . in the eyes of the aver- age Washington officeholder to insure that much government time is consumed in courting favor with them and in dressing up ideas and programs so that they look as saleable as possible." Reporters, Ike wrote, "have little sense of humor and, because of this, they deal in negative criticism rather than in any attempt toward constructive helpfulness." (Murray Kempton, in some ways the first Eisenhower revisionist, recalled how journalists had ridiculed Ike's amiability in the 1950s, while the president actually had intelligently confused and hood- winked them. Kempton decided that Eisenhower was a cunning politician whose purpose was "never to be seen in what he did.")

The people Ike did like, aside from his millionaire friends, were those men who in his view rose above politics, including Milton Eisenhower, Robert Ander- son, and Earl Warren. Of Milton, Ike wrote in 1953, "I believe him to be the most knowledgeable and widely informed of all the people with whom I deal. . . . So far as I am concerned, he is at this moment the most highly qualified man in the United States to be president. This most emphatically makes no exception of me. . . ." Had he not shrunk from exposing Milton to a charge of benefiting from nepotism, Ike would have made his younger brother a member of his cabinet.

In 1966, during an interview in Eisenhower's Gettysburg office, I asked him who was the most intelligent man he had ever met, expecting a long pause while he ran such names as Marshall, Roosevelt, de Gaulle, Churchill, Truman, or Khrushchev through his mind. But Ike never hesitated: "Robert Anderson," he said emphatically. Anderson, a Texan and a Democrat, served Ike in various capacities, including secretary of the navy and secretary of the treasury. Now Ewald reveals for the first time that Eisenhower offered Anderson the second spot on the Republican ticket for 1956 and wanted Anderson to be his successor. Anderson turned down the president because he thought the offer was politically unrealistic.

Which inevitably brings up the subject of Richard Nixon. Eisenhower's relations with Nixon have long been a puzzle. Ike tried to get Nixon to resign during the 1952 campaign, but Nixon saved himself with the Checkers speech. In 1956 Ike attempted to maneuver Nixon off the ticket by offering him a high-level cabinet post, but Nixon dug in his heels and used his connections with the right wing of the party to stay in place. And in 1960, Ike's campaign speeches for Nixon were distinctly unenthusiastic. Still, Eisenhower and Nixon never severed their ties. Ike stuck with Nixon throughout his life. He often remarked that Nixon's defeat by Kennedy was one of his greatest disappointments. And, of course, his grandson married one of Nixon's daughters. Sad to say, neither the diary nor the private correspondence offers any insights into Eisenhower's gut feelings toward Nixon. The relationship between the two men remains a puzzle.

Some writers used to say the same about the Eisenhower-Earl Warren relationship, but thanks to Ike's dairy, Ewald's book, and the correspondence, we now have a better understanding of Eisenhower's feelings toward Warren personally, and toward his Court. In December 1955, Jim Hagerty suggested that if Ike could not run for a second term for reasons of health, Warren might make a good nominee. "Not a chance," Ike snapped back, "and I'll tell you why. I know that the Chief Justice is very happy right where he is. He wants to go down in history as a great Chief Justice, and he certainly is becoming one. He is dedicated to the Court and is getting the Court back on its feet and back in respectable standing again."

Eisenhower and Warren were never friends; as Ewald writes, "For more than seven years they sat, each on his eminence, at opposite ends of Pennsylvania Avenue, by far the two most towering figures in Washington, each playing out a noble role, in tragic inevitable estrangement." And he quotes Attorney General Herbert Brownell as saying, "Both Eisenhower and Warren were very reserved men. If you'd try to put your arm around either of them, he'd remember it for sixty days."

Ike had a great deal of difficulty with *Brown v. Topeka,* but more because of his temperament than for any racist reasons. He was always an evolutionist who wanted to move forward through agreement and compromise, not command and force. Ike much perferred consensus to conflict. Yet Ewald argues that he privately recognized the necessity and justice of *Brown v. Topeka.* Even had that not been so, he would have supported the Court, because — as he carefully explained to one of his oldest and closest friends, Sweed Hazlett, in a private letter — "I hold to the basic purpose. There must be respect for the Constitution — which means the Supreme Court's interpretation of the Constitution — or we shall have chaos. This I believe with all my heart — and shall always act accordingly."

Precisely because of that feeling, Eisenhower never made a public declaration of support for the *Brown v. Topeka* decision, despite the pleas of liberals, intellectuals, and many members of the White House staff that he do so. He felt that once the Supreme Court had spoken, the president had no right to second guess nor any duty to support the decision. The law was the law. That Ike was always ready to uphold the law, he demonstrated decisively when he sent the U.S. Army into Little Rock in 1957 to enforce court-ordered desegregation.

Despite his respect for Warren and the Court, when I asked Eisenhower in 1965 what was his biggest mistake, he replied heatedly, "The appointment of that S.O.B. Earl Warren." Shocked, I replied, "General, I always thought that was your best appointment." "Let's not talk about it," he responded, and we did not. Now that I have seen the flattering and thoughtful references to Warren in the diary, I can only conclude that Eisenhower's anger at Warren was the result of the criminal rights cases of the early 1960s, not the desegregation decisions of the 1950s.

As everyone knows, Ike also refused publicly to condemn Senator McCarthy, again despite the pleas of many of his own people, including his most trusted adviser, Milton. Ike told Milton, "I will not get into a pissing contest with that skunk."

The revisionists now tell us that the president was working behind the scenes, using the "hidden hand" to encourage peaceful desegregation and to censure McCarthy. He helped Attorney General Brownell prepare a brief from the Justice Department for the Court on *Brown v. Topeka* that attacked the constitutionality of segregation in the schools. As for McCarthy, Greenstein writes that Eisenhower,

> working most closely with Press Secretary Hagerty, conducted a virtual day-to-day campaign via the media and congressional allies to end McCarthy's political effectiveness. The overall strategy was to avoid *direct mention* of McCarthy in the president's public statements, lest McCarthy win sympathy as a spunky David battling against the presidential Goliath. Instead Eisenhower systematically condemned the *types* of actions in which McCarthy engaged.

Eisenhower revisionism is full of nostalgia for the 1950s, and it is certainly true that if you were white, male, and middle class or better, it was the best decade of the century. The 1950s saw peace and prosperity, no riots, relatively high employment, a growing GNP, virtually no inflation, no arms race, no great reforms, no great changes, low taxes, little government regulation of industry or commerce, and a president who was trusted and admired. Politics were middle-of-the-road — Eisenhower was the least partisan president of the century. In an essay entitled "Good-By to the 'Fifties — and Good Riddance," historian Eric Goldman called the Eisenhower years possibly "the dullest and dreariest in all our history." After the turmoil of the 1960s and 1970s — war, inflation, riots, higher taxes, an arms race, all accompanied by a startling growth in the size, cost, and scope of the federal government — many Americans may find the dullness and dreariness of the 1950s appealing.

Next to peace, the most appealing fact was the 1.5 percent inflation rate. The revisionists claim that Ike deserved much of the credit for that accomplishment because of his insistence on a balanced budget (which he actually achieved only twice, but he did hold down the deficits). Ike kept down the costs by refusing to expand the New Deal welfare services — to the disgruntlement of the Republican right wing, he was equally firm about refusing to dismantle the New Deal programs — and, far more important, by holding down defense spending.

This was, indeed, Ike's special triumph. He feared that an arms race with the Soviet Union would lead to uncontrollable inflation and eventually bankrupt the United States, without providing any additional security. In Ike's view, the more bombs and missiles we built, the less secure we would be, not just because of the economic impact, but because the more bombs we built, the more the Soviets would build. In short, Ike's fundamental strategy was based on his recognition that in nuclear warfare, there is no defense and can be no winner. In that situation, one did not need to be superior to the enemy in order to deter him.

The Democrats, led by Senator John F. Kennedy, criticized Ike for putting a balanced budget ahead of national defense. They accused him of allowing a "bomber gap" and, later, a "missile gap" to develop, and spoke of the need to "get America moving again." Nelson Rockefeller and Richard Nixon added to the hue and cry during the 1960 campaign, when they promised to expand defense spending. But as long as Eisenhower was president, there was no arms race. Neither the politicians nor the military-industrial complex could persuade Eisenhower to spend more money on the military. Inheriting a $50 billion defense budget from Truman, he reduced it to $40 billion and held it there for the eight years of his tenure.

Holding down defense costs was a longstanding theme of Ike's. As early as December 1945, just after he replaced George Marshall as army chief of staff, he jotted in his diary, "I'm astounded and appalled at the size and scope of plans the staff sees as necessary to maintain our security position now and in the future." And in 1951, before he became a candidate, he wrote in his diary that if the Congress and military could not be restrained about "this armament business, we will go broke and still have inefficient defenses."

President Eisenhower was unassailable on the subject. As one senator complained, "How in hell can I argue with Ike Eisenhower on a military matter?" But as Ike wrote in 1956 to his friend Hazlett, "Some day there is going to be a man sitting in my present chair who has not been raised in the military services and who will have little understanding of where slashes in their estimates can be made with little or no damage. If that should happen while we still have the state of tension that now exists in the world, I shudder to think of what could happen in this country."

One reason why Ike was able to reduce the military in a time of great tension was his intimate knowledge of the Soviet military situation. From 1956 on, he directed a series of flights by the U-2 spy plane over the Soviet Union. He had personally taken the lead in getting the U-2 program started, and he kept a tight personal control over the flights — he gave his approval to the individual flights only after a thorough briefing on where in the U.S.S.R. the planes were going and what the CIA wanted to discover. Here too the revisionists have shown that the contemporary feeling, especially after Francis Gary Powers was shot down in 1960, that Ike was not in charge and hardly knew what was going on inside his own government is altogether wrong. He was absolutely in charge, not only of broad policy on the use of the U-2, but of implementing details as well.

The major factor in Eisenhower's ability to restrain defense spending was keeping the peace. His record here is clear and impressive — he signed an armistice in Korea less than half a year after taking office, stayed out of Vietnam, and managed to avoid war despite such crisis situations as Hungary and the Suez, Quemoy and Matsu, Berlin and Cuba. The revisionists insist that the credit must go to Ike, and they equally insist that Eisenhower, not Secretary of State John Foster Dulles, was in command of American foreign policy in the 1950s. Dulles, says Greenstein, "was assigned the 'get tough' side of foreign-policy enunciation, thus placating the fervently anti-Communist wing of the Republican party." Ike, meanwhile, appeared to be above the battle, while actually directing it on a day-to-day basis.

"In essence, Eisenhower used Dulles." So writes Robert Divine, one of America's leading diplomatic historians, in his provocative new book, *Eisenhower and the Cold War* (Oxford University Press). Divine concludes that "far from being the do-nothing President of legend, Ike was skillful and active in directing American foreign policy." All the revisionists agree that the contemporary idea that Dulles led Ike by the nose was a myth that Eisenhower himself did the most to encourage. Nevertheless, Eisenhower did have a high opinion of his secretary of state. Divine quotes Ike's comment to Emmet Hughes on Dulles: "There's only one man I know who has seen *more* of the world and talked with more people and *knows* more than he does — and that's me."

The quotation illustrates another often overlooked Eisenhower characteristic — his immense self-confidence. He had worked with some of the great men of the century — Churchill, Roosevelt, Stalin, de Gaulle, Montgomery, and many others — long before he became president. His diary entry for the day after his inauguration speaks to the point: "My first day at the president's desk.. Plenty of worries and difficult problems. But such has been my portion for a long time — the result is that this just seems (today) like a continuation of all I've been doing since July 1941 — even before that."

Ike's vast experience in war and peace made him confident in crises. People naturally looked to him for leadership. No matter how serious the crisis seemed to be, Ike rarely got flustered. During a war scare in the Formosa Straits in 1955, he wrote in his diary, "I have so often been through these periods of strain that I have become accustomed to the fact that most of the calamities that we anticipate really never occur."

Ike's self-confidence was so great that, Greenstein writes, he had "neither a need nor a desire" to capture headlines. "He employed his skills to achieve his ends by inconspicuous means." In foreign policy, this meant he did not issue strident warnings, did not — in public — threaten Russia or China with specific reprisals for specific actions. Instead, he retained his room for maneuver by deliberately spreading confusion. He did not care if editorial writers criticized him for jumbled syntax; he wanted to keep possible opponents guessing, and he did. For example, when asked at a March 1955 press conference if he would use atomic bombs to defend Quemoy and Matsu, he replied:

> Every war is going to astonish you in the way it occurred, and in the way it is carried out. So that for a man to predict, particularly if he has the responsibility for making the decision, to predict what he is going to use, how he is going to do it, would I think exhibit his ignorance of war; that is what I believe.

As he intended, the Chinese found such statements inscrutable, as they had in Korea two years earlier. When truce talks in Korea reached an impasse in mid-May 1953, Ike put the pressure on the Chinese, hinting to them that the United States might use atomic weapons if a truce could not be arranged, and backing this up by transferring atomic warheads to American bases in Okinawa. The Chinese then accepted a truce. As Divine writes, "Perhaps the best testimony to the shrewdness of the President's policy is the impossibility of telling even now whether or not he was bluffing."

Nearly all observers agree that one of Ike's greatest accomplishments was staying out of Vietnam in the face of intense pressure from his closest advisers to save the French position there or, after July 1954, to go in alone to defeat Ho Chi Minh. Ike was never tempted. As early as March 1951 he wrote in his diary, "I'm convinced that no military victory is possible in that kind of theater." And in a first draft of his memoirs, written in 1963 but not published until 1981 by Ewald, Ike wrote:

> The jungles of Indochina would have swallowed up division after division of United States troops, who, unaccustomed to this kind of warfare, would have sustained heavy casualties until they had learned to live in a new environment.

Furthermore, the presence of ever more numbers of white men in uniform probably would have aggravated rather than assuaged Asiatic resentments.

That was hardheaded military reasoning by General Eisenhower. But President Eisenhower stayed out of Vietnam as much for moral as for military reasons. When the Joint Chiefs suggested to him in 1954 that the United States use an atomic bomb against the Vietminh around Dien Bien Phu, the president said he would not be a party to using that "terrible thing" against Asians for the second time in less than a decade. And in another previously unpublished draft of his memoirs, he wrote:

> The strongest reason of all for the United States refusal to [intervene] is the fact that among all the powerful nations of the world the United States is the only one with a tradition of anti-colonialism. . . . The standing of the United States as the most powerful of the anti-colonial powers is an asset of incalculable value to the Free World. . . . Thus it is that the moral position of the United States was more to be guarded than the Tonkin Delta, indeed than all of Indochina.

Ike's international outlook, already well known, is highlighted by the new documents. He believed that the bonds that tied Western Europe and the United States together were so tight that the fate of one was the fate of the other. In May 1947, one year before the Marshall Plan, he wrote in his diary, in reference to Western Europe:

> I personally believe that the best thing we could now do would be to post 5 billion to the credit of the secretary of state and tell him to use it to support democratic movements wherever our vital interests indicate. Money should be used to promote possibilities of self-sustaining economies, not merely to prevent immediate starvation.

Ike also anticipated Kennedy's Alliance for Progress. Historian Burton Kaufman, in the narrowest but perhaps most important study reviewed here, *Trade and Aid: Eisenhower's Foreign Economic Policy* (Johns Hopkins University Press), concludes: "Not only did Eisenhower reorient the mutual security program away from military and toward economic assistance, he was also the first president to alter the geographical direction of American foreign aid toward the developing world." After an exhaustive examination, Kaufman also gives Ike high marks for resisting Nelson Rockefeller and others who wanted the president to encourage private investment overseas through tax breaks, while reducing or eliminating all forms of public foreign aid. Kaufman's basic theme is "the transition of a foreign economic program based on the concept of 'trade not aid' when Eisenhower took office to one predicated on the principle of 'trade and aid,' with the emphasis clearly on the flow of public capital abroad, by the time he left the White House."

That Ike himself was in charge of this transition, Kaufman leaves no doubt. That Kaufman likes Ike is equally clear: the foreign aid and trade program, Kaufman writes, "demonstrates the quality and character of Eisenhower's intellect and the cogency and forcefulness of his arguments in defense of administration policy. Finally, it emphasizes Eisenhower's flexibility as president and his capacity to alter his views in response to changing world conditions."

Kaufman, however, is critical of Ike on a number of points. Eisenhower himself, it turns out, could be as hypocritical as the "politicians" he scorned. In his speeches, Ike espoused the principles of free trade with sincerity and conviction; in his actions, he supported a protectionist agricultural policy and made broad concessions to the protectionist forces in Congress. Kaufman reaches the conclusion that "he often retreated on trade and tariff matters; he gave up the struggle with hardly a whimper."

And, as Blanche Wiesen Cook, another of the new Eisenhower scholars (but no revisionist), points out in *The Declassified Eisenhower* (Doubleday), Ike's vision of a peaceful world was based on a sophisticated version of Henry Luce's "American Century." Cook argues that Eisenhower's "blueprint . . . involved a determination to pursue political warfare, psychological warfare, and economic warfare everywhere and at all times." Under Ike's direction, she writes, the CIA and other branches of the government "ended all pretensions about territorial integrity, national sovereignty and international law. Covert operatives were everywhere, and they were active. From bribery to assassination, no activity was unacceptable short of nuclear war."

Cook does stress the importance of Eisenhower's stance against general war and his opposition to an arms race, but insists that these positions have to be placed in context, a context that includes the CIA-inspired and -led governmental overthrows in Iran and Guatemala, covert operations of all types in Vietnam and Eastern Europe, and assassination attempts against political leaders in the Congo and Cuba. Returning to an earlier view of Ike, Cook regards him as a "captive hero," the "chosen instrument" of the leaders of the great multinational corporations "to fight for the world they wanted."

One does not have to accept Cook's "captive hero" view to realize that it may indeed be time, as Kaufman indicates, to blow the whistle on Eisenhower revisionism. Ike had his shortcomings and he suffered serious setbacks. For all his openness to new ideas, he was rigid and dogmatic in his anti-Communism. The darker side of Eisenhower's refusal to condemn McCarthy was that Ike himself agreed with the senator on the nature, if not the extent, of the problem, and he shared the senator's goals, if not his methods. After his first year in office, Ike made a list of his major accomplishments to date. Peace in Korea was first, the new defense policy second. Third on the list: "The highest security standards are being insisted upon for those employed in government service," a bland way of saying that under his direction, the Civil Service Commission had fired 2,611 "security risks" and reported that 4,315 other government workers had resigned when they learned they were under investigation. That was the true "hidden hand" at work, and the true difference between Ike and McCarthy — Ike got rid of Communists and fellow travelers (and many liberals) quietly and effectively, while McCarthy, for all his noise, accomplished nothing.

Thus, no matter how thoroughly the revisionists document Ike's opposition to McCarthy personally or his support for Warren, it remains true that his failure to speak out directly on McCarthy encouraged the witch hunters, just as his failure to speak out directly on the *Brown v. Topeka* decision encouraged the segregationists. The old general never admitted that it was impossible for him to be truly above the battle, never seemed to understand that the president is inevitably a part of the battle, so much so that his inaction can have as great an impact as his action.

With McCarthy and *Brown v. Topeka* in mind, there is a sad quality to the following Eisenhower diary passage, written in January 1954, about a number of Republican senators whom Ike was criticizing for being more inclined to trade votes than to provide clear leadership:

> They do not seem to realize when there arrives that moment at which soft speaking should be abandoned and a fight to the end undertaken. Any man who hopes to exercise leadership must be ready to meet this requirement face to face when it arises; unless he is ready to fight when necessary, people will finally begin to ignore him.

One of Ike's greatest disappointments was his failure to liberalize and modernize the Republican party, in order to make it the majority party in the United States. "The Republican party must be known as a progressive organization or it is sunk," he wrote in his diary in November 1954. "I believe this so emphatically that far from appeasing or reasoning with the dyed-in-the-wool reactionary fringe, we should completely ignore it and when necessary, repudiate it." Responding to cries of "impeach Earl Warren," Ike wrote in his diary, "If the Republicans as a body should try to repudiate him, I shall leave the Republican Party and try to organize an intelligent group of independents, however small." He was always threatening to break with the Republican party, or at least re-name it; in March 1954, he told Hagerty, "You know, what we ought to do is get a word to put ahead of Republican — something like 'new' or 'modern' or something. We just can't work with fellows like McCarthy, Bricker, Jenner and that bunch."

A favorite revisionist quotation, which is used to show Ike's political astuteness, comes from a 1954 letter to his brother Edgar:

> Should any political party attempt to abolish social security and eliminate labor laws and farm programs, you would not hear of that party again in our political history. There is a tiny splinter group, of course, that believes that you can do these things. Among them are H. L. Hunt, a few other Texas oil millionaires, and an occasional politician and businessman from other areas. Their number is negligible and they are stupid.

Good enough, but a critic would be quick to point out that Ike's "tiny splinter group" managed to play a large role in the nominations of Barry Goldwater, Richard Nixon, and Ronald Reagan. In short, although Ike saw great dangers to the right in the Republican party, he did little to counter the reactionary influence in his own organization. Franklin Roosevelt did a far better job of curbing the left wing in the Democratic party, and generally in building his party, than anything Ike did for the Republicans.

The Eisenhower legacy for the Reagan administration, in brief, is mixed. Reagan can choose to emphasize the darker side of Ike's foreign policy, with its emphasis on CIA activities and reflexive opposition to communism, or he can follow Ike's lead and reject any thought of general war while searching for a genuine peace. Similarly, on the domestic front he can ignore the poor and the minorities in an attempt to balance the budget and curb inflation, or he can again emulate Ike and insist on retaining a strong Social Security system backed by the federal government. He could also recall that Ike presided over the largest public works program in the history of mankind, the Interstate Highway System.

What Reagan cannot do, and still remain faithful to Eisenhower's legacy, is spend increasing sums on the military. From the end of World War II to his last day in the White House, Eisenhower resisted swollen military budgets. In January 1952 he noted in his diary his fear of "the danger of internal deterioration through the annual expenditure of unconscionable sums on a program of indefinite duration, extending far into the future." Or, as he told some members of Congress, "It is perfectly clear that you can't provide security just with a check book. You've got to be prepared to live with a series of [crises] for the next 40 years. If these people decide to put another $3 billion into the budget every time Russia tries to push, they might as well go all the way to a garrison state." The style and rhetoric of the Reagan administration might well be those of the Eisenhower administration — the quick and easy smile, low-key cabinet government on the Whig model, practical businessmen in charge, balanced budgets and lower taxes, stern opposition to communism — but so long as the Reagan people insist on expanded military expenditures the reality can never be the same. Ike's legacy means more than presidential style; he also bequeathed us a record of achievement.

Shortly after Ike left office, a group of leading American historians was asked to rate the presidents. Ike came in near the bottom of the poll. That result was primarily a reflection of how enamored the professors were with FDR and Harry Truman. Today, those same historians would compare Ike with his successors rather than his predecessors and place him in the top ten, if not the top five, of all our presidents. No matter how much one qualifies that record by pointing to this or that shortcoming or failure of the Eisenhower administration, it remains an enviable record. No wonder the people like Ike.

SOURCE: This article, originally entitled "The Ike Age," appeared in *The New Republic* (May 9, 1981). Reprinted by permission of *The New Republic*, © 1981.

# Presidential Power

# *IV*

**9. The President's Constitutional Position**
*C. Herman Pritchett*

**10. Presidential Power and the Crisis
of Modernization**
*Alan Wolfe*

# 9. The President's Constitutional Position

## C. Herman Pritchett

The presidency looms so large in our national history, and we are so accustomed to the president as a necessary and familiar fact of life, that it is difficult to conceive of any other way we could institutionalize the executive power. For that reason, it may be helpful to the reader to begin this survey of current constitutional problems with respect to *presidential powers* by returning to 1787 and reviewing the alternatives as the founders saw them and the proposals from among which they made the choices that created the presidency.

What were the attitudes toward executive power in the founding period? The fear of monarchy was basic to all considerations of the executive office. The shadow of George III was heavy on the land. Executive authority was symbolized by the royal governors. As Corwin says, "The colonial period ended with the belief prevalent that 'the executive magistracy' was the natural enemy, the legislative assembly the natural friend of liberty." [1] The Virginia constitution of 1776 stipulated that the executive powers of government were to be exercised according to the laws of the commonwealth, and that no power of prerogative was ever to be claimed "by virtue of any law, statute, or custom of England." The intention was to cut the executive power off entirely from the resources of the common law and of English constitutional usage.

But, between 1776 and 1787, there was enough experience with state legislatures to destroy naïve assumptions about their inherent goodness. Madison was critical of the state constitutions, which, in their concern with the "over-grown and all-grasping prerogative of an hereditary magistrate," did not realize the "danger from legislative usurpation, which, by assembling all power in the same hands, must lead to the same tyranny as is threatened by executive usurpations." [2] Gouverneur Morris, reversing the earlier pattern, saw the executive as the protector and the legislature as the threat, saying the "Executive Magistrate should be the guardian of the people, even of the lower classes, agst. Legislative tyranny, against the Great & the wealthy who in the course of things will necessarily compose — the Legislative body." [3]

The principal theoretical writers with whom the founders were familiar likewise supplied support for a strong executive. Particularly impressive is Locke's description of "prerogative" in Chapter 14 of his *Second Treatise of Government,* which argues that

*C. Herman Pritchett, a past president of the American Political Science Association, has authored several books, including* The Roosevelt Court *and* The American Constitution *and coauthored* Judges and Politics.

... the good of the society requires that several things should be left to the discretion of him that has the executive power.... For the legislators not being able to foresee and provide by laws for all that may be useful to the community, the executor of the laws, having the power in his hands, has by the common law of Nature a right to make use of it for the good of the society.

Montesquieu's doctrine of the separation of powers, holding that the three departments of government must be kept separate and that each must be able to defend its characteristic functions from intrusion by either of the other departments, provided another source of defense for the executive against legislative supremacy.

The problem, then, as the founders saw it, was how to secure an executive power capable of penetrating to the remotest parts of the Union for the purpose of enforcing national laws and bringing assistance to the states in emergencies of domestic disorder, yet avoiding, at the same time, stirring up the widespread popular fear of monarchy.

On one side was the preference for an executive which would be nothing more than an institution for carrying the will of the legislature into effect, with an incumbent appointed by and accountable to the legislature. On the other side was the strong-executive faction, which wanted a single-headed office independent of the legislature. As the convention deliberated, the key decisions increasingly favored the latter view.

## The Decisions that Established the Constitutional Dimensions of the Presidency

*Rejection of a collegial executive or a council.* The one decision about the executive that was basic to all others was that it should be an individual and not a board or committee. Some thought a one-person executive would be too much like a monarch. In the discussions at the convention, Sherman said that the number of the executive should "not be fixed, but ... the legislature should be at liberty to appoint one or more as experience might dictate." Randolph then proposed an executive council of three men, contending that "unity in the Executive magistracy" would be the "foetus of monarchy." But Gerry thought that, in military matters, a plural executive would be a "general with three heads." [4]

James Wilson was the leader of the strong executive faction. He wanted a "single magistrate, as giving most energy, dispatch, and responsibility to the office." [5] Unity in the executive would be the "best safeguard against tyranny." As chairman of the Committee of Detail, Wilson had the opportunity to incorporate his conception of the office into the draft. In Articles VI and X of the committee's report of August 6, 1787, the issue was settled in favor of a single executive.

There was still the issue of restraining the executive by a Council. On September 7, while discussing the provision for the president to require the opinion in writing of the heads of departments, Mason said that, in rejecting a Council to the president, "we were about to try an experiment on which the most despotic Governments had never ventured — the Grand Signor himself had his Divan." He proposed a Council of State for the president, made up of six members — two from the Eastern, two from the Middle, and two from the Southern states — with a rotation and duration of office similar to those of the Senate, and appointed by Congress or the Senate. Franklin approved; he thought a Council "would not only be a check on a bad President but be a relief to a good one." Morris replied that the committee had considered a Council and rejected the idea; "it was judged that the President by persuading his Council — to concur in his wrong measures, would acquire their protection for them." The proposal was defeated, eight to three.[6]

*Rejection of election by the legislature.* Election of the president by the legislature, which was very nearly adopted, would inevitably have made the presidency a much different institution. There was a close relationship between the method of election and the term of office. If the executive were to be chosen by Congress, then a fairly long term, with no reeligibility, was favored, to reduce the possibility of intrigue with Congress for a second term. If the president could be chosen in some other fashion, then reeligibility was not objectionable, and a shorter term was possible.

The Virginia Plan called for a national executive to be named by electors chosen by Congress. Sherman wanted the executive to be only an "institution for carrying the will of the legislature into effect," and consequently executive officials should be "persons . . . appointed by and accountable to the legislature only." [7] Early discussion by the Committee of the Whole left the Virginia Plan unchanged.

Choice of the president by electors chosen by the people was proposed by Wilson on June 2 and defeated, eight to two. Morris again proposed popular election on July 17, at which time Mason made his famous comment that "it would be as unnatural to refer the choice of a proper character for chief Magistrate to the people, as it would, to refer a trial of colours to a blind man." [8] The popular-election plan failed, and the convention then reaffirmed legislative election unanimously. But Morris and Madison contended that the executive should be independent of the legislature. The convention then switched to electors, but provided for their choice by the state legislatures.

On July 24, the convention flopped back to the original scheme for legislative election, with a seven-year term and no reeligibility. In this posture, the matter went to the Committee of Detail, which had to decide how Congress would vote for president. Would the houses vote separately (they might not agree) or jointly (the larger states would dominate)? Joint election was adopted on August 24, but an effort to have the votes cast by states, each with one vote, failed by a six-to-five margin. Here, Morris again urged popular election and lost only by six to five. The matter was so completely in dispute that it was turned over to the Committee of Eleven, including Morris. This committee proposed the plan that was finally adopted — electors equaling in number senators and representatives from the states and appointed by the states.

*A broad appointing power for the president.* The appointing power went to the president only after prolonged opposition. The Virginia Plan called for the election of judges as well as the president by the Congress, but the judicial provision was soon eliminated. On June 5, Wilson argued for appointment of judges by the president. "A principal reason for unity in the Executive was that officers might be appointed by a single, responsible person." [9] Madison inclined toward appointment of judges by the Senate, as the more stable and independent branch of the legislature.

On July 18, Gorham's proposal for executive appointment, with Senate advice and consent, was rejected by a tie vote. Senate appointment was reaffirmed on July 21, and the decision then went to the Committee of Detail. Its report gave the general appointing power to the president, but left judges and ambassadors with the Senate. The Committee of Eleven, reporting on September 4, gave the appointment of Supreme Court justices and ambassadors, and all other officers of the United States whose appointment was not otherwise provided for, to the president, with Senate advice and consent. This formula was accepted by the convention on September 7.

*The grant of power as commander in chief to the president and the power to declare war to Congress.* In giving Congress the power to declare war, the Convention clearly intended to vest the power to embark on a war in the body most representative of the people, in contrast to the power of the British sovereign to initiate war on his own prerogative. In the draft that came from the Committee of Detail, the language was that Congress should have the power to "make" war. This clause remained in its original form in the committee drafts for several weeks after other foreign relations powers had been transferred from the whole Congress to the Senate and then to the president.

On August 17, Pinckney opposed the vesting of this power in Congress — "its proceedings were too slow." He thought the "Senate would be the best depositary, being more acquainted with foreign affairs." Butler was "for resting the power in the President, who will have all the requisite qualities, and will not make war but when the Nation will support it." But Gerry said he "never expected to hear in a republic a motion to empower the Executive alone to declare war." [10]

It was Gerry and Madison who moved to substitute "declare" for "make," "leaving to the Executive the power to repel sudden attacks." Mason supported the change; he was against "giving the power of war to the Executive, because [he could] not (safely) . . . be trusted with it." King pointed out that the phrase "make war" might be understood to mean "conduct war," which was clearly an executive function — an argument Ellsworth found convincing. The change was made by a vote of seven to two.[11] Thus, the purpose of the change from "make" to "declare" was by no means to limit the role of Congress to a declaratory formality; the intention was to vest in Congress the full power and responsibility of initiating war.[12]

The power of the president to act as commander in chief was not much discussed, according to Madison's notes. There is no evidence that it was thought of as a source of power for the president. Since the clause contains nothing to indicate the purposes for which the president may exercise the power thus granted to command the troops, these purposes must ultimately be found in other provisions of Article II. According to Hamilton, in No. 69 of the *Federalist,* the power "would amount to nothing more than the supreme command and direction of the military and naval forces, as first General and admiral of the Confederacy."

*The power to make treaties.* The draft of the Constitution, as reported by the Committee of Detail on August 6, gave the Senate the power to make treaties as well as to appoint ambassadors and judges of the Supreme Court. On August 15, Mercer objected. The power of treaties, he contended, "belonged to the Executive department," adding that "Treaties would not be final so as to alter the laws of the land, till ratified by legislative authority." Madison, on August 23, agreed, saying "that the Senate represented the States alone, and that for this as well as other obvious reasons it was proper that the President should be an agent in Treaties." [13]

On September 4, the Committee of Eleven reported the new language giving the president the power to make treaties by and with the advice and consent of the Senate, with a two-thirds vote required. It was adopted on September 7, unanimously, after the convention voted down, ten to one, Wilson's proposal that treaties be approved by the House of Representatives also.

*The president's power to take care that the laws be faithfully executed.* The most general statement of presidential power to come from the founders was the provision that the president should take care that the laws be faithfully executed. Obviously, the executive had to have some general authorization to enforce the laws. The only question was how this grant of power was to be phrased. The original Virginia Plan gave the national executive a "general authority to execute the National laws," as well as the "Executive rights vested in Congress by the Confederation." [14] On June 1, this language was amended in the Committee of the Whole to read "with power to carry into execution the national laws." The additional provision, "to execute such powers, not legislative or judiciary in their nature, as may from time to time be delegated by the national legislature," was voted down.[15] The subsequent change to the present language was a change in style, not in content or intention.

## The Constitutional Setting

The creation of the presidency by the constitutional convention was political invention of a very high order. While there can have been in 1787 no conception of the powerful and multifaceted office which history and practice were to make of the presidency, the basis was laid for this development by the bold decisions of the founders.

In the controversy over ratification of the Constitution, fear of a strong executive was one of the motives most widely exploited by opponents of the new charter. Hamilton in No. 67 of *The Federalist* ridiculed the efforts that had been made to present the office as possessed of practically royal prerogatives. As for the unity of the executive, he contended that far from being a danger, it made the institution more susceptible to popular surveillance and control, while at the same time guaranteeing energy in the office, "a leading character of good government."

The "energy" of George Washington and his successors has translated the language of Article II into the world's most powerful executive. Our concern here is briefly to relate the constitutional language on executive structure and powers to the development of the presidential office. Realistically considered, the constitutional powers of the president are those which successive incumbents have asserted and in the exercise of which Congress has acquiesced. Where Congress has refused to acquiesce, the separation of powers has produced some classic constitutional struggles. Occasionally, and recently with increasing frequency, the Supreme Court has been called on to adjudicate issues of presidential authority.

## Presidential Election and Term

The unitary nature of the presidency is, of course, the foundation on which the entire subsequent development of the Executive Office rests. A collegial executive surely would have collapsed almost immediately. Under President Washington's wise and responsible exploration of presidential powers, fears of an executive monarchy gradually faded away. While the institution of the cabinet developed, it hardly filled the role of a council to the president that some had urged in the convention. Executive responsibility rested solely on the president, and each incumbent has had ample opportunity to recreate the office in his own image.

Equally portentous was the convention's rejection of congressional election of the president. Such an arrangement would certainly have diminished the potential of the office, making the president subservient to Congress, and perhaps opening the way to some version of the parliamentary system.[16]

The choice the convention made, as close to popular election as seemed feasible at the time, proved to be rather readily adaptable to a system of full popular election (with the necessary qualifications that the electoral college system requires). The direct link between the president and the national electorate must be regarded as the primary condition of presidential power, providing him with a legitimacy possessed by no other official of the government. This legitimacy is slightly diminished when the president is elected with less than 50 percent of the popular vote, or when the margin between the two leading candidates is very narrow. It would be seriously eroded if, in a future election, the workings of the electoral college awarded the presidency to a candidate who actually secured fewer popular votes than his opponent.

Another electoral concern is that the House of Representatives, voting by states, would have to choose a president in case no candidate achieved a majority in the electoral college. Moreover, electoral votes are weighted in favor of the smaller states, and there is no guarantee that electors will vote as instructed by the electorate. While these are substantial problems, the system has so far worked to general satisfaction, and efforts to abolish the electoral college in favor of a system of direct national election have failed to win the necessary support in Congress. In fact, current dissatisfaction centers on presidential campaign and nominating procedures rather than on the electoral college.

After the two-term tradition had been breached by Franklin Roosevelt, Republicans and conservative Democrats locked the barn door by authoring the Twenty-second amendment. During the Carter administration some support developed for a single presidential term of six years, the argument being that, with a second term foreclosed, the president could concentrate on promoting the public interest without considering the impact on his electoral fortunes.

The Twenty-fifth amendment was adopted to insure that the post of vice-president would never become vacant because of the incumbent's succession to the presidency or for any other reason. It provides for presidential nomination when a vacancy occurs, with confirmation by majority vote of both houses of Congress. The amendment was invoked for the first time in 1973 as President Nixon named Gerald Ford to fill the vacancy in the vice-presidency caused by the resignation of Spiro Agnew. Then, in August 1974, Ford succeeded to the presidency on Nixon's resignation and named as vice-president, Nelson Rockefeller, who was confirmed by Congress after a four-month delay. Thus the Twenty-fifth amendment did not succeed in its intention never to permit a vacancy in the vice-presidency, and resulted for almost two and one-half years in a president and a vice-president, neither of whom had been elected by the people.

Watergate led to the inauguration of impeachment proceedings against a president for only the second time in American history. The unsavory character of the impeachment effort against President Andrew Johnson a century earlier was generally thought to have so discredited the impeachment device as to preclude its future use against a president. But as evidence of Nixon's participation in the Watergate cover-up accumulated, impeachment proceedings were begun before the House Judiciary Committee, and three articles of impeachment were ultimately voted. Although impeachment action was dropped after Nixon's resignation, the Judiciary Committee did clarify a long-disputed issue as to the meaning of "high crimes and misdemeanors," the terms used by the Constitution to define impeachable offenses.

One possible view is that an impeachable offense is whatever a majority of the House of Representatives considers it to be. The opposite position is that impeachment can be voted only on proof of serious, indictable crimes. The Judiciary Committee majority adopted a middle position — that violation of a criminal statute is not a prerequisite for impeachment, as long as the offense is a serious one.[17]

One month after assuming office, President Ford granted a full pardon to Nixon for any crimes he "has committed or may have committed" during his presidency, though Nixon had not been indicted for crime or admitted any criminal acts. While the pardon was strongly criticized, there was no way of challenging its validity, and as a precedent it seemed to establish that pardons can be granted for criminal offenses in advance of any legal proceedings.

## Executive Power

That the president possesses not only the specific powers mentioned in the Constitution but also the powers necessary and proper for the performance of the executive function finds the broadest support in the first sentence of Article II: "The executive power shall be vested in a President of the United States." It has always been a nice constitutional question whether these words constitute a grant of power or are a mere designation of an office. The former interpretation is consistent with the Lockean notion of executive power as "residual," and it is also supported by the so-called "decision of 1789," in which the First Congress relied on the "executive power" provision in deciding that the president already had the power of removal under the Constitution without any authorization by Congress.

The constitutional directive to the president to "take care that the laws be faithfully executed" has been a significant reliance in support of presidential actions, and it is a principal support for the theory of implied presidential powers. The clause was authoritatively interpreted by the Supreme Court in the well-known case of *In re Neagle* (1890), where it held that the "laws" that the president was to execute included not only statutes enacted by Congress but also "any obligation fairly and properly inferrible from [the Constitution], or any duty . . . to be derived from the general scope of . . . duties under the laws of the United States." The president's duty to see that the laws are faithfully executed, the Court went on, is not "limited to the enforcement of acts of Congress . . . according to their express terms," but includes also "the rights, duties and obligations growing out of the Constitution itself, our international relations, and all the protection implied by the nature of the government under the Constitution."

The same position was taken by the Court in *In re Debs* (1895), where it upheld the power of the president to order his attorney general to secure a court injunction against the Pullman railroad strike despite the fact that there was no explicit statutory basis for the injunction.

The principal Supreme Court ruling limiting the implied powers of the presidency is the famous steel-seizure case of 1952, in which President Truman's seizure of the steel mills to prevent a strike that would impair the flow of munitions to the troops in Korea was invalidated. That decision, however, turned on the special circumstances of the case and should not be read as imposing any serious limitations on the president's emergency powers. It was the fact that Congress, in passing the Taft-Hartley Act, had specifically considered giving seizure powers to the president and decided against it (though adopting no language at all on the subject) that convinced the swing justices, Jackson and Frankfurter, that this nonaction had stripped the president of powers he might otherwise have had.

In *New York Times Co.* v. *United States* (1971), involving the Nixon Administration's attempt to enjoin the press from publishing the so-called Pentagon Papers,[18] the Court likewise rejected, by a vote of six to three, a presidential claim to inherent power that was unsupported by statutory authorization. But two of the majority justices, Stewart and White, were willing to grant the existence of a "sovereign prerogative power" to protect the confidentiality of materials related to the national defense, and only voted against the president because they could not say that disclosure of the Pentagon Papers would "surely result in direct, immediate, and irreparable damage to our Nation or its people." Speaking for the three dissenters, Harlan would have granted the president's inherent power to act, subject only to a judicial determination that the issue lay within the "proper compass of the president's foreign relations power," and a determination by the secretary of state or secretary of defense that "disclosure of the subject matter would irreparably impair the national security."

President Carter's agreement with Iran which secured the release of 52 American hostages early in 1981 was unanimously upheld by the Court in *Dames & Moore* v. *Regan* (1981). The agreement cancelled all attachments against Iranian assets in the United States, and transferred from U.S. courts to an international tribunal all legal claims by American firms against Iran. After only eight days of deliberation at the close of the term in 1981, the Court concluded that the 1977 Emergency Economic Powers Act explicitly gave the president authority to void attachments against Iranian assets. As for the transfer of legal claims out of the United States, the Court found no statutory authorization, but held that Congress had "implicitly" approved of Carter's action by a longstanding pattern of acquiescence in presidential settlement of claims disputes with other nations. Should any firms be dissatisfied with treatment of their claims by the international tribunal, they were authorized by the Court to sue the United States in the Court of Claims. The ruling attests to the continuing judicial disposition to support broad presidential authority by resort either to statute or history.

## Executive Privilege

The Watergate scandals destroyed Nixon's "imperial presidency" and provoked an unprecedented reconsideration of presidential powers. One major issue was the validity of the claim of "executive privilege," which Nixon had initially put forth to justify refusal to respond to congressional requests for information, and later in denying White House tapes and other records demanded by congressional investigating committees, the Watergate special prosecutor, and judges in the several Watergate cases. In *United States* v. *Nixon* (1974), the Supreme Court unanimously denied the president's right to make a final, nonreviewable claim of executive privilege, saying:

> Neither the doctrine of separation of powers, nor the need for confidentiality of high-level communications, without more, can sustain an absolute, unqualified, presidential privilege of immunity from judicial process under all circumstances.

The Court did grant that there was a limited executive privilege with a constitutional base, mentioning particularly the need to protect military, diplomatic, or sensitive national-security secrets, and assured that the Court would recognize claims of confidentiality related to the president's ability to discharge his constitutional powers effectively. But no national-security claims were involved in this case, which concerned White House tapes subpoenaed in connection with the trial of former Attorney General John Mitchell and White House aides H. R. Haldeman and John Ehrlichman.[19]

*United States* v. *Nixon,* as well as a ruling by the Court of Appeals for the District of Columbia in *Nixon* v. *Sirica* (1973), established that the president is subject to subpoena. There had been some doubt on this subject because of the obvious enforcement problem if he chose to resist. The principal precedent was Chief Justice Marshall's subpoena to President Jefferson in the 1807 treason trial of Aaron Burr. Although Marshall's opinion clearly asserted the president was not immune from subpoena, later developments in the case were confused, and the subpoena was not actually enforced.[20]

Later, in *Mississippi* v. *Johnson* (1867), the Supreme Court declined to issue an injunction against the President, pointing out that if he refused obedience, the Court would be "without power to enforce its process." When Judge John J. Sirica subpoenaed Nixon's tapes in 1973 for use by the Watergate grand jury, he considered it immaterial "that the court has not physical power to enforce its order to the President." He simply relied on the "good faith of the executive branch." In fact Nixon did yield to both subpoenas.

Another constitutional issue raised by Watergate was whether a president is subject to criminal indictment while in office. The Watergate grand jury was convinced by the evidence it received that Nixon had participated in the cover-up and proposed to indict him along with the other principals. It was dissuaded, however, by Special Prosecutor Leon Jaworski, who told the grand jury that the president was constitutionally protected against indictment.

Whether a president may be the subject of a civil suit because of official actions that damage someone's constitutional rights was at issue in the case of *Kissinger* v. *Halperin* (1981). Halperin, a political scientist, was a former National Security Council staff member during the Nixon administration whose home telephone was illegally wiretapped by presidential order, and Halperin sought damages from Nixon, his national security adviser, Henry A. Kissinger, and former Attorney General John N. Mitchell. Reviewing a lower court decision which had upheld Nixon's liability to suit, the Supreme Court divided four to four. The tie vote left the lower court ruling in effect and permitted the assessment of damages to go forward, but the issue of presidential liability remained unsettled at the Supreme Court level.[21]

## Legislative Role

Clearly Congress has failed to live up to the original constitutional expectations in the field of legislative performance, encouraging the president to assume a greater role than was anticipated in the formulation of legislative programs. In fact, a presidential candidate campaigns for office on the basis of the legislation he will propose, and his success in office is largely determined by his ability to secure favorable congressional action on his program. The classic example is the first one hundred days of Franklin Roosevelt's administration, during which the Great Depression was turned around by force of presidential personality and a program of far-reaching economic and social legislation adopted by Congress.

President Carter's inability to influence Congress was made all the more glaring by comparison with the initial achievements of his successor. President Reagan used his "election mandate," personal charm, and communication skills to carry through Congress a revolutionary legislative "package" reversing decades of well-established social policy and aiming towards a fundamental shift in the balance of power between the federal government and the states.

Executive authority over fiscal policy goes back to the Budget and Accounting Act of 1921, which gave the president responsibility for preparation of the budget. Congress of course still made the final decisions, though the growth of the federal government rendered the legislative budget review increasingly ineffective. President Nixon challenged the integrity of legislative spending decisions when between 1971 and 1973 he sought to impound some $25 billion in appropriations for projects he disapproved or in amounts he deemed unwise. This assertion of executive power was too blatant, however, and was partially countered by judicial decisions and legislative reaction.[22] Congress recognized that its own slipshod fiscal practices, which never required appropriations to be considered in relation to anticipated revenues, had furnished the President with some justification for his actions. Consequently a serious effort was made to reform congressional budget procedures by adoption of the Congressional Budget and Impoundment Control Act of 1974. Briefly, the act created budget committees in each house to oversee expenditures and revenues, and established a congressional budget office to give Congress the type of expertise available to the President through his Office of Management and Budget. The act also specified procedures by which Congress could force the president to spend funds he had impounded.

These efforts by Congress to recapture some of its lost authority over the budget were stunningly reversed by President Reagan. He had barely taken office before he unleashed a blitzkrieg against the Congress, calling for deep cuts in social programs, increased defense outlays, and a three-year tax cut. Under intense White House pressure, Congress adopted a budget resolution setting slashed fiscal targets and containing "reconciliation" instructions obligating House and Senate committees to cut over $36 billion in existing programs. Over ineffective Democratic opposition in the House, the detailed budget reductions demanded by the President's budget director were adopted. Thus, a reform originally intended to control the executive was put to use to control the Congress.

As for organization of the federal establishment, Congress has since the 1930s largely abdicated to the president by a series of reorganization acts giving the president the power to set up new organizational structures, retaining only the power to refuse to approve reorganization plans — the so-called "legislative veto." This authority was used, for example, by President Nixon to create the Office of Management and Budget. However, the newest departmental unit, the Department of Education, was created directly by statute.

The legislative veto, invented for use with reorganization plans, has proved increasingly attractive to Congress as a device for controlling acts of the president and bureaucratic regulations. The Lend-Lease Act of 1941 contained a congressional veto provision, and during World War II Congress adopted the veto to check on the broad war-making power it had delegated to the administration. From 1932 to 1975 almost 200 statutes carried some form of provision for the congressional veto, and it was a favorite tactic against Carter.

Every president since Hoover has charged that the legislative veto is unconstitutional. During his campaign in 1980 Reagan favored greater legislative authority to veto administrative regulations, but once in office his attorney general indicated he would consider legislative vetoes unconstitutional if they intruded on the presidential power to manage the executive branch.[23]

## Administrative Head

The appointment power is the president's most important instrument for effectuating his control of the executive branch and ensuring that the laws are faithfully executed. The principal limitations on this power derive from the necessity of securing Senate confirmation for his appointments to a very large number of offices, a number extending far beyond positions with substantial policy-forming powers. However, the great bulk of these appointments are confirmed routinely.

The occasional Senate rejection of a presidential appointee takes place under two circumstances. First, nominees who are to fill positions in a state may be rejected because a senator from that state announces to the Senate that the nominee is personally obnoxious to him, in which event the rule of senatorial courtesy almost invariably results in rejection of the nomination. Second, a majority of the Senate may reject a nominee because he is deemed unqualified for the post or, for some other reason, personally unfit or politically undesirable. Examples are the rejections of Nixon nominees Clement F. Haynsworth and G. Harrold Carswell for the Supreme Court, Kennedy nominee Francis X. Morrissey for the federal district bench, Eisenhower nominee Lewis B. Strauss as secretary of commerce, and Reagan nominee Ernest W. Lefever for assistant secretary of state.

Another technique Congress might employ to limit presidential discretion in appointments has been used very seldom, and that is to specify qualifications that nominees for a position must have. Thus, members of federal regulatory commissions must come from both parties, and members of the boards of the Federal Reserve banks must come from certain occupational areas. The various proposals that have been made to require the president to appoint only persons with prior judicial experience to the Supreme Court have all failed.

The president's appointing power was interpreted and safeguarded by the Supreme Court in *Buckley* v. *Valeo* (1976). When setting up the Federal Election Commission in 1974 to supervise the new plan for public financing of presidential elections, Congress provided that four of its six voting members should be appointed by the president pro tempore of the Senate and the speaker of the house, with only two being presidential appointees. The Court ruled that the commission was an administrative agency with wide rule-making and enforcement powers, and that under Article II, section 2, clause 2, its members must be appointed by the president. Congress then amended the act accordingly.

Attempts to limit the president's power of removal have led to some classic and well-known constitutional arguments, but any restraints imposed as a result are of greater theoretical than practical significance. The requirement that the Senate be consulted on removals as on appointments was declared unconstitutional by Chief Justice Taft in *Myers* v. *United States* (1926). An exception for officials in quasi-judicial positions, where Congress had manifested an intention that they be removable only for cause, was created by the Court in *Humphrey's Executor* v. *United States* (1935), an exception extended in *Wiener* v. *United States* (1958) to all positions created by Congress with quasi-judicial duties, whether or not the legislature specified removal only for cause. While these rulings suggest to the president a certain caution in removing members of the regulatory commissions, their practical effect on the president's control over personnel is otherwise negligible.

In spite of the constitutional powers and position of the executive, all recent presidents have found it difficult to exercise policy control over the federal establishment because of its size, bureaucratic rigidity, and ties to protectors and sponsors in Congress. Beginning with the development of the Executive Office of the President under Franklin Roosevelt, efforts have been made to achieve a greater measure of executive control, without marked success. Again it remained for President Nixon to make a frontal assault on the problem by greatly increasing the Executive Office staff and by an unprecedented concentration of administrative control in the White House by the appointment as cabinet members of men who had no independent political base, by placing in key positions in the departments and independent agencies men who had proved their loyalty to the president in service on the White House staff, and by setting up four super-department heads directly under the president. These arrangements collapsed in the Watergate holocaust.

President Carter surrounded himself with a White House staff of native Georgians with little or no previous Washington experience, thus creating problems in relations with Congress and his department heads. President Reagan gave the usual promises to use his cabinet for decision-making purposes and to allow department heads to run their own departments. But policy control was firmly in the hands of his major White House aides, and unparalleled authority was delegated to Reagan's director of the budget.

## The President and Foreign Relations

Although Congress has the constitutional power to declare war, and the Senate shares responsibility for the ratification of treaties and the appointment of ambassadors, the president's role in the conduct of foreign affairs is much more expansive than in domestic matters. His powers of initiative are greater, and the possibilities of restraint fewer. Some of the reasons for this contrast are suggested in the following summary:

1. The president monopolizes the sources of information about foreign affairs to a much greater degree than he does the sources of domestic information, and much of it is not made public, so that the president can always contend that his actions are based on data not available to Congress or the public.
2. The president directs diplomatic negotiations, which must proceed largely in secret.
3. The necessity for emergency action, not permitting consultation, is much greater, the ultimate example being the need to counter a threatened nuclear attack.
4. As commander-in-chief, the president is in control of a vast engine of force that can move into immediate operation on his command, as compared with the civil establishment, which the president can put in motion or redirect much more slowly, and sometimes not at all.
5. Recommendations for military action come up to the president through a military hierarchy that typically presents specific and coordinated policy proposals, compared with the conflicting and uncoordinated advice he usually receives on domestic matters.
6. The doctrine of political questions generally prevents the Supreme Court from reviewing any challenges to the constitutionality of executive action in the field of foreign affairs, in contrast to the full power of judicial review over domestic controversies.[24]

In certain foreign-policy matters, Congress does participate fully, and admittedly its record is not always one to inspire great confidence in congressional capacity. The Senate's action, or inaction, in the ratification of treaties has been a long-standing cause for complaint. The annual foreign-aid appropriation is another field where Congress has not been reluctant to substitute its judgment for that of the president. There are matters with domestic ramifications, such as the closing of military posts, where Congress has often reversed presidential judgment. On the other hand, appropriations for the CIA are hidden completely from the public and from most members of Congress, and the general appropriations for military supply and procurement are seldom seriously questioned.[25]

*The treaty power.* To be sure, the requirement that treaties secure ratification by a two-thirds vote of the Senate has been a substantial limitation on the president's initiative in foreign affairs. But this challenge has often been met by the extensive use of executive agreements, which have the same legal effect as treaties. The principal limitations on their use are political in nature — the degree to which it is wise to exclude the Senate from this constitutional foreign-policy role. The serious but unsuccessful drive for the Bricker Amendment in the early 1950s sought to prevent the use of executive agreements as alternatives to treaties. In 1972 discovery by the Senate of a number of secret foreign commitments, particularly an agreement permitting American use of Spanish bases in return for substantial grants, led Congress to adopt the Case Act, which requires the secretary of state to submit to Congress within sixty days the text of any international agreement.

President Carter secured ratification of the controversial Panama Canal Treaty in 1978, but with only one vote to spare and all 100 members of the Senate voting. Carter had the assistance of the Supreme Court, which rejected several efforts by opponents of the treaty to assert constitutional objections, the principal contention being that the House also had to approve the treaty because the disposition of federal property was involved.[26]

Forceful constitutional objections were also lodged against Carter's termination of the American mutual defense treaty with Taiwan. A sense-of-the-Senate resolution condemning the President's action was adopted by a vote of 59 to 35, but it had no legal effect on Carter's establishment of diplomatic relations with Peking and termination of the defense pact after one year's notice.

President Carter was less successful in securing Senate ratification of the SALT II Treaty (Strategic Arms Limitation Treaty) with Russia, which he withdrew from Senate consideration on January 3, 1980, following the Soviet invasion of Afghanistan. His major diplomatic triumph in bringing Israel and Egypt into the Camp David accord of course required no Senate approval, but the secretary of state subsequently entered into a memorandum of agreement with Israel providing specific American assurances to Israel in the event that the treaty fell apart.

*Commander-in-chief.* The power that the president has asserted as commander-in-chief would probably have surprised the founders. The Hamiltonian view, that this provision merely placed the president at the top of the military hierarchy, was endorsed half a century later by Story, who interpreted this power in his *Commentaries* as "to give orders and have a general superintendency" over the armed forces. In a Supreme Court opinion by Chief Justice Taney (*Fleming* v. *Page* [1850]), the Court spoke of the president's duty and power as "purely military."

Corwin describes the transformation that occurred in 1861, as Lincoln met the secession crisis:

> The sudden emergence of the "Commander-in-Chief" clause as one of the most highly charged provisions of the Constitution occurred almost overnight in consequence of Lincoln's wedding it to the clause that makes it the duty of the President "to take care that the laws be faithfully executed." From these two clauses thus united, Lincoln proceeded to derive what he termed the "war power," to justify the series of extraordinary measures that he took in the interval between the fall of Fort Sumter and the convening of Congress in special session on July 4, 1861.[27]

In World War I, no such reliance had to be placed on the commander-in-chief power, since the war was initiated by a congressional declaration, and Congress provided authority to the president to conduct the war either by substantive legislation or by broad delegation of legislative power. Even so, Wilson called on his power as commander-in-chief to create such war agencies as the Committee on Public Information, the War Industries Board, and the War Labor Board. He invoked the same authority at the outbreak of the war in closing German wireless stations and subjecting communications companies to regulation with respect to messages received from or going abroad.

The World War II situation was similar, but the emergency started before the declaration of war and extended further beyond the termination of hostilities. The destroyer deal with Britain on September 3, 1940, was directly in violation of at least two statutes and represented an exercise by the president of a power specifically assigned to Congress, but it was defended by Attorney General Jackson as based on the president's powers as commander-in-chief. During the war, President Roosevelt created no fewer than thirty-five executive agencies, generally invoking as authority his powers as "commander-in-chief in time of war." In only one case, involving the War Labor Board, was the constitutional legitimacy of these agencies questioned, and then unsuccessfully.[28]

When the president uses American armed forces abroad in the *absence* of a congressionally declared war, his reliance on the commander-in-chief power is even more crucial. It seems likely that the framers never intended troops to be used outside the country without congressional consent. Since neither a standing army nor a navy was contemplated, naturally any military operations abroad would necessarily require congressional participation in securing the troops and providing the funds. However, the availability of a navy made possible three undeclared naval wars — the war with France (1798–1800) and the first (1801–1805) and second (1815) Barbary wars. But Jefferson forbade the navy to attack Tripoli in 1801 on the ground that Congress had not declared war, and Madison, in 1812, refused to retaliate against British provocations until Congress declared war.

By the latter half of the nineteenth century, it had become a well-established presidential practice to use troops abroad for the purpose of protecting American lives and property. In the present century, both Roosevelts, Wilson, Truman, Eisenhower, Kennedy, Johnson, and Nixon all moved American troops into action or across national frontiers with little or no effort to secure advance congressional assent. Since 1950, there have been presidential moves into Korea, Lebanon, Cuba, the Dominican Republic, Vietnam, Cambodia, and Laos, as well as distant naval operations, undercover plots, military advisory programs, and aerial overflights of foreign countries that risked conflict — all with no opportunity for congressional review.

The two major examples of undeclared wars are of course the Korean War (1950–1953) and the Vietnam War (1964–1975). In the Korean War, justification for the executive action was provided by the U.N. resolution condemning aggression by North Korea. In 1955, President Eisenhower secured from Congress a joint resolution authorizing his employment of the armed forces, if required, to protect Taiwan from Chinese attack. Again, in 1957, he requested from Congress authorization to use force against Communist aggression in the Middle East when asked to do so by a victim of such aggression. Under Democratic leadership, the Senate concluded that it would be constitutionally improper to "authorize" the president to take action he already had power to take as commander-in-chief, and so changed the language to read that, "if the president determines the necessity thereof, the United States is prepared to use armed forces" on behalf of nations requesting assistance against armed aggression.

These precedents were used by President Johnson in 1964. At a time when there were only twenty thousand American troops in Vietnam, and after alleged North Vietnamese torpedo-boat attacks on two U.S. destroyers in the Gulf of Tonkin, the President asked Congress for a joint resolution of support to strengthen his hand in dealing with the Vietnam situation. Almost unanimously, Congress adopted the Tonkin Gulf Resolution, approving and supporting the "determination of the President, as Commander-in-Chief, to take all necessary measures to repel any armed attack against the forces of the United States and to prevent further aggression."

President Johnson subsequently relied on this resolution as authorizing and justifying the tremendous escalation of military operations in Vietnam and the bombing of North Vietnam. Assistant Secretary of State Nicholas Katzenbach argued before the Senate Foreign Relations Committee that the resolution gave the president as much authority as a declaration of war. In fact, he alarmed the senators by referring to declarations of war as "outmoded," and contended that a declaration of war would not "correctly reflect the very limited objectives of the United States with respect to Vietnam." [29]

Efforts by members and committees of Congress to recapture some control of the war-making power were tremendously accelerated in 1970 by President Nixon's precipitate expansion of military activities into Cambodia with no prior consultation with Congress, but they had only limited success. Congress did repeal the Tonkin Gulf Resolution in 1970, but this action had no effect, because by then the official justification for continued military operations was the necessity to protect American troops until they could be withdrawn. Various "end the war" and withdrawal resolutions failed, but Congress did eventually order the bombing of Cambodia stopped by August 15, 1973. Efforts to involve the Supreme Court failed, as it rejected all attempts to have it consider whether the Vietnam War was unconstitutional because there had been no declaration of war by Congress.[30]

Congress's frustration over its impotence in attempting to end the Vietnam War ultimately resulted in adoption of the War Powers Act, passed in 1973 over President Nixon's veto. The law sets a sixty-day limit on any presidential commitment of U.S. troops abroad without specific congressional authorization. The commitment can be extended for another thirty days if necessary for the safe withdrawal of troops. Unauthorized commitments can be terminated before the sixty-day deadline by congressional adoption of a concurrent resolution, a measure that does not require presidential signature. Moreover, the act requires the president to consult with Congress in every possible situation before introducing armed forces into hostilities or areas where imminent involvement in hostilities is clearly indicated. Whereas President Nixon condemned the statute as an unconstitutional and dangerous restriction on the power of the commander-in-chief to meet emergencies, some liberal members of Congress voted against it on the opposite ground that the statute, in fact, recognized the president's right to start a war.

The collapse of the South Vietnamese regime in April 1975 was so sudden that Congress was precluded from acting on President Ford's request for authorization to use U.S. troops to evacuate American citizens from Vietnam. But within two weeks another situation arose calling for application of the War Powers Act — the seizure of the American merchant vessel *Mayaguez* by Cambodian naval forces. Not until the sea and air rescue operation ordered by President Ford, including bombing of the Cambodian mainland, was under way did Ford call congressional leaders to the White House to "advise" them of the military moves. After he left office Ford stated that it was literally impossible in six major crises during his presidency to consult with Congress in a meaningful way, and he characterized the War Powers Act as a "serious mistake." [31]

Congress did, however, find other methods of participating more actively in the field of foreign affairs, highlighted by a congressionally imposed arms embargo against Turkey in 1974, in response to the Turkish invasion of Cyprus, and a ban on funds and military aid to factions in the Angolan civil war in 1975. Both actions were strongly condemned by the executive as congressional meddling in foreign affairs. Disclosure of CIA covert activities and assassination plots led both the House and Senate to create special intelligence committees in

1975 to investigate these reports. As a result the Senate in 1976 created a new fifteen-member select committee charged with oversight of all the nation's secret intelligence services, with absolute authority to approve the CIA budget. Subsequently a more favorable attitude toward the CIA made such review largely ineffective.

President Carter avoided the issue of use of the armed forces abroad except for the disastrous effort to rescue the hostages in Iran. After a speech in which Carter said he would not rule out the use of force to release the hostages, members of the Senate Foreign Relations Committee asked the Secretary of State to consult with the committee in accordance with the terms of the War Powers Act, but the request was disregarded.[32]

President Reagan's Secretary of State, Alexander M. Haig, Jr., during his confirmation hearings proposed a "partnership" with the Senate in the conduct of foreign affairs.[33] But within two months the Reagan administration had sent military advisers, arms and equipment into El Salvador, which was in a state of virtual civil war, leading to charges that the War Powers Act and the Arms Export Control Act had been violated. Any "partnership" between the administration and Congress on foreign relations issues is likely to be very one-sided and the War Powers Act an ineffective limitation on presidential military initiatives.

## Balance Sheet on Presidential Power

The conventional wisdom on the American presidency, confirmed by our review of the decisions made by the framers in 1787, is that the presidency was intended to be an office of great power, and that the successful operation of the American constitutional system requires that this power be used. Presidents who do not use their power vigorously are condemned as weak and as failures in office. The unity, dispatch, and national outlook of the president are contrasted with the divisiveness, the delay, and the parochialism of the legislature. Concern about the "imperial presidency," which Nixon's concept of the office generated, was largely dissipated during the Ford and Carter years and replaced by worry about presidential inadequacy.

But President Reagan demonstrated during his first "one hundred days" that the potentialities in the office were as great as ever. The incumbent occupies incomparably the "best bully pulpit" in the land, particularly if he is an effective performer on television. His role as administrative chief is guaranteed by control over personnel, organization, and funds. He has, by virtue of his election, the extra-constitutional role of leader of his party, though both Nixon and Carter played this role poorly.

The president gains support for his other roles from his status as symbolic and ceremonial head of the nation. On the other hand, his performance as head of state is handicapped because he is partisan for whom almost half of the electorate did not vote. No practical plan has ever been suggested for providing the

Republic with a nonpartisan chief of state. Thus, the ultimate symbols of unity have to be inanimate objects — the flag and the Constitution.

This summary view of the powers of the president in and through his different roles affords some measure of understanding of his resources for performing his domestic functions. His great powers of leadership, initiative, and action are balanced by countervailing forces inherent in the separation-of-powers system. No president is ever able to develop a domestic program without working within this system. Neither for Roosevelt nor Reagan was Congress for long willing to be a rubber stamp.

When we consider the president's foreign-policy functions and his access to the war power, however, the situation becomes quite different. Here, there is a real basis for concern whether the system is in balance, for events have repeatedly demonstrated that presidential powers of initiative are greater and the possibilities of restraint fewer. Because of the inherent differences between domestic and foreign problems, the president may legitimately claim greater freedom of action in the foreign field, particularly the right as commander in chief to take emergency action in the use of military forces. However, broad claims for executive autonomy in the use of military forces in other than emergency situations, though they may find support in practices of the past hundred years, are not justified by the intentions of the framers and are not consistent with the American system of checks and balances.

Congress cannot run foreign policy, but it has the right and the obligation to use its appropriating and legislating power to fix outer limits for American foreign and military policy and to review and revise ongoing foreign and military commitments. Under present conditions, the congressional declaration of war, which was relied upon so strongly by the framers as a limitation on the executive, is probably obsolete, for it encourages what is no longer acceptable — the use of unlimited force. Limited war is all that can now be contemplated, and the determination of those limits is a matter for joint action by the president and Congress.

SOURCE: An earlier version of this essay appeared in Thomas E. Cronin and Rexford G. Tugwell, eds., *The Presidency Reappraised,* New York, Praeger, 1977.

## Notes

1. Edward S. Corwin, *The President: Office and Powers, 1787–1957* (New York: New York University Press, 1957), pp. 5–6.
2. *The Federalist,* No. 48.
3. Max Farrand, *The Framing of the Constitution of the United States* (New Haven, Conn.: Yale University Press, 1913), vol. II, p. 52.
4. *Ibid.,* vol. I, pp. 65, 66, 97.
5. *Ibid.,* p. 65.
6. *Ibid.,* vol. II, pp. 541–42.
7. *Ibid.,* vol. I, p. 65.

8. *Ibid.,* vol. II, p. 31.
9. *Ibid.,* vol. I, p. 119.
10. *Ibid.,* vol. II, p. 318.
11. *Ibid.,* p. 319.
12. See Charles A. Lofgren, "War-Making Under the Constitution: The Original Understanding," 81 *Yale Law Journal* 672 (1972).
13. Farrand, *op. cit.,* vol. II, pp. 297, 392.
14. *Ibid.,* vol. I, p. 21.
15. *Ibid.,* pp. 63–64.
16. There have been periodic proposals for grafting features of the parliamentary system onto the American system of separate powers. The most common suggestion has been for congressional question periods during which cabinet members would appear before the House or Senate to defend administration policies. Representative Henry Reuss's proposal for a congressional vote of no confidence in the President is the subject of a symposium in 43 *George Washington Law Review* 327 (1975).
17. Raoul Berger, *Impeachment: The Constitutional Problems* (Cambridge, Mass.: Harvard University Press, 1973); Charles L. Black, Jr., *Impeachment: A Handbook* (New Haven, Conn.: Yale University Press, 1974); House Committee on the Judiciary, 93d Cong., 1st sess., *Impeachment: Selected Materials* (Washington, D.C.: U.S. Government Printing Office, 1973).
18. Martin Shapiro, *The Pentagon Papers and the Courts* (San Francisco: Chandler, 1972); Louis Henkin, "The Right to Know and the Duty to Withhold: The Case of the Pentagon Papers," 120 *University of Pennsylvania Law Review* 271 (1971); Peter D. Junger, "Down Memory Lane: The Case of the Pentagon Papers," 23 *Case Western Reserve Law Review* 3 (1971).
19. See "Symposium: *United States* v. *Nixon,*" 22 *UCLA Law Review* 1 (1974); Paul A. Freund, "On Presidential Privilege," 88 *Harvard Law Review* 13 (1974); Raoul Berger, *Executive Privilege: A Constitutional Myth* (Cambridge, Mass.: Harvard University Press, 1974). All the documents in the case are collected in Leon Friedman (ed.), *United States* v. *Nixon: The President Before the Supreme Court* (New York: Chelsea House, 1974).
20. Raoul Berger, "The President, Congress, and the Courts — Subpoenaing the President: *Jefferson* v. *Marshall* in the Burr Case," 83 *Yale Law Journal* 1111 (1974).
21. In 1981 the Court accepted for review the case of *Nixon* v. *Fitzgerald,* in which a lower court had held Nixon liable for damages in dismissing an Air Force official after he had publicized massive cost overruns on a Pentagon air transport project.
22. *Train* v. *City of New York* (1975); Louis Fisher, *Presidential Spending Power* (Princeton, N.J.: Princeton University Press, 1975), chaps. 7–8.
23. Louis Fisher, *The Constitution Between Friends* (New York: St. Martin's Press, 1978), pp. 99–108; *New York Times,* March 19, 1981.
24. See Louis Henkin, "Is There a 'Political Question' Doctrine?" 85 *Yale Law Journal* 597 (1976); Michael Tigar, "Judicial Power, the 'Political Question' Doctrine, and Foreign Relations," 17 *UCLA Law Review* 1135 (1970).
25. In *United States* v. *Richardson* (1974), the Supreme Court rebuffed an effort to make the CIA budget public. See also "The CIA's Secret Funding and the Constitution," 84 *Yale Law Journal* 608 (1975).
26. *Helms* v. *Vance,* 432 U.S. 907 (1977); *Idaho* v. *Vance,* 434 U.S. 1031 (1978); *Edwards* v. *Carter,* 436 U.S. 907 (1978).
27. Corwin, *op. cit.,* p. 229.
28. *Ibid.,* p. 243.
29. *New York Times,* August 18, 1967.

30. Anthony A. D'Amato and Robert M. O'Neil, *The Judiciary and Vietnam* (New York: St. Martin's Press, 1972). The Supreme Court denied certiorari in a number of cases, including *Mora* v. *McNamara* (1967), *Mitchell* v. *United States* (1967), and *Sarnoff* v. *Shultz* (1972). See also *Massachusetts* v. *Laird* (1970) and *Holtzman* v. *Schlesinger* (1973).
31. *New York Times,* April 12, 1977.
32. *Congressional Quarterly Weekly Report,* May 3, 1980, p. 1200.
33. James Reston, *New York Times,* March 4, 1981.

# 10. Presidential Power and the Crisis of Modernization

## Alan Wolfe

The presidency — once called by Charles Beard the "dark continent of American constitutionalism" — remains a puzzle, both to those who seek it and to those who seek to understand it. At once all powerful yet curiously impotent, majestic if suspect, and meritocratic while astoundingly incompetent, the president reflects the contradictions of American democracy writ large. If neither our presidents nor the American people seem to know what the presidency is for, this is because in America it is unclear what government is for.

There was a time in the first century of the Republic when the man shaped the office. The most ambiguous sentence in the Constitution — "The executive power shall be vested in a President of the United States" — allowed the Polks and the Lincolns to develop the institution according to their own lights. Now the office shapes the man. Candidates run, not only to be president, but to be "presidential." Jimmy Carter, though possessed of the advantage of four years of incumbency, never convinced the American people that he fit their conception of the office. Ronald Reagan, even though elected, spends considerable time — perhaps it will take an entire first term — demonstrating that he is indeed "presidential" material. It is unclear whether the office has increased in stature or whether the stature of those who seek it has diminished; it is clear that the gap between what Americans expect of their president and whom they elect has never been greater. It would be a challenge worthy of even the most passionate defender of the American electoral process to make the claim that Ronald Reagan is the most competent man to serve as president of the United States in the 1980s, *Time* magazine's "Man of the Year" award notwithstanding.

In some respects, Ronald Reagan was chosen president by an overwhelmingly democratic process, at least as conventionally understood in the United States. His nomination was deserved, for he campaigned longest and hardest for it and demonstrated his appeal, within his party, over all other possible challengers. Similarly, Jimmy Carter campaigned against a seemingly popular challenger in his party and won the bulk of the primaries fair and square. (By contrast, John Kennedy entered only seven of the eighteen primaries in 1960, faced meaningful competition in two, and was chosen by a convention, a majority of

*Alan Wolfe teaches sociology at Queens College (CUNY) in New York and is the author of several books, including* The Limits of Legitimacy *and* The Rise and Fall of the Soviet Thrust.

whose delegates were not popularly elected.) And if a large number of citizens were unhappy with the two major candidates, they were free to vote for an experienced and attractive independent, or, failing that, for any one of two or three minor-party candidates with clear programs. The 1980 election may have been a debacle, but it was a democratic debacle. The problem lies not in an aberration in the process, but in the process working as best it can. There may be something amiss in the conception of democracy that undergirds the way people select the president of the United States.

Even though Ronald Reagan was a clear winner in 1980, the feeling of having somehow been cheated lies just beneath the placid surface of the public's mood. Throughout the campaign, the general attitude was one of disgust at the candidates, and Reagan was preferred, not because he gained respect, but because his opponent lost so much. If the people were contemptuous of the candidates, moreover, the candidates were also contemptuous of the people. Carter expressed his disdain for the American people by professing his love for them; who can love an aggregate? Meanwhile Reagan, Iago-like, flattered the public out of disdain for its wisdom. Appealing to prejudice and searching out the lowest common denominator, Reagan paid the people the ultimate insult of telling them what they wanted to hear. Working as best it could, American democracy produced the worst it could. Nineteen-eighty may be recalled not as the year in which Reagan won, but as the year in which respect for the office of the president was finally lost.

The people and the presidency, it would seem, are at odds. Unhappy with the choices offered them, Americans increasingly either do not vote or do so only after forcing themselves to go through with the act. Unhappy without a "mandate," presidents from Johnson to Reagan have lied to the people, violated their trust, sermonized about their habits, and pandered to their prejudices. America has encountered a conundrum with respect to presidential power: understanding its need, distrusting its exercise. Arousing themselves out of a stupor every four years, the people choose a new leader, only to repudiate him once he begins to act. The leader, in turn, contemplates trying to govern, only to retreat as the next election rolls around, often apologizing for the indiscretion of actually having tried to do something. In order to understand this deterioration of the presidency from the ideal of just two decades ago, one must first discover how the people and the president came to distrust each other so much.

Waking up from his twenty-year nap, Rip Van Winkle, in Washington Irving's tale, heads for his village inn, recognizing on its sign the face of King George, only to discover on closer examination that the face actually belongs to George Washington. While he was sleeping, the framers of the Constitution, protecting the people from a hereditary monarchy, created the structure for an elected one.

From the start, two opposing conceptions of the presidency have existed side by side in the collective conscience of the United States. Distrust of power has always been great, and distrust of executive power has been even greater. On five consecutive votes, the advocates of a single executive lost at the Constitutional Convention, finally prevailing out of weariness as much as political philosophy. Edmund Randolph articulated the general sentiment when he called a single executive "the foetus of monarchy." "If the president is possessed of ambition," wrote anti-Federalist Governor George Clinton of New York, "he has the power and time sufficient to ruin the country." Nonsense, replied Alexander Hamilton, in the process writing the definitive words on the other side of this particularly American schizophrenia. Because, he said, "energy in the Executive is a leading character of the definition of good government," there must be an office created that will permit the State to carry out the tasks entrusted to it. The authors of Article II of the Constitution, bitterly divided between those fearful of executive power and those desiring to see it exercised, wrote some general-sounding phrases and hoped that history would take care of the rest.

History did, so to speak. The American presidency has been a product of practice, not theory. Concrete struggles between economic and political forces have been responsible for shaping it, not maxims from Montesquieu. So much is generally acknowledged, yet there is much debate about what those forces were. To a writer like Samuel P. Huntington, petty-commodity production and Lockean liberalism, with their emphasis on marketlike checks on power and belief in the inherent virtue of smallness, predisposed the American people to accept a weak executive. This predisposition then demands that neo-Hamiltonian conservatives like himself must never cease their agitation for a stronger one. Huntington's argument has much to commend it, but it is also true that opposition to executive power frequently came from a conservative tradition that was more comfortable with slavery, a limited franchise, and a cramped vision of human nature than it was with Lockean optimism. From George Mason ("it will be impossible without a revolution, to displace him") to Henry Clay ("We are in the midst of a revolution, hitherto bloodless, but tending rapidly toward a total concentration of power in the hands of one man") to Robert A. Taft ("The President [in Korea] simply usurped authority, in violation of the laws and the Constitution"), attacks on the presidency have been led by men who fail to fit even the more protean definitions of American liberalism.

Whereas to Huntington, the presidency represents a conservative institution in a liberal world, to writers like James MacGregor Burns and Arthur Schlesinger, Jr., writing before Watergate, the presidency embodies everything liberal. For both of these men, writing under a Rooseveltian spell, the presidency grew as a democratic response to the oligarchic structure of other institutions, especially state legislatures and the courts. Containing some truth also, this account demonstrates as much hero worship as analysis. Hamilton, Gouverneur Morris, and James Wilson, the leading advocates of presidential power at the Constitutional Convention, were hardly liberals, and neither was John Marshall, who may be the man most responsible for the creation of a strong executive. Nationalism has strengthened the presidency more than liberalism has, and sectionalism has weakened it more than conservatism. Even as Burns wrote his peroration to presidential power, he was outdone by a self-professed conservative (Clinton Rossiter). When Hobbes triumphed over Locke in the form of Richard Nixon, Burns and Schlesinger changed their ways, only, in the case of Burns, to renew the praise of leadership once the crisis had passed.

The truth seems to be that our political vocabulary is inappropriate for discussing presidential power. Words like *conservative* and *liberal* do not correlate in any simple way with the expansion and retrenchment of the executive, despite mighty attempts to show that they do. An alternative account would be to suggest that it is all a matter of whose ox is being gored, that opposition to the presidency is in reality opposition to what any particular president plans to do. This version, a bit closer to reality, still suffers from not talking about the stakes at issue. The struggles over the presidency have been more economic struggles over distribution than political battles over rights, but one would be mistaken to reduce the matter to cost/benefit calculations about economic advantage. Central to conceptions of the presidency has been the notion of modernization, which subsumes both political and economic concerns.

The American presidency has been the major instrument by means of which modernizing elites have sought to overcome or remove obstacles to the expansion and revitalization of American capitalism. Modernization can be defined as the process by which industry, and with it public life, is brought to ever higher stages of integration and sophistication, first on a national scale, currently on an international one. Modernization brings with it the division of labor, rationalization, managerialism, control over markets, and homogenization. Ideologically ambiguous, modernization is progressive in the sense that it undermines the authority of conservative defenders of outmoded productive arrangements, but it is also regressive in that it undermines community, diversity, and democracy as well. A modernized polity provides its citizens with more consumer goods and fewer rights.

One of the sources of resistance to modernization has been a form of political Luddism — the use of the state, traditionally dependent on older and economically displaced elites, to delay the introduction of new social forces. The obstacles to modernization vary from period to period: agrarianism, slavery, protectionism, resistance to labor legislation, competition, opposition to globalism. The tactics used to overcome these obstacles have also changed from one period to another. But the one thread of consistency running through these struggles has been the notion that the expansion of the presidency is the triumph of the general interest over the particular. Modernizers, both conservative and liberal, have supported a strong executive; political Luddites, both conservative and liberal, have opposed one. The presidency is the locus of modernization, and the crisis of the presidency is a crisis of modernization.

Modernization did not come smoothly to the United States. A market economy was lodged in a Tudorlike state. Whereas in some European monarchies the state became the instrument by which feudal resistance to primitive accumulation was crushed, in America the separation of powers and federalism placed substantial veto powers in the hands of precapitalist elites. The courts (under its Tawneys, not its Marshalls), the state governments, the Senate filibuster, and later the congressional committee system were instruments grabbed by local elites to delay introduction of new social and political relationships. By default, then, the presidency — the sole national institution in a regional system of government — became the one vehicle capable of running roughshod over the realms of local interests in order to establish the political conditions for dynamic growth. Arguing before the Supreme Court in *Mississippi v. Johnson* (1867), Attorney General Stanberry spoke for all those seeking the expansion of American political and economic power when he pointed out that the president "represents the majesty of law and of the people as fully and as essentially, and with the same dignity, as does any absolute monarch or the head of any independent government in the world."

So long as local elites maintained sufficient power to delay the triumph of modernization, the presidency could not be established as the hegemonic force within the state. Instead, an unstable political cycle was created, not dissimilar to the cyclical ups and downs of the economy, in which periods of presidential domination would set in motion succeeding periods of congressional supremacy. Jefferson, a traitor to his class in the act of becoming a patriot to his country, promoted modernization, which then slackened with the advent of an era of good feelings. (Rapid accumulation creates feelings that are anything but good.) The cycle of expansion resumed again with Jackson, whose Indian policy, as Michael Rogin has pointed out, was primitive accumulation with a vengeance. This movement was then followed by a series of attempts to appease slavery. Just as a modern economy was forged through crises, with each panic centralizing a bit more power in the hands of a new class, so each political cycle would leave the presidency somewhat stronger as an instrument of modernization.

It was always a question how much crisis the system could absorb, especially when the Civil War threatened to tear the whole enterprise part. Lincoln, of course, greatly expanded the scope of presidential power, leaving behind him more tools of modernization than any previous occupant of the office. But not even civil war put an end to the cycles; the attempts by radical Republicans to complete the capitalist revolution were once again stymied by agrarian, working-class, and mercantile resistance. After the Hays-Tilden standoff, a political stalemate that reflected the equilibrium of class forces in the country at large, it became clear that the post–Civil War presidency, by itself, was still not strong enough to lead the struggle for industrial supremacy. The Civil War may have been America's bourgeois revolution, but like the Prussian, it was incomplete. The presidency needed an ally before it could emerge in all its modernizing glory.

At first an attempt was made by the emerging capitalist elite to assume and consolidate political power without the help of the state. Government being paralyzed in any case, it seemed to make more sense to rely on the industrial corporation as an agency of modernization, since it was more unified and nationalistic than the state gave any promise of being. The Republican Ascendancy at the end of the nineteenth century represented the rebirth of laissez-faire, an implicit confession that presidentially inspired modernization à la Hamilton was inappropriate to the political and economic realities of the period. Satisfying the urge to profit, laissez-faire did not solve the problem of how to govern. Rule by corporate power created as many problems as it solved: corporate authority was illegitimate in the eyes of the working class; carefully worked-out negotiations would collapse because no mechanism of enforcement existed to compel obedience; and resistance to modernization provoked disagreement on such vital issues as tariff policy and the creation of an American empire. During the period of the Republican Ascendancy, the problem of the state and the role of the presidency within it was never resolved but was simply postponed.

By the turn of the century, any further development of a political authority appropriate to modern capitalism had to include the use of governmental power. The presidency remained available for the task, but still viable as well were the traditions of federalism and of the separation of powers that formed obstacles to such a use of presidential power. Between one Roosevelt and the other, the impasse would finally be resolved in the form of an alliance between the president and the people directed against the realm of interests in the middle. As Henry Jones Ford demonstrated in his book *Rise and Growth of American Politics* (1898), democracy was the key to effective presidential leadership. The alliance between the president and the people represented, in Mosca's phrase, a new political formula, a solution to the political instability that had plagued capitalist development for a century. Modernization could be assured by overruling the realm of interests in plebiscitary fashion. So long as the link between the president and the people was secure, the United States could finally be governed. But when, as in recent years, the link began to fray, then the crisis would return again.

The new political formula that was developed in the first three decades of the present century, aptly termed the Roosevelt Revolution by Rexford G. Tugwell, was premised upon a political bargain: the people would give the president their support for the reforms necessary to insure the transition to advanced capitalism, and the president would offer the people security from the tensions induced by this transition. Specifically, the presidency became the focal point for two major features of contemporary economic modernization: first, a domestic economy rationalized through centralization and economic concentration; and second, a global free-trade system organized by American power. At the same time, the president provided the people with welfare to protect them from the dislocations of the first change and with a military apparatus to lessen the instabilities of the second. This bargain was not settled without considerable turmoil and many delays, and was culminated only after World War II. The institution of the presidency that emerged from the struggle was considerably different from the one that had existed previously.

Modernizing elites in America have traditionally been sympathetic to economic rationalization achieved through the concentration of industry. Theodore Roosevelt's trust-busting rhetoric was designed to make the point that "responsible" corporations willing to look past the bottom line to the needs of the economy as a whole were essential to the functioning of modern America. Similarly, the corporate liberals of the early twentieth century were critical of the market to the degree that it encouraged waste and destructive labor relations. From this perspective, the major change during the course of the New Deal was the substitution of Berle for Brandeis. Instead of symbolizing "the curse of bigness," the corporation was hailed as an institution that, if properly regulated, would bring enormous social and economic benefits. Old progressives, with their anachronistic faith in competition and their stress on civic virtue, seemed redundant to an economy in crisis, in which the encouragement of production took on supreme importance. The New Deal transformed American liberalism as much as it changed the economy; from this time forward, liberals became advocates of executive power, because only the president had the authority to shape the market so that it would not destroy itself. During the 1930s, state intervention implied presidential intervention.

The same movement took place in international affairs. Competitive capitalism in the United States had been both isolationist and protectionist, neither of which was appropriate to a rapidly developing economy. Because protectionist sentiment was lodged as securely in Congress as the seniority system, the promotion of free trade became a presidential prerogative. After Roosevelt shifted away from the protectionist position of the progressives, he had little choice but to rely on the free-trade advocacy of Cordell Hull and Will Clayton. Legislation like the Reciprocal Trade Agreements Act (1934), which gave the president broad discretionary authority to lower tariff rates, was to the global economy what the National Recovery Administration was to the domestic: both were attempts to use executive flexibility to overcome the realm of interests in the name of capitalist development.

Industrial concentration and globalism demanded their price. Specific sectors of the economy lost markets and profits. Protected industries that could not compete in a free-trade world and competitive firms unable to match the economies of scale generated by the monopolies were forced to close. In addition, a rationalized agricultural sector resulted in more displaced farmers who had to look for jobs in the cities. Financial reorganization created personal insecurity. Under these circumstances, Rooseveltian liberalism worked to soften the impact on people of these economic changes. The right of labor to organize, particularly in the monopoly sector, and domestic reforms like the establishment of social security were undoubtedly popular victories for ordinary people. They also strengthened the link between the president and the people. So long as the people were given some security *against* the market, they were willing to support a restructuring *of* the market.

It took a long time before America entered the world economy under the guidance of its president. Indeed, free trade did not become American policy until after World War II, and when it did, the president was unable to secure domestic support for it without projecting the Soviet threat as its rationale. Consequently, globalism came to the United States in the form of militarism, a movement directly counter to the intentions of men like Hull and Clayton. The Marshall Plan, support for the British loan, foreign aid, support for the European Economic Community — none of these innovations in international economics would have been possible without the atmosphere of the cold war. Just as *social* security consolidated the domestic transformations of the economy, *national* security insured the global ones. The same president who attempted to curb the anarchy of the market at home both guided and softened the anarchy of the system of nation-states. Popular and congressional support for globalism in isolationist America was won only by offering economic relief in the form of expenditures on national defense. Government spending orchestrated by means of presidential power would protect the people against insecurities coming from abroad, just as it bought protection against the effects of economic depression at home.

By the late 1940s, a sharply new formula for the exercise of presidential power had been created. The president would have to be a leader, not because his personality disposed him that way, but because the structure of national and international economics demanded it. Obstacles to the exercise of presidential leadership — federalism, an independent judiciary, a watchdog press, the seniority system in Congress, even the party system — were, one by one, modified to account for the new realities. Meanwhile, the president, now embodying the people's security, came to be viewed by the people as beyond the realm of ordinary mortals. Having lost their own security — both their ability to protect themselves against depression through economic self-sufficiency and their ability to protect themselves against war by a local militia — the people reified the institution onto which they had displaced their needs. The president would lead the people through the harsh realities of the modern world, just as the magic flute led Tamino. In return for the president's guidance, the people would join the new order.

There can be little doubt that the new political formula was a great success, for it survived two potential catastrophes: the death of Roosevelt and the rebirth of the Republican Party. Understanding the need to put his regionalism behind him, [Harry] Truman adopted the mantle of New Deal liberalism and shared in the commencement of the cold war. Even more significantly, Eisenhower, who in another era would have signaled a return to the down phase of the presidential cycle, held firm against campaigns to repeal both the welfare and the warfare state and, most extraordinarily, used federal troops to insure compliance with national law in the American South. As a result, the formula constructed in the 1930s and 1940s reached its fulfillment during the Kennedy/Johnson years. For one half of a decade, everything seemed to come together. The president proposed and Congress, after its fashion, disposed. Meanwhile, public faith in the institution of the presidency was high, for the office had come to symbolize the struggle against poverty on the one hand and against alien external forces on the other. America, after fighting its own modernizing instincts for a century, finally entered the world of corporate growth and global responsibility, coaxed and cajoled by its benevolent leader. "The President," wrote Clinton Rossiter in 1960, "is not a Gulliver, immobilized by ten thousand tiny cords, nor even a Prometheus, chained to a rock of frustration. He is, rather, a kind of magnificent lion who can roam freely and do great deeds so long as he does not try to break loose from his broad reservation." [1]

Yet Kennedy and Johnson, the men who first came to benefit from this increased popular support for the presidency, also set in motion the events that initiated another cycle of the disintegration of presidential power. Implicit in the bargain that made the Rooseveltian formula possible were two conditions that could not be sustained indefinitely: continuous economic growth at home and persistent U.S. hegemony abroad. So long as those conditions held, the people supported presidential modernization and the president possessed enough resources, financial and otherwise, to offer the people domestic and international security. As those conditions collapsed, the bargain began to unravel. But so intertwined had the economy become with the expansion of presidential power that the expectations surrounding the office were perpetuated, even though the assumptions presupposed conditions that no longer existed. This growing imbalance intensified a set of illusions about the nature of the presidency and the economy that only made matters worse. In actual fact, the president was not protecting the best interests of the people, and the people withdrew their support for presidentially inspired modernization. In their political rhetoric, however, both sides professed the opposite. The result of the increasing gap between a domestic political formula based on one set of conditions and a world economy rooted in another was the rapid delegitimation of the presidency.

Welfare states are expected to provide economic security for their citizens so that the misfortunes caused by the market are mitigated. As every economist knows, the funds to pay for social welfare can come from redistributing a fairly steady national income or from expanding the size of the economy so that the poor can benefit without threatening the privileges of the rich. Pursuit of the latter course was well nigh inevitable in postwar America, given the absence of a social democratic ideology and political coalition at the national level. After the New Deal shifted to a course of economic rationalization, liberal modernizers became dependent on corporate support to finance the economic growth that would enable them to pay off their promises to their working-class constituencies. Given this collaboration, the chief domestic role of liberal Democratic presidents was to act as a cheerleader for economic growth. "This country," John F. Kennedy noted in 1961, "cannot prosper unless business prospers. This country cannot meet its obligations and tax obligations and all the rest unless business is doing well. Business will not do well and we will not have full employment unless there is a chance to make a profit. So there is no long-run hostility between business and government. There cannot be. We cannot succeed unless they succeed." [2]

Growth worked. The fantastic expansion of the economy in the early 1960s, which took place with minimal inflation, provided exactly the kind of fiscal dividend that economists hoped would pay for social welfare programs for the poor. High growth rates financed the modern formula for presidential power, enabling the executive to make good its promises of security while at the same time consolidating the monopoly sector of the economy. The only problem was that growth had a huge appetite. To feed the beast, structural reforms in the economy, such as Sweden's manpower policy or Britain's nationalization, were taken off the legislative agenda. (Redistribution of income was held to undermine business confidence.) As a result, when the growth gave out, so did the security. Few institutionalized mechanisms had been created that could protect the people from unemployment, from inflation, and (worst of all) from both together.

The record with regard to national security was not much better. Globalism has never been overwhelmingly popular in American political culture, and popular support for an internationalist stance could be won only by offering peace. Yet peace could be secured only in one of two ways, either through a restrucuring of the world's political and economic relationships or through an attempt by one hegemonic power to enforce order. In retrospect, in light of the balance of political forces within the United States at the time, the adoption of the latter course seems to have been as inevitable as was the substitution of growth for welfare. In order to win public support for Bretton Woods, free trade, the United Nations, foreign aid, and other such global innovations, the president had to link them to threats from abroad, particularly from the Soviet Union. Internationally, the president became the cheerleader for American power, guiding the military establishment as commander in chief, coaxing reluctant allies, confronting the Alien Other, and inspiring the poor and downtrodden. America's military might became a force for modernization in the world at large, developing other capitalist economies, "showing the path" for the Third World, and keeping the alternative Marxist model of modernization out of the picture.

American hegemony brought all the advantages of economic growth, and all the problems as well. Use of the dollar as the world's currency reserve enabled the United States to spend other peoples' money. Free trade seemed too good to be true, so long as it was American firms that reaped the benefits. Most importantly, the illusion of peace itself was preserved, since no country in the world could match American military power. Yet once again the failure to reform international power arrangements upset the political formula at home. Hegemony never lasts forever. To protect its security interests, America undermined its economic interests. The dollar began to collapse under its overextended role. As America used its strategic superiority, it only convinced the Russians of the need to eliminate it. Germany and Japan, not dependent on inefficient military spending, increased their productivity, giving rise to protectionist sentiment within the United States. In short, when the hegemony withered away, so did feelings of international security. Americans were once again exposed to a world in crisis, and no president seemed able to win their trust for a program to restore order.

Richard Nixon was the first president to govern as the conditions that made possible the modern formula for presidential leadership deteriorated. One can never know what Nixon's fate would have been had Watergate not intervened, but there can be little doubt that the United States was structurally prepared for a crisis of the presidency during the Nixon years. The two most blatant economic realities of the Nixon years were stagflation at home, which required some restructuring of the domestic economy; and the transformation of the world economy (increasing oil prices, currency imbalances, Eurodollar speculation, and the drying up of grain reserves, for example), which demanded an alteration in foreign policy. To govern effectively, Nixon would have had to move the American people into a new position, all the while insisting that he was keeping the old verities alive. It was an excruciatingly difficult task, and Nixon almost managed to accomplish it. Had he not given his enemies everything they needed, Nixon might have been able to transform American politics to accord with the emerging economic realities. Wage and price controls at home and détente abroad were certainly important first steps.

As it happened, Nixon's failure to realign American politics made it more difficult for anyone else to carry out the task. Gerald Ford retreated to traditional Republicanism, an insufficient basis upon which to get himself reelected, and Jimmy Carter, after some Trilateralist feints, resumed the usual Democratic course of public works and military spending, no matter what the inflationary costs to the economy. Stagflation in the realm of production was matched by stagflation in the realm of government. The presidency had come to attract men who could campaign, but not men who could govern. Although it was an outlet for ambition, the office retained no place for vision. Presidents simply abdicated from trying to govern and concentrated their efforts on reelection, while the people tired of giving the president their unquestioned support and retreated into a cynical and grudging privatism. Holding power but unable to exercise it, the president had become what Nixon hoped would never be America's fate: a crippled giant, powerful enough to matter, but no longer mattering enough to be powerful.

The bargain is off. Presidents can no longer offer the people material security against a malfunctioning economy or unquestioned national security in a hostile international environment. The people, as a result, have withdrawn their worship of the institution, barely listening to speeches, voting uninformed when voting at all, expressing to anyone who asks their dismay at recent candidates for the office. The United States has entered one of its periodic retreats from presidential power. But this one is different. The expansion of the executive during the 1930s and 1940s had a stronger economic foundation than any previous expansion of presidential power. It represented the last gasp of unplanned modernization in the United States. The current crisis of the presidency derives from the fact that the presidency has been a vehicle for world modernization, but the current world economic crisis indicates a situation in which other countries have taken the lead in modernizing the forces of production. The American presidency requires economic growth to work; when economic growth cannot be generated, the presidency cannot work.

A host of explanations for America's economic crisis exists, but it is beyond the scope of this essay to evaluate them. Suffice it to say that the very techniques once used to insure the triumph of modernization are now themselves undercutting the expansion they once facilitated. Modernization never comes easy. To insure the transition to a global-oriented, industrially concentrated form of advanced capitalism, two options were present in the postwar period. In Europe, the change was facilitated by social democratic coalitions that supported a structural reorganization of the economy along neocorporatist lines. But in America, where business ideology is so strong and the labor movement so weak, such an option could not be exercised. Instead, the state encouraged the rapid, unplanned expansion of the private sector, both at home and abroad, and then agreed to pay for the external costs generated by that expansion in the form of welfare, unemployment benefits, and, later, pollution controls and import quotas. In the 1980s, America has encountered the limits of this strategy, and the president, who is charged with the responsibility for managing it, is caught in the middle.

Neither at home nor overseas does the postwar conception of allowing unplanned corporate expansion actually work to produce domestic economic benefits. The leading sectors of the postwar growth wave, autos and steel, have become inefficient, complacent industries, easily undermined by foreign competition. Meanwhile, the expansion of multinational corporations overseas has contributed to domestic unemployment and to a weakened role for the dollar. Unplanned expansion, in short, leads directly to higher rates of inflation and unemployment. At the same time, the lack of economic growth in the private sector makes it impossible for the public sector to pay for the externalities. Consequently, public goods are cut back, the social infrastructure of the society is allowed to deteriorate, and the state is helpless to prevent the export of jobs and capital. Once having been the beneficiary of the expansion induced by private-sector freedom, the president is now the victim of the stagflation that follows from that freedom. Those who gave their enthusiastic support to the president when matters went smoothly now withhold their respect when matters go poorly.

The American president is truly in an awkward position. Presidential popularity without economic growth is no longer possible. Yet to achieve growth, a president is now forced to intervene in the private sector, for one of the major causes of stagnation is the extraordinary freedom that the private sector gained under the postwar political formula. But were a president to attempt to plan the economy at home or to set limits on multinational operations overseas, the private sector would treat him with the same combination of threats and blackmail with which the banks in Cleveland treated former Mayor Dennis Kucinich. When the president, whether Carter or Reagan, offers even greater freedom for the private sector, and thereby gains the support of influential people, such a program is a certain recipe for worsened economic conditions, and bound to undermine his general popularity. The president cannot win. His role is reduced to one of promising economic growth in order to be elected but then breaking his promise in order to govern. The president is trapped between a political formula that demands prosperity and economic practices that insure austerity. No wonder the institution deteriorates.

Thus it becomes possible to understand how the system, working as democratically as it could, nevertheless produced candidates and a victor that nobody seemed to want. The problem *does* lie with the conception of democracy inherent in the modern political formula for the exercise of presidential power. Under conditions of economic growth, the people and the president entered into a relationship of mutual dependence. The people needed the president to protect them and the president needed the people to bring about modernization over the opposition of congressional and local elites. When the growth disappeared, the dependency remained. People and president are trapped in a passive relationship with each other. Dependent on the president, the people cannot think critically, or vote for more imaginative alternative candidates, or develop for themselves new sources of political power. Dependent on the people, the president cannot correctly formulate his own true judgments, or exercise creative leadership, or engage in the actual process of making policy relevant to the real world. Each side responds to the other's fantasies; neither side responds to the other's true needs.

There are ways by which the mutual dependency between the people and the president could be broken, but they would require a fairly substantial structural transformation of the economy. Balanced and planned growth, combined with an effort to stabilize international relationships around something other than an arms race, could bring about the security that would, on the one hand, enable the people to begin to exercise political judgment once more and, on the other, allow the president some scope for trying to govern. But so long as Americans keep their faith in uncontrolled business freedom at home and an unstable world abroad, the president will fail to live up to the expectations that have been generated about him. If anything, the cycle will intensify, replaying (as happened under Carter) in four years a presidential cycle that used to occupy a generation. The American people will either have to accept a presidency as contained and narrow-based as their economic system or they will have to democratize their economy to match their grandiose vision of presidential leadership. That choice, and not the one between candidates running for an office that is incapable of satisfying the contradictory demands placed upon it, is the only one that can solve the puzzle of presidential power in the United States.

SOURCE: From *Democracy: A Journal of Political Renewal and Radical Change,* April 1981. Reprinted with permission.

## Notes

1. Cited in Godfrey Hodgson, *All Things to All Men* (New York: Simon and Schuster, 1980), p. 71.
2. Cited in Ronald F. King, "The Politics of Regressive Taxation Changes," paper prepared for delivery at the 1977 Annual Meeting of the Midwest Political Science Association, p. 12.

# Rethinking the
# Separation of Powers Doctrine

# V

**11. The Doctrine of Separated Powers**
*Louis Fisher*

**12. To Form a Government—
On the Defects of Separation of Powers**
*Lloyd N. Cutler*

**13. In Defense of Separation of Powers  I**
*Thomas E. Mann and Norman J. Ornstein*

**14. In Defense of Separation of Powers  II**
*James Q. Wilson*

# 11. The Doctrine of Separated Powers

## Louis Fisher

The doctrine of separated powers has been heavily attacked in the twentieth century, first for impeding the flow of power to public administrators (who supposedly possessed expertise not found among legislators), and secondly for interfering with the demand for centralized authority during World War II. Carl Friedrich warned that "Many who today belittle the separation of powers seem unaware of the fact that their clamor for efficiency and expediency easily leads to dictatorship . . ." [1]

The abuse of power by recent presidents, particularly Lyndon Johnson and Richard Nixon, generated some conventional and convenient arguments about the separation doctrine. Opponents of presidential power claimed that the framers distrusted government (especially the executive) and attempted to fashion an instrument of checks and balances to prevent tyranny. While the framers did indeed construct a system designed to restrain power, that was only part of their intention. It would be inaccurate and a disservice to their labors at the Philadelphia convention to believe that they created a document primarily for the purpose of obstructing and hampering the operation of government.

It is important to understand the practical forces that led to the creation of separated branches. Our structure of government owes its existence to the experiences of the framers, not the theory of Montesquieu or precedents borrowed from England. The framers used Montesquieu selectively, adopting what they knew from their own experience to be useful and rejecting what they knew to be inapplicable. The product was more theirs than his. Having served in public life for many years, both in the colonies and in the fledgling republic, they knew firsthand the practical duties and problems of running a government. They were continuously and intimately involved in the mundane, down-to-earth matters of conducting a war and laying the foundation for a more perfect union. Their close familiarity with the classics in history and government, combined with the daily experience of public office, marked their special genius. It gave them vision without becoming visionaries.

British history, while valuable for the study of private and individual rights, is of marginal interest for the study of executive-legislative relationships in

*Louis Fisher is an American government specialist on the staff of the Congressional Research Service at the Library of Congress and is the author of several books, including* The Constitution Between Friends *and* The Politics of Shared Power.

America. Questions of executive privilege, impoundment, and the war power cannot be resolved by harkening back to British practices. The Supreme Court made this valid observation in 1850:

> [I]n the distribution of political power between the great departments of government, there is such a wide difference between the power conferred on the President of the United States, and the authority and sovereignty which belongs to the English crown, that it would be altogether unsafe to reason from any supposed resemblance between them, either as regards conquest in war, or any other subject where the right and powers of the executive arm of the government are brought into question.[2]

It is said that powers are separated to preserve liberties. But separation can also destroy liberties. The French constitutions of 1791 and 1848 represented ambitious efforts to erect a rigid and dogmatic separation of powers. The first document produced the reign of Napoleon Bonaparte; the next effort led to the Second Empire.[3]

Instead of indiscriminately championing the virtues of the separation doctrine, we should remember that it can satisfy a number of objectives, not all of them worth seeking. The framers of the American Constitution did not want a political system so fragmented in structure, so divided in authority, that government could not function. Justice Story pointed out in his *Commentaries* that the framers adopted a separation of power but "endeavored to prove that a rigid adherence to it in all cases would be subversive of the efficiency of the government, and result in the destruction of the public liberties." [4] His observation has been underscored by others. Justice Jackson correctly identified the multiple goals that motivated the framers: "While the Constitution diffuses power the better to secure liberty, it also contemplates that the practice will integrate the dispersed powers into a workable government. It enjoins upon its branches separateness but interdependence, autonomy but reciprocity." [5]

Had this understanding prevailed in the 1960s and 1970s, we might have been spared some of the stark, corrosive confrontations between president and Congress. More recently, in *Buckley v. Valeo* (1976), the Supreme Court noted that the framers recognized that a "hermetic sealing off of the three branches of Government from one another would preclude the establishment of a Nation capable of governing itself effectively." [6]

This conclusion is driven home by studying the political climate in which the framers produced their document. If they wanted weak government, if they wanted it shackled and ineffective, they could have retained the Articles of Confederation. They decided against this, for very good reason. The framers had labored under a weak government from 1774 to 1787, and deliberately rejected that model in favor of stronger central powers. Consciously, at the national level, they vested greater powers in an executive.

The distrust of executive power in 1776 — against the king of England and the royal governors — was tempered by two developments in the following decade. Americans discovered that state legislative bodies could be as oppressive and capricious toward individual rights as executive bodies. Also, many delegates to 'the Continental Congress watched with growing apprehension as the Congress found itself incapable of discharging its duties and responsibilities. Support began to grow for an independent executive, in large part for the purpose of assuring efficiency.

This interpretation challenges a famous dissent by Justice Brandeis, who claimed that the separation of powers doctrine was adopted *not* for efficiency but to preclude the exercise of arbitrary power.[7] Brandeis's dictum, invoked regularly by those who urged legislative reassertion in the 1960s, is a half-truth. The historical record is clear and persuasive that the inefficiency of the Continental Congress convinced the framers of the need for a separate and independent executive.[8]

The practical source of the separation doctrine is generally overlooked or ignored. Much more satisfying, emotionally if not intellectually, is the belief that the Constitution was pounded into shape from abstract principles, with the name of Montesquieu leading the list of theorists. Gladstone reinforced this impression by describing the American Constitution as the most wonderful document ever "struck off at a given time" by the mind of man.[9] But the framers did not create out of whole cloth the document that guides us today. They were alert to the excesses and injustices committed by state legislators. They were sensitive, very sensitive, to the demonstrated ineptitude of the Continental Congress, which had to administer and adjudicate while trying to legislate. One branch of government performed all the tasks.

Because of the repeated failings of the Congress, it soon began to delegate power — first to committees, then to boards staffed by people from outside the legislature, and finally, in 1781, to single executive officers.[10] These events occurred prior to the Philadelphia convention. The Constitution marked a continuity with political developments already underway. John Jay, after serving as secretary of foreign affairs under the Continental Congress, remained in office in the Washington administration until Thomas Jefferson could take his place. Henry Knox was secretary of war under the Continental Congress and under President Washington. Because of this orderly transition it has been said that the Constitution did not create a system of separated powers; rather, a system of separated powers created the Constitution.[11]

Several delegates to the ratifying conventions objected to the fact that the branches of government — legislative, executive, and judicial — had been intermingled instead of being kept separate. "How is the executive?" demanded one irate delegate at Virginia's ratifying convention. "Contrary to the opinion of all the best writers, blended with the legislature. We have asked for bread, and they have given us a stone." [12] This outcry enlisted some support, but not much. By the time of the Philadelphia convention the doctrine of separated powers had been modified to allow for checks and balances. One contemporary pamphleteer called the separation doctrine, in its pure form, a "hackneyed princi-

ple" and a "trite maxim." [13] Madison devoted several of his *Federalist* essays
to the need for overlapping powers, claiming that the concept was superior to the
impracticable partitioning of powers demanded by some of the anti-federalists.[14]

The system of checks and balances is not a contradiction to the separation
doctrine. The two are complementary. Without the power to withstand en-
croachments by another branch, a department might find its powers drained to
the point of extinction. The Constitution allocated separate functions to separate branches, but "parchment barriers" were not dependable. It was necessary, Madison concluded in *Federalist* 51, that "ambition must be made to
counteract ambition," while in *Federalist* 48 he warned: "unless these departments be so far connected and blended as to give to each a constitutional control over the others, the degree of separation which the maxim requires, as
essential to a free government, can never in practice be duly maintained."

The case for a strict separation of powers was tested in the form of an amendment to the Constitution. Three states — Virginia, North Carolina, and Pennsylvania — wanted to add a separation clause to the national bill of rights.[15]
The proposed language read as follows: "The powers delegated by this constitution are appropriated to the departments to which they are respectively distributed: so that the legislative department shall never exercise the powers
vested in the executive or judicial [,] nor the executive exercise the powers vested
in the legislative or judicial, nor the judicial exercise the powers vested in the
legislative or executive departments." [16] Congress rejected this proposal, as well
as a substitute amendment to make the three departments "separate and distinct." [17]

Although powers are not separated in a pure sense, it does not help to characterize the federal government as a "blend of powers." The branches have distinctly different responsibilities, practices, and traditions. A certain distance between the branches is preserved by Article I, Section 6 of the Constitution,
which prohibits members of either house from holding appointive office. Congress is prohibited from reducing the compensation of the president and members of the judiciary. The Speech or Debate Clause was designed to protect
legislators from executive or judicial harassment.[18]

Any occupant of the White House, after a short time in office, appreciates
the degree to which an institutional separation exists, whether Congress is in
the hands of the president's party or the opposition party. That is as it should
be. The president does not share with Congress his pardoning power, nor does
Congress share with the courts its taxing and appropriations powers (although
the judiciary is participating in the outer fringes). In 1974 the Supreme Court
highlighted the separation that exists in the federal government by stating that
the judicial power vested in the federal courts by Article III of the Constitution
"can no more be shared with the Executive Branch than the Chief Executive,
for example, can share with the Judiciary the veto power, or the Congress share
with the Judiciary the power to override a Presidential veto." [19] Even in administrative agencies that discharge executive, legislative, and judicial duties, those

tasks are kept separate. Someone who prosecutes a case, for example, would not be called upon to render a decision on the dispute.[20]


## The Durability of the Separation Doctrine

Has the balance among political institutions, as fashioned by the framers, failed to meet the test of time? Have events overtaken theory? Tocqueville, quoting with approval a passage from Jefferson, believed that the "tyranny of the legislature" in America would continue for a number of years before being replaced by a tyranny of the executive.[21] Yet presidential power, after cresting with Abraham Lincoln, subsided in the face of a determined and resurgent Congress. Writing in 1885, Woodrow Wilson believed that Congress had become the dominant branch. He said that the Constitution of 1787 was a form of government in name rather than in reality, "the form of the Constitution being one of nicely adjusted, ideal balances, whilst the actual form of our present government is simply a scheme of congressional supremacy." [22]

Two decades later, glancing with covetous eyes at the White House, Wilson predicted that the president "must always, henceforth, be one of the great powers of the world. . . . We have but begun to see the presidential office in this light; but it is the light which will more and more beat upon it. . . ." [23] The new wellspring of presidential power, according to his analysis, was the burden of international responsibilities thrust upon the United States. The Great Depression of the 1930s, joined with the personal qualities of Franklin D. Roosevelt, gave further impetus to executive power.

The reputation of Congress plummeted with such swiftness that Samuel P. Huntington, in an influential study published in 1965, suggested that unless Congress drastically altered its mode of operation it should abandon its legislative role and concentrate on serving constituents and overseeing the agencies.[24] The condition of Congress appeared to deteriorate even further, for in 1968 Philip B. Kurland charged that it did not have the "guts to stand up to its responsibilities." Congress was prostrate, the president transcendent. Kurland invited us to visit the "sickbed of another constitutional concept — the notion of separation of powers." Not only was the patient diseased, the affliction seemed terminal. Theoretically a cure was possible, but Kurland saw no grounds for optimism. To him the patient had lost the will to live.[25]

These dire predictions suggest that the imbalance between president and Congress is chronic and permanent. At no time, however, has either branch been as all-powerful or as defective as critics maintained. Congress, though its particular life style may offend our tastes, is alive and well. The political system has shown a capacity for self-correction. Two presidents, testing the limits of their power during the 1960s and 1970s, were driven from office. Congress, flexing its muscles during this time of reassertion, ran into barriers erected by the courts. In 1976 the Supreme Court ruled against the Federal Election Commission because Congress had staked out a role for itself in the appointment of four of the commission's six members. The court held this procedure contrary to the separation doctrine. Congress could not both legislate and enforce.[26]

The separation doctrine, subjected to ridicule for much of the twentieth century, still retains vitality. A longer view of American history provides room for confidence. Senator George Wharton Pepper offered this sound perspective: "[I]f the geometers of 1787 hoped for perfect peace and if the psychologists of that day feared disastrous conflicts, history, as so often happens, has proved that hopes were dupes and fears were liars. There has not been perfect peace; but the conflicts have not proved disastrous." [27]

SOURCE: From Louis Fisher, *The Constitution Between Friends: Congress, the President, and the Law,* New York, St. Martin's Press, Inc., and Macmillan & Co., Ltd., 1978. Reprinted by permission.

## Notes

1. Carl Friedrich, *Constitutional Government and Democracy* 175 (1946). See his "Constitutions and Constitutionalism," *Int'l Encyc. Soc. Sci.* (1968) and "Separation of Powers," *Encyc. Soc. Sci.,* XIII, 664 (1935), as well as Charles H. Wilson, "The Separation of Powers under Democracy and Fascism," 52 *Pol. Sci. Q.* 481 (1937). Arthur T. Vanderbilt, in the introduction to his *Doctrine of the Separation of Powers and Its Present-Day Significance* (1953), has written that individual freedom and the progress of civilization were attainable only by adhering to the principles of the separation of powers.
2. *Fleming v. Page,* 50 U.S. (9 How.) 602, 618 (1850).
3. M. J. C. Vile, *Constitutionalism and the Separation of Powers* 176–211 (1967).
4. Joseph Story, *Commentaries on the Constitution of the United States,* 5th ed. (1905), I, 396.
5. *Youngstown Co. v. Sawyer,* 343 U.S. 579, 635 (1952).
6. *Buckley v. Valeo,* 424 U.S. 1, 121 (1976).
7. *Myers v. United States,* 272 U.S. 52, 293 (1926).
8. See Louis Fisher, *President and Congress* 1–27, 241–270 (1972).
9. "Kin Beyond the Sea," *North Am. Rev.,* Vol. 127, No. 264 (Sept.-Oct. 1878), at 185.
10. I trace this process in *President and Congress.*
11. Francis Wharton, *The Revolutionary Diplomatic Correspondence of the United States,* I, 663 (1889).
12. Quoted in Elliot, *Debates,* III, 280.
13. Quoted in Vile at 153.
14. *Federalist* 37 and 47 attempted to rebut some of the Antifederalist objections regarding blended powers. For the latter see Morton Borden, ed., *The Antifederalist Papers* (1965), papers 47, 48, 64, 67, 73, and 75.
15. Elliot, *Debates,* III, 280, and IV, 116, 121; John Bach McMaster and Frederick D. Stone, eds., *Pennsylvania and the Federal Constitution* 475–477 (1888).
16. Edward Dumbauld, *The Bill of Rights and What It Means Today* 174–175, 183, 199 (1957).
17. For the congressional debates, see *Annals of Congress,* I, 453–454 (June 8, 1789) and 789–790 (Aug. 18, 1789). For action by the Senate, see U.S. Senate, *Journals, 1789–1794,* I, 64, 73–74 (1820).

18. *United States* v. *Johnson,* 383 U.S. 169, 179 (1966).
19. *United States* v. *Nixon,* 418 U.S. 683, 704 (1974).
20. Kenneth Culp Davis, *Administrative Law and Government* 174–191 (1975).
21. Tocqueville, *Democracy in America,* I, 280 (1945 ed.).
22. Woodrow Wilson, *Congressional Government* 6 (1885).
23. Woodrow Wilson, *Constitutional Government in the United States* 78 (1908).
24. Samuel P. Huntington, "Congressional Responses to the Twentieth Century," in David B. Truman, ed., *The Congress and America's Future* 5–31 (1965). Writing a year later, however, Ralph K. Huitt argued that Congress played a more important part in legislation than its critics realized. See his "Congress, the Durable Partner," originally published in 1966 and reprinted in Ralph K. Huitt and Robert L. Peabody, *Congress: Two Decades of Analysis* 209–229 (1969).
25. Philip B. Kurland, "The Impotence of Reticence," 1968 *Duke L.J.* 619, 621 (1968).
26. *Buckley* v. *Valeo,* 424 U.S. 1 (1976).
27. George Wharton Pepper, *Family Quarrels: the President, the Senate, the House* viii (1931).

# 12. To Form a Government—
# On the Defects of Separation of Powers

## Lloyd N. Cutler

[On May 10, 1940, Winston Churchill was summoned to Buckingham Palace.] His Majesty received me most graciously and bade me sit down. He looked at me searchingly and quizzically for some moments, and then said: "I suppose you don't know why I have sent for you?" Adopting his mood, I replied: "Sir, I simply couldn't imagine why." He laughed and said: "I want to ask you to form a Government." I said I would certainly do so.

— Winston S. Churchill
*The Gathering Storm* (1948)

Our society was one of the first to write a Constitution. This reflected the confident conviction of the Enlightenment that explicit written arrangements could be devised to structure a government that would be neither tyrannical nor impotent in its time, and to allow for future amendment as experience and change might require.

We are all children of this faith in a rational written arrangement for governing. Our faith should encourage us to consider changes in our Constitution — for which the framers explicitly allowed — that would assist us in adjusting to the changes in the world in which the Constitution must function. Yet we tend to resist suggestions that amendments to our existing constitutional framework are needed to govern our portion of the interdependent world society we have become, and to cope with the resulting problems that all contemporary governments must resolve.

A particular shortcoming in need of a remedy is the structural inability of our government to propose, legislate and administer a balanced program for governing. In parliamentary terms, one might say that under the U.S. Constitution it is not now feasible to "form a Government." The separation of powers between the legislative and executive branches, whatever its merits in 1793, has become a structure that almost guarantees stalemate today. As we wonder why we are having such a difficult time making decisions we all know must be made, and projecting our power and leadership, we should reflect on whether this is one big reason.

We elect one presidential candidate over another on the basis of our judgment of the overall program he presents, his ability to carry it out, and his ca-

*Lloyd Cutler, a prominent Washington lawyer, served as counsel to President Carter and has frequently advised Congress and presidents.*

pacity to adapt his program to new developments as they arise. We elected President Carter, whose program included, as one of its most important elements, the successful completion of the SALT II negotiations that his two predecessors had been conducting since 1972. President Carter did complete and sign a SALT II Treaty, in June 1979, which he and his Cabinet regarded as very much in the national security interests of the United States. Notwithstanding [subsequent] . . . events, the President and his Cabinet still [held] that view — indeed they [believed] the mounting intensity of our confrontation with the Soviet Union [made] it even more important for the two superpowers to adopt and abide by explicit rules as to the size and quality of each side's strategic nuclear arsenal, and as to how each side [could] verify what the other side [was] doing.

But because we do not "form a Government," it [was] not . . . possible for President Carter to carry out this major part of his program.

Of course the constitutional requirement of Senate advice and consent to treaties presents a special situation. The case for the two-thirds rule was much stronger in 1793, when events abroad rarely affected this isolated continent, and when "entangling foreign alliances" were viewed with a skeptical eye. Whether it should be maintained in an age when most treaties deal with such subjects as taxation and trade is open to question. No parliamentary regime anywhere in the world has a similar provision. But in the American case — at least for major issues like SALT — there is merit to the view that treaties should indeed require the careful bipartisan consultation essential to win a two-thirds majority. This is the principle that Woodrow Wilson fatally neglected in 1919. But it has been carefully observed by recent presidents, including President Carter for the Panama Canal Treaties and the SALT II Treaty. In each of these cases there was a clear prior record of support by previous Republican Administrations, and there would surely have been enough votes for fairly rapid ratification if the president could have counted on the total or near-total support of his own party — if, in short, he had truly formed a Government, with a legislative majority which takes the responsibility for governing.

Treaties may indeed present special cases, and I do not argue here for any change in the historic two-thirds requirement. But our inability to "form a Government" able to ratify SALT II is replicated regularly over the whole range of legislation required to carry out any president's overall program, foreign and domestic. Although the enactment of legislation takes only a simple majority of both Houses, that majority is very difficult to achieve. Any part of the president's legislative program may be defeated, or amended into an entirely different measure, so that the legislative record of any presidency may bear little resemblance to the overall program the president wanted to carry out. Energy and the budget provide two . . . critical examples [from the Carter presidency]. Indeed, SALT II itself could have been presented for approval by a simple majority of each House under existing arms control legislation, but the administration deemed this task even more difficult than achieving a two-thirds vote in the Senate. And this difficulty is of course compounded when the president's party does not even hold the majority of the seats in both Houses, as was the case from 1946 to 1948, from 1954 to 1960 and from 1968 to 1976 — or almost half the duration of the last seven administrations.

The Constitution does not require or even permit in such a case the holding of a new election, in which those who oppose the president can seek office to carry out their own overall program. Indeed, the opponents of each element of the president's overall program usually have a different makeup from one element to another. They would probably be unable to get together on any overall program of their own, or to obtain the congressional votes to carry it out. As a result the stalemate continues, and because we do not form a Government, we have no overall program at all. We cannot fairly hold the president accountable for the success or failure of his overall program, because he lacks the constitutional power to put that program into effect.

Compare this with the structure of parliamentary governments. A parliamentary government may have no written constitution, as in the United Kingdom. Or it may have a written constitution, as in West Germany, Japan and Ireland, that in other respects — such as an independent judiciary and an entrenched Bill of Rights — closely resembles our own. But while there may be a ceremonial president or, as in Japan, an Emperor, the executive consists of those members of the legislature chosen by the elected legislative majority. The majority elects a Premier or Prime Minister from among its number, and he selects other leading members of the majority as the members of his Cabinet. The majority as a whole is responsible for forming and conducting the "government." If any key part of its overall program is rejected by the legislature, or if a vote of "no confidence" is carried, the "Government" must resign and either a new "Government" must be formed out of the existing legislature or a new legislative election must be held. If the program *is* legislated, the public can judge the results, and can decide at the next regular election whether to reelect the majority or turn it out. At all times the voting public knows who is in charge, and whom to hold accountable for success or failure.

Operating under a parliamentary system, Chancellor Helmut Schmidt formed the present West German Government with a majority of only four, but he has succeeded in carrying out his overall program these past five years. [In 1979] Mrs. Thatcher won a majority of some 30 to 40 in the British Parliament. She has a very radical program, one that can make fundamental changes in the economy, social fabric and foreign policy of the United Kingdom. There is room for legitimate doubt as to whether her overall program will achieve its objectives and, even if it does, whether it will prove popular enough to reelect her Government at the next election. But there is not the slightest doubt that she will be able to legislate her entire program, including any modifications she makes to meet new problems. In a parliamentary system, it is the duty of each majority member of the legislature to vote for each element of the Government's program, and the Government possesses the means to punish members if they do not. In a very real sense, each member's political and electoral future is tied to the fate of the Government his majority has formed. Politically speaking, he lives or dies by whether that Government lives or dies.

President Carter's party [had] a much larger majority percentage in both Houses of Congress than Chancellor Schmidt or Mrs. Thatcher. But [such] comfortable [majorities do] not even begin to assure that President Carter or any other president can rely on [those majorities] to vote for each element of his program. No member of [a] majority has the constitutional duty or the practical political need to vote for each element of the president's program. Neither the president nor the leaders of the legislative majority have the means to punish him if he does not. In the famous phrase of Joe Jacobs, the fight manager, "it's every man for theirself."

Let me cite one example. In the British House of Commons, just as in our own House, some of the majority leaders are called the Whips. In the Commons, the Whips do just what their title implies. If the government cares about the pending vote, they "whip" the fellow members of the majority into compliance, under pain of party discipline if a member disobeys. On the most important votes, the leaders invoke what is called a three-line whip, which must be obeyed on pain of resignation or expulsion from the party.

In our House, the Majority Whip, who happens to be one of our very best Democratic legislators, can himself feel free to leave his Democratic president and the rest of the House Democratic leadership on a crucial vote, if he believes it important to his constituency and his conscience to vote the other way. When he does so, he is not expected or required to resign his leadership post; indeed he is back a few hours later "whipping" his fellow members of the majority to vote with the president and the leadership on some other issue. But all other members are equally free to vote against the president and the leadership when they feel it important to do so. The president and the leaders have a few sticks and carrots they can use to punish or reward, but nothing even approaching the power that Mrs. Thatcher's Government or Chancellor Schmidt's Government can wield against any errant member of the majority.

I am hardly the first to notice this fault. As Judge Carl McGowan has reminded us, that "young and rising academic star in the field of political science, Woodrow Wilson — happily unaware of what the future held for him in terms of successive domination of, and defeat by, the Congress — despaired in the late nineteenth century of the weakness of the Executive Branch vis-à-vis the Legislative, so much so that he concluded that a coalescence of the two in the style of English parliamentary government was the only hope." [1]

As Wilson put it, "power and strict accountability for its use are the essential constituents of good Government." [2] Our separation of executive and legislative power fractions power and prevents accountability.

In drawing this comparison, I am not blind to the proven weaknesses of parliamentary government, or to the virtues which our forefathers saw in separating the executive from the legislature. In particular, the parliamentary system lacks the ability of a separate and vigilant legislature to investigate and curb the abuse of power by an arbitrary or corrupt executive. Our own recent history has underscored this virtue of separating these two branches.

Moreover, our division of executive from legislative responsibility also means that a great many more voters are represented in positions of power, rather than as mere members of a "loyal opposition." If I am a Democrat in a Republican district, my vote in the presidential election may still give me a proportional impact. And if my party elects a president, I do not feel — as almost half the voters in a parliamentary constituency like Oxford must feel — wholly unrepresented. One result of this division is a sort of permanent centrism. While this means that no extreme or Thatcher-like program can be legislated, it means also that there are fewer wild swings in statutory policy.

This is also a virtue of the constitutional division of responsibility. It is perhaps what John Adams had in mind when, at the end of his life, he wrote to his old friend and adversary, Thomas Jefferson, that "checks and balances, Jefferson, . . . are our only Security, for the progress of Mind, as well as the Security of Body." [3]

But these virtues of separation are not without their costs. I believe these costs have been mounting in the last half-century, and that it is time to examine whether we can reduce the costs of separation without losing its virtues.

During this century, other nations have adopted written constitutions, sometimes with our help, that blend the virtues of our system with those of the parliamentary system. The Irish Constitution contains a replica of our Bill of Rights, an independent Supreme Court that can declare acts of the government unconstitutional, a figurehead president, and a parliamentary system. The postwar German and Japanese Constitutions, which we helped to draft, are essentially the same. While the Gaullist French Constitution contains a Bill of Rights somewhat weaker than ours, it provides for a strong president who can dismiss the legislature and call for new elections. But it also retains the parliamentary system and its blend of executive and legislative power achieved by forming a Government out of the elected legislative majority. The president, however, appoints the premier or first minister.

## II

We are not about to revise our own Constitution so as to incorporate a true parliamentary system. But we do need to find a way of coming closer to the parliamentary concept of "forming a Government," under which the elected majority is able to carry out an overall program, and is held accountable for its success or failure.

There are several reasons why it is far more important in [the 1980s] than it was in 1940, 1900 or 1800 for our government to have the capability to formulate and carry out an overall program.

1) The first reason is that government is now constantly required to make a different kind of choice than usually in the past, a kind for which it is difficult

to obtain a broad consensus. That kind of choice, which one may call "allocative," has become the fundamental challenge to government today. As a recent newspaper article put it:

> The domestic programs of the last two decades are no longer seen as broad campaigns to curb pollution or end poverty or improve health care. As these programs have filtered down through an expanding network of regulation, they single out winners and losers. The losers may be workers who blame a lost promotion on equal employment programs; a chemical plant fighting a tough pollution control order; a contractor who bids unsuccessfully for a government contract, or a gas station owner who wants a larger fuel allotment.[4]

This is a way of recognizing that, in giving government great responsibilities, we have forced a series of choices among these responsibilities.

During the second half of this century, our government has adopted a wide variety of national goals. Many of these goals — checking inflation, spurring economic growth, reducing unemployment, protecting our national security, assuring equal opportunity, increasing social security, cleaning up the environment, improving energy efficiency — conflict with one another, and all of them compete for the same resources. There may have been a time when we could simultaneously pursue all of these goals to the utmost. But even in a country as rich as this one, that time is now past. One of the central tasks of modern government is to make wise balancing choices among courses of action that pursue one or more of our many conflicting and competing objectives.

Furthermore, as new economic or social problems are recognized, a responsible government must *adjust* these priorities. In the case of energy policy, the need to accept realistic oil prices has had to be balanced against the immediate impact of drastic price increases on consumers and affected industries, and on the overall rate of inflation. And to cope with the energy crisis, earlier objectives of policy have had to be accommodated along the way. Reconciling one goal with another is a continuous process. A critical regulatory goal of 1965 (auto safety) had to be reconciled with an equally critical regulatory goal of 1970 (clean air) long before the auto safety goal had been achieved, just as both these critical goals had to be reconciled with 1975's key goal (closing the energy gap) long before either auto safety or clean air had lost their importance. Reconciliation was needed because many auto safety regulations had the effect of increasing vehicle size and weight and therefore increasing gasoline consumption and undesirable emissions, and also because auto emission control devices tend to increase gasoline consumption. Moreover, throughout this 15-year period, we have had to reconcile all three of these goals with another critical national objective — wage and price stability — when in pursuit of these other goals we make vehicles more costly to purchase and operate.

And now, in 1980, we find our auto industry at a serious competitive disadvantage vis-à-vis Japanese and European imports, making it necessary to limit those regulatory burdens which aggravate the extent of the disadvantage. A responsible government must be able to adapt its programs to achieve the best balance among its conflicting goals as each new development arises.

For balancing choices like these, a kind of political triage, it is almost impossible to achieve a broad consensus. Every group will be against some part of the balance. If the "losers" on each item are given a veto on that part of the balance, a sensible balance cannot be struck.

2) The second reason is that we live in an increasingly interdependent world. What happens in distant places is now just as consequential for our security and our economy as what happens in Seattle or Miami. No one today would use the term "Afghanistanism," as the Opposition benches did in the British Parliament a century ago, to deride the Government's preoccupation with a war in that distant land. No one would say today, as President Wilson said in 1914, that general European war could not affect us and is no concern of ours. We are now an integral part of a closely interconnected world economic and political system. We have to respond as quickly and decisively to what happens abroad as to what happens within the portion of this world system that is governed under our Constitution.

New problems requiring new adjustments come up even more frequently over the foreign horizon than the domestic one. Consider the rapid succession of events and crises since President Carter took up the relay baton for his leg of the SALT II negotiations back in 1977: the signing of the Egyptian-Israeli Peace Treaty over Soviet and Arab opposition, the Soviet-Cuban assistance to guerrilla forces in Africa and the Arabian peninsula, the recognition of the People's Republic of China, the final agreement on the SALT II terms and the signing of the Treaty in Vienna, the revolution in Iran and the later seizure of our hostages, the military coup in Korea, the Soviet-supported Vietnamese invasion of Kampuchea, our growing dependence on foreign oil from politically undependable sources, the affair of the Soviet brigade in Cuba, the polarization of rightist and leftist elements in Central America, and finally (that is, until the next crisis a month or two from now) the Soviet invasion of Afghanistan and the added threat it poses to the states of Southwest Asia and to the vital oil supplies of Europe, Japan and the United States.

Each of these portentous events required a prompt reaction and response from our Government, including in many cases a decision as to how it would affect our position on the SALT II Treaty. The government has to be able to adapt its overall program to deal with each such event as it arises, and it has to be able to execute the adapted program with reasonable dispatch. Many of these adaptations — such as changes in the levels and direction of military and economic assistance — require joint action by the president and the Congress, something that is far from automatic under our system. And when Congress does act, it is prone to impose statutory conditions or prohibitions that fetter the president's policy discretion to negotiate an appropriate assistance package or to adapt it to fit even later developments. The congressional bans on military assistance to Turkey, any form of assistance to the contending forces in Angola, and any aid to Argentina if it did not meet our human rights criteria by a deadline now past, are typical examples.

Indeed, the doubt that Congress will approve a presidential foreign policy initiative has seriously compromised our ability to make binding agreements with nations that "form a Government." Given the fate of SALT II and lesser treaties, and the frequent congressional vetoes of other foreign policy actions, other nations now realize that our executive branch commitments are not as binding as theirs, that Congress may block any agreement at all, and that at the very least they must hold something back for a subsequent round of bargaining with the Congress.

3) The third reason is the change in Congress and its relationship to the Executive. When the Federalist and Democratic Republican parties held power, a Hamilton or a Gallatin would serve in the Cabinet, but they continued to lead rather than report to their party colleagues in the Houses of Congress. Even when the locus of congressional leadership shifted from the Cabinet to the leaders of Congress itself, in the early nineteenth century, it was a congressional leadership capable of collaboration with the executive. This was true until very recently. The Johnson-Rayburn collaboration with Eisenhower a generation ago is an instructive example. But now Congress itself has changed.

There have been the well-intended democratic reforms of Congress, and the enormous growth of the professional legislative staff. The former ability of the president to sit down with ten or fifteen leaders in each House, and to agree on a program which those leaders could carry through Congress, has virtually disappeared. The committee chairmen and the leaders no longer have the instruments of power that once enabled them to lead. A Lyndon Johnson would have a much harder time getting his way as Majority Leader today than when he did hold and pull these strings of power in the 1950s. When Senator Mansfield became Majority Leader in 1961, he changed the practice of awarding committee chairmanships on the basis of seniority. He declared that all Senators are created equal. He gave every Democratic Senator a major committee assignment and then a subcommittee chairmanship, adding to the sharing of power by reducing the leadership's control.

In the House the seniority system was scrapped. Now the House Majority Caucus — not the leadership — picks the committee chairmen and the subcommittee chairmen as well. The House parliamentarian has lost the critical power to refer bills to a single committee selected by the speaker. Now bills like the energy bills go to several committees which then report conflicting versions back to the floor. Now mark-up sessions take place in public; indeed, even the House-Senate joint conference committees, at which differing versions of the same measure are reconciled, must meet and barter in public. . . .

There is also the decline of party discipline and the decline of the political party itself. Presidential candidates are no longer selected, as Adlai Stevenson was selected, by the leaders or bosses of their party. Who are the party leaders today? There are no such people. The party is no longer the instrument that selects the candidate. Indeed, the party today, as a practical matter, is no more than a neutral open forum that holds the primary or caucus in which candidates for president and for Congress may compete for favor and be elected. The party does not dispense most of the money needed for campaigning, the way the European and Japanese parties do. The candidates raise most of their own money. To the extent that money influences legislative votes, it comes not from a party with a balanced program, but from a variety of single-interest groups.

We now have a great many diverse and highly organized interest groups — not just broad-based agriculture, labor, business and ethnic groups interested in a wide variety of issues affecting their members. We now have single-issue groups — environmental, consumer, abortion, right to life, pro- and anti-SALT, pro- and anti-nuclear, that stand ready to lobby for their single issue and to reward or punish legislators, both in cash and at the ballot box, according to how they respond on the single issue that is the group's raison d'être. And on many specific foreign policy issues involving particular countries, there are exceptionally strong voting blocs in this wonderful melting pot of a nation that exert a great deal of influence on individual senators and congressmen.

## III

It is useful to compare this modern failure of our governmental structure with its earlier classic successes. There can be no structural fault, it might be said, so long as an FDR could put through an entire anti-depression program in 100 days, or an LBJ could enact a broad program for social justice three decades later. These infrequent exceptions, however, confirm the general rule of stalemate.

If we look closely we will find that in this century the system has succeeded only on the rare occasions when there is an unusual event that brings us together, and creates substantial consensus throughout the country on the need for a whole new program. FDR had such a consensus in the early days of the New Deal, and from Pearl Harbor to the end of World War II. But we tend to forget that in 1937 his court-packing plan was justifiably rejected by Congress — a good point for those who favor complete separation of the executive from the legislature[5] — and that as late as August 1941, when President Roosevelt called on Congress to pass a renewal of the Selective Service Act, passage was gained by a single vote in the House. Lyndon Johnson had such a consensus for both his domestic and his Vietnam initiatives during the first three years after the shock of John Kennedy's assassination brought us together. . . .

When the great crisis and the resulting large consensus are not there — when the country is divided somewhere between 55–45 and 45–55 on each of a wide set of issues, and when the makeup of the majority is different on every issue — it has not been possible for any modern president to "form a Government" that could legislate and carry out his overall program.

Yet modern government has to respond promptly to a wide range of new challenges. Its responses cannot be limited to those for which there is a large consensus induced by some great crisis. Modern government also has to work in every presidency, not just in one presidency out of four, when a Wilson, an FDR or an LBJ comes along. It also has to work for the president's full time in office, as it did not even for Wilson and LBJ. When they needed congressional support for the most important issue of their presidencies, they could not get it.

When the president gets only "half a loaf" of his overall program, this half a loaf is not necessarily better than none, because it may lack the essential quality of balance. And half a loaf leaves both the president and the public in the worst of all possible worlds. The public — and the press — still expect the president to govern. But the president cannot achieve his overall program, and the public cannot fairly blame the president because he does not have the power to legislate and execute his program. Nor can the public fairly blame the individual members of Congress, because the Constitution allows them to disclaim any responsibility for forming a Government and hence any accountability for its failures.

Of course the presidency always has been and will continue to be what Theodore Roosevelt called "a bully pulpit" — not a place from which to "bully" in the sense of intimidating the Congress and the public, but in the idiom of TR's day a marvelous place from which to exhort and lift up Congress and the public. All presidents have used the bully pulpit in this way, and this is one reason why the American people continue to revere the office and almost always revere its incumbent. Television has probably amplified the power of the bully pulpit, but it has also shortened the time span of power; few television performers can hold their audiences for four consecutive years. In any event, a bully pulpit, while a glorious thing to have and to employ, is not a Government, and it has not been enough to enable any postwar president to "form a Government" for his entire term.

Finally, the myth persists that the existing system can be made to work satisfactorily if only the president will take the trouble to consult closely with the Congress. If one looks back at the period between 1947 and 1965 there were indeed remarkable cases, at least in the field of foreign policy, where such consultation worked to great effect, even across party lines. The relationships between Senator Vandenberg and Secretaries Marshall and Acheson, and between Senator George and Secretary Dulles, come readily to mind. But these examples were in an era of strong leadership within the Congress, and of unusual national consensus on the overall objectives of foreign policy and the measures needed to carry it out.

Even when these elements have not been present, every president has indeed tried to work with the majority in Congress, and the majority in every Congress has tried to work with the president. . . .

Except on the rare issues where there is . . . a consensus, the structural problems usually prove too difficult to overcome. In each administration, it becomes progressively more difficult to make the present system work effectively on the range of issues, both domestic and foreign, that the United States must now manage even though there is no large consensus.

## IV

If we decide we want the capability of forming a Government, the only way to do so is to amend the Constitution. Amending the Constitution, of course, is extremely difficult. Since 1793, when the Bill of Rights was added, we have amended the Constitution only 16 times.... But none has touched the basic separation of executive and legislative powers.

The most one can hope for is a set of modest changes that would make our structure work somewhat more in the manner of a parliamentary system, with somewhat less separation between the executive and the legislature than now exists.

There are several candidate proposals. Here are some of the more interesting ideas:

1) We now vote for a presidential candidate and a vice-presidential candidate as an inseparable team. We could provide that in presidential election years, voters in each congressional district would be required to vote for a trio of candidates, as a team, for president, vice-president and the House of Representatives. This would tie the political fortunes of the party's presidential and congressional candidates to one another, and provide some incentive for sticking together after they are elected. Such a proposal could be combined with a four-year term for members of the House of Representatives. This would tie the presidential and congressional candidates even more closely, and has the added virtue of providing members with greater protection against the pressures of single-issue political groups. This combination is the brainchild of Congressman Jonathan Bingham of New York, and is now pending before the Congress.

In our bicameral legislature, the logic of the Bingham proposal would suggest that the inseparable trio of candidates for president, vice-president and member of Congress be expanded to a quintet including the two Senators, who would also have the same four-year term. But no one has challenged the gods of the Olympian Senate by advancing such a proposal.

2) Another idea is to permit or require the president to select 50 percent of his Cabinet from among the members of his party in the Senate and House, who would retain their seats while serving in the Cabinet. This would be only a minor infringement on the constitutional principle of separation of powers, but it would require a change in Article I, Section 6, which provides that "no person holding any office under the United States shall be a member of either house during his continuance in office." It would tend to increase the intimacy between the executive and the legislature, and add to their sense of collective responsibility. The 50-percent test would leave the president adequate room to bring other qualified persons into his Cabinet, even though they do not hold elective office.

3) A third intriguing suggestion is to provide the president with the power, to be exercised not more than once in his term, to dissolve Congress and call for new congressional elections. This is the power now vested in the president under the French Constitution. It would provide the opportunity that does not now exist to break an executive-legislative impasse, and to let the public decide whether it wishes to elect Senators and Congressmen who *will* legislate the president's overall program.

For obvious reasons, the president would invoke such a power only as a last resort, but his potential ability to do so could have a powerful influence on congressional responses to his initiatives. This would of course be a radical and highly controversial proposal, and it involves a number of technical difficulties relating to the timing and conduct of the new election, the staggering of senatorial terms, and similar matters. But it would significantly enhance the president's power to form a Government.

On the other hand, the experience of presidents — one recalls Nixon in 1970 — who sought to use the mid-term election as a referendum on their programs suggests that any such dissolution and new election would be equally as likely to continue the impasse as to break it. Perhaps any exercise of the power to dissolve Congress should automatically require a new presidential election as well. But even then, the American public might be perverse enough to reelect all the incumbents to office.

4) Another variant on the same idea is that in addition to empowering the president to call for new congressional elections, we might empower a majority or two-thirds of both Houses to call for new presidential elections. . . .

5) There are other proposals that deserve consideration. There could be a single six-year presidential term, an idea with many supporters, among them Presidents Eisenhower, Johnson and Carter, to say nothing of a great many political scientists. (The French Constitution provides a seven-year term for the president, but permits reelection.) Of course presidents would like to be elected and then forget about politics and get to the high ground of saving the world. But if first-term presidents did not have the leverage of reelection, we might institutionalize for every presidency the lame duck impotence we now see when a president is not running for reelection.

6) It may be that one combination involving elements of the third, fourth and fifth proposals would be worthy of further study. It would be roughly as follows:

A. The president, vice-president, Senators and Congressmen would all be elected for simultaneous six-year terms.
B. On one occasion each term, the president could dissolve Congress and call for new congressional elections for the remainder of the term. If he did so, Congress, by majority vote of both Houses within 30 days of

the president's action, could call for simultaneous new elections for president and vice-president for the remainder of the term.

C. All state primaries and state conventions for any required mid-term elections would be held 60 days after the first call for new elections. Any required national presidential nominating conventions would be held 30 days later. The national elections would be held 60 days after the state primary elections and state conventions. The entire cycle would take 120 days. The dissolved Congress would be free to remain in session for part or all of this period.

D. Presidents would be allowed to serve only one full six-year term. If a mid-term presidential election is called, the incumbent would be eligible to run and, if reelected, to serve the balance of his six-year term.

Limiting each president to one six-year term would enhance the objectivity and public acceptance of the measures he urges in the national interest. He would not be regarded as a lame duck because of his continuing power to dissolve Congress. Our capacity to "form a Government" would be enhanced if the president could break an impasse by calling for a new congressional election and by the power of Congress to respond by calling for a new presidential election.

Six-year terms for Senators and Congressmen would diminish the power of single-interest groups to veto balanced programs for governing. Because any mid-term elections would have to be held promptly, a single national primary, a shorter campaign cycle and public financing of congressional campaigns — three reforms with independent virtues of their own — would become a necessity for the mid-term election. Once tried in a mid-term election, they might well be adopted for regular elections as well. . . .

## V

How can these proposals be evaluated? How can better proposals be devised? Above all, how can the public be educated to understand the costs of the present separation between our executive and legislative branches, to weigh these costs against the benefits, and to decide whether a change is needed?

One obvious possibility is the widely feared constitutional convention — something for which the Constitution itself provides — to be called by Congress itself or two-thirds of the states. Jefferson expected one to occur every generation. Conventions are commonplace to revise state constitutions. But Congress has never even legislated the applicable rules for electing and conducting a national constitutional convention, even though more than 30 states have now called for one to adopt an amendment limiting federal taxes and expenditures. Because of the concern generated by this proposal, any idea of a national constitutional convention on the separation of powers is probably a non-starter.

A more practicable first step would be the appointment of a bipartisan presidential commission . . . to analyze the issues, compare how other constitutions work, hold public hearings, and make a full report. The presidential commission could include ranking members of the House and Senate, or perhaps Congress could establish a parallel joint commission of its own.

[My] point [here] is not to persuade the reader of the virtue of any particular amendment. I am far from persuaded myself. But I am convinced of these propositions:

> We need to do better than we have in "forming a Government" for this country, and this need is becoming more acute.
> The structure of our Constitution prevents us from doing significantly better.
> It is time to start thinking and debating about whether and how to correct this structural fault.

SOURCE: Excerpted by permission of *Foreign Affairs,* Fall 1980. Copyright 1980 by the Council on Foreign Relations, Inc.

## Notes

1. Carl McGowan, "Congress, Court, and Control of Delegated Power," *Columbia Law Review,* Vol. 77, No. 8 (1977) pp. 1119–20.
2. *Congressional Government: A Study in American Politics,* Boston and New York: Houghton Mifflin, 1913, p. 284.
3. *The Adams-Jefferson Letters,* Vol. II, (Lester J. Cappon, ed.), Chapel Hill: University of North Carolina Press, 1959, p. 134.
4. Quoted from Carl P. Leubsdorf, "Contemporary Problems Leave U.S. Political System Straining to Cope," reprinted in the *Congressional Record,* October 31, 1979, pp. S15593–94.
5. The mention of this historic example may strike some readers as sharply impairing the general thesis of this article in favor of disciplined party voting in the Congress. But one can readily envisage a category of issues — analogous to mutual defense treaties — where an Administration would not be entitled to apply party discipline. (In Britain, for example, votes on such issues as capital punishment have traditionally not been subject to the party whip.) Any measure amending the Constitution or affecting the separation of powers (as the 1937 Court Plan did) should probably be exempted, as well as any issue of religious conscience, such as legislation bearing on abortion.

# 13. In Defense of Separation of Powers  I

## Thomas E. Mann and Norman J. Ornstein

Lloyd N. Cutler, in his "To Form a Government," has highlighted an important set of developments: the instruments of collective authority and accountability in American politics have been weakened in recent years at the same time that the problems facing government have become more complex. However, Mr. Cutler, in the course of his essay, manages at one and the same time to gloss over the difficulties of parliamentary systems, overstate the intractability of modern American government, misrepresent the changes that have swept Congress in the last decade, and lend credibility to a laundry list of unworkable and infeasible constitutional reforms.

In any society, structural arrangements alone do not determine the quality or direction of policy — the political, geographic, cultural and social variables are equally important. The vacillation, disarray, and misdirection at various times in the foreign and domestic policies of parliamentary Britain and Italy are cases in point. One need look only at the zigs and zags over the years in Britain's response to membership in the European Economic Community and the Labour Party's potential move in the coming months to urge withdrawal to see that indecision on an important foreign policy question is not restricted to the American system. Italy's parliamentary system, of course, has had great success in forming governments — several dozen, at last count, in the postwar era. This is not to suggest that these countries should scotch *their* political institutions and adopt ours or any others — only that structural reforms are not panaceas.

Moreover, in the United States the recent deadlocks or failures of policy initiatives have been as much failures of political will and skill as anything else. The new, more diffuse Congress *can* be worked with — the diffusion of power creates opportunities as well as constraints. But it puts a premium not just on the consultation that Mr. Cutler so easily dismisses, but on the skills of political management. A case in point is the successful handling of the Multilateral Trade Negotiations.

Here the Carter Administration had a clear policy leader on MTN — Robert Strauss — who developed a politically sustainable substantive position, was sen-

*Thomas E. Mann is Executive Director of the American Political Science Association and is the author of* Unsafe at Any Margin. *Norman J. Ornstein teaches political science at Catholic University and is the author and editor of several books on Congress. Mann and Ornstein are coeditors of* The New Congress.

sitive to the congressional climate and to individual members' needs, and culti-
vated an image of toughness. These elements of successful political management
were missing from SALT II, the Energy Mobilization Board and other notorious
Carter failures. Better bills and better leadership could provide different results.

Even in the current context, there are virtues to an active Congress — virtues
unappreciated by Mr. Cutler, who would prefer to make Congress a "silent
partner." Our system of separation of powers provides multiple channels for
assessing policy options and for rejecting those that are misguided or altering
those that are misdirected. Many constituencies have a voice — and the outcomes, more often than not, are the better for it. For example, the two-year
struggle on Capitol Hill over natural gas deregulation served both to correct
problems with President Carter's proposal and to develop a consensus that made
it possible later to deregulate oil. In spite of the temporary setbacks, the strife,
and the seeming irrationality of the legislative process, we now have an energy
policy, the broad outlines of which will survive any change in administrations.
In many ways, this compares favorably with Britain, where dramatic policy reversals often follow a change in government: witness the Conservative and Labour governments' struggle over nationalizing, denationalizing and renationaliz-
ing the same industries.

In any case, if discussion of the problems and limits of Congress takes place,
it ought to be on an accurate factual basis. Mr. Cutler's discussion of changes
in Congress has numerous inaccuracies that require clarification. Senator Mike
Mansfield did not in 1961 change the practice of awarding committee chairmanships; nor was he the first to give every Democratic Senator a major committee assignment. The latter was an innovation of Lyndon Johnson. The
former was altered by the Senate Democratic Conference in the 1970s, but the
norm of seniority has never been violated. The statement that the seniority system in the House was "scrapped" is hyperbole — virtually every chairman
selected since the reform has been the most senior. The House Majority Caucus
does not pick subcommittee chairmen (except for the Appropriations Committee). While jurisdictional overlap among committees has further decentralized
the process, the procedural change allowing the leadership to refer bills to multiple committees and to appoint ad hoc committees to coordinate these efforts
was instituted to enhance, not weaken, the Speaker's power — and it has worked
that way for the most part (witness the Ad Hoc Energy Committee).

Finally, we disagree with Mr. Cutler's interpretation of the historical role of
Congress. Mr. Cutler portrays a rosy period of two decades ago and more, when
a president could "sit down with ten or fifteen leaders in each House, and . . .
agree on a program which those leaders could carry through Congress." If John
Kennedy were with us today, he would be amused to learn about his supposed
ability to work out his program with Congress. President Kennedy couldn't
simply tell Congress what to do; more often he had to wait for congressional
leaders to tell *him* what was possible or impossible. Their assessments were reliable too — the bulk of President Kennedy's civil rights, poverty, education, and

health proposals foundered in Congress during his three years in the White House.

Mr. Cutler's proposals for constitutional reform are likely to lead to unanticipated consequences worse than the original malady. Suppose, for example, that in 1960 the candidates for president, vice-president and the House of Representatives had, as he suggests, run for election in each district as a team, with voters making a single choice. John Kennedy, who actually carried well under half of the congressional districts, would have faced a Republican majority in the House strongly tied to Richard Nixon! The same condition almost prevailed in 1976.

Other Cutler suggestions, such as the proposal to have 50 percent of the Cabinet selected from members of the House and Senate, could easily lead to a divided executive and *increased* tension between the branches. Mr. Cutler also endorses the shopworn idea of a single six-year term for the president, stating that "Limiting each president to one six-year term would enhance the objectivity and public acceptance of the measures he urges in the national interest." Why? Have the proposals of second-term presidents received greater public acceptance since the ratification of the 22nd Amendment? Obviously not.

Let us not allow pipe dreams of constitutional reform to blind us to the positive virtues of a true separation of powers or distract us from the task of making our political system work.

SOURCE: This article appeared in the letters to the editor column of *Foreign Affairs* as a critical commentary and rebuttal to Lloyd Cutler, "To Form a Government."

# 14. In Defense of Separation of Powers   II

## James Q. Wilson

... To paraphrase Winston Churchill, the separation of powers is a poor philosophy of government, except in comparison with all others. It has its defects, ... perhaps notably with respect to the conduct of foreign affairs, but it has the virtues of those defects as well. It facilitates scrutiny, sometimes at the expense of action; it protects the particular and the individual, sometimes at the expense of the general. But it has brought about the capacity to engage in great national commitments when important national emergencies arise, and above all it has permitted a union to be created out of great diversity by providing separate constitutional places on which individuals could focus their loyalties. ...

Mr. Cutler has a philosophy of governance that is at odds with what the framers of the Constitution embodied in that document. To Mr. Cutler good policy or good government is the product or the act of a single will. It is an act of management, of allocation, of balance. The framers, by contrast, thought that good policy could be recognized when it appeared, but to achieve it in the real world required a process of ambition counteracting ambition, leading thereby to the formation of coalitions — coalitions of partial, self-interested groups. They hoped the Constitution would lead these coalitions to emerge only on the principle of the common good.

This has not always happened, but it is a first approximation of their effort. The difficulty and magnitude of our problems are admittedly great, but no greater than the problems other presidents in post centuries have had to deal with, and intellectually it is unlikely that we can devise a program that corresponds to a theory of governance based on the act of a single will or intelligence. Politically, it is unlikely that we can devise institutions that could translate that will, if formulated, into a desirable result.

Consider Great Britain. ... I do not see that great steady hand, that even philosophy of governance, that striking for balances emerging from the parliamentary system. Great Britain has nationalized and denationalized industry at a dizzying rate. It has perhaps the worst labor-management relations of any western democracy. It has had extraordinary difficulties in deciding whether it will remain part of the European Community. I have profound sympathies with Britain's difficulties, because we would have had as many; those difficulties do not suggest that, once the appropriate parliamentary devices are in place there is a will, which, when revealed, will produce altogether good effects. ...

*James Q. Wilson teaches political science at Harvard University and is the author of several books including* Thinking about Crime *and* Political Organizations.

I grant some force to [Mr. Cutler's] argument with respect to the conduct of foreign affairs, but in general it does not correspond to what the American people expect. They do not wish to have an opportunity to vote yes or no on a party's cohesive performance in office, in which it takes responsibility for the policies that have been put in place, because the American public does not exist as a public. It is a collection of separate publics that have discovered, or would readily admit if it were pointed out, that if they have to vote yes or no on a comprehensive set of policies, they cannot do so. They are torn with too many internal contradictions.

During the last 200 years, the people more or less successfuly have modified policies by taking up the various constitutional opportunities presented to them — off-term elections for the House, six-year terms for the Senate, presidential elections, the congressional oversight process, the lobbying process, campaign contributions — as a way of giving expression to particular preferences, which the unlucky folk in Washington must cope with and try to put together into a coalition around each issue. This creates great difficulties for those who govern, difficulties so great that many persons, especially those associated with activist presidents, have regularly published books about "the deadlock of democracy." Whenever the deadlock is broken, however, as they allege it has been in recent years, they then write about the imperial presidency. That does not seem to be desirable, either. I agree that an imperial presidency is a mistake, but we have not had an imperial presidency, with perhaps a few exceptions.

The deadlock of democracy is not a deadlock at all; in the 1930s, the 1960s, and [now more recently], our system produced an extraordinary outpouring of legislative innovation because certain ideas were sufficiently coherent to permit change to occur.

The people are unwilling to vote simply yes or no in a national referendum about the record of a party because the people are too various. They want these diverse opportunities to peck and chip and constrain in order to moderate policy. If we compare American policy with that of most parliamentary democracies, its leading characteristic is its moderation. There are many policies I do not approve of and regularly call immoderate. Taken as a whole, however, we tend to temper the enthusiasm of temporary majorities by the need constantly to reformulate that majority. . . .

I wish we would not agree so readily that America has a foreign policy that is a hodgepodge. I disagree with many elements of it and certain tendencies of it, but we are speaking now of a country that won World War II, that put in place European reconstruction, that rearmed the West, that created the NATO alliance, that gave aid to Greece and Turkey, that established a ring of alliances that gave some hope to democratic regimes in all parts of the world, and that fought Communist interventionism when it was not in our material interests to do so. Although we have surely made mistakes in the pursuit of all these objectives, that is not such bad policy. Would a stronger president have been a better one? Did General de Gaulle have a better policy when he was president of France, with certainly all the power he could have wished?

With respect to the budget, I agree that the budget cycle, which Mr. Cutler accurately describes, proves conclusively that the public interest differs from the summation of private wants (something that my colleagues in political science like to deny, but this fact establishes it). The question is, How do we deal with that? I am not sure it is by having a stronger president who can say, "This is my budget, take it or leave it." President Johnson did this during the Vietnam war and decided to print money to finance the deficit.

Perhaps we must have a sharper restriction on the budget. Though we have not mentioned it so far, if constitutional revision is to occur, perhaps we should consider a budget limitation linked to gross national product and public expenditures. . . .

Once you start unraveling [a] sweater, it all starts coming apart. You cannot change one part of the system without, as Mr. Cutler has indicated, thinking about changing all parts of the system. If we have the president calling a congressional election or the Congress forcing a presidential election, we have to change the party system. This means we have to change the degree of control the national government has over state governments, because ultimately they control the local party systems. We have to force a different kind of primary or convention system. This alters the relationship between the state governments and the parties. I cannot, because I lack the wit, imagine all of the additional permutations that are implied. My point is simple: There are no simple changes in the Constitution. . . .

I am not confident there are institutional strategies to achieve [a sustained national consensus]. Among the reasons why there is not only disagreement but in some quarters disaffection about the government is that the government has promised more than it could achieve and has done so at the expense of inflating the currency and harming, in a very visible way, a style of life that most Americans thought was their birthright.

The source of my ultimate skepticism about Mr. Cutler's proposal is doubt that institutional reforms of the sort he proposes would do anything more than feed this process by enlarging expectations, enlarging the role of the president as a national leader conducting not an election but a plebiscite. The president's proposals would be put forward, based on assembling a coalition by offering as much as possible to as many as possible. Though this would sound good in the short run, it would lead to enlarged, and ultimately frustrated, expectations.

The problem is that government is too large. . . . I am looking for ways of making government more modest and, at the same time, more moderate. Perhaps this can be done by constitutional limitations on spending; perhaps it can be done by other, less drastic means to force choices. I am not convinced, however, that this process will be facilitated by enhancing the power of the executive to ask for a yes-or-no vote on his program, because those programs that have received yes votes have produced this problem we now face. . . .

I am ordinarily not cast in the role of reformer, but if reforms are to be sought, we should seek them from within the American experience on the basis of those institutional arrangements to which the American people have become accustomed. We should not reach overseas for an approximation of the parliamentary system; we should look at state and city governments in this country and ask what modifications in federal arrangements already tested at the city and state levels might commend themselves. Many governors have, in fact, line-item vetos awarded to them by state constitutions. Many city charters deny to city councils the right to increase the executive budget.

None of them, so far as I know, allows the governor or the mayor to force a new election, or vice versa, nor does any require the abolition of the separation of powers. These modest changes, which would require, as Mr. Cutler says, constitutional change, are the sorts of changes on which we could focus attention with a greater confidence that we know what we would get as a result.

SOURCE: James Q. Wilson's remarks are taken from a dialogue in which he, along with others, discussed Lloyd Cutler's proposals; reprinted in AEI Forum, *President vs. Congress: Does the Separation of Powers Still Work?* Reprinted with permission.

# Presidents and the Public

# VI

**15. Great Expectations:
What People Want from Presidents**

*Stephen J. Wayne*

**16. Presidential Manipulation
of Public Opinion**

*George C. Edwards III*

**17. Monopolizing the Public Space:
The President as a Problem
for Democratic Politics**

*Bruce Miroff*

**18. The Rise of the Rhetorical Presidency**

*James Ceaser
Glen E. Thurow
Jeffrey Tulis
Joseph M. Bessette*

# 15. Great Expectations: What People Want from Presidents

## Stephen J. Wayne

What do Americans expect from a president? How have these expectations and demands changed over the years? What do they suggest about public values, needs, and support for the president?

How Americans view the president affects what he does, how he does it, and whether he is thought to have succeeded or failed. It affects the scope of his job, the extent of his power and his ability to lead or be led. It influences his appearance, his manner, even his behavior in office. Expectations shape evaluations, and evaluations, in turn, affect the capacity to get things done.

Knowing what these expectations are is important for the president. It gives him a sense of critical needs, a prescription for governing, and a means for anticipating reactions to his policies. It provides guidelines for representation and criteria for judging performance in office.

Surprisingly, there have been few studies that have focused on expectations per se. While there is a substantial literature on the public aspects of the presidency, it has been primarily concerned with approval ratings, information acquisition, and attitude formation. This literature, however, contributes to an understanding of expectations by identifying, and to a limited extent, measuring the forces that affect perceptions, attitudes, and evaluations of the president.

### Studies of Public Opinion

Leadership of public opinion has long been considered an important source of presidential power. As early as 1908, Professor Woodrow Wilson said that a president's ability to persuade the country contributed mightily to his capacity to influence Congress:

> The President is at liberty, both in law and conscience, to be as big a man as he can. His capacity will set the limit; and if Congress be overborne by him, it will be no fault of the makers of the Constitution, — it will be from no lack of constitutional powers on its part, but only because the President has the nation behind him, and Congress has not. He has no means of compelling Congress except through public opinion.[1]

*Stephen J. Wayne teaches political science at George Washington University and is the author of* The Legislative Presidency *and* The Road to the White House.

Wilson took his own words literally as president. While he probably over-estimated his ability to sway the nation behind the Versailles Treaty and League of Nations, he did show the potential of public opinion as an important source of presidential influence, one which Franklin Roosevelt used so successfully during the Depression and World War Two. Roosevelt's mobilization of public opinion became the example for others to emulate.

Professor Richard E. Neustadt described the Rooseveltian model in his 1960 classic, *Presidential Power.* Neustadt argued that prestige with the public was an important determinant of whether a president could get his way:

> Presidential influence on government becomes, in part, a matter of direct relationships with special-purpose publics. And the members of a special public . . . are often swayed by what they think the general public thinks of him.[2]
>
> A President's prestige is thus a factor in his influence of roughly the same sort as his professional reputation: a fact that may not decide the outcome in a given case but can affect the likelihoods in every case and therefore is strategically important to his power.[3]

Subsequent presidents have attempted to heed Neustadt's words and well they should. Political scientists have found that popularity and public support do contribute to a president's influence, particularly with Congress.[4]

What causes variations in public support? Are these variations a consequence of what the president does or are they a product of forces not subject to his direct or even indirect control? Political scientists have labored long and hard to find the answers.

### Measuring Support for the President

In one of the earlier and more influential attempts to identify the forces that affect presidential popularity, John Mueller suggested that the international situation and the state of the economy contributed to short-run changes in public approval of the president. He added, however, that it was actions by the president himself that ultimately explained why he became less popular in the long run.[5] By making decisions, Mueller theorized, a president will inevitably alienate some of the electoral coalition that supported him. Defections from this coalition will thus reduce his popularity. Mueller labeled this the "coalition of minorities" variable.[6]

The inevitability of declining popularity led another political scientist, James Stimson, to conclude that only time mattered in explaining the drop in presidential support from the time a person enters office until the time he leaves.[7] According to Stimson, people hold unrealistic expectations of a newly elected president. When these expectations are not realized, the public becomes disillusioned and its support for the president declines. A quest for reelection might temporarily increase it, but the popularity of an incumbent who is reelected can be expected to drop during his second term.

While Mueller and Stimson agreed on the importance of time in assessing changes in presidential popularity, they disagreed over the cause of these changes. For Mueller, it was presidential actions and decisions; for Stimson it could have been the lack of decisions, or, at least, the inability to meet expectations.

The problem with both these studies is the meaning of the word "time." [8] As used by Mueller and Stimson, it clouds more than it reveals. In a sense, time explains everything, but in another sense, it explains nothing. Presidential support may decline in the long run, but what causes it to rise and fall in the short run? Is it something within the environment or endemic to the office itself?

One way to answer this question is to examine the relationship between external events and short-term fluctuations in evaluations of the president. In doing so, political scientists have looked at three types of environmental factors: those that pertain to *the economy,* those that relate to *international affairs,* and those that draw attention to *the president himself.* Considered as independent variables, these factors have been proposed as the causes for changes in the approval/disapproval ratings of the president. Approval/disapproval has been considered, for the most part, the dependent variable — the item that needs to be explained. In most studies, it is measured by responses to the frequently asked Gallup Poll question: Do you approve or disapprove of the way President ———————— is handling his job? Figure 1 summarizes the order of these relationships.

The economic measures that have been used include rate of inflation, level of unemployment, amount of real personal income, consumer price increases, private consumption expenditures, even the stock market performance. Of these, the rate of inflation has been the one found to be most closely related to approval or disapproval of the president.[9] The higher the rate of inflation, the greater the disapproval. The response of the public to changing economic conditions, however, tends to be sluggish.[10] This has led some researchers to conclude that it is the perception of these conditions rather than the conditions themselves that affects the evaluation of the job the president is doing.[11]

The presence or absence of war, the progress of armed conflict, the number of

*Figure 1. The Dynamics of Presidential Support*

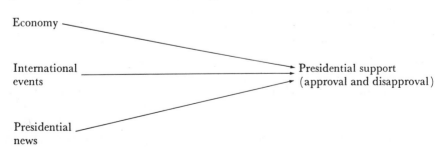

Americans killed in action, and the amount of military expenditures have all been explored as possible indicators of how international affairs can affect the president.[12] Of these, conflict situations have the greatest long-term impact, although most salient international events will affect presidential support, at least in the short run. The events, particularly those that threaten national security, become rallying points for the citizenry. People are not indiscriminate, however, in their support of the president. International set-backs will decrease his support, even in the short run.[13]

The third group of variables pertains to the president himself: the amount of news about him, the portion that is good, and the public's evaluation of his performance in office. Being popular contributes to public approval as does good news.[14]

In short, a variety of external factors, some of which a president can influence directly and some of which he cannot, affects his popularity and, ultimately, his political support. The range of these factors testifies to the size of the office. Getting credit for good times and blame for bad times indicates how large presidential roles and responsibilities have become, at least in the public's mind.

The effect of external events on the president's popularity, however, is not immediate or necessarily uniform among the population. There is often a lag between a condition and a change in the public's evaluation of the president.[15] Moreover, segments within the society often respond in different ways. This suggests that environmental forces alone are not the only variables that explain how a president is perceived or what is expected of him. The beliefs, attitudes, and values people have also color their expectations and affect their evaluations. These beliefs, attitudes, and values constitute a conceptual framework in which events are interpreted and judgments formed. That is why it is important to consider their development in understanding public perceptions of the president.

### Discerning Beliefs and Attitudes

A considerable body of literature has focused on the ways in which people learn about government. Since learning begins at a young age, many of these so called "socialization" studies concern children and the formation of their beliefs.[16]

In their early years, children possess a benevolent, almost idealistic view of government. They see it largely in personal terms. The president is the best known and most admired official to come to their attention initially. Seen as a kind, dependable, powerful person (a father figure), he is the embodiment of the national government.[17]

As children become older, they begin to acquire critical skills and analytic abilities. The critical skills provide them with the capacity to evaluate leaders on the basis of what they do rather than simply on the basis of what positions they hold. The analytic abilities enable them to distinguish between people and institutions. While the tendency to evaluate the government in personal terms persists, even for adults, the gap between the person in the office and the office itself tends to widen. It is the office that becomes conceived in ideal terms, and the person who is appraised on a more human dimension (i.e., with warts and all).

Evaluative skills and conceptual processes are not developed uniformly. People mature at different speeds and ultimately reach different levels of understanding. Why some are better able than others to reason and make critical judgments may be in part a product of their education, their age, even their socioeconomic environment. It may also be related to their ethnic background, sex, or race.

In general, the more educated people are, the more knowledgeable and sophisticated they tend to be about government. That is why increases in education, in age (particularly for preadolescents), and in socioeconomic status should not only result in greater information and awareness, but in more political participation. The better people understand how the government affects them, the more likely they are to attempt to influence it. Ignorance, on the other hand, tends to breed apathy and disinterest.

Political support is also related to education, but inversely related. More educated people tend to be more critical.[18] The greater the capacity to use critical skills, the less blind adoration is placed in leaders and the less confidence in their ability to solve complex national problems.

While education may be the most important variable in explaining levels of support for the president, it is not the only one. The ability to reason and evaluate varies with age, at least through school years. Similarly, socioeconomic status, race, and even sex affect beliefs and values. While status (including income, profession, and class) tends to vary directly with education, it may also have an independent effect on the opinions and priorities people have. For instance, high social position and/or professional occupation may substitute for the lack of education among some, or it may produce additional shared values among others.

To the extent that people are influenced by their associations and their roles, they often adopt common traits that affect and, more importantly, differentiate their values and beliefs from one another. Women, for example, have tended to place a higher priority on compassion and concern for the less fortunate, while men often rate power, strength, and decisiveness as more important leadership attributes.[19] These respective orientations naturally affect expectations of what a president should do and judgments of how well he is doing it.

Social, racial, and ethnic groupings also lead to differing perceptions and judgments, even among children. Researchers have found that black and rural Appalachian children adopt less positive evaluations of the president than do others of similar ages. They were more negative toward Richard Nixon and Ronald Reagan than were white children, but they were on the other hand more positive toward John Kennedy and Lyndon Johnson.[20]

In general, those who have suffered racial discrimination and/or economic deprivation tend to have a more ambivalent attitude toward leadership. On the one hand, they are less trusting toward those with whom they cannot identify and might even regard as adversaries. On the other, their concentration in the lower educational and socioeconomic levels provides them with less incentive and capacity to evaluate performance critically. In the end, this can produce greater fluctuations in their approval/disapproval ratings.[21]

Finally, psychological factors also influence how people feel about their leaders. The president serves certain psychological needs of the public,[22] but the public's psychological needs also condition attitudes toward the president. To cite but one example, people who are inflexible tend to be most supportive of strong leadership. Their "authoritarian personalities" generate a desire for direction and a sympathy for concentrated power. Moreover, those with less flexible personalities tend to be less tolerant of behavior that digresses from the norm.

How does this all affect expectations and evaluations? How much confidence do people have in the president? Can he expect increasing or decreasing support in the years ahead? According to three California political scientists, presidential support is likely to decline. Writing in 1975, they stated:

> Presidential support is disproportionately located among citizens who are older, of fundamentalist religious persuasion, have fewer years of formal schooling, and may be described as psychologically inflexible. Yet the population is becoming younger, less likely to belong to fundamentalist sects, possessing additional years of formal education, and is more likely to be psychologically flexible. Other things being equal, therefore, these long-term, secular changes in the population would lead to a drop in support for Presidents.[23]

If the thesis of declining support is true, then it augurs trouble for the president.

The remainder of this essay will explore confidence in the president and support for his leadership. It will do so by examining the ingredients of presidential leadership today: the range of expectations concerning the office; the qualities and characteristics deemed essential for him to possess; levels of tolerance for various kinds of behavior by the president. Both the aggregate beliefs of the general public and the disaggregated views of groups within it will be presented. The objective will be to identify those sociodemographic and attitudinal variables that affect contemporary expectations and evaluations. In this way, the potential for future presidential support can be assessed.

## Contemporary Expectations and Evaluations

In the fall of 1979 a nationwide poll, conducted by the Gallup organization, elicited information on public perceptions and attitudes toward the president. The survey, commissioned by WHYY-TV (Philadelphia-Wilmington) for its public television series, *Every Four Years,* included 45 open and closed-ended questions on the president. In addition, data on the demographic characteristics, partisan attitudes and regional distribution of the sample was also collected. The responses of 1520 adults, 18 years of age and older, were analyzed.[24] Here are some of the more interesting findings.

## Responsibilities and Powers

The American public demands a lot from the president and is willing to entrust him with considerable authority. Expectations of his roles and responsibilities have grown substantially in recent years, while public satisfaction in job performance has declined.

What is the president's job? Almost half the sample saw the making of foreign policy primarily as a presidential responsibility,[25] but opinion was divided whether the president or Congress should handle domestic affairs.

The willingness to rely on the president's initiative for policy-making varied with the level of education. College graduates were much more likely to be supportive of congressional responsibilities, particularly in the domestic arena, than were those with only grade school or high school educations. College graduates were also more likely to perceive the impact of the president on their daily lives, although most respondents acknowledged that presidential actions and policies had some effect.

While expectations of what the president should do have increased, and perceptions of impact remain large, satisfaction in his job performance declined. A majority of people expressed little or no confidence in Congress or in President Carter's ability to handle what they perceived as the nation's most critical problem, and almost one third of the respondents believed that no president could effectively deal with this issue.

While variations occurred among sexual, racial, and partisan groupings, the greatest distinctions were among education and income levels. Those with the lowest income and the least formal education displayed the most confidence in Carter and Congress, and, conversely, those with higher income and more education were more critical. This conforms to findings in the literature that sug-

*Table 1. The Policy-making Responsibilities of Congress and the Presidency*

**Survey Question:**
Some people think that the president ought to have the major responsibility for making policy, while other people think that Congress ought to have the major responsibilities. In general, which do you think should have the major responsibility for setting (foreign) (economic) (energy) policy?

**Responses:**

| | *Policy* | | | |
|---|---|---|---|---|
| *Institution* | *Foreign policy* | *Economic policy* | *Energy policy* | *General responsibility* |
| President | 49% | 34% | 35% | 37% |
| Equal | 18 | 20 | 19 | 22 |
| Congress | 27 | 40 | 40 | 36 |
| Don't know | 6 | 6 | 6 | 5 |

gest education generates greater substantive knowledge and more highly developed analytic and critical skills.

The association between education and awareness was confirmed by the responses to two other questions: one that asked people to indicate the number of aides on the president's staff and the other that asked them to identify some of them. In both instances, those with college educations provided the largest percentage of correct responses. However, the amount of information revealed even by these educated respondents was still low, very low. Forty percent of the sample could not even guess the size of the president's staff, while another forty percent said it was 100 or less. Despite the concern which is periodically voiced about the size of the White House, only 4 percent of the respondents thought the president had 600 or more people working for him. Even less was known about the people themselves. Fifty-seven percent could not name one single presidential aide!

## Personal Qualities

While no single factor stood out in the public's mind as the main reason why contemporary presidents were having difficulties, many people saw the need for increased power as part of the solution.

Interestingly, those with less education and lower incomes were more disposed to a stronger presidency. Similarly, nonwhites expressed greater willingness to enlarge the scope of the president's powers than did whites. A strong association between role and power was also evident. Those perceiving larger presidential responsibilities were more willing to invest the office with greater power.

Associated with the desire for a stronger institution was a reordering of the most important qualities for the head of the institution to have. Being politically savvy, demonstrating forcefulness and decisiveness, inspiring public confidence, and exercising sound judgment during crises were cited more frequently than they had been five years earlier when Gallup included a similar item on a nationwide survey.

With the exception of crisis judgment, the emphasis placed on the other attributes seemed to reflect a good deal of dissatisfaction with President Carter. It is not surprising that perceptions of leadership are inevitably influenced and often made concrete by events of the present and memories of the past. In order to determine the extent to which presidents have shaped contemporary conceptions of the office, people were asked to name the president they wished were in office and the reasons why they believed such an individual would make a good president. Table 2 lists the responses to the first question by sex, race, party and age. Table 3 lists the responses to the second question by sex, race, party and education.

Table 2 contains some surprises. Supporters of Harry Truman were almost equally divided among Democrats, Republicans, and Independents. Blacks overwhelmingly preferred Kennedy to Franklin Roosevelt. They also provided John-

*Table 2. Preferences for Past Presidents*

**Survey Question:**

Of all the presidents we have ever had, whom do you wish were president today?

**Responses:**

| | | | | | | | | | | | |
|---|---|---|---|---|---|---|---|---|---|---|---|
| | | | | | | *Respondents* | | | | | |
| | *All* | *Sex* | | *Race* | | *Party* | | | *Age* | | |
| *Presidents* | | *M* | *F* | *W* | *NW* | *R* | *D* | *I* | *18–34* | *35–49* | *50–64* | *65+* |
| Kennedy | 33% | 29 | 36 | 29 | 62 | 14 | 42 | 30 | 44 | 35 | 23 | 16 |
| Roosevelt, F. | 16 | 16 | 17 | 16 | 17 | 11 | 24 | 11 | 9 | 12 | 23 | 31 |
| Truman | 13 | 16 | 11 | 15 | 2 | 12 | 13 | 15 | 6 | 17 | 20 | 16 |
| Eisenhower | 6 | 6 | 6 | 7 | 1 | 15 | 2 | 7 | 5 | 8 | 6 | 8 |
| Lincoln | 5 | 5 | 6 | 6 | 2 | 10 | 2 | 7 | 7 | 5 | 3 | 4 |
| Ford | 4 | 4 | 4 | 4 | — | 10 | 1 | 4 | 4 | 4 | 4 | 4 |
| Nixon | 3 | 4 | 2 | 3 | — | 5 | 2 | 3 | 4 | 1 | 2 | 3 |
| Roosevelt, T. | 2 | 3 | 2 | 2 | — | 7 | 1 | 1 | 2 | 3 | 2 | 2 |
| Carter | 2 | 2 | 2 | 2 | 4 | — | 2 | 3 | 2 | 2 | 2 | 2 |
| Johnson, L. | 1 | 1 | 2 | 1 | 6 | 1 | 2 | 1 | 1 | 2 | 1 | 2 |
| Washington | 1 | 2 | 1 | 1 | 1 | 1 | 1 | 3 | 2 | 1 | 1 | 1 |
| Jefferson | 1 | 1 | 1 | 1 | — | 1 | — | — | — | 1 | — | — |
| Other | 2 | 3 | 1 | 2 | — | 3 | 1 | 2 | 2 | 1 | 2 | 1 |
| Don't know | 11 | 10 | 12 | 12 | 5 | 11 | 8 | 13 | 13 | 9 | 10 | 10 |

NOTE: Total percentages do not equal 100% due to rounding.

son and Carter with more backing than did any other group. Younger people, particularly those in the 18–34 age bracket, chose Kennedy, while those 50 to 64 were divided among Roosevelt, Truman, and Kennedy supporters. Those 65 and over fondly remember FDR, but that is where their memory ended. The heroes of the more distant past received scant mention from any group.

The specificity of the responses in Table 3 seems to be explained largely by the level of education. Those who had not attended college tended to provide more general assessments while college graduates were more precise, citing strong leadership and forcefulness in office as the most redeeming qualities of their particular president. Only one other trait received more frequent mention than strong leadership. More than one-third of the black respondents indicated that concern for the average citizen was the reason they believe their favorite president would be good today, an understandable reaction in the light of the social and economic discrimination they have suffered over the years.

Individually, these responses hint at the reasons for group preferences. Collectively, they contribute to a profile of the most desirable presidential traits. These traits present what might be regarded as a masculine view of leadership

Table 3. *Desirable Qualities of Past Presidents*

**Survey Question:**
Why would he (past president) make a good president today?

**Responses:**

| | | Respondents | | | | | | | | | |
|---|---|---|---|---|---|---|---|---|---|---|---|
| | | Sex | | Race | | Party ID | | | Education | | |
| Quality | All | M | F | W | NW | R | D | I | Grade school | High school | College |
| *General* | | | | | | | | | | | |
| Was a good/better president | 21% | 17 | 26 | 21 | 28 | 19 | 22 | 23 | 23 | 24 | 16 |
| *Leadership* | | | | | | | | | | | |
| Strong | 21 | 25 | 18 | 23 | 13 | 26 | 20 | 20 | 17 | 18 | 30 |
| Forceful | 12 | 13 | 11 | 13 | 5 | 12 | 11 | 14 | 10 | 11 | 15 |
| Ability to get things done | 11 | 12 | 9 | 11 | 7 | 14 | 10 | 9 | 12 | 11 | 9 |
| Decisive | 10 | 13 | 7 | 10 | 5 | 10 | 9 | 10 | 5 | 10 | 11 |
| In control | 3 | 3 | 2 | 3 | 3 | 3 | 3 | 2 | 2 | 3 | 3 |
| *Personal* | | | | | | | | | | | |
| Concern for average citizen | 16 | 12 | 19 | 13 | 35 | 9 | 17 | 17 | 18 | 17 | 10 |
| Honest | 12 | 10 | 14 | 13 | 8 | 12 | 10 | 15 | 7 | 13 | 12 |
| Forthright | 7 | 8 | 6 | 7 | 3 | 10 | 6 | 6 | 7 | 6 | 8 |
| Placed country's interest ahead of politics | 4 | 5 | 4 | 4 | 4 | 4 | 4 | 6 | 6 | 3 | 6 |
| Intelligent | 4 | 4 | 4 | 4 | 2 | 3 | 4 | 5 | 3 | 4 | 5 |
| *Abilities* | | | | | | | | | | | |
| Had confidence of people | 11 | 10 | 11 | 12 | 5 | 12 | 12 | 9 | 9 | 11 | 11 |
| Good policies | 10 | 10 | 9 | 9 | 14 | 8 | 11 | 7 | 10 | 9 | 10 |
| Handle the economy | 9 | 8 | 9 | 8 | 13 | 8 | 9 | 8 | 12 | 9 | 7 |
| Foreign policy | 5 | 6 | 4 | 6 | 4 | 6 | 6 | 4 | 5 | 5 | 7 |
| *Don't know* | 2 | 1 | 2 | 2 | 1 | 1 | 1 | 3 | 2 | 2 | 1 |

on the part of most of the population. Being strong, forceful and decisive, inspiring confidence, and solving policy problems were seen as the keys to success.

## Standards of Behavior

A president is expected to conform to acceptable standards of appearance and behavior. In government, as in politics, the norm is often considered the ideal. Thus a president must embody society's most redeeming values, certainly not flout them.

This is not to suggest, however, that values and mores do not change. The 1960s witnessed a significant evolution in a variety of social behaviors. This evolution appears to have altered the public's conception of what is acceptable for the president.

The survey inquired whether people would strongly object if the president engaged in behavior long considered taboo. If he: smoked marijuana occasionally; told ethnic or racial jokes in private; was not a member of a church; used tranquilizers occasionally; used profane language in private; had seen a psychiatrist; wore blue jeans occasionally in the Oval Office; were divorced; had a cocktail before dinner each night. A majority of respondents said yes to only one of them — the occasional smoking of marijuana.

The analysis of these responses revealed that a larger percentage of women than men objected strongly to each of the activities except seeing a psychiatrist. A larger percentage of nonwhites than whites objected strongly to each of these behaviors except the occasional smoking of pot, although a majority of nonwhites objected to this as well. The percentage of objectors, those with the less tolerance, seemed to vary directly with age and indirectly with education. The older people were and the less formal education they had, the more likely they would object strongly to the specified behavior. In general, those with lower incomes also voiced greater objection.

Levels of tolerance also varied among regions of the country. A larger percentage of respondents in the South and Midwest voiced strong objection to each of the behaviors mentioned with the exception of the president occasionally wearing blue jeans in the Oval Office. Of these two regions, the South appeared to be slightly less tolerant, particularly with respect to the president drinking a nightly cocktail and using profane language in private.

Interesting differences among party identifiers were also apparent. A larger percentage of Republicans than Democrats or Independents objected to the smoking of marijuana, wearing of blue jeans, and not belonging to a church. Of all the presidential supporters, those who wished Eisenhower were president registered the most objection. Almost one-fourth of Eisenhower's supporters raised strong objections to a president's having a cocktail before dinner and almost one-half to his using profane language in private. But according to scholars, Eisenhower frequently had a cocktail before dinner. And when angry, Ike allegedly could curse like a trooper.

## Conclusion

The presidency continues to be viewed as a large multifaceted office and the president as the wearer of many hats. Job expectations have grown, probably beyond the collective and individual capacities of the institution and the incumbent to respond. This has produced growing public disenchantment which in the short run has contributed to decline in the popularity of recent presidents and a loss of confidence in their ability (and also that of the Congress) to deal with the nation's most pressing problems. In the long run, however, it may actually increase patience with existing leadership.

Because of the perceived gap between expectations and performance, there seems to be more support for strengthening the presidency. In contrast to the post-Watergate era when abuses of power were uppermost in the public's mind, respondents at the end of the 1970s expressed the view that the presidency might not be powerful enough, that strong leadership is more desirable than it is dangerous.

Strength is only one of the leadership skills that have been reevaluated in the light of contemporary events. Political expertise has also increased in importance. The ability to be forceful and decisive, to make good policy, and to inspire confidence are remembered as the qualities of previous presidents that would be most useful today.

The survey does not indicate, however, that all the lessons of the late 1960s and the early to mid-1970s have been forgotten. High ethical standards, integrity, candor, honesty, empathy, and compassion are still considered necessary attributes. The public continues to evaluate a president on the basis of an ideal type, except perhaps during an election, when comparison is made to his opponent.

Differences persist in attitudes, expectations and evaluations within the population. A key explanation of these differences is the level of education. Variations in knowledge of the presidency, perceptions of impact, confidence in leadership and even tolerance for nonstandard behavior were evident among grade school, high school and college graduates. In general, those with more education were more informed, more critical, and at the same time more tolerant.

These findings are consistent with the studies that suggest that the amount of information and the capacity to evaluate increase with education. If confidence in the president can be considered an indicator of presidential approval (and hence, a measure of support), then the results of this study also at least partially confirm the inverse relationship which analysts have found between presidential support and level of education. However, it does not necessarily follow that simply because the population is becoming better educated, support for the president will inevitably decline.

A variety of factors could have the effect of actually increasing public support in the long run. In addition to the psychological, political, and social forces that contribute to a president's prestige and reputation, tolerance of the president may be enhanced and expectations of the office lessened by increased education. Changes are already in the wind. There is some recognition on the part of the general public that certain problems are beyond the capacity of any president to solve. Moreover, there seems to be a willingness to tolerate a range of personal behavior long considered taboo. In short, disappointment over time may lower expectations.

Other characteristics such as sex and race were also associated with expectations and attitudes toward the president. Sexual differences fell along largely predictable lines. Men desired a more powerful president than women. They remembered the virtues of past leaders in terms of their strength, forcefulness, and decisiveness, while women placed greater emphasis on the president's compassion and his concern for the average citizen. Consistent with their more macho view of leadership, male respondents tended to be less satisfied with the extent of the institution's powers, more desirous of entrusting the president with greater authority, and less fearful that strong leadership would be dangerous. These sexual differences also conform to findings in much of the literature that men are more power-oriented and more willing to use force than women who, in turn, have been found to be more sensitive to social and economic needs than men.

Finally, the responses of nonwhites indicate more ambivalence toward power than whites. Nonwhites were *more* likely to believe the president had too little power but also *more* likely to believe strong leadership might be dangerous and *less* likely to conclude such leadership was necessary. Placing greater emphasis than whites on the president's need to provide economic leadership and be responsive to the average citizen, they also voiced more confidence in Congress's and President Carter's ability to deal with the most important national problems.

In sum, expectations of the president reflect group attitudes. How people are socialized colors their perceptions of government and their expectations of its leaders. The socialization process provides stability for these perceptions and expectations. It does not, however, preclude their change.

Environmental conditions, institutional relationships and individual behavior, particularly of those in office, alter beliefs over time and affect judgment of what can and should be done. There have been shifts in attitudes toward the presidency, but there have been continuities as well. The shifts relate principally to the characteristics, qualities, and behavior that would be most desirable, or at least acceptable, for the president. The continuities pertain primarily to the responsibilities of the office, the function of the president, and his standards of performance. With respect to the job, past expectations guide present performance and serve as the major criteria for evaluating it. With respect to the individual, traditional standards as modified by evolving social mores condition his qualifications for office, qualities of leadership, and behavior as president.

A president must be aware of these expectations if he is to act responsibly. That is part of what democratic leadership is all about. But the public has responsibilities too, responsibilities that pertain to the acquisition of information about public affairs and to participation in the political process. People need to know what a president says and does if they are to judge him accurately. Unrealistic expectations produce disappointment and frustration on the part of both the citizenry and its leaders. For the system to operate successfully, the gap between expectations and performance should not be wide.

SOURCE: Revision of a paper entitled "Expectations of the President," presented at the 1980 Annual Meeting of the American Political Science Association, Washington, D.C., August 28–31, 1980. Copyright by the Americal Political Science Association. The author gratefully acknowledges permission of WHYY-TV (Philadelphia-Wilmington) to use data collected by the Gallup organization for its television series, *Every Four Years,* aired in January and February, 1980.

## Notes

1. Woodrow Wilson, *Constitutional Government in the United States* (New York: Columbia University Press, 1980), pp. 70–71.
2. Richard E. Neustadt, *Presidential Power* (New York: John Wiley, 1976), pp. 158–159.
3. Ibid., 160–161.
4. George C. Edwards III, *Presidential Influence in Congress* (San Francisco: W.H. Freeman, 1980), pp. 86–115; Harvey G. Zeidenstein, "Presidential Popularity and Presidential Support in Congress: Eisenhower to Carter," *Presidential Studies Quarterly,* 10 (Summer 1980), 224–233.
5. John E. Mueller, *War, Presidents and Public Opinion* (New York: John Wiley, 1973).
6. If a president seeks reelection, he rebuilds this coalition. But after his victory, his popularity begins to wane as his new decisions adversely affect some of his supporters. Mueller's theory suggests that those presidents who champion fewer causes are likely to remain more popular. Dwight Eisenhower is the obvious example; Reagan may be another. (*Ibid.,* pp. 196–241.)
7. James A Stimson, "Public Support for American Presidents: A Cyclical Model," *Public Opinion Quarterly,* 40 (Spring 1976), 1–21.
8. According to Samuel Kernell "Time... has no inherent theoretical meaning." It acts as a summary measure, one that synthesizes all the forces that affect presidential popularity. If Kernell is correct, then time can be used to confirm the validity of any thesis that explains a decline in popularity. Kernell goes on to explain that it is necessary to disaggregate the forces that may affect popularity and attempt to measure their impact on short-term movements in the president's standing with the general public. Samuel Kernell, "Explaining Presidential Popularity," *American Political Science Review,* 72 (June 1978), 508.
9. Henry C. Kenski, "Inflation and Presidential Popularity," *Public Opinion Quarterly,* 41 (Spring 1977), 86–90.
10. Kernell, "Explaining Presidential Popularity," p. 515. In addition to the lag between economic conditions and changes in public support for the president, it has also been suggested that the public responds to cumulative change. The president is held responsible for sustained inflation, not for brief intervals in which prices rise. Kristen R. Monroe, "Inflation and Presidential Popularity," *Presidential Studies Quarterly,* 9 (Summer 1979), 339.
11. Robert Y. Shapiro and Bruce M. Conforto, "Presidential Performance, the Economy and the Public's Evaluation of Economic Conditions," *Journal of Politics,* 42 (February 1980), 49–67.

12. Jong R. Lee and Jeffrey S. Milstein, "A Political Economy of the Vietnam War, 1965–1977," Papers, *Peace Science Society* (International, 21 (1973), 41–63. Jeffrey S. Milstein, *Dynamics of the Vietnam War: A Quantitative Analysis and Predictive Computer Simulation* (Columbus: Ohio State University Press, 1974).

13. John E. Mueller, *War, Presidents and Public Opinion,* pp. 208–213; Jong R. Lee, "Rallying Around the Flag: Foreign Policy Events and Presidential Popularity," *Presidential Studies Quarterly,* 7 (Fall 1977), 252–256.

14. Richard A. Brody and Benjamin I. Page, "The Impact of Events on Presidential Popularity: The Johnson and Nixon Administrations," in Aaron Wildavsky, ed., *Perspectives on the Presidency* (Boston: Little, Brown, 1975), pp. 136–148; Samuel Kernell, "Explaining Presidential Popularity," pp. 515–521.

15. Kernell estimates, "the president's current popularity reflects the level of approval during the preceding month." *Ibid.,* pp. 515.

16. David Easton and Jack Dennis, "The Child's Image of Government," *Annals of the American Academy of Political and Social Science,* Vol. 361 (1965), 40–57; Fred I. Greenstein, *Children and Politics,* (New Haven, Conn.: Yale University Press, 1965); Robert D. Hess and Judith V. Torney, *The Development of Basic Attitudes and Values Toward Government and Citizenship During the Elementary School Years,* Part I (Chicago: University of Chicago Press, 1965).

17. *Ibid.* See also Dean Jaros, "Children's Orientations Toward the President: Some Additional Theoretical Considerations and Data," *Journal of Politics,* 29 (May 1967), 368–387.

18. Samuel Kernell, Peter W. Sperlich, and Aaron Wildavsky, "Public Support for Presidents," in Aaron Wildavsky (ed.), *The Presidency* (Boston: Little, Brown, 1969), pp. 154–156.

19. Angus Campbell, et al., *The American Voter* (New York: John Wiley, 1960), pp. 489–493; Greenstein, *Children and Politics,* pp. 115–120; Anthony Orum, et al., "The Problem of Being a Minority: Sex, Socialization, and Politics," in *A Portrait of Marginality,* Marianne Githens and Jewel L. Prestage (eds.) (New York: David McKay, 1977), pp. 17–37.

20. David O. Sears, "Political Socialization" in Fred I. Greenstein and Nelson Polsby (eds.), *Handbook of Political Science, II* (Reading, Mass.: Addison-Wesley, 1975), pp. 107–108.

21. Roberta Sigel, "Image of the American Presidency, Part II of an Exploration into Popular Views of Presidential Power," *Midwest Journal of Political Science,* Vol. 10 (February 1966), pp. 123–137. David O. Sears and John B. McConahay, *The Politics of Violence: The New Urban Blacks and the Watts Riot* (Boston: Houghton Mifflin, 1973).

22. Fred I. Greenstein lists five such needs: a cognitive aid; an outlet for affect; a means of vicarious participation; a symbol of national unity; and a symbol of stability and predictability. Fred I. Greenstein, "Popular Images of the President," *American Journal of Psychiatry,* 122 (November, 1965), pp. 523–529.

23. Kernell, Sperlich and Wildavsky, "Public Support for Presidents," p. 178.

24. For the sample as a whole, the error is estimated to be within the range of two to three percent at .05 level of significance.

25. The perception of presidential dominance in foreign affairs begins early. Thus Greenstein notes that two-fifths of the American children in his sample saw the president having an international role in contrast to British and French children, who rarely mentioned foreign affairs as an important function of their head of government. Fred I. Greenstein, "The Benevolent Leader Revisited: Children's Images of Political Leaders in Three Democracies," *American Political Science Review,* 69 (December 1975), p. 1383.

# 16. Presidential Manipulation of Public Opinion

## George C. Edwards III

Presidents have generally not been content to follow public opinion on issues or to placidly allow their popularity to reach some "natural" level. Instead, they have usually devoted substantial energy to attempting to influence the public's attitudes. Some of their actions, such as direct appeal for support and attempts to educate the public, fall under the respectable heading of "leadership." In this essay, however, we shall examine part of the darker side of these efforts, information control and deceptive public relations, that more properly fall into the category of "manipulation."

### Information Control

Presidents rather commonly engage in manipulating what they want the public to know. Such information control comes in many forms, ranging from withholding information from the public to lying to it. If the public is unaware of a situation or has a distorted view of it, then a president may have more flexibility in achieving what he desires. Often a president desires public passivity as much as he wants direct public support.

#### Withholding Information

One means of influencing public opinion through information control is to withhold information from the public, information it needs to evaluate the president and his policies. The war in Vietnam provides many examples of the president and other high officials withholding crucial information from the American people about very important policy matters.

In 1962, the U.S. military commander in Vietnam was ordered to try to prevent reporters from learning that American soldiers were directing combat missions.[1] That same year the Pentagon for the first time revealed that there were several thousand American troops in South Vietnam. In early 1963 the public learned that there had been 11,000 U.S. military personnel there six months earlier. All of this information, it must be stressed, was revealed *after* the actions

*George C. Edwards III teaches political science at Texas A & M University and is the author of several books, including* Presidential Influence in Congress *and* Implementing Public Policy.

were taken, precluding any chance for public debate before the soldiers were sent.

During the 1964 presidential campaign President Lyndon B. Johnson failed to tell the American public his administration was planning possible bombing raids and troop actions against North Vietnam.[2] Instead he publicly advocated American restraint in the war.[3] When he decided to commit a significantly greater number of troops to South Vietnam, he ordered officials to keep the decision secret and play down the change in policy. The public was not alerted to the serious military situation facing South Vietnam. No announcement was made that American troops had taken offensive combat roles in addition to their advisory functions. Similarly, efforts were made to hide the fact that the bombing of North Vietnam had changed from reprisals for specific enemy acts to a long-run strategy.[4] Finally, throughout the 1960s and into the 1970s the C.I.A. financed Laotian tribesmen to fight the Pathet Lao, but the American public was never notified that its tax dollars were being used for this purpose.[5]

In other areas of foreign policy the public was kept equally in the dark. Americans were not informed that between 1962 and 1974 the United States engaged in covert actions to prevent Salvador Allende from coming to power in Chile and then to remove him from power once he was elected.[6] In 1975 the U.S. secretly intervened in the civil war in Angola.[7]

Pertinent information is also withheld on domestic policies. President Richard Nixon favored federal subsidies for the Supersonic Transport plane (better known as the SST) and therefore withheld a negative assessment of the airplane by his own advisers (done at public expense).[8] He also failed to make public a $7 million government study projecting the nation's recreational needs and presenting a detailed program to meet them.[9] In the Johnson administration attempts were made to keep secret the results of the Coleman report on educational opportunity as well as an evaluation of Head Start programs.[10]

The presidents perceived the information contained in these reports to be contrary to their self-interest. Each of these reports was eventually released, but not until members of Congress or the media had discovered them and applied pressure for their publication. The public received some of the information only after it was no longer relevant for the formulation of public policy.

The classification of information under the rubric of "national security" is a frequently used means of withholding information from the public. Most people support secrecy in handling national security affairs, especially in matters such as defense plans and strategy, weapons technology, troop movements, the details of current diplomatic negotiations, the methods and sources of covert intelligence gathering, and similar information about the defense, negotiations, and intelligence gathering of other nations. Secrecy in these matters is directly related to our national security, is essential to provide flexibility and bargaining potential in international negotiations, or is necessary for maintaining our relationships with other countries.

The question is whether too much information is classified and whether classification is used by the president and other high officials to influence public opinion. By withholding information that might aid the public in evaluating their performance in office and questions of public policy in general but that might prove embarrassing to themselves if made public, officials may provide a distorted view of reality and increase or maintain support for themselves.

The classification system is set up by executive order of the president and is implemented by many thousands of bureaucrats. In 1972, after a major campaign to reduce the number of official classifiers of secrets, there were still 1,647 persons in the State Department alone who could classify material.[11] Many thousands more exercise similar authority in the Defense Department, CIA, FBI, and other federal agencies. The discretion bureaucrats have in classifying information, no matter what the guidelines might say, was dramatically demonstrated in Daniel Ellsberg's trial for releasing the *Pentagon Papers,* the secret study of decision-making about the war in Vietnam. The director of the study and the man responsible for its classification testified that he was unaware of official classification guidelines and made the decision to classify it "top secret" very quickly, without regard for the government's own rules and regulations for the protection of national defense.[12]

It is also interesting to note that the Ford administration found there were no clear rules for responding to congressional demands for classified documents. One committee could subpoena the same document from several different agencies, each of which would censor what it considered information too sensitive to be made public. The committee would then receive six different versions. Pasting them together, it could get most of the original document.[13] This shows the lack of consensus even among those doing the classification on what should and should not be classified.

At the end of 1978 an executive order issued by President Carter and designed to limit classification and accelerate declassification took effect. The new procedures ordered by the president established narrower, more explicit criteria for restricting public access to government information. Thus a document can now be classified only if its unauthorized disclosure reasonably could be expected to cause "identifiable" damage to national security. The previous standard allowed classification if any damage could be reasonably expected.[14] What impact these new procedures will have on classification and its abuse remains to be seen.

It appears that much of what has been classified really ought not to have been. Lyndon Johnson said there was little he knew as president that was not also in the press.[15] In 1972 Richard Nixon complained about excessive secrecy and pointed out that even the menus of official dinners for visiting heads of state came to the White House marked "top secret." The previous year a former Pentagon security officer testified that only one-half of one percent of all classified Defense Department material contained genuine secrets that should be kept from the public.[16] In the *Pentagon Papers* case discussed above, the government claimed that public disclosures of the study would cause "irreparable injury to the defense interests of the United States." [17] A decade later, however, evidence to support such a contention has not been produced.

Reason to doubt the necessity of much of classification stems from officials' leaking classified information to the press for their own purposes. The following quote from a top Johnson aide illustrates the extent of such leaks.

> Presidents and White House national security advisors at presidential direction have leaked more classified information since 1960 than all the disaffected State Department, Defense Department, and Central Intelligence Agency employees combined. During the Nixon administration, Henry Kissinger provided more classified information to selected reporters than they had ever before received.[18]

During part of the Nixon administration a Navy yeoman, assigned to the Washington Special Action Group's staff "retained" copies of secret notes and minutes and gave them to the Chairman of the Joint Chiefs of Staff, Admiral Thomas Moore.[19] The Special Action Group was a very high-level group dealing with national security matters, and the nation's highest ranking military officer evidently felt it appropriate that classification rules would not apply to him.

The classification system does more than simply deny information to foreign adversaries and the American public, as the following excerpt from congressional testimony by Rear Admiral (ret.) Gene LaRocque illustrates.

> Classification is made for a variety of reasons. First, to prevent it from falling into the hands of a potential enemy; this ... accounts for only a small portion of the material classified. Other reasons for classifying material are: to keep it from the other military services; from civilians in their own service; from civilians in the Defense Department; from the State Department; and, of course, from the Congress. Sometimes, information is classified to withhold it for later release to maximize the effect on the public or the Congress.
>
> Frequently, information is classified so that only portions of it can be released selectively to the press to influence the public or the Congress. These time-released capsules have a lasting effect.[20]

In other words, classification is sometimes used to attempt, either directly or indirectly, to manipulate public opinion. The president and his advisers can selectively leak classified information that will be to their advantage.

Naturally, classification may also be used to cover up mistakes. We really do not know what errors in judgment and what policies have been obscured because of their being classified, but there is little doubt that many have been hidden from the public. As we might expect, national security was a rationale used by the Nixon White House to support its efforts to deny evidence on the Watergate cover-up to Congress, the courts, and the American people.

"Executive privilege," whereby presidential aides are shielded from testifying before Congress, is yet another means by which the president controls the public's access to information. Although Cabinet members regularly testify before Congress, Henry Kissinger, who functioned as the most important foreign policy figure besides the president in Richard Nixon's first term, refused to testify because of this doctrine. At one point Attorney General Richard Kleindienst claimed executive privilege for the entire executive branch.[21] Although this extreme opinion was later rescinded, it points up the problems of this extra-constitutional doctrine which has no clearly delineated boundaries.

### De-emphasis

A president can also employ more subtle methods of manipulating information in an effort to influence public opinion. He can, for example, order that information collected by the government be de-emphasized. When the economy was not doing well in 1971, the White House ordered the Bureau of Labor Statistics to discontinue its monthly briefing of the press on prices and unemployment. Similarly, during the war in Vietnam the Defense Department gave much more attention in its public announcements to deserters from enemy forces than to deserters from the armed forces of our South Vietnamese allies. In each case the government possessed information that might negatively influence public perceptions of the president and his administration. Thus, it chose not to emphasize this "bad news."

### Collection

Going a step further, a president can simply not order that information on a policy be collected. This, of course, prevents the public from fully evaluating his performance. President Johnson had invested a great deal in his Great Society domestic programs and did not want to cut back on them when large amounts of funds were needed for the war in Vietnam. Although warned by the Council of Economic Advisors at the end of 1965 of the need for a tax increase to avoid the inflation that would result from having both guns *and* butter, he refused to request one. He also refused to seek wage and price controls. Instead Johnson kept the precise costs of the war from Congress and the public. No serious effort was ever made to determine the true costs of U.S. involvement in the war in Vietnam, and Americans felt the ravages of inflation for years to come.

### Timing

Sometimes information is provided, but the timing of its release is used to try to influence public opinion. On November 2, 1970, the White House announced the most recent casualty figures from Vietnam. They were at a five-year low and their announcement was made on Monday instead of Thursday as usual — presumably because the 1970 congressional elections were being held the next day. The Carter administration revealed the Pentagon had developed a new technology that made aircraft virtually invisible to enemy detection devices. This disclosure coincided with an administration effort during the 1980 presidential election campaign to show that it was working to strengthen national defense.

Taking the opposite tack, the Ford administration announced that the country was in a recession one week after the 1974 congressional elections.[22]

## Obfuscation

Presidents and their aides may also attempt to obscure or distort the truth in order to confuse or mislead the public. President Eisenhower regularly gave purposefully ambiguous answers at his press conferences.[23] In a classic exercise in obfuscation a U.S. spokesman in Vietnam once declared that "it became necessary to destroy the town to save it." [24]

Distortion comes in many forms. One of the most common is to provide impressive statistics without going into the details of how they were compiled. President Johnson once proudly claimed that under his guidance the Eighty-ninth Congress had appropriated a record $9.6 billion for education. What he failed to tell the American public was that this impressive figure included about $2 billion for military training plus the budgets of the Library of Congress, the Agricultural Extension Service, most of the Office of Economic Opportunity, and the Smithsonian Institution. Although each of these agencies or programs is related to education in one way or another, they do not fall under the heading of "education" as most people who heard the aggregate figure would define it.

Johnson used a similar tactic when he claimed that the fiscal year 1968 budget provided $26.6 billion for "poor people." Included in these figures were billions of dollars for social security benefits and veterans' pensions, plus funds for highway construction and urban renewal. Again, these policies are not those which we generally think of as aimed at "poor people."

Presidents have also used tricks to make overall spending appear small. In his last year in office President Johnson introduced the "unified budget," which included trust funds previously *excluded* from the budget, such as those for social security, unemployment, highway construction, and retirement pensions of railroad workers. The fact that the trust funds were running a surplus allowed him to cut the size of the projected federal deficit — at least on paper. (The surplus trust funds could not be used to cover the deficit in the regular budget.) President Nixon introduced the "full employment" budget in fiscal 1972. His ruse was to calculate the federal revenues not at what was expected but at what they would be if there were full employment (which there was not). This subterfuge allowed him to show a smaller overall deficit.

It is not only what goes into compiling a "fact" that is important for the public's evaluation of it, but also the context of events in which the "fact" occurs. For example, U.S. sustained bombing of North Vietnam was begun after an attack on U.S. barracks at Pleiku, South Vietnam. The bombing was supposed to be in response to the enemy's attack on U.S. forces. However, the administration had already decided to bomb the North and was just waiting for the proper pretext.[25]

In 1964 Lyndon Johnson went before Congress to ask for a resolution supporting U.S. retaliation against North Vietnam for two attacks on U.S. ships in the

Gulf of Tonkin. The Gulf of Tonkin Resolution was subsequently passed with only two dissenting votes and marked the watershed of U.S. military actions in Vietnam. As the president desired, it was passed in the context of strong public support for retaliating against "unprovoked" attacks against Americans.

The public may have been less enthusiastic in its backing of military reprisals, however, if it had known what the president knew about the context in which the North Vietnamese actions took place. First, the United States had secretly been engaged in intelligence gathering and in supporting covert South Vietnamese operations against North Vietnam for several years before the incidents in the Gulf of Tonkin. Some were going on in the vicinity at the time of the attacks on the U.S. ships, and the North Vietnamese might have thought our ships were involved.[26]

The second piece of crucial contextual information that was withheld from the American people was that there was considerable reason to doubt that the second attack ever occurred at all! As President Johnson later said (in private, of course), "For all I know, our Navy was shooting whales out there." [27] Although it is possible that at the time the President had honestly concluded that the attack had in fact occurred,[28] there is little doubt that the public's approval of U.S. retaliatory actions would have been more restrained if it had had this information. As the authors of a leading study of the war later concluded, "the second attack...had quite possibly been a figment of the jittery destroyer crews' imaginations.[29]

Distortion may also be a matter of emphasis as the following statement about official U.S. statements about the war in Vietnam indicates:

> At the same time U.S. leaders gave a creditable public accounting of their inside estimates and duly noted the long road ahead, they also fostered precisely the opposite impression — that things were going well and that the end was in sight. To be sure, the right cautionary words appeared in the formal statements, but the stress was on the brighter side, the upbeat note. In a few instances some officials made outrageously optimistic predictions...which tended to linger in the public mind. Of equal importance, leaders in Washington did nothing to damp down the perpetual outpouring of optimism from the field. They also went out of their way to attack deeply pessimistic press accounts of the war....[30]

When the 1968 Tet offensive began the president wanted the U.S. commander in Vietnam to "make a brief personal comment to the press at least once each day...to convey to the American public your confidence in our ability to blunt these enemy moves, and to reassure the public here that you have the situation under control." [31]

Attempts to distort information are not always successful. In 1971 the United States supported a South Vietnamese invasion of Laos. It was unsuccessful, and the South Vietnamese retreated six weeks ahead of their own timetable for withdrawal. Nevertheless, the administration denied that there was a rout, and the deputy assistant secretary of defense for public affairs said the South Vietnamese were engaged in "mobile maneuvering" and proceeding according to plan. However, every night on television the American public could see South Vietnamese soldiers clinging to the skids of overloaded helicopters in an attempt to escape from their enemy.

On a wider plane, by 1967 two-thirds of the people felt the Johnson administration was not telling them all it should know about the Vietnam War. In 1971 a similar percentage felt the same way about the Nixon administration.[32] Out of such attitudes emerged the credibility gap and low levels of popular standing for these presidents.

### Lying

The most extreme form of information control is lying. Do presidents lie? The answer is yes. Before discussing this situation let us look at some examples of presidential lies, i.e., lies told directly by the president or by high-level government officials speaking for the president. In the Truman administration there was a gap between what officials were telling the American people and what they really knew about the situation in Vietnam. In 1952, for example, Secretary of State Dean Acheson privately reported that it was "futile and a mistake to defend Indochina in Indochina," but the next day he publicly stated that communist "aggression has been checked" and that the "tide is now moving in our favor."[33]

The Eisenhower administration falsely claimed it had no role in the 1954 coup in Guatemala. It also said the U-2 spy plane shot down over the Soviet Union was there by accident, then that it was not authorized to be there. Both of these statements were false.

The Kennedy administration also had several Cold-War-oriented lies. In 1961 it claimed the U.S. had no role in the Bay of Pigs invasion of Cuba; in 1962 it said it had no information on Soviet missiles in Cuba; and in 1963 it argued that it had no role in the coup that overthrew President Diem of South Vietnam. Each of these claims was untrue.[34]

The number of prevarications expanded considerably in the Johnson presidency. Thus shortly after taking office Johnson let his secretary of defense mislead the American people about the situation in South Vietnam as the latter told the press that the South Vietnamese could cope (on the same day he told the president that South Vietnam might fall to the communists even with U.S. aid).[35]

1965 found several lies emanating from the Johnson administration. First, the day before he appointed Abe Fortas to the Supreme Court, Johnson told reporters he had not even considered whom to appoint. Second, the U.S. claimed a CIA agent never offered a $5 million bribe to the prime minister of Singapore. Unfortunately for the U.S., the prime minister produced a letter of apology from Secretary of State Dean Rusk — predating the disavowal. Finally, the president justified our invasion of the Dominican Republic as necessary to save American lives because "some fifteen hundred innocent people were murdered and shot, and their heads cut off . . . ," and the United States ambassador there had phoned the President while sitting under his desk as bullets were whizzing overhead. None of this was true, nor was the claim that we were neutral. We really invaded the island to prevent a possible communist takeover.

Two years later, in a particularly fascinating but nevertheless tragic episode, the *USS Liberty* was attacked by our Israeli allies, and 34 Americans were killed and 75 were wounded. When asked why it was stationed so close to the fighting in the Arab-Israeli war, the Pentagon said it was to assist in relaying information concerning the evacuation of Americans from the Middle East and so the moon could be used as a passive reflector for communications. This was an attempt to hide the fact that the *Liberty* was a spy ship monitoring battlefield communications.[36]

In congressional hearings in 1968, the Chairman of the Joint Chiefs of Staff lied when he testified that the joint chiefs of staff had made no recommendations for a bombing program before the Gulf of Tonkin crisis occurred.[37]

There were countless other prevarications from the Johnson White House, some large and some small. The President lied when he told reporters that he had known the massive North Vietnamese Tet offensive of 1968 was coming[38] and when he claimed that there was no connection between a price increase in aluminum and his decision to sell some of the government's stockpile of that metal. He also repeatedly lied about matters such as appointments, his travel plans, future policies, not knowing his former protégé Bobby Baker when he got into trouble, his wealth, what he drank, and so on.

The Nixon administration may hold the record for lying to the American people. Continuing a pattern set in the Johnson years, the Nixon administration issued a constant stream of statements assuring the public that we were winning the war in Vietnam. These statements included inaccurate information on the effects of bombing, counts of enemy casualties, "secure" areas, U.S. losses of planes, and the capabilities of the South Vietnamese army.

In 1969 and 1970 the White House denied that the U.S. was bombing in Cambodia, although it was doing so and engaging in a large-scale effort to cover up this fact. In 1970 it falsely denied that it was providing air and logistical support for South Vietnamese operations in Cambodia after the U.S. invasion of Cambodia had ended. The next year the secretary of defense displayed a piece of pipe at a news conference that he said had been severed from an enemy fuel line in Laos during the U.S.-supported South Vietnamese invasion of that country. Later it was revealed that the pipe came from an earlier, unreported operation in Laos.[39]

There were yet other lies. In 1973 the government claimed the U.S. had made no attempts to prevent the election of Marxist Salvador Allende as President of Chile in 1970. Nevertheless, in 1977 former CIA director Richard Helms was convicted on two counts of failing to testify fully about these activities before Congress. The President lied about an entirely different matter when he said his lawyer (John Dean) had advised him capital punishment was constitutional. Dean, however, had simply never looked into the matter.[40]

Last, but certainly not least, we must not forget Watergate. Over a period of more than two years, from mid-1972 through August 1974, the White House claimed the President had no role in the break-in of the Democratic National Committee headquarters or its subsequent cover-up. This same claim was made on behalf of many top administration officials. As we now know the President and his chief of staff, chief domestic policy adviser, personal attorney, White House counsel, two attorney generals, leading campaign officials, and numerous other aides were guilty of a wide variety of Watergate-related crimes. The Watergate tapes even captured the President coaching his chief of staff and White House counsel to tell investigators that they could "not recall" answers to crucial questions.[41]

Although the Ford administration was considerably more forthright with the public than its immediate predecessors, it still issued some lies. When the President fired Secretary of Defense James Schlesinger in November 1975, he claimed there were no policy differences between Schlesinger and Secretary of State Henry Kissinger. Later on a nationally televised interview, however, Ford admitted policy differences were a major consideration in his action.[42] Further, both of the President's press secretaries have reported they were sometimes provided with less than the whole truth by the President's advisers. Thus, at times they inadvertently misled reporters because they themselves did not know the truth.[43]

What can we conclude from these examples of lying? Perhaps the most obvious pattern revealed by them is that lying is most common in the national security area. The reason is simple: it is difficult for the public to challenge official statements about events in other countries, especially military activities, which often are shrouded in secrecy. It is much easier to be skeptical about domestic activities that American reporters can scrutinize and to which they can provide alternative views. In addition, the public can relate many domestic policies to their own experiences more easily than they can relate to most foreign and military policies. When officials' statements do not correspond to their experiences, they have a built-in basis for skepticism.

Another point to remember about government lying is that lies are not told only to deny information to a foreign adversary. They are also told to deny information to the American public. In virtually all of the disproven claims involving national security policy, from the U-2 flight over the Soviet Union to the secret bombing of Cambodia, the "enemy" knew the truth. The Soviet Union, for example, was well aware of the reconnaissance flights and the Cambodians, and North Vietnamese certainly knew that they were being bombed by the U.S. Only the American people were not told the truth.

Sometimes presidents and their aides lie for only a short time, presumably to avoid public panic or to confuse a foreign adversary, as in the Cuban missile crisis. President Kennedy had no intention of keeping the presence of Soviet missiles in Cuba a permanent secret. But in the short run he did not want the public to panic, and he did not want the Soviet Union to know that the U.S. was aware of the missiles until he had reached a conclusion about the proper response.

In most of the cases cited here, lies have had a negative impact on the presidency and the country. We have been embarrassed before the rest of the world when caught in our lies about the U-2 flights, the Bay of Pigs invasion, and similar events. The President has been embarrassed before the country and often developed credibility problems through lies on both major issues and minor events. It is not at all clear that the benefits of lying are worth the costs.

There are also a range of "white" lies which presidents sometimes tell. Lyndon Johnson claimed that his great-great-grandfather died at the Alamo. This seems to have satisfied some personal need for the President and had little impact on public policy. It did little for his general credibility however. Gerald Ford's press secretary told the press the President was playing in a golf tournament because he was in Florida anyway to attend a community leaders conference. Actually, the conference was arranged as an excuse for him to play in the tournament. Jimmy Carter falsely told Bill Moyers in a televised interview that he never reviewed requests to use the White House tennis courts.[44]

No one really knows how many overt lies are made by government officials or how many official lies have significance for public policy. But in the face of several confirmed lies it is reasonable to assume there are many more that we do not know about. This conclusion is supported by the following two examples. In 1966 several reporters met with Assistant Secretary of Defense for Public Affairs Arthur Sylvester. One reporter raised a question about the credibility of American officials on the war in Vietnam. Sylvester responded, "Look, if you think any American official is going to tell you the truth, then you're stupid. Did you hear that? — stupid." [45] In 1974 Senator Edward Kennedy requested information on the commitments entailed in plans for military aid to South Vietnam. When he heard of this, American Ambassador to South Vietnam Graham Martin cabled his superiors in the State Department that it would be foolish to give the senator an "honest and detailed answer." [46]

## Public Relations

In its efforts to mold public opinion, the White House sometimes employs public relations techniques modeled after those of commercial advertising agencies. In other words, it attempts to portray the president and his administration in a positive light through publicity and the provision of information. Much of this involves "getting the word out" about the president and his policies through press releases, news conferences, meetings with news executives, and the like. At other times the White House orchestrates "media events" such as pictures with the national spelling bee winner, supposedly candid views of the president at work, foreign travels amidst cheering masses, and speeches at home before wildly enthusiastic audiences.

Although the information the public receives in this manner is not balanced and media events generally involve a large component of "staging," it is not necessarily fair to label them as deceptions. Some public relations activities clearly distort or hide the truth, however, and these are our concern here.

One indicator of the importance of public relations to contemporary presidents is the presence of advertising specialists in the White House. President Carter put Gerald Rafshoon, the advertising director for his 1976 campaign, on the White House staff. His role was that of a general adviser with special responsibilities for developing and coordinating public relations. These included orchestrating the President's public appearances and scheduling and coordinating public appearances by other Administration officials to help ensure both that they publicized the President's policies and that their public postures were consistent.[47]

This use of public relations specialists was hardly novel. One of President Johnson's closest aides, Jack Valenti, was in the advertising business. Richard Nixon carried the hiring of public relations experts further than any other president. His chief of staff, H. R. Haldeman; his press secretary and later close adviser, Ron Ziegler; and several other aides came to the White House from the advertising business.[48]

Aside from serving as an indicator of the importance presidents place on public relations, the presence of these aides may influence the substance and especially the timing of policy. Since no president will admit to making policy decisions on the basis of advice from image-makers, this is difficult to pin down. Carter aide Gerald Rafshoon told one reporter, "I try to tell the President how these things [policies] will be perceived, but I have nothing to do with making up policy." [49]

Nevertheless, being human, all presidents are subject to the temptation to do the most popular things. Now people whose main concern is to make the president popular and whose vocational orientation is to view decisions in terms of their popular reception have regular and immediate access to the president's ear. Thus, one Nixon aide reports that White House aides were less concerned with the qualifications of Supreme Court nominee G. Harrold Carswell than with obtaining support for his confirmation.[50] The potential for subordinating substance to style is clearly present.

So is the potential for running the White House like an advertising agency. Since an advertising person's orientation is to stress a uniform image, the power of such persons can be a centralizing force in an administration. Emphasis on "team play" inevitably leads to the discouragement of dissent and irregularity because it blunts the impact of the president's image. The parallels between this description and the Nixon White House are striking.

The re-election campaigns of incumbent presidents are often prime opportunities for the White House to flex its public relations muscles. The 1972 Republican National Convention was carefully planned from the public relations viewpoint. Orchestrated by the White House, it was treated as a television show and gave viewers drama, spectacle, and celebrities. Speeches were kept short and were written in advance by campaign officials to meet the President's needs. Roll calls, parliamentary debate, and other boring aspects of a convention were kept to a minimum and out of prime time. Instead the public saw a film of President Nixon's foreign trips, a pro-Nixon demonstration by young people, or some other interesting "entertainment." In other words, a minute-by-minute scenario for the convention was planned and followed.[51]

Although Gerald Ford was less in control of the Republican party in 1976 than his predecessor had been four years earlier, he and his aides still tried to fully exploit its public relations opportunities. His arrival at the convention was timed so that he was welcomed by large crowds and so that the television networks had to cut into their prime time television offerings to cover it live on the scene. During the convention the President's television adviser made sure Ford received maximum and positive television coverage. During a movie on Ford's career *all* the lights in the auditorium were turned off so the networks were forced to carry it and not switch to interviews of delegates or campaign officials. When potentially damaging developments were taking place or during convention lulls, the Ford camp had people ready to rush before the television cameras for interviews to direct attention from or spice up the convention.[52]

In the first debate between President Ford and Jimmy Carter in the 1976 election campaign the President had prepared his opening remarks ahead of time and would have given a variation of it no matter what Carter's first remarks had been. Answers to questions were also preplanned. No matter what the specific question the president was asked, he was to answer it briefly and then slip into one of seven prepared points and use some of his prepared quotable expressions. Rehearsals were held before the debate on a replica of the stage which would be used, and these were videotaped and replayed for the President and his advisers to try to improve Ford's performance. Thus, the "spontaneous" debate was much less so than it seemed.[53]

Public relations efforts sometimes go to extraordinary lengths to attempt to influence public opinion. During the 1972 presidential election campaign President Nixon's reelection committee (run from the White House) led counter demonstrations to antiwar demonstrations; set up mock presidential elections on college campuses but kept the turnout low so that Nixon would have a greater chance of winning — and demonstrating his support among young voters; and spied on and disrupted opponents' campaigns.[54] Perhaps most intriguing was the committee's actions following the President's decision to mine Haiphong's harbor. The committee spent $8200 on telegrams which it sent to the White House (in effect, the President sent telegrams to himself) and advertisements to make it appear as though there were widespread support for his decision. When the *New York Times* opposed the decision in an editorial, the committee placed an ad in the paper entitled "The People vs. the *New York Times*." It was signed by ten people who supposedly spent their own money for it. Actually, the money came from the same secret fund that paid the "hush money" to the Watergate burglars.[55]

Efforts to simulate public support for the President occurred at other times. An extensive letter writing program was organized by the Nixon White House. It had women in Washington writing fifty or sixty individualized letters each week and then sent them to Republicans around the country to be signed and sent to various publications which had criticized the President in one way or another. One presidential aide estimated that 15 or 20 percent of these letters were published. The White House also worked with state committees to set up grass-roots letter-writing operations. Following one of the President's televised speeches on Vietnam, the White House sent itself telegrams of support. The telegrams stacked in piles on the president's desk the morning after his speech made for impressive wire-service and television pictures, indicating intense public support for his actions. Frequently, H. R. Haldeman, the White House chief of staff, ordered individually worded telegrams sent to members of Congress from around the country thanking or criticizing them, depending upon their support of the administration. Calls and letters also went out to critics. The President himself was aware of and interested in these tactics.[56]

When President Nixon decided to make the first of the White House tapes public, he and his aides sought to impress the public with the extensiveness of his disclosures. Twin stacks of notebooks, each bearing the presidential seal, were displayed at the President's side as he spoke on national television. However, each of the 50 three-ring binders contained only about 25 typewritten transcript pages. The same material, when prepared for the news media, composes a single 8-by-10-inch book, two and one-half inches thick. It can be purchased as a paperback in most college bookstores.

This distortion was not enough for the White House, however. Instead of simply sending a set of transcripts to each member of the House Judiciary Committee, which was investigating the charges against the President, Nixon's aides delivered them in a manner which again emphasized their volume. A station wagon was driven to the front of the White House and, while reporters watched and photographers snapped pictures, the car was filled with 38 sets of transcripts (one for each member of the Judiciary Committee) plus four large briefcases containing the single set bound in notebooks. Naturally, all this filled the back of the vehicle as it drove down Pennsylvania Avenue to the Capitol.

Presidents also use public relations to attempt to have their interpretation of events accepted by the public. President Ford once hailed as a "hundred-percent" victory a vaguely worded promise from Congress to hold down spending. As his press secretary wrote later, the congressional action "wasn't a victory at all." Similarly, the President told his staff not to be unduly optimistic about the economy so that when things were better the White House would appear in a better light and be more credible.[57]

Public relations can be used to discredit opponents as well as to build support for a president or his policies. In September 1977, White House Press Secretary Jody Powell passed along to at least two newspapers unsubstantiated allegations (which later proved to be false) that Republican Senator Charles Percy has improperly used corporate aircraft and the facilities of a Chicago bank in his 1972 reelection campaign. At the time this occurred Percy was a persistent critic of Office of Management and Budget Director and Carter confidant Bert Lance. Powell said he had not conferred with the President before passing the rumors and apologized personally to Percy and told a press conference his action had been "inappropriate, regrettable, and dumb." Earlier in the year Powell told a reporter that a close inquiry would uncover improper actions of Representative Morris Udall of Arizona regarding a water project in his state. Udall had been critical of the President's efforts to end funding for some water projects and had been a steadfast opponent of Carter for the 1976 Democratic presidential nomination.[58]

Unfortunately, this use of the press to discredit opponents is not unique to the incidents described above. Charles Colson, a high-ranking aide to Richard Nixon, planted a story in *Life* magazine on Senator Joseph Tydings of Maryland in 1970 when the Senator was up for reelection. The story falsely accused him of financial misdeeds and may well have contributed to his defeat. Similarly, the White House got hold of a picture of Senator Edward Kennedy dancing with an unknown beautiful woman in Rome. This was planted in the *National Enquirer* and then picked up by other magazines. During the debate over the confirmation of Nixon's appointment of G. Harrold Carswell to the Supreme Court, the White House spread word that opponent Senator Birch Bayh had once flunked his bar examination and that Senators Hubert Humphrey and George McGovern had restrictive covenants in the deeds to their homes (limiting the sale of the property to caucasians).[59]

Members of Congress who attempt to compete with the president in shaping public opinion may face formidable public relations obstacles. In early 1967 while Senator Robert Kennedy was preparing to deliver a speech attacking President Johnson's policy toward Vietnam, the President engaged in a whirlwind of activity to divert attention: he suddenly called a press conference to announce the progress of United States–Soviet negotiations on antiballistic missiles, gave an address on civil rights at Howard University, and delivered a speech at the Office of Education about the state of the nation's schools. At the same time, Senator Henry Jackson produced a letter from the President defending his Vietnam policy; Secretary of State Dean Rusk dismissed Kennedy's proposals as nothing new; and General William Westmoreland issued a rebuttal from South Vietnam. All of these activities and opinions were reported in the morning newspapers, which diminished the impact of the reports of Kennedy's opposition. An even more spectacular example of the executive's manipulation of events as a public relations move to counter opposition took place in early 1966 when the Senate Foreign Relations Committee was holding hearings on Vietnam. The hearings, which received wide publicity, were not supportive of the President's policy. He therefore hastily arranged a "summit meeting" in Honolulu with the leaders of South Vietnam.[60]

## Conclusion

Presidents are not content to follow public opinion. Instead they use techniques ranging from direct appeals to the manipulation of the information and public relations to try to influence it. There is no guarantee of success in these efforts, however, and they often fail to achieve their desired effects. Nevertheless, presidents continue to employ these tactics, adding their own wrinkles to those of their predecessors as they seek public support.

SOURCE: "Presidential Manipulation of Public Opinion" was written for this volume. It is part of a larger study of the presidency by Professor George C. Edwards III, to be published. Copyright © 1982 by George C. Edwards III.

## Notes

1. William McGaffin and Erwin Knoll, *Anything but the Truth* (New York: Putnam's, 1968), p. 79.
2. Leslie H. Gelb with Richard K. Betts, *The Irony of Vietnam: The System Worked* (Washington, D.C.: Brookings Institution, 1979), pp. 103–104; *The Pentagon Papers* (New York: Bantam, 1971), chap. 5.
3. See, for example, John M. Orman, *Presidential Secrecy and Deception: Beyond the Power to Persuade* (Westport, Conn.: Greenwood Press, 1980), p. 98.
4. Gelb with Betts, *Irony of Vietnam,* p. 315; Robert L. Gallucci, *Neither Peace nor Honor: The Politics of American Military Policy in Viet-Nam* (Baltimore, Md.: Johns Hopkins University Press, 1975), pp. 40–41; Herbert Y. Schandler, *The Unmaking of a President: Lyndon Johnson and Vietnam* (Princeton, N.J.: Princeton University Press, 1977), pp. 15, 21–22.
5. Orman, *Presidential Secrecy,* pp. 99–106; William Colby, *Honorable Men: My Life in the CIA* (New York: Simon and Schuster, 1978), chap. 6.
6. Orman, *Presidential Secrecy,* pp. 126–132.
7. See Morton H. Halperin and David H. Hoffman, *Top Secret: National Security and the Right to Know* (Washington, D.C.: New Republic Books, 1977), pp. 21–24.
8. "SST Report," *Congressional Quarterly Weekly Report,* August 28, 1971, p. 1830.
9. Jack Anderson, "A Blueprint for Recreation," *Washington Post,* July 21, 1974, Section C, p. 7.
10. James S. Coleman, *Policy Research in the Social Sciences* (Morristown, N.J.: General Learning Press, 1972), pp. 13–14.
11. United States Department of State, *Freedom of Information* (Washington, D.C.: U.S. Government Printing-Office, 1974).
12. " 'Top Secret' Tag Routine Jury Is Told," *Washington Post,* April 24, 1973, Section A, pp. 1, 15.
13. Ron Nessen, *It Sure Looks Different from the Inside* (Chicago: Playboy Press, 1978), p. 61.
14. "New Rules for Classifying Information Set by Carter," *Congressional Quarterly Weekly Report,* July 8, 1978, p. 1747.
15. Patrick J. McGarvey, *C.I.A.: The Myth and the Madness* (Baltimore, Md.: Penguin Books, 1973), pp. 31–32.

16. Testimony of William G. Florence before the House Subcommittee on Foreign Operations and Government Information, June 24, 1971. Cited in Richard L. Worsnop, "Secrecy in Government," *Editorial Research Reports,* August 18, 1971, p. 648.
17. William E. Porter, *Assault on the Media: The Nixon Years* (Ann Arbor: University of Michigan Press, 1976), p. 88.
18. Joseph A. Califano, Jr., *A Presidential Nation* (New York: Norton, 1975), p. 193.
19. Porter, *Assault on the Media,* pp. 141–142.
20. Quoted in Norman Dorsen and Stephen Gillers, eds., *None of Your Business: Government Secrecy in America* (New York: Penguin Books, 1974), p. 73.
21. Raoul Berger, *Executive Privilege: A Constitutional Myth* (Cambridge, Mass.: Harvard University Press, 1974), pp. 254–255.
22. Nessen, *It Sure Looks Different,* p. 76.
23. Fred I. Greenstein, "Eisenhower as an Activist President: A Look at New Evidence," *Political Science Quarterly* 94 (Winter 1979–80), pp. 588–590.
24. Don Oberdorfer, *TET!* (Garden City, N.Y.: Doubleday, 1971), p. 185.
25. Gelb with Betts, *Irony of Vietnam,* p. 105; Wise, *Politics of Lying,* p. 41; Townsend Hoopes, *The Limits of Intervention,* rev. ed. (New York: McKay, 1973), p. 30.
26. Gelb with Betts, *Irony of Vietnam,* pp. 102–103; *Pentagon Papers,* chapter 3 and pp. 259–260; David Wise, *The Politics of Lying: Government Deception, Secrecy and Power* (New York: Vintage, 1973), pp. 62–66; Joseph C. Goulden, *Truth Is the First Casualty* (Chicago: Rand McNally, 1969), chapter 3 and pp. 122–141.
27. Quoted in Goulden, *Truth Is the First Casualty,* p. 160. See also pp. 142–180.
28. See, for example, *Pentagon Papers,* pp. 262–263.
29. Gelb with Betts, *Irony of Vietnam,* p. 104.
30. *Ibid.,* pp. 320–321.
31. Schandler, *Unmaking of a President,* p. 83.
32. John E. Mueller, *War, President and Public Opinion* (New York: Wiley, 1973), pp. 112–113.
33. Gelb with Betts, *Irony of Vietnam,* pp. 48–49, 311.
34. *Ibid.,* pp. 86–91; Wise, *Politics of Lying,* pp. 58–59; *Pentagon Papers,* chap. 4.
35. Paul Freedenberg, "The Rhetoric of Vietnam: Reaction to Adversity" (Unpublished dissertation, University of Chicago, 1972), p. 48; "Secretary McNamara Reports on the Situation in Vietnam," *Department of State Bulletin,* January 13, 1964, p. 46.
36. Goulden, *Truth Is the First Casualty,* pp. 100–104; Phil G. Goulding, *Confirm or Deny* (New York: Harper & Row, 1970), chap. 4.
37. Gelb with Betts, *Irony of Vietnam,* p. 104, fn. 31.
38. *Pentagon Papers,* p. 592.
39. Wise, *Politics of Lying,* pp. 71–72.
40. John Dean, *Blind Ambition: The White House Years* (New York: Simon and Schuster, 1976), p. 138.
41. *The White House Transcripts* (New York: Bantam Books, 1974), p. 171.
42. Gerald R. Ford, *Time to Heal* (New York: Harper & Row and Reader's Digest, 1974), p. 330.
43. Nessen, *Sure Looks Different,* p. 132; J.F. TerHorst, "What the Press Must Do," *Newsweek,* December 9, 1974, p. 15.
44. James Fallows, "The Passionless Presidency: The Trouble with Jimmy Carter's Administration," *Atlantic Monthly,* May 1979, p. 44.
45. Quoted in MacGaffin and Knoll, *Anything but the Truth,* p. 86.

46. Carl P. Leubsdorf, "Kennedy Tells of Envoy Cable," *New Orleans Times-Pica-yune,* April 3, 1974, Section 1, p. 3.
47. "Rafshoon and Co.," *Newsweek,* January 29, 1979, pp. 22–23; "Carter's No 'Good Ole Boy,'" *Houston Chronicle,* September 3, 1978, Section 1, p. 14; Dom Bonafede, "Has the Rafshoon Touch Left Its Mark on the White House?" *National Journal,* April 14, 1979, pp. 588–593; Dom Bonafede, "Carter Sounds Retreat from 'Cabinet Government,'" *National Journal,* November 18, 1978, p. 1857.
48. Jeb Stuart Magruder, *An American Life: One Man's Road to Watergate* (New York: Pocket Books, 1975), p. 6.
49. Bonafede, "Rafshoon and Co.," p. 22.
50. Magruder, *American Life,* p. 129.
51. Magruder, *American Life,* pp. 310–311.
52. Nessen, *It Sure Looks Different,* pp. 227, 241–242. But the President was not in complete control, giving his acceptance speech at 11:40 P.M. E.S.T.
53. *Ibid.,* pp. 262–263, 265.
54. Magruder, *American Life,* pp. 187, 244–245, chaps. 8–9.
55. Carl Bernstein and Bob Woodward, *All the President's Men* (New York: Warner, 1975), pp. 293–294.
56. Magruder, *American Life,* pp. 62, 92–93, 111.
57. Nessen, *It Sure Looks Different,* pp. 88–89.
58. Charles Mohr, "Powell Apologizes for Attempting to Spread Rumor Harmful to Percy," *New York Times,* September 15, 1977, pp. 1, 62.
59. Magruder, *American Life,* pp. 77, 130, 149.
60. Bruce Ladd, *Crisis in Credibility* (New York: New American Library, 1968), pp. 174–175; Chester L. Cooper, *The Lost Crusade: America in Vietnam* (New York: Dodd, Mead, 1970), p. 301.

# 17. Monopolizing the Public Space: The President as a Problem for Democratic Politics

## Bruce Miroff

In the early 1970s a rapidly swelling chorus of political commentators warned against an "imperial presidency." By the end of the decade warnings of a quite different sort were heard. Few observers of the presidency continued to focus on abuses of power or undemocratic behavior; the complaints now revolved around ineffectual leadership. With their lackluster styles and limited accomplishments, Gerald Ford and Jimmy Carter convinced many that American politics required not a more circumscribed but a more imposing figure in the White House.

This shift of opinion is somewhat premature. Even if the once "imperial presidency" has been brought back to within constitutional and political limits, the presidency remains an impediment to democratic politics in America. This impediment does not depend upon abuses of power. In fact, it is only in part a question of power at all.

The problem I address is the monopolization of public space in America by presidents; i.e., their dominant position in that visible realm of political action that is ostensibly to be shared not only with other representative institutions but with citizens as well. Democratic politics requires an open public space, one where all potentially may enter, display and express themselves, and be seen and heard. When one political figure dominates this space, and engrosses its proceedings, the possibilities for a democratic politics are greatly diminished. The modern president is such a figure.[1]

Since the concept of a democratic public space is integral to my argument,[2] I will introduce it by way of an example that reveals its possibilities: the civil rights movement of the early 1960s. The civil rights movement was able to mobilize numerous blacks whose prior experience had been one of enforced political submission and passivity. Breaking open a hitherto closed public space in the South, these individuals found their voices and articulated what had long had to be kept inside. Through their commitment to action, their willingness to take and to share risks, they began to develop political power. But generating power was not the whole of their enterprise; equally important was the dignity they earned through their actions in the public space they had opened. Whatever the later vicissitudes of the movement, those individuals who had participated in it learned from their experiences what it meant to be democratic citizens.

*Bruce Miroff teaches political science at the State University of New York at Albany and is the author of* Pragmatic Illusions: The Presidential Politics of John F. Kennedy.

My concern in this article is not with the opening of such public spaces, but with their foreclosure. For most Americans, the presidency has come to be nearly all there is to democratic politics. The president's monopoly over the public space reduces the incentives to political action for most citizens, and makes it more difficult for those who do assume a political stance to be seen and understood. That same monopoly distorts the public space itself, creating a mystified political realm where dramaturgy and individual will supplant the democratic features of openness, dialogue, and shared decision.

To avoid misunderstanding, I should make clear at the outset what my argument does *not* intend to claim. In emphasizing the presidential monopoly over the public space, I am not constructing an argument about overwhelming presidential power. The president who dominates our public space is considerably less potent in the less-visible workings of national politics; here he is challenged, frustrated, and often overmatched by Congress, the bureaucracy, private power. Nor am I making a claim about the wide popularity of contemporary presidents. Analyses of poll data have demonstrated the fragility of presidential popularity, especially its tendency to decline over the course of a four-year term.[3]

Nevertheless, when declining popularity takes the form of criticism that is preoccupied with the president's personality, style, or agenda, it still reveals a fixation on him as the preeminent figure in the public space. As Michael Novak has observed: "It is not necessary to accept the symbols generated by a president's words and actions; to tear them to shreds bit by bit is sufficient evidence of engagement." [4] As presidential difficulties mount, the political questions most widely asked may change in character, but they will still be directed at the White House: can this president recoup his fortunes, or will he have to yield the public space to another aspirant for the unmatched eminence of his position?

## The Main Character

If we consider the public, visible dimension of American national politics, the preeminent position of the president is readily apparent. His words and actions receive far more coverage from the mass media than the efforts of other political actors or institutions. His access to the political consciousness of ordinary American citizens is unmatched for directness and immediacy. This preeminent position does not guarantee that a president will win his political contests; it does mean that the majority of those contests will be ones that he has chosen.

In a political system where the weight of inertia and complexity is considerable, the capacity to launch something new is scarce. The president stands out among American political actors for an ability to initiate action. Our political calendar is structured around his initiatives and departures from routine. His State of the Union message, Budget, Economic Report, and special messages form the heart of the yearly national agenda; they determine, in large part, what public policies Congress, the media, and the attentive public will debate over the course of the year. The results of the debate will generally be uncertain, but its character will not be; almost all the programs at issue will carry the name of the incumbent president and be judged as part of his overall record.

There is some factual distortion in this personalization of the national agenda. Many of the proposals that bear the president's name will have actually taken shape in the far reaches of the executive bureaucracy. Further, scholars have increasingly recognized that a number of the ideas publicly credited to the White House have congressional origins; "policy incubation" in Congress may precede presidential action by several years.[5] In both cases, however, proposals don't ordinarily enter the public space, don't become politically visible, until the president adopts them as his own.

In initiating political action the president gains an unparalleled advantage in defining political reality for most Americans. Whatever revelations about presidential deceptions or White House public-relations campaigns have taught us, the terms in which informed political discussion in America takes place are still largely set by presidential pronouncements. Presidents cannot always choose their issues; problems may be forced upon them by public pressures, economic disturbances, international crises. But whether an issue they emphasize is voluntarily or reluctantly addressed, they will generally be the ones who establish the context for its further consideration. The bulk of public attention will be directed toward those facets of either the problem or the proposed solution that they have highlighted. Especially when congressional participation can be minimized — through executive orders or in certain areas of foreign policy — presidential ability to shape public understanding can be quite extensive.

It might seem something of an exaggeration to portray the president as a potent definer of reality during a period when so much criticism has been leveled at the White House. Despite an upsurge of press and popular skepticism, however, as well as the usual strain of partisan criticism, the central aspects of what recent presidents have depicted as reality have remained undisturbed in the public eye. Nixon's claim to be the architect of a structure of global peace was scarcely tarnished by revelations of a secret air war in Southeast Asia and a covert attempt at counterrevolution in Chile. Carter's energy program was generally treated as a future-oriented national plan beleaguered by parochial interests, and his human-rights crusade was seen as a reassertion of traditional American ideals in spite of such obvious contradictions as support for the Shah of Iran. Press or partisan criticism may challenge a president on the form or the details of his actions, but the outline of reality that he has sketched is usually left intact. When alternative definitions of reality are put forward (e.g., by critics on the left), they generally receive so little exposure in the public space that they cannot call into question definitions emanating from the White House.

A president's ability to initiate action and to shape the terms within which action will be understood are bound up with his preeminent dramatic role in American politics. He is our perennial main character, occupying center stage during almost all dramas in national political life. Presidents clearly vary in dramatic skills; some are natural, if hard-working, performers, while others woodenly enact gestures scripted by expert advisers. Whatever the caliber of their skills, theirs is the performance upon which all eyes will be fixed.

The chief tool of presidential drama is, of course, television. Television's significance for the presidency has been widely noted. Here, with only slight hyperbole, is Fred W. Friendly:

> No mighty King, no ambitious emperor, no pope, or prophet ever dreamt of such an awesome pulpit, so potent a magic wand. In the American experiment with its delicate checks and balances, this device permits the First Amendment and the very heart of the Constitution to be breached, as it bestows on one politician a weapon denied to all others. . . . The President, in his ability to command the national attention, (has) diminished the power of all other politicians. . . .[6]

Television, with its emphasis on the personal and the visual, finds the president a natural focus for its political coverage. The major newsmagazines, whose audience is less extensive but more politically attentive, have much the same orientation. When I examined *Time* and *Newsweek* for each of two calendar years (1975 and 1977), I found that more than half of the lead stories in each magazine dealt primarily with presidential activities. Gerald Ford was the chief subject of 50 percent of *Time*'s lead stories and 54 percent of those in *Newsweek*; Jimmy Carter was featured in 63 percent of *Time*'s lead stories and 65 percent of those in *Newsweek*. The headlines for these stories were striking in their evocation of presidential drama. Thus, American foreign and military policy became a series of presidential adventures ("Ford's Rescue Operation" — *Newsweek*, May 26, 1975; "Carter v. Brezhnev: The SALT Standoff" — *Time*, April 11, 1977). American prospects rested on presidential risk-taking ("Ford's Risky Plan Against Slumpflation" — *Time*, January 27, 1975; "Ford's Big Gamble on Detente" — *Newsweek*, August 4, 1975). Presidential power itself oscillated with dramatic rises and falls in the incumbent's fortunes ("Why Is Jimmy Smiling? Why Not?" — *Time*, April 4, 1977; "Can Jimmy Carter Cope?" — *Newsweek*, October 24, 1977).

That presidents dominate media coverage of national politics is not simply a function of their importance in the American political system. Recent administrations have built up substantial organizational capabilities for projecting a favorable presidential image. While the successors to Richard Nixon have not shared his obsession with public relations, they too have considered television and advertising specialists to be indispensable in presidential politics. These specialists counsel presidents on the timing and the form of actions; they provide expert advice on how to shape images that the media will play up and sell to the public.[7]

By means of television and other media a conception of the presidential character — of face and voice, of gestures and style, of themes and ideals — is created. Soon after the start of a new administration (with the election campaign as background) the public becomes extremely familiar with this presidential character. With ample prodding from the media, it comes to watch ongoing political events as episodes in the story of this character. It hears, from television commentators and Washington columnists, of the successful stratagems and the botched plans, of the grievous defeats and the exciting comebacks of this character. Portrayal of national politics as a drama of presidential character has become such a commonplace that the media appear reluctant to depart from it. Beneath much of its disappointment in Jimmy Carter could be heard the complaint that this main character was undramatic and this story unexciting.[8] Presidential drama is *expected* to fill up the public space; presidential dominance over visible public action is now as much demanded by the media as it is sought by the president.

## Surrogate for the People

That one public figure has so great an advantage over all others in initiating action, defining political reality, and dramatizing his own character might be expected to trouble a democratic polity. Americans, one might think, should wonder why one man should dominate a public space that in other western democracies is largely filled with the clash of political parties. Yet, apart from some worries expressed during the Nixon administration about "presidential television," [9] concern over this phenomenon has rarely been voiced. I suspect we fail to be concerned partly because presidential monopoly over the public space is now largely taken for granted. In addition, however, there are several traditional, widely-held arguments that support presidential preeminence.

The need, in a complex and cumbersome political system, for decisive and effective leadership is one of the most powerful of these arguments. Alexander Hamilton's pronouncement that "decision, activity, secrecy, and dispatch will generally characterize the proceedings of one man in a much more eminent degree than the proceedings of any greater number. . . ." [10] has become a fundamental maxim of American thought. Presidents are supposed to supply those qualities of leadership without which the American republic would be confused and feeble. But leadership is an intangible phenomenon; to be credible it has to be publicly manifested. A presidential character who can fill the public space with impressive spectacles of action provides a reassuring statement of leadership.

A second traditional argument casts the president as the sole representative of a national constituency. Whereas other political figures represent partial and presumably self-seeking interests, the president, this argument goes, occupies a unique vantage point. His lofty eminence brings with it the perspective of the public welfare. Even self-seeking motives are transformed by his position; pursuing power and fame rather than material gain, his personal success requires broad public accomplishments. (Scholars have sometimes questioned the equation of presidential purposes with the public interest. But presidents continue to paint themselves as champions of the general good combatting selfish "special interests" — witness Carter's efforts on behalf of his energy program and Reagan's campaign for massive budget cuts.)

Arguments about the president's leadership and representation functions gain a good deal of their persuasiveness from an underlying premise that is common to both. The premise states that the president is a surrogate for a mass public that cannot act for itself. This idea of the president as a democratic surrogate can be traced back to the first self-proclaimed champion of the people, Andrew Jackson. Reversing James Madison's famous warning about majority factions, Jackson insisted that only selfish and corrupted elites had the capacity to act in a concerted fashion; ordinary citizens were incapable (due to the conditions of their daily existence) of taking collective action, and could have their interests protected only through the actions of their defender in the White House.[11] Jackson's image of the president as surrogate for a citizenry incapable of action has recurred frequently in American history. It can be seen in Theodore Roosevelt's "stewardship" theory, in Franklin Roosevelt's personal (albeit mainly rhetorical) war upon "economic royalists," in Richard Nixon's "silent majority."

Jackson had described a citizenry too dispersed in space and absorbed in making a living to act as a collective force; modern arguments tend to emphasize that size and complexity make organized mass participation unrealistic. Whatever reasons are presented, such arguments have led to a belief that presidential action is the only kind of democratic action possible on a national scale. Presidential action thus becomes — in a symbolic sense — our action; a scattered, divided, uncertain people are made one and exercise their popular power through their surrogate. No wonder, then, that it becomes difficult to perceive the kind of problem the presidency poses for democratic politics, when presidential monopoly over the public space has so often been confused with democratic politics.

## Vicarious Participation

If presidential monopoly over the public space is justified by the difficulties of actual citizen participation in politics, it is made appealing by the outlet it offers for vicarious participation. Taught by our "realists" that the significant issues of our times are above and beyond ordinary citizens, who couldn't make much of a difference even if they could understand, those same citizens are offered compensation in the form of a presidential spectacle enacted in their name. The drama, the power, the sense of mastery derived from that spectacle, even though vicarious, provide many Americans with the only meaningful experience of political action they have.[12]

Before I discuss the subject of vicarious participation, some qualifications are in order. There are many Americans who are not attracted to presidential spectacles; some are indifferent, others resistant, while a smaller number are actively skeptical.[13] Further, the amount of vicarious participation that any particular president encourages is dependent upon the skill with which he utilizes the personal and institutional symbols available to him. A symbolically awkward president (e.g., Gerald Ford) can make vicarious participation difficult. If his performances become too soporific, he may even induce boredom with politics in general.

Notwithstanding these limiting factors, vicarious participation in presidential performances remains an important phenomenon. For many Americans, it serves as a way of making sense out of a confusing political world. Murray Edelman's comment about leadership is especially applicable to the president: "Because it is apparently intolerable for men to admit the key role of accident, of ignorance, and of unplanned processes in their affairs, the leader serves a vital function by personifying and reifying the processes." [14] Through presidential words and actions a familiar political landscape is established; relevant problems are defined, conflicting forces are identified, historic designs (a "New Deal," a "Great Society") are charted. Political meaning, one-sided or inflated as it might be, is thereby made accessible to the public.

Even more important at times than this provision of meaning may be the provision of a sense of personal power. Through skillful dramatic efforts, combined with projection on the part of the audience, a president can exhibit admirable and heroic qualities — such as decisiveness and courage — that most people cannot exhibit, or even feel, in their own lives. In the presence of the president — seen on television or perhaps on tour — ordinary citizens may feel touched and inspirited by these qualities. Apart from his presence, however, the experience of personal powerlessness recurs. Watching absorbing presidential spectacles (like those of FDR, Eisenhower, Kennedy, or Reagan), many Americans believe that they inhabit not only an intelligible, but a satisfying political world.[15]

Many presidential performances fall short of these absorbing spectacles. For spectacle to be achieved, for vicarious participation to be heightened, an impressive presidential character — in part real, in part contrived — must be crystallized. Presidents who try to modify their character to please diverse constituencies, to be different men to different audiences, usually come across as unconvincing to most of those they wish to impress. Johnson, Nixon, and Carter each suffered in this regard; their public character appeared variable, vague, or even distasteful, suggesting to many spectators that the real presidential character must be hidden from view.

When vicarious participation is attracted by presidential performances, there are several consequences for the character of American political life. One consequence is a disinterest in actual political participation. How often do the modes of political action available to ordinary citizens match the color, the drama, or the grand scale of presidential politics? When contrasted with presidential action, citizen participation usually looks drab and petty. It is thus easier to concentrate on private affairs and to restrict politics to conversations with friends and co-workers about the president than it is to seek out opportunities for one's own action.

A second consequence of vicarious participation is a diversion of citizens from their own needs and interests. The dramatic ebb and flow of presidential action distracts the audience from a careful consideration of the substance of action. It obscures the beneficiaries and the losers in presidential policies.[16] American audiences are not especially naïve; to the extent that they become aware of the social and economic stakes they will vote or act accordingly. The proliferation of "single-issue" groups in recent years testifies to how attuned Americans can be (though often in an overly narrow fashion) to their own interests. Yet, while a presidential performance may not be diverting to the committed on an issue close to their hearts, it can be diverting to the majority of onlookers, for whom the drama is presented as primary and the concrete meaning is left vague.

A third consequence of vicarious participation in presidential performances is a mystification of existing power relationships in America. An audience accustomed to seeing one dominant figure in the public space, and habituated to finding its political satisfactions or disappointments through that figure, comes to believe that his are the powers of action that matter the most. But as presidential powers of action stand out, other forms of power are obscured. There are plenty of reasons to downgrade the actual capacity of presidents to achieve their objectives. Circumscribing and sometimes surpassing presidenital powers are not only the powers of Congress, the federal bureaucracy, and the courts, but also concentrated economic power. Yet these forms of power, because they are overshadowed in the public space, are not as well understood by the public. The public is thus ill-prepared to recognize, much less to hold accountable, what in many cases are the most influential actors and institutions in American politics.

## *Will*

What happens to American politics when the president monopolizes the public space as a democratic surrogate through whom citizens achieve vicarious participation? It becomes a politics in which personal will replaces public choice, in which the public space itself becomes only the visible representation of a largely unknowable realm where real action takes place. It becomes a politics whose central features stand in contradiction to the features of an authentic democratic politics.

While presidential preeminence has been justified in' terms of the public functions of leadership and representation, it has been asserted primarily in the language of personal will. Presidential "will" has been understood in several senses: e.g., as the strength of the president's resolve in international affairs (a major preoccupation for both John Kennedy and Richard Nixon) and the impulse to political mastery in Washington politics (the will to power described by Richard E. Neustadt in his classic *Presidential Power*). The form of presidential will that holds the greatest import for the nature of the public space, however, is the impulse to political mystery: the will as impenetrable.

Especially during important controversies, the presidential will may emerge as the unknowable personal element that has ultimately determined a decision. This form of will can be contrived; many routine presidential decisions are merely ratifications of decisions already made elsewhere, while even in the case of important decisions presidential choice is influenced by the play of what Graham Allison and others have termed "bureaucratic politics." Yet whatever advances have been made in the study of the decision-making process, the most critical moments of choice frequently remain draped in obscurity. As John Kennedy wrote, in a frequently cited passage: "The presidential office is the vortex into which all the elements of national decision are irresistibly drawn. And it is mysterious because the essence of ultimate decision remains impenetrable to the observer — often, indeed, to the decider himself." [17]

Decision-making is generally regarded as the center of presidential activity. The information and advice that a president receives before making a decision can sometimes be unearthed by journalists or reproduced by scholars. Similarly, public justifications for a decision can be evaluated, and analyses of its effects undertaken. But the ultimate reasons for the decision will remain personal, internal, and largely invisible. Hence neither the public, nor even institutional actors and elites, can safely predict or fully explain presidential choice.

Jimmy Carter's decision on the B-1 bomber provides an illustration of the uses presidents make of this impenetrability of will. For weeks before Carter's announced time of decision the media was filled with excited speculation: Would he or would he not choose to construct the B-1? Carter artfully built up the suspense. When a reporter suggested to him at a press conference two weeks before the time of decision that his views on the B-1 appeared to have shifted, Carter replied: "I don't think that you could detect what my view might be." [18] The drama was played out to the end; Carter's announcement of his decision, to quote *Newsweek,* "stunned and confounded both opponents and backers of the supersonic bomber." [19] A similar desire to maintain the impenetrability of decision can be noted in many administrations. Lyndon Johnson, for example, was reportedly so intent on suspense that he would reverse a decision already made if reports of it prematurely reached the press.

The obscurity of decision is further buttressed by the imagery of official secrecy. The president sits atop a maze within which numerous accumulators and guardians of state secrets conduct their unseen business. He alone is presumed to have at least potential knowledge of everything that anyone else in the federal government secretly knows. While the contents of his more important secrets are tightly held, the fact of their possession is not hidden. On the contrary, one of the president's most valuable public attributes is his presumed mastery of secrets of state.

Since the heart of presidential activity is decision-making, which revolves around an impenetrable act of will, a split emerges between the public space and the space of choice and power. What appears in the public space are not presidential decisions, but rather dramas that presidents enact to signify their previous acts of will. Sometimes these dramas reveal a substantial amount about the bases and motives for a decision. At other times they reveal little, or counterfeit the considerations that entered into presidential choice.

Visible presidential drama, it should be emphasized, retains its impact despite the existence of a prior, mysterious realm of will. The mass audience, while offered an intelligible presidential drama, is also provided with hints that it cannot know the reality behind the drama. It can watch, it can participate vicariously, but it can never attain the vantage point of the president. The result is not to cast doubt upon the drama; rather, the presidential character who enacts that drama is made to appear even more fascinating and profound.

If the effectiveness of presidential performances is not undermined by their distance from the realm of secrecy, decision, and power, the same cannot be said of the public space itself. When what appears in public is mainly dramatic representation, possessing an indeterminate degree of truth, the public space becomes a shadow of a more vital, hidden realm. Dominated by presidential performances, the public space is simultaneously diminished by the president's paramount role in this hidden realm.

If we consider, for a moment, the elements that are necessary for democratic decisions, the processes of dialogue, debate, and deliberation are, I would propose, essential. These processes in turn necessitate an open space, one to which citizens have access, whether they wish to participate or merely to observe. The decisions that result under democratic conditions are, critics have long pointed out, not always the best decisions; they often prove to be mistaken or unwise. But they cannot be willful, idiosyncratic, or mysterious decisions; their hallmark is a clear, shared judgment arrived at through open discussion and deliberation. A democratic decision can thus be understood, criticized, redone.

When the sphere of important decisions is impenetrable to citizens, the foundations for democratic decision-making collapse. Citizens may still react with favor or disapproval to what presidents do in the public space, but their reactions remain ignorant of many of the factors actually shaping decisions. Confronting this mystified political world, where public intelligibility is edged with reminders of a deeper obscurity, most Americans can, I suspect, sense that they remain out of touch with the real roots of presidential action, and with politics itself.

## Rivals for the Public Space

Presidents, I have suggested, both dominate and diminish the public space. But they do not, of course, monopolize publicly visible action in any absolute sense. Other candidates for public attention can be seen and heard. Congressional leaders, spokesmen for the opposition party, challengers within the president's own party have channels for expressing and dramatizing their positions. Organized interests or grass-roots groups can sometimes garner attention, especially in areas of substantial controversy. The president is the towering figure in the national political landscape, but he is by no means the only figure.[20]

Nevertheless, presidential dominance is sufficient to present difficulties for other individuals or groups who are seeking a public stage or a public forum. Drawing attention away from the president can prove to be a formidable task. Media coverage is centered on him; he is frequently the focus of the opening segments of nationally televised news, the front page of newspapers, the lead stories in the national newsmagazines. Public awareness of issues is largely governed by the problems he has defined and the battles he is engaged in fighting. His role in the public space is so prominent that it is sometimes hard for others simply to be seen on any large scale.

His most widely publicized rivals for the public space are presidential aspirants from the other political party. Especially when a president's popularity ratings are low, and speculation is rampant about his reelection worries, the media may begin to pay considerable attention to these rivals. Yet the competitors must stake out their positions and indicate their merits in the language of promises for the future; a president can take action in the present that dramatizes his position and illustrates his merit. The capacity of a president to undercut his rivals' talk with action has been demonstrated on numerous occasions. Witness, for example, the collapse of George McGovern's major issue when the Nixon Administration announced that "peace is at hand" in Vietnam.

One available path to public visibility is to dramatize an issue that falls outside the presidential agenda. But when an individual or group has carved out a place in the public space by bringing to public attention a hitherto neglected issue, their visibility can still be undercut by the president. For he can take over an issue and add it to his own agenda; indeed, he is likely to co-opt an issue once it gains a wide and favorable audience. When, for example, a president like Jimmy Carter identifies himself publicly with causes such as environmental and consumer protection, the political efforts of environmental and consumer groups begin to be overshadowed. Media interest in advocates for the "public interest," such as Common Cause or Ralph Nader and his associates, is diminished. With a "friend" in the White House, such groups find themselves attracting less public attention than they did when previous presidents appeared indifferent or hostile to them.[21]

Rather than staking out an independent position, some groups try to win a public endorsement from the president. They pay obeisance to presidential dominance over the public space by concentrating their efforts on obtaining a part in his dramas. The White House is the focal point for an extraordinary amount of group activity, ranging from letter writing to lobbying. The scope of this activity attests not only to presidential power, but to the presidential ability to bestow public visibility on individuals and groups.

Obeisance to presidential dominance is also paid, ironically, by those who are the most strongly opposed to existing policies. Groups at loggerheads with major policies pursued by an administration often become preoccupied with the person of the president. Their efforts come to center around getting to the president and persuading him to change his mind, or — if that appears impossible — attacking him in public. Much of the antiwar movement, for example, developed a fixation on the figures of Lyndon Johnson and Richard Nixon. The character and the dramas of these presidents drew mounting outbursts of anger and loathing that were, in most regards, as politically sterile as the more positive responses to presidential spectacles. Abandoning the solid (though less emotionally appealing) grounds of structural and political analyses, American dissenters have often accepted the terms of presidential drama. On occasion, they have even served as its foils. The Nixon Administration admitted angry demonstrators to campaign rallies to enhance its argument about impending anarchy.[22]

Despite the barriers to independent action in the public space, some groups have managed to mount actions that rivalled presidential performances in visibility and drama. The civil rights movement, to take the most notable modern example, seized its own public space in the early 1960s with displays of commitment and courage that presidents were hard put to match. Facing this situation, Presidents Kennedy and Johnson responded not only with dramatic civil rights gestures of their own, but also with various behind-the-scenes maneuvers aimed at guiding the civil rights movement in a more moderate direction. Each was concerned that the public actions of the movement might prove embarrassing to his own public stance; each hoped that those actions, once properly channeled, could be used to embellish presidential drama. A memo from presidential aide Hobart Taylor, Jr., to Lyndon Johnson in July, 1964 reflects this characteristic White House approach:

> I am disturbed about the continued demonstrations and what I see on radio and TV. I am convinced that a great deal of the Negro leadership simply does not understand the facts of life. . . . We have not done with the Negro leaders what we did with the business community and with southern public officials — i.e., make a major and organized effort to direct their thinking along a proper course. . . .[23]

The president cannot bar entry into the public space. He cannot control most of the activities that go on in that space; he cannot avoid public opposition and criticism. But his preeminent role makes it possible for him to overshadow, to distort, or to guide the public roles that others develop. Even when challenged, he can act to reassert the primacy of his drama. The president, in short, has substantial power to ensure that, in the realm of visible action at least, he has no real peers, no full-scale rivals.

## Conclusion

Some readers may react to the foregoing analysis by citing all the difficulties that Gerald Ford and Jimmy Carter encountered in the "post-Watergate" era.

Recent experiences, they may suggest, indicate that presidents are no longer the awesome figures that they seemed a few years back. According to this view, the presidency today is simply not the spectacle that it once was.

I suggest that this view is shortsighted. Even in the recent disenchantment with the presidency, and amid the often healthy skepticism about presidential actions, sophisticated observers and ordinary citizens alike remained fixated on the office and its occupant. Far more energy was devoted to criticisms of Jimmy Carter's personal failings than to analyses of systemic failures, such as the deterioration of neo-Keynesian economic management or the breakup of interest-group liberalism. Most commentators remained bound to the assumption that everything ultimately depends on the presidency. Much of the criticism of Carter's presidency was, in fact, rooted in this assumption; it called for more decisive leadership, a firmer will, even a restoration of presidential mystique. Presidential dramas may have become disappointing or disconcerting to many Americans, but those dramas still dominate the public space. Few people yet perceive the possibilities for other forms of public action.

It thus remains important to understand the presidential monopoly over the public space, and to examine the consequences of our fixation on presidential drama. It is one of the ironies of American political thought that the cost, for citizen politics, of presidential dominance was hinted at a long time ago, during the proceedings which first fashioned the executive office. Responding to James Wilson's arguments for a unitary executive, George Mason voiced his doubts to the Constitutional Convention:

> The chief advantages which have been urged in favor of unity in the Executive, are the secrecy, the dispatch, the vigor and energy which the government will derive from it, especially in time of war. That these are great advantages, I shall most readily allow.... Yet perhaps a little reflection may incline us to doubt whether these advantages are not greater in theory than in practice, or lead us to enquire whether there is not some pervading principle in republican government which sets at naught and tramples upon this boasted superiority.... This invincible principle is to be found in the love, the affection, the attachment of the citizens to their laws, to their freedom, and to their country.[24]

Although Mason was primarily discussing military affairs, his comments held broader implications. It was possible for Americans to become so impressed by executive capabilities that they would come to denigrate their own capabilities. It was possible for presidents to take over so much of the public space that citizens would perceive the political world chiefly through presidential actions. The principle that Mason rejected has indeed proven to be more successful than the "invincible principle" that he invoked. Presidential action has come to overshadow other actions in the public space. In the name of democracy as well as leadership, in the garb of drama as well as will, the presidency now stands as an impediment to democratic politics.

## Notes

1. My argument in this essay is not that presidents are the only impediment to a
   more democratic political life. Other factors — economic, ideological, technological — also hinder mass political understanding and participation. I focus on the
   president's part because it is so little understood and so often mystified.
2. My use of the term "public space" is derived primarily from the work of Hannah
   Arendt, but I do not agree with all of Arendt's stipulations about the term (e.g.,
   her separation of political from economic and social questions).
3. See, for example, John E. Mueller, *War, Presidents, and Public Opinion* (New
   York: John Wiley, 1973); Richard A. Brody and Benjamin I. Page, "The Impact
   of Events on Presidential Popularity: The Johnson and Nixon Administrations,"
   in *Perspectives on the Presidency,* ed. by Aaron Wildavsky (Boston: Little, Brown,
   1975), pp. 136–48; James A. Stimson, "Public Support for American Presidents:
   A Cyclical Model," *Public Opinion Quarterly* (Spring 1976), pp. 1–21; Samuel
   Kernell, "Explaining Presidential Popularity," *The American Political Science
   Review* (June 1978), pp. 506–22.
4. Michael Novak, *Choosing Our King: Powerful Symbols in Presidential Politics*
   (New York: Macmillan, 1974), p. 10.
5. For an argument that the congressional role in legislative innovation is generally
   underrated, see Ronald C. Moe and Steven C. Teel, "Congress as Policy-Maker:
   A Necessary Reappraisal," *Political Science Quarterly* (September 1970), pp.
   443–70. The congressional role in innovation has been more perceptible in the
   face of a conservative president. On this score, see Gary Orfield, *Congressional
   Power: Congress and Social Change* (New York: Harcourt, Brace, Jovanovich,
   1975).
6. Fred W. Friendly, foreword to Newton N. Minow, John Bartlow Martin, and
   Lee M. Mitchell, *Presidential Television* (New York: Basic Books, 1973), pp.
   vii–viii.
7. See Michael Baruch Grossman and Martha Joynt Kumar, *Portraying the President: The White House and the News Media* (Baltimore, Md.: Johns Hopkins
   University Press, 1981), especially pp. 81–156, 226–249.
8. Russell Baker captured this phenomenon satirically: "If the Carter Administration were a television show it would have been canceled months ago. There are
   no chases, no shoot-outs, no jokes, no spectacles, no drama, no mystery, no comedy
   and no star performer." Russell Baker, "The Jimmy Carter Show," *New York
   Times Magazine,* December 18, 1977.
9. See Minow, Martin, and Mitchell, *Presidential Television,* passim; Novak, *Choosing Our King,* pp. 258–269.
10. Alexander Hamilton, James Madison, and John Jay, *The Federalist Papers* (New
    York: Mentor, 1961), p. 424.
11. Andrew Jackson, "Farewell Address," in *Social Theories of Jacksonian Democ-
    racy,* ed. by Joseph L. Blau (Indianapolis: Bobbs-Merrill, 1954), p. 17. Also see
    Michael Paul Rogin, *Fathers and Children: Andrew Jackson and the Subjugation
    of the American Indian* (New York: Knopf, 1975), pp. 278–79.

12. Fred Greenstein has detailed a number of psychological uses which citizens make of presidents. See Fred I. Greenstein, "Popular Images of the President," in *The Presidency*, ed. by Aaron Wildavsky (Boston: Little, Brown, 1969), pp. 292–95; and "What the President Means to Americans: Presidential 'Choice' Between Elections," in *Choosing the President*, ed. by James David Barber (Englewood Cliffs, N.J.: Prentice-Hall, 1974), pp. 142–47.

13. See Samuel Kernell, Peter W. Sperlich, and Aaron Wildavsky, "Public Support for Presidents," in *Perspectives on the Presidency*, ed. by Wildavsky, pp. 148–81.

14. Murray Edelman, *The Symbolic Uses of Politics* (Urbana, Illinois: University of Illinois Press, 1964), p. 78.

15. My analysis here has been influenced by Richard Sennett's provocative account of the relationship between a dominant public personality and a passive audience. See Richard Sennett, *The Fall of Public Man* (New York: Knopf, 1977), pp. 195–218.

16. See Sennett, *The Fall of Public Man*, pp. 224–37.

17. John F. Kennedy, foreword to Theodore C. Sorensen, *Decision-Making in the White House* (New York: Columbia University Press, 1963), p. xi.

18. *Weekly Compilation of Presidential Documents*, Vol. 13, No. 25 (June 20, 1977), p. 881.

19. Susan Fraker et al., "B-1 No, Cruise Yes," *Newsweek*, July 11, 1977, p. 15.

20. There are moments when presidents wish they were not such towering figures. In the midst of foreign policy fiascos, legislative defeats, administrative disarray, or scandals, the enormous amount of attention focused on the White House can be costly to a president in both political and personal terms. But these moments are ephemeral; no recent administration has dismantled its public-relations operations and tried to remove a president from the limelight.

21. The Carter example was suggested by Thomas E. Cronin. Franklin Roosevelt was the acknowledged master at taking over others' issues. Witness his moves in 1935 to undercut the Townsend Clubs with a social security plan and to "steal the thunder" from Huey Long's "Share the Wealth" movement with his media-dubbed "soak the rich" tax program.

22. Jonathan Schell, *The Time of Illusion* (New York: Vintage, 1976), pp. 128–29.

23. Hobart Taylor, Jr., Memorandum to the President, July 17, 1964 (Lyndon Baines Johnson Library, White House Central Files, EX HU 2, Box 3).

24. Max Farrand, ed., *The Records of the Federal Convention of 1787, Vol. 1* (New Haven, Conn.: Yale University Press, 1937), p. 112.

# 18. The Rise of the Rhetorical Presidency

James W. Ceaser
Glen E. Thurow
Jeffrey Tulis
Joseph M. Bessette

One of the most revealing periods of President Carter's tenure in office — and perhaps of the modern presidency itself — occurred during the summer of 1979. Falling to a new low in the public's approval ratings and facing criticism from all quarters for his leadership, the President dramatically cancelled a scheduled televised speech on energy and gathered his advisers together for a so-called domestic summit. Discussions moved beyond energy and economics to a reappraisal of the nature of presidential leadership and to an analysis of what, for want of a better term, can only be called the state of the national consciousness. Having served already more than half of his term, the President came to the conclusion that he had been mistaken in his understanding of the presidential office; he had, as he told David Broder, fallen into the trap of being "head of the government" rather than "leader of the people." As for the state of the national consciousness, the President concluded that the nation was experiencing a crisis of spirit or "malaise" that went deeper and was more ominous than the economic challenges at hand. Yet difficult as this problem of malaise was, the President believed it could be tackled, and by the very same means that would correct his own failures of leadership. By engaging in a rhetorical campaign to "wake up" the American people, the President hoped both to save his presidency and begin the long process of national moral revival. As a *Washington Post* front page headline proclaimed on the day preceding his newly scheduled national address: "CARTER SEEKING ORATORY TO MOVE AN ENTIRE NATION."[1]

Looking back today at these unusual events, one must surely be surprised that all of this self-analysis and deep introspection was so quickly forgotten. True, his July 15th, 1979, speech was no classic of American oratory; but it did receive an extraordinary amount of attention at the time and was commonly thought to mark a "turning point" in the Carter presidency, at least as measured by the President's own intentions. Yet just three months afterward, no one in the Administration was mentioning the crisis of malaise, and the President, after the Iranian hostage crisis, returned to the White House and began deliberately

*James Ceaser teaches political science at the University of Virginia and is the author of* Presidential Selection: Theory and Development. *Glen E. Thurow teaches political science at the University of Dallas; Jeffrey Tulis teaches political science at Princeton University; Joseph Bessette teaches political science at Catholic University. Bessette and Tulis are the coeditors of* The Presidency in the Constitutional Order.

acting "presidential," which is to say more like "the head of the government" than the "leader of the people."

Were these events merely a peculiar "story" of the Carter presidency? Perhaps. On the other hand, it might be argued that they are revealing in an exaggerated form of a major institutional development in this century — the rise of the rhetorical presidency — and of some of the problems inherent in that development.

Popular or mass rhetoric, which presidents once employed only rarely, now serves as one of their principal tools in attempting to govern the nation. Whatever doubts Americans may now entertain about the limitations of presidential leadership, they do not consider it unfitting or inappropriate for presidents to attempt to "move" the public by programmatic speeches that exhort and set forth grand and ennobling views.

It was not always so. Prior to this century, popular leadership through rhetoric was suspect. Presidents rarely spoke directly to the people, preferring communications between the branches of the government. Washington seldom delivered more than one major speech per year of his administration, and that one — the Annual Address — was almost mandated by the Constitution and was addressed to Congress. Jefferson even ceased delivering the address in person, a precedent that continued until Woodrow Wilson's appearance before Congress in 1913. The spirit of these early presidents' examples was followed throughout the nineteenth century. The relatively few popular speeches that were made differed in character from today's addresses. Most were patriotic orations, some raised constitutional issues, and several spoke to the conduct of war. Very few were domestic "policy speeches" of the sort so common today, and attempts to move the nation by means of an exalted picture of a perfect ideal were almost unknown. Indeed, in the conspicuous case where a president did "go to the people" in a "modern" sense — Andrew Johnson's speaking tour in the summer before the 1866 Congressional elections — the campaign not only failed, but was considered highly irregular.[2] It was not until well into the present century that presidential speeches addressed to the people became commonplace and presidents began to think that they were not effective leaders unless they constantly exhorted the public.[3]

Today, a president has an assembly line of speechwriters efficiently producing words that enable him to say something on every conceivable occasion. Unless a president is deliberately "hiding" in the White House, a week scarcely goes by without at least one major news story devoted to coverage of a radio or TV speech, an address to Congress, a speech to a convention, a press conference, a news release, or some other presidential utterance. But more important even than the quantity of popular rhetoric is the fact that presidential speech and action increasingly reflect the opinion that speaking *is* governing. Speeches are written to become the events to which people react no less than "real" events themselves.

The use of rhetoric by some of our recent presidents is revealing of this development. During his campaign and through the first few months of his presidency, President Kennedy spoke continually of the existence of a national crisis and of the need for sacrifice and commitment, only to find it difficult at times to explain just what the crisis was and where the sacrifice and commitment were actually needed. Today, seen in perspective, much of Kennedy's talk about our "hour of national peril" has a nice ring but a hollow sound, as if it were fashioned to meet the imperatives of a certain rhetorical style and not those of the concrete situation he faced.[4] It seems to reflect the view expressed by a former Kennedy White House aide: "It will be less important in years to come for presidents to work out programs and serve as administrators than it will be for presidents through the means of television to serve as educational and psychic leaders." [5]

President Johnson followed with a steady stream of oratory that swelled popular expectations of governmental capacity to a level that even his apologists now concede far exceeded what government could possibly achieve. What Harry McPherson, one of Johnson's chief aides and speechwriters, said of the goals of the Johnson administration characterizes perfectly the tone of its rhetoric:

> People were [seen to be] suffering from a sense of alienation from one another, of anomie, of powerlessness. This affected the well-to-do as much as it did the poor. Middle-class women, bored and friendless in the suburban afternoons; fathers, working at "meaningless" jobs, or slumped before the television set; sons and daughters desperate for "relevance" — all were in need of community beauty, and purpose, all were guilty because so many others were deprived while they, rich beyond their ancestors' dreams, were depressed. What would change all this was a creative public effort....[6]

President Nixon sensed people's reaction to the feverish pitch of the midsixties and countered with an antirhetoric rhetoric that soberly promised to "lower our voices":

> In these difficult years, America has suffered from a fever of words; from inflated rhetoric that promises more than it can deliver;...from bombastic rhetoric that postures instead of persuading.[7]

But this calm and mature pose, typical of Nixon's political superego, could not contain his own desire to strike back at his detractors, and together with Vice-President Agnew, Nixon launched his own rhetorical counteroffensive. If they enjoyed, up to a point at least, a great deal of success with their oratory, it was because much of it had the self-contained purpose of calling into question the rhetoric of their liberal opponents. With Agnew in particular, the privilege of holding public office was less important for what it could allow him to do than for what it could allow him to say.

President Carter, the outsider who came to Washington promising to bring a simple honesty and decency to government, began his term speaking in a voice lowered to a point where many felt that it had become inaudible. By mid-term, falling in the polls and urged on by his media adviser, Gerald Rafshoon, the President began to look for more opportunities to display rhetorical forcefulness. And by the time of his July oratorical campaign he emerged with an assertive tone and vigorous body movement, his theme being the decline and revitalization of America:

> [We face] a crisis that strikes at the very heart and soul and spirit of our national will. We can see this crisis in the growing doubt about the meaning of our own lives and in the loss of unity of purpose for our nation. . . . The erosion of our confidence in the future is threatening to destroy the social and political fabric of America. . . . [What] we must do is to regenerate our sense of unity, joining hands with each other in a sense of commitment to a national purpose. . . . We must bring together the different elements in America — producers, consumers, labor, business — bring us all together from the battlefield of selfishness to a table of common purpose.[8]

In the face of no tangible crisis on the order of a war or domestic upheaval, Carter was seeking nevertheless to define a subtler crisis and, linking it to the pragmatic issues of energy politics, to lead a domestic cultural revival. As one of his aides claimed, "I think we have seen both the rebirth of the American spirit that he talks about and the rebirth of the Carter presidency as well." [9]

Much of this rhetoric is undoubtedly, as many say today, "mere rhetoric." The excess of speech has perhaps fed a cynicism about it that is the opposite of the boundless faith in rhetoric that has been so far portrayed. Yet, despite this cynicism, it seems increasingly the case that for many who comment on and form opinions about the presidency, word rivals deed as the measure of presidential performance. The standard set for presidents has in large degree become an artifact of their own inflated rhetoric and one to which they frequently fall victim.[10] While part of this difficulty can be blamed on the ineptness of certain presidents' rhetorical strategies, it is also the case that presidents operate in a context that gives them much less discretion over their rhetoric than one might think. The problem is thus not one simply of individual rhetorics, but is rather an institutional dilemma for the modern presidency. Beginning with the campaign, the candidates are obliged to demonstrate their leadership capacity through an ever growing number of rhetorical performances, with the potential impact of their words on future problems of governing often being the least of their concerns. The pressure to "say something" continues after the president has begun to govern. Presidents not only face the demand to explain what they have done and intend to do, but they also have come under increasing pressure to speak out on perceived crises and to minister to the moods and emotions of the populace. In the end, it may be the office of the presidency that is weakened by this form of leadership, puffed up by false expectations that bear little relationship to the practical tasks of governing and undermined by the resulting cynicism.[11]

How did the rhetorical presidency come into existence? What are its strengths and weaknesses? Can presidents escape its burdens, and to what extent should they try to do so? These are some of the important questions that need addressing.

## I

The rise of the rhetorical presidency has been primarily the result of three factors: (1) a modern doctrine of presidential leadership, (2) the modern mass media, and (3) the modern presidential campaign. Of these three, doctrine is probably the most important.

As strange as it may seem to us today, the framers of our Constitution looked with great suspicion on popular rhetoric. Their fear was that mass oratory, whether crudely demogogic or highly inspirational, would undermine the rational and enlightened self-interest of the citizenry which their system was designed to foster and on which it was thought to depend for its stability. The framers' well-known mistrust of "pure" democracy by an assembly — and by extension, of the kind of representative government that looked only to public opinion as its guide — was not based, as is generally supposed, on a simple doubt about the people's capacity to govern, but on a more complex case concerning the evils that would result from the interplay between the public and popular orators.

In democracies, they reasoned, political success and fame are won by those orators who most skillfully give expression to transient, often inchoate, public opinion.[12] Governing by this means, if indeed it can be called governing, leads to constant instability as leaders compete with each other to tap the latest mood passing through the public. The paradox of government by mood is that it fosters neither democratic accountability nor statesmanly efficiency. Freed from the necessity to consult public opinion, understood as "the cool and deliberate sense of the community," popular orators would be so chained to public opinion, understood as "mood," that discretion and flexibility essential to statesmanship would be undermined.[13]

The framers were not so impractical as to think that popular rhetoric could be entirely avoided in a republican system. But the government they designed was intended to minimize reliance on popular oratory and to establish institutions which could operate effectively without the immediate support of transient opinion. All of the powers of governing were to be given, not directly to the people, but to their representatives. These representatives would find themselves in a tripartite government in which the various tasks of governing would be clearly discernible and assigned, and in which they would be forced to deal with knowledgeable and determined men not easily impressed by facile oratory. As part of their solution, the framers were counting on the large size of the nation, which at the time erected a communication barrier that would mute the impact of national popular rhetoric, whether written or oral. Beyond this, the framers instituted a presidential selection system that was designed to preclude active campaigning by the candidates. As for the presidency itself, the framers discouraged any idea that the president should serve as a leader of the people who would stir mass opinion by rhetoric; their conception was rather that of a constitutional officer who would rely for his authority on the formal powers granted by the Constitution and on the informal authority that would flow from the office's strategic position.

These limitations on popular rhetoric did not mean, however, that presidents were expected to govern in silence. Ceremonial occasions presented a proper forum for reminding the public of the nation's basic principles; and communications to Congress, explicitly provided for by the Constitution, offered a mechanism by which the people also could be informed on matters of policy. Yet this intrabranch rhetoric, though public, was not meant to be popular. Addressed in the first instance to a body of informed representatives, it would possess a reasoned and deliberative character; and insofar as some in the public would read these speeches and state papers, they would implicitly be called on to raise their understanding to the level of characteristic deliberative speech.

Nineteenth century politics in America did not, of course, follow exactly the framer's model of an essentially nonrhetorical regime. Campaigns quickly changed from their intended place as quiet affairs into spirited events replete with fanfare and highly charged popular rhetoric, though it is important to observe that the rhetoric was produced not by the candidates but by surrogates arranged for by the parties. Moreover, certain presidents — most notably Jackson and Lincoln — used their communications with Congress and some of their speeches and proclamations to address the people more or less directly. Yet the amount of nineteenth century presidential rhetoric that even loosely could be called popular is very little indeed, and the presidency remained, with some slight alterations, a constitutional office rather than the seat of popular leadership.[14]

The Inaugural and the Annual Address (now called the State of the Union) were the principal speeches of a president given wide dissemination. The character of the Inaugural Address illustrates the general character of presidential popular speech during the period. Given on a formal occasion, it tended to follow a pattern which was set by Jefferson's First Inaugural Address in which he delivered an exposition of the principles of the Union and its republican character. Although Jefferson's speech might in one sense be considered a partisan document, in fact he sought to be conciliatory toward his opponents. More important still, he presented his case not as an attempt to win support for the particular policies of a party but rather as an effort to instruct the people in, and fortify their attachment to, true republican political principles. The form of inaugural address perfected by Jefferson proved a lasting model throughout the century. Although subsequent addresses did not often match the eloquence or understanding of Jefferson's — Lincoln's Second Inaugural, of course, being the most conspicuous exception — they consistently attempted to show how the actions of the new administrations would conform to constitutional and republican principles.

Against this tradition Woodrow Wilson gave the Inaugural Address (and presidential speech generally) a new theme. Instead of showing how the policies of the incoming administration reflected the principles of our form of government, Wilson sought to articulate the unspoken desires of the people by holding out a vision of their fulfillment. Presidential speech, in Wilson's view, should articulate what is "in our hearts" and not necessarily what is in our Constitution.[15]

Theodore Roosevelt had presaged this change by his remarkable ability to capture the nation's attention through his understanding of the character of the new mass press and through his artful manipulation of the national press corps.[16] It was Wilson, however, who brought popular speech to the forefront of American politics by his dramatic appearances before Congress — breaking more than a century's precedent of presidential nonattendance — and by his famous speaking tour on behalf of the League of Nations. Most importantly, Wilson articulated the doctrinal foundation of the rhetorical presidency and thereby provided an alternative theoretical model to that of the framers. In Wilson's view, the greatest power in modern democratic regimes lay potentially with the popular leader who could sway or — to use his word — "interpret" the wishes of the people. After some indecision Wilson finally concluded that the presidency was the institution best suited to assume this role: "There is but one national voice in the country and that is the voice of the President." And it is the "voice" that is most important for governing: "It is natural that orators should be the leaders of a self-governing people. . . ."[17]

The Wilsonian concept of the rhetorical presidency consists of two interfused elements. First, the president should employ oratory to create an active public opinion that, if necessary, will pressure Congress into accepting his program: "He [the president] has no means of compelling Congress except through public opinion."[18] In advancing policy, deliberative, intrabranch rhetoric thus becomes secondary to popular rhetoric, and the president "speaks" to Congress not directly but through his popular addresses. Second, in order to reach and move the public, the character of the rhetoric must tap the public's feelings and articulate its wishes. Rhetoric does not instill old and established principles as much as it seeks to infuse a sense of vision into the president's particular legislative program.

> A nation is led by a man who . . . speaks, not the rumors of the street, but a new principle for a new age; a man in whose ears the voices of the nation do not sound like the accidental and discordant notes that come from the voice of a mob, but concurrent and concordant like the united voices of a chorus, whose many meanings, spoken by melodious tongues, unite in his understanding in a single meaning and reveal to him a single vision, so that he can speak what no man else knows, the common meaning of the common voice.[19]

Much the same idea, though stripped of some of its eloquence, was expressed by President Carter in his convention acceptance speech when he promised to be a president "who is not isolated from the people, but who feels your pain and shares your dreams and takes his strength and his wisdom and his courage from you." [20] Presidents have not always found it easy to bring these two elements — policy and mood — together. Carter's "malaise" address of July 1979 again illustrates the point. The first half of the speech portrayed a national malaise of sweeping and profound proportions; the second half incongruously implied that we could secure our redemption by conserving energy and taxing the oil companies.

The Wilsonian concept of presidential leadership was echoed in FDR's claim that the presidency is "pre-eminently a place of moral leadership" and subsequently canonized in the scholarly literature by Clinton Rossiter's characterization of the presidency as the nation's "trumpet." [21] To be sure, not all presidents since Wilson have embraced this grandiloquent conception of their role, but as a doctrine the rhetorical presidency has become the predominant model. What these metaphorical terms like "voice of the nation," "moral leader" and "trumpet" all suggest is a form of presidential speech that soars above the realm of calm and deliberate discussion of reasons of state or appeals to enlightened self-interest. Rather, the picture of leadership that emerges under the influence of this doctrine is one that constantly exhorts in the name of a common purpose and a spirit of idealism.

If the doctrine of the rhetorical presidency leaves us today with the occasional feeling that it is hollow or outworn, it is not because of a decline in its influence but because of the inevitable consequences of its ascendancy. Presidents such as Wilson, Franklin Roosevelt, and John Kennedy found in the doctrine a novelty which they could exploit to win attention — if not always success — for their programs. Exercised against the prevailing expectation of moral leadership, however, presidents may find that the doctrine is sometimes more of a burden than an opportunity. Presidents can speak and exhort, but will anyone genuinely heed what they say?

The events leading up to President Carter's address in July 1979 are instructive. Late in June, the President received a memo from his chief domestic policy adviser, Stuart Eizenstat, recommending what has become by now the standard use of the rhetorical presidency:

> Every day you need to be dealing with — and publicly be seen as dealing with — the major energy problems now facing us.... You have a variety of speeches scheduled after your return.... Each of those occasions should be used to talk about energy.... The windfall tax campaign was successful because of your repeated discussion of it during a short time. With strong steps we can mobilize the nation around a real crisis and with a clear enemy.[22]

But on the day before his originally scheduled TV address, the President decided to cancel it because, in columnist David Broder's words, "He believed that neither the country nor the Congress would heed or respond to another energy speech — the fifth of his term — from him." [23] If a nationally televised presidential address, itself once a dramatic event, must be cancelled as a way of recapturing a sense of drama, one wonders what expedient presidents will turn to next.

## II

The second factor that accounts for the rise of the rhetorical presidency is the modern mass media. The media did not create the rhetorical presidency — doctrine did — but it facilitated its development and has given to it some of its special characteristics. The mass media, meaning here primarily radio and television, must be understood first from the perspective of its technical capacities. It has given the president the means by which to communicate directly and instantaneously with a large national audience, thus tearing down the communications barrier on which the framers had relied to insulate representative institutions from direct contact with the populace. Besides increasing the size of the president's audience, the mass media have changed the mode by which he communicates with the public, replacing the written with the spoken word delivered in a dramatic visible performance. The written word formerly provided a partial screen or check against the most simplistic argumentations, as it allowed more control of the text by the reader and limited the audience to those with the most interest in politics.

One might reply, of course, that presidents today produce more written documents than ever before and that all of their speeches are recorded and transcribed. But this matters little, as few in the public ever bother to peruse, let alone read, the president's words. Significant messages are delivered today in speeches, and presidents understand that it is the visible performance, not the tangible text, that creates the public impression. Under the constant demand for new information that characterizes audiences of the media age, what is not seen or heard today does not exist. Presidents accordingly feel the pressure to speak more and to engage in what Eizenstat called "campaigns" to keep their message before the public. Words come to have an ephemeral quality to them, and the more the president speaks the less value can be put on any one speech he delivers. One of the great ironies of the modern presidency is that as the president relies more on rhetoric to govern, he finds it more difficult to deliver a truly important speech, one that will stand by itself and continue to shape events.

The influence of the mass media on presidential rhetoric is not limited to its technical capacities. The mass media have also created a new power center in American politics in the form of television news. If the technical aspect of the media has given the president an advantage or an opportunity, the existence of television news often serves as a rival or an impediment. Journalists are filters in the communication process, deciding what portions of the president's non-televised speeches they will show and how their arguments will be interpreted. When presidents speak in public today, their most important audience is not the one they are personally addressing, but rather the public as it is reached through the brief cuts aired on the news. Speeches accordingly tend to be written so that any segment can be taken to stand by itself — as a self-contained lead. Argument gives way to aphorism.

The direct impact of the news media's interpretation of the president's words is perhaps less important for presidential rhetoric than the indirect influence that derives from the character of news itself. Television news not only carries the messages of governing officials to the people; it also selects the issues that are presented to the government for "action" of some sort. "Real" expressions of mass opinion, which in the past were sporadic, are replaced by the news media's continuous "sophisticated" analyses that serve as a surrogate audience, speaking to the government and supposedly representing to it what the people are saying and thinking. Driven by its own inner dynamic to find and sustain exciting issues and to present them in dramatic terms, the news media create — or give the impression of creating — national moods and currents of opinion which appear to call for some form of action by the government and especially by the president.

The media and the modern presidency feed on each other. The media have found in the presidency a focal point on which to concentrate their peculiarly simplistic and dramatic interpretation of events; and the presidency has found a vehicle in the media that allows it to win public attention and with that attention the reality, but more often the pretense, of enhanced power.[24] What this two-sided relationship signifies is a change in the rhetorical context in which the president now operates, the implications of which extend beyond the question of how much power the president has to the issue of how he attempts to govern. Constitutional government, which was established in contradistinction to government by assembly, now has become a kind of government by assembly, with TV "speaking" to the president and the president responding to the demands and moods that it creates. The new government by assembly — operating without a genuine assembling of the people — makes it increasingly difficult for presidents to present an appearance of stability and to allow time for policies to mature and for events to respond to their measures. Instead, the president is under more pressure to act — or to appear to act — to respond to the moods generated by the news.

Partly as a result of these pressures from the media for more and more presidential speech, a major new staff capacity has been added to the White House to enable the president to produce the large number of speeches and messages that he speaks or writes. While not a major cause of the rhetorical presidency, like any staff capacity its existence becomes a reason for its continual use. Once known as "ghosts" and hidden in the presidential closet, rhetoric-makers today have come out into the full light of day and are openly employed under the title of speechwriters.[25] We have perhaps passed beyond the point of naïveté where we shudder at exposés which reveal that the personal convictions of the president are written by someone else, but it is worth noting the paradox that at a time when presidents are judged more by their rhetoric, they play less of a role in its actual formulation. If, as Francis Bacon once wrote, only writing makes a man exact, the incoherence of much presidential policy-making may owe something to the fact that presidents do so little of their own writing and sometimes schedule more speeches than they can possibly supervise closely.[26] Certain rapid shifts that occurred during 1978 in President Carter's pronounced foreign policy, which Senator Edward Kennedy attempted to make into an important campaign issue, are attributable to different viewpoints of the authors of his speeches, which the President either did not want or did not have the time to integrate.[27] An institutionalized speechwriting staff may bring to presidential speeches interests of its own that conflict with presidential policy or, to the extent that the staff becomes divorced from the president's chief political advisers, it may be incapable of resisting pressure from others for the inclusion of remarks in speeches at the expense of presidential coherence. Finally the speechwriting task has come more and more to be influenced by pollsters and admen whose understanding of rhetoric derives from the premises of modern advertising and its offshoot, political consulting. Such influence is even more visible in the modern presidential campaign.

## III

The modern presidential campaign is the third factor that accounts for the rise of the rhetorical presidency. The roots of the modern campaign go back to Wilson and the Progressives and to many of the same ideas that helped to create the rhetorical presidency. Prior to 1912, the parties were largely responsible for conducting the campaigns, and the candidates, with few execptions, restricted their communications to letters of acceptance of the nomination. Wilson was the first victorious presidential candidate to have engaged in a full-scale speaking tour during the campaign. In his view, it was essential that the candidates replace the parties as the main rhetorical instruments of the campaign. This change would serve not only to downgrade the influence of traditional parties but also to prepare the people for the new kind of presidency that he hoped to establish. Indeed, with Wilson the distinction between campaigning and governing is blurred, as both involve the same essential function of persuading through popular oratory.

Although Wilson himself did not campaign extensively in the preconvention period, he supported the idea of a preconvention campaign and pushed for nomination by national primaries. His ideal of a truly open presidential nomination campaign in which all candidates must take the "outside" route was not fully realized, however, until after the reforms that followed the 1968 election. Over the past three campaigns (1972, 1976 and 1980) we have seen the development of one of the most peculiarly irresponsible rhetorical processes ever devised. For a period of what is now well over a year, the various contenders have little else to offer except their rhetoric. Undisciplined by the responsibility of matching word to deed, they seek to create events out of their speeches, all the while operating under the constant media-created pressure to say something new. As their goal is to win power, and as that goal, especially in the preconvention period, is remote, candidates can easily afford to disregard the impact of their speech on the demands of governing and instead craft their rhetoric with a view merely to persuading.

Scholars of the electoral process, interested in such issues as accountability and democratic voting theory, have sought to determine just how much of the candidates' rhetoric goes into spelling out stands on issues as compared to other kinds of appeals, e.g., character or vaguely formed interpretation of events. If there is an operative normative theory to some of these inquiries, it is based on the premise that it would be desirable for the voters to know the candidate's stand on the full range of issues and to make up their minds on the basis of a rational calculation of their position as it compares to those of the candidates.[28] However, if one does not focus exclusively in campaigns but tries to see campaigns as part of the total process of governing, there is cause for wondering whether what is ideal from the standpoint of democratic voting theory is very helpful for promoting effective governing: too many specific commitments might, if taken seriously, undermine a necessary degree of discretion, or, if blatantly ignored, add to public cynicism. It is the empirical findings of such research that are, perhaps, of most interest, and here one discovers two contrasting tendencies. Benjamin Page has shown that candidates devote little time in their speeches to spelling out anything like concrete policy stands; instead most of their effort goes into general interpretations of past records and highly ambiguous statements about future goals.[29] On the other hand, Jeff Fishel has found that the number of specific promises that candidates make over the course of a campaign has been increasing dramatically since 1952.[30] This paradox is easily explicable if one bears in mind that while candidates may discuss little of substance in their speeches, they speak (and write) much more than they ever did in the past and thus accumulate more pledges. This research suggests, then, that we have the worst of both worlds — vague and uninstructive speeches on the one hand and more and more specific promises on the other. In this result one finds the perfect marriage of media and special interest politics.

It may also be that the distinctions scholars make in regard to "issue stands" and "image making" are increasingly irrelevant. For the candidates and their political consultants the campaign is often seen as a whole, with the most sophisticated campaigns today being run on the premise that the candidates must tap and express a popular mood. Issues and images are both fit into this general theme. As Jimmy Carter remarked in 1976, "Insofar as my political campaign has been successful, it is because I have learned from our people and have accurately reflected their concerns, their frustrations and their desires." [31] Reflecting but not necessarily educating the people's moods has in some instances been the order of the day. The old case against the political consultants and admen — that they build up an image of the candidate's person — largely underestimates their impact. Today, they are definitely in the "business" of dealing with "issues" no less than images, and both frequently are subordinated to mood.

Actually, the efforts that candidates do make in some of their speeches to address the issues are often passed over and ignored in the media. Although it may take the public a long time to learn the candidates' basic themes — and many never learn them — the reporters covering the campaign often tire of repetitive stories and resist putting comments from formal speeches on the air. As Thomas Patterson has shown, the press, and especially television news coverage, looks for the "new" in the campaigns, and thus tends to cover those comments of candidates that are made in impromptu sessions. Indeed, journalists attempt to stimulate "campaign issues" — e.g., off-the-cuff responses to charges or to contemporary news events — rather than to cover what the candidates seek to communicate in their own rhetoric.[32] This form of news coverage may well help us learn something about the candidates' "character" or ability to think in public, but it hardly does much to encourage among the people a respect for the formal rhetorical mode. That speeches might, if heard, be a helpful way of judging candidates, however, is suggested by the importance of the one main campaign speech that the public can view in its entirety — the campaign acceptance speech.

The presidential campaign is important for the kinds of inflated expectations it raises, but it is even more important for the effects it has on the process of governing. So formative has the campaign become of our tastes for oratory and of our conception of leadership that presidential speech and governing have come more and more to imitate the model of the campaign. In a dramatic reversal, campaigns set the tone for governing rather than governing for campaigns. This trend, which is becoming more embedded in public expectations, is furthered by another dynamic that works on the president and his staff. Both may think of the campaign as their finest hour, to the extent that its techniques become internalized in their conception of governing. As Pollster Pat Caddell advised Carter at the beginning of his term, "governing with public approval requires a continuing political campaign." [33] In a memo that led up to the Camp David speech, Caddell suggested that "Carter should return to the style that had marked his campaign for the presidency, at least in its early stages: to address the nation's mood and to touch on the 'intangible' problems in our society." [34] Some of the President's political advisers, Vice-President Mondale among them, opposed the whole idea of a campaign while holding office. But the political consultants stood together and won the day. As Gerald Rafshoon told Elizabeth Drew, "It was important for the President to be 'relevant,' which meant showing people he understood what was bothering them." [35]

The growing intrusion of the mentality of the campaign consultants into the governing process recalls the ancient philosophical battle between the original founders of the art of rhetoric — the sophists — and the political scientists. When rhetoric was first discovered as a teachable art in ancient Greece, its masters emphasized its purely persuasive powers; and because rhetoric claimed to be able to instruct politicians on how to win power, it quickly began to pass itself off as the most important kind of political education. As Carnes Lord has stated, ". . . by encouraging the supposition that the exercise of political responsibility requires little substantive knowledge beyond rhetorical expertise itself, rhetoric as taught by the sophists tended to make men oblivious to the very need for a science of politics." The threat that the art of rhetoric so defined posed to political science, yet the evident necessity of politicians to use rhetoric, led Aristotle to write a rhetoric of his own. It was designed to recast the nature of the discipline so as to emphasize, within the realm of the potentially persuasive, the role of rational argumentation and to encourage politicians "to view rhetoric not as an instrument of personal aggrandizement in the sophistic manner, but rather as an instrument of responsible or prudent statesmanship." [36] This view, which came to constitute the rhetorical tradition of the West through its central place in a liberal arts education, exerted a powerful influence on our founding. Many of the framers, as Gordon Wood has pointed out, were schooled in this tradition of rhetoric, and one of our presidents, John Quincy Adams, wrote a treatise on rhetoric that reflected many of its premises.[37] Clearly, however, under the impact of the modern campaign, this tradition has lost ground to a modern-day version of the sophistic tradition. Under the tutelage of political consultants and pollsters, the understanding of rhetoric as mere persuasion has come to be almost second nature to many of our politicians. The devolution of governing into campaigning is thus even more ominous than it first appeared, for it represents not just a change in the purpose of speeches but a decay in the standard of speech itself.

## IV

President Carter's formulation of July 1979, that a president should be "the leader of the people" rather than "the head of the government," was a perfect expression of his support for the doctrine of the rhetorical presidency. Acting explicitly on this doctrine, the president pledged to spend more time with the people and launched a campaign of speeches, largely inspirational in tone, that were designed to mobilize a popular constituency which supposedly would translate into higher opinion ratings and more power in Washington. The evident failure of this campaign, however, should perhaps have given the President pause about the effectiveness of his newly discovered conception of his office. For all the momentary attention lavished on the President's words, they did not succeed — or come close to succeeding — in creating "a rebirth of the American spirit." Nor is this surprising.

As the name implies, the rhetorical presidency is based on words, not power. When connected in a practical way with the exercise of power, speech can be effective, but when used merely to generate public support it is apt to fail. However much attention and enthusiasm a president can momentarily garner, there is little assurance that the Congress will accede. As Henry Fairlie once observed, "There is in fact very little that the people can do to assist a President while he is in office; brought together at a general election, they are dispersed between elections; brought together in the evening by a television address, they are dispersed the next day." [38] Although a president may sometimes find that he can make the greatest public impression by attacking Congress for failing to pass his preferred programs, or by attributing such failures to archaic procedures or undue influence and power of special interests, such appeals are not likely to win friends in that body which still retains ultimate authority over legislation. Moreover, to the extent that presidents *can* pressure Congress through popular appeals, such a strategy, like crying wolf, is likely to work less well the more often it is used.

The inflated expectations engendered by the rhetorical presidency have by now become a matter of serious concern among those who study the presidency. In response to this problem, a growing number of scholars have begun to argue that presidents should remove themselves from much of the day-to-day management of government and reserve themselves for crisis management.[39] If this argument means only that presidents should not immerse themselves in details or spread themselves too thin, no one could quarrel with it. But if it means that the president should abandon the articulation of a broad legislative program or avoid general management of the bureaucracy at a time when the bureaucracy is becoming more and more unmanageable, then the argument is misguided. If the president does not give coherence to policy or enforce discipline on the Executive branch, who will? Certainly not Congress. The president remains our only national officer who, as Jefferson once said, "commands a view of the whole ground." [40] A retrenched presidency that cedes much of its authority to others and merely reacts to crisis is hardly the answer to our difficulties. Nor is it the only possible response to the doctrine of the rhetorical presidency. Advocates of the retrenched presidency contend that to reduce the expectations on the office, its authority must be diminished. But the high expectations for the office are not the result of its authority, but rather of the inflated conception of presidential leadership that governs our thinking. It is the publicly proclaimed pretensions of presidential power, not the power itself, that is the source of the problem.

The roots of the rhetorical presidency extend so deeply into our political structure and national consciousness that talk of change may seem futile; and yet the evident failures of the current doctrine, together with the growing scholarly debate about the crisis of the presidency, suggest that the moment has arrived for a discussion of alternatives. It should not be forgotten that the foundations of the rhetorical presidency were deliberately laid by Woodrow Wilson and that other presidents might establish new doctrines. If a sensible reform of the institution is ever possible, the key will be found in reversing the order of President Carter's July 1979, formulation — that is, in restoring the president to his natural place as the head of government, and subordinating his awkward role of an itinerant leader of the people. But how could such change take place, and what would the contours of the office look like?

First, since the modern campaign is the source of so many of the problems of the presidency, it is evident that no reform of the office can hope to succeed without a change in the selection process. The operative theoretical principle that must govern this change is that the selection process should be thought of not as an end in itself, but as a means of promoting, or at least not undermining, the character of the presidential office. Construed in practical terms, this principle translates into a call for electoral reform that would reduce the duration of the campaign, especially in the preconvention period. The elimination or dramatic reduction in the number of presidential primaries and the return of the power of selection to the parties would be helpful. This change would not eliminate the campaign, but it would reduce its public phase to a shorter period and thus focus public attention on the speechmaking that takes place after the nomination. Indeed, as Thomas Patterson has recently shown, the longer campaigns of recent years have *not* increased the level of public knowledge of the candidates' stands; and the psychology of mass attention may well be such that, after a certain point, there is an inverse relationship between information and learning.[41] Rhetorical performances may lose their drama as they become simply another in a long and expected series.

Second, presidents should reduce the number of their speeches. As they speak less, there is at least the chance that their words will carry more weight; and if their words carry more weight, then perhaps more thought will be given to speech that can sensibly direct action. What applies to speeches applies equally to press conferences. Press conferences without cameras would probably allow for a more detailed exchange of information between the president and the press corps and avoid the pressures on the president (and the journalists) to make each news conference dramatic and newsworthy.[42] Written messages might replace many presently oral performances, and personal television appearances would be reserved for truly important issues of public concern.

Third, it is obvious that a reduction in the quantity of rhetoric itself is not enough; its character must also change. To avoid inspirational rhetoric does not mean that the president must abandon firm principles, practical ideals or even a political poetry that connects this generation with the moorings of our political system. Indeed, such a rhetoric is perfectly consistent with the dignity of a head of state and the character of our political order. In respect to policy, however, presidents must recapture the capacity to address the nation's enlightened self-interest no less than its sense of idealism and the related capacity to approach Congress directly rather than through the people.

The gravest problem of the rhetorical presidency, however, goes deeper than any issue confined to presidential practice. It extends to the basic questions of how our nation can be governed. No one would deny that presidents need to hold up America's basic principles and on occasion mobilize the public to meet genuine challenges. Indeed, in a liberal system of government that frees men's acquisitive instincts and allows them to devote their energies to individual material improvement, there is room on occasion for presidents to lift up the public's vision to something beyond the clash of interests. But under the influence of the rhetorical presidency, we have seen an ever-increasing reliance on inspirational rhetoric to deal with the normal problems of politics. If there is a place for such rhetoric, it is necessary also to be aware of its danger and of the corresponding need to keep it within limits. By itself, rhetoric does not possess the power to make citizens devote themselves selflessly to the common weal, particularly where the basic principles of society protect and encourage men's independent and private activities. The founders of our country created a complex representative government designed to foster a knowledgeable concern for the common good in the concrete circumstances of political life that would be difficult, if not impossible, to elicit directly from a people led by orators. What the continued use of inspirational rhetoric fosters is not a simple credibility problem, but a deep tension between the publicly articulated understanding of the nature of our politics and the actual springs that move the system. No wonder, then, that some politicians, deceived by their own rhetoric, find it difficult to come to terms with the job of governing a nation of complex multiple interests. Far from reinforcing our country's principles and protecting its institutions, the rhetorical presidency leads us to neglect our principles for our hopes and to ignore the benefits and needs of our institutions for a fleeting sense of oneness with our leaders.

SOURCE: This essay originally appeared in *Presidential Studies Quarterly* (Spring 1981) and is reprinted with permission. The author wishes to thank the National Endowment for the Humanities and the White Burkett Miller Center of Public Affairs at the University of Virginia.

## Notes

1. *The Washington Post,* July 14, 15, and 16, 1979.
2. For a discussion of Johnson's "swing around the circle," see Albert Castel, *The Presidency of Andrew Johnson* (Lawrence, Kans.: Regents Press, 1979).
3. Joseph Kallenbach, *The American Chief Executive* (New York: Harper & Row, 1966), pp. 333–340.
4. *Public Papers of the Presidents, John F. Kennedy 1961* (Washington, D.C.: U.S. Government Printing Office, 1961), p. 19; see also Henry Fairlie, *The Kennedy Promise: The Politics of Expectation* (Garden City, N.J.: Doubleday, 1973).
5. Cited in Thomas E. Cronin, *The State of the Presidency* (Boston: Little, Brown, 1975), p. 72. The identification of the aide is not revealed.
6. Harry McPherson, *A Political Education* (Boston: Little, Brown, 1972), p. 301–2.
7. *The Public Papers of the Presidents, Richard Nixon 1969* (Washington, D.C.: U.S. Government Printing Office, 1969), p. 2.

8. President Carter, Speeches of July 15, 1979, (National Television Address) and July 16, 1979, (Detroit). *Presidential Documents, Annual Index,* 1979, p. 1237 and 1248.

9. *The Washington Post,* July 17, 1979, p. A14.

10. See for example, Theodore Lowi, *The End of Liberalism* (New York: Norton, 1969), p. 182.

11. In discussing matters that "force" presidents to make decisions by specified dates, Richard Neustadt concludes: "It is hardly to be wondered at that during Truman's years such matters became focal points for policy development, especially in the domestic sphere." See Richard Neustadt, "Presidency and Legislation: Planning the Presidents Program" *American Political Science Review* (December 1955), p. 1021. It is also interesting to note here that in reference to John Kennedy's decision to implement the moon shot program, Theodore Sorensen has implied that the decision was largely made "because we felt we were in need of some display of action." See Theodore Sorensen, Kennedy Library oral history.

12. Alexander Hamilton, James Madison and John Jay, *The Federalist Papers,* ed., Clinton Rossiter (New York: New American Library, 1962), p. 360 (#58).

13. *Ibid.,* p. 384 (#63).

14. See Marvin R. Weisbord, *Campaigning for President* (Washington: Public Affairs Press, 1964), pp. 1–55; Arthur Schlesinger, *Introduction to Schlesinger and Israel,* eds., *The State of the Union Messages of the President* (New York: Chelsea House, 1966).

15. Woodrow Wilson, *Papers,* ed. Arthur S. Link (Princeton, N.J.: Princeton University Press, 1978) vol. 27, p. 150.

16. Elmer Cornwell, Jr., *Presidential Leadership and Public Opinion* (Bloomington, Ind.: Indiana University Press, 1965), pp. 1–30.

17. Woodrow Wilson, *Constitutional Government in the United States* (New York: Columbia University Press, 1908), p. 67; Woodrow Wilson, Congressional Government (Cambridge, Mass.: Riverside Press, 1885), p. 209.

18. Wilson, *Constitutional Government,* p. 65.

19. Wilson, *Papers,* ed. Link, Vol. 19, p. 42.

20. *Congressional Quarterly Almanac,* 1976, pp. 852–53.

21. Kallenbach, p. 253; and Clinton Rossiter, *The American Presidency* (New York: Harcourt Brace, 1960), p. 34.

22. *The Washington Post,* July 10, 1979.

23. *The Washington Post,* July 14, 1979, p. A1.

24. See Michael J. Robinson, "Television and American Politics, 1956–1976," *The Public Interest* (Summer 1972), pp. 3–39; Michael Baruch Grossman and Martha Joynt Kumar, *Portraying the President: The White House and the News Media* (Baltimore, Md.: Johns Hopkins University Press, 1981); and Robert Entman, "The Imperial Media," in Arnold J. Meltsner, ed., *Politics and the Oval Office* (Washington, D.C.: Institute for Contemporary Studies, 1981).

25. For a review of the transformation of speechwriters from secret aides to openly identified advisers, see Marie Hochmuth Nichols; *Rhetoric and Criticism,* (Baton Rouge: Louisiana State University Press, 1963), pp. 35–48.

26. Francis Bacon, *A Selection of His Works,* ed. by Sidney Warhaft (Indianapolis: Odyssey Press, 1965), p. 42.

27. James Fallows, Personal Interview, March 10, 1979. Also see James Fallows, "The Passionless Presidency" and "The Passionless Presidency, Part II," *Atlantic,* May and June, 1979.

28. Benjamin I. Page, *Choices and Echoes in Presidential Elections* (Chicago: University of Chicago Press, 1979), pp. 10–61.

29. *Ibid.,* pp. 152–192.
30. Jeffrey Fishel, "From Campaign Promise to Presidential Performance," A paper prepared for a Colloquium at the Woodrow Wilson Center, June 20, 1979.
31. *The Campaign of 1976 Jimmy Carter* (Washington, D.C.: U.S. Government Printing Office, 1976), vol. 2, p. 274.
32. See Thomas Patterson, *The Mass Media Election* (New York: Praeger, 1980).
33. Patrick H. Caddell, "Initial Working Paper on Political Strategy," mimeo. Dec. 10, 1976.
34. Elizabeth Drew, "Phase: In Search of a Definition," *The New Yorker Magazine,* Aug. 27, 1979, p. 49–73.
35. *Ibid.,* p. 59.
36. Carnes Lord, "On Aristotle's Rhetoric," conference paper delivered at the White Burkett Miller Center, July 1979.
37. John Quincy Adams, *Lectures on Rhetoric and Oratory* (Cambridge, Mass., 1810).
38. Cited in Cronin, p. 73.
39. See David Broder's column, "Making the Presidency Man-sized," *The Washington Post,* Dec. 5, 1979, p. A27. Broder summarizes the consensus of a conference on the presidency held at the White Burkett Miller Center of Public Affairs at the University of Virginia.
40. Richardson, p. 3.
41. Patterson, pp. 67–75 and 173–181.
42. See Cornwell, op. cit., for the history of the press conference. In a series of forums on the press conference sponsored by the White Burkett Miller Center, most of the reporters present who have covered the president were of the opinion that, while television conferences were helpful on occasion, they often were superficial and did not allow for a genuine and in-depth exchange with the president. Most felt that greater use of the "reporters around the desk" format would improve the reading public's knowledge of the president.

# Presidents as Politicians

# VII

**19. Presidential Leadership of Congress**
*Reo M. Christenson*

**20. The President as Coalition Builder:
Reagan's First Year**
*Hedrick Smith*

**21. Presidents and Political Parties**
*Thomas E. Cronin*

# 19. Presidential Leadership of Congress

## Reo M. Christenson

"The classic test of greatness in the White House," James MacGregor Burns once wrote, "has been the chief executive's capacity to lead Congress." [1] . . .

It was not always so. In Whig days, presidential attempts to shape the legislative product were resented as impertinent, a dangerous violation of separation of powers which savored of incipient despotism. Even though Washington (through Hamilton) and Jefferson had exercised such leadership, the self-confidence of later congressional leaders, combined with hatred of Jackson's aggressive behavior, created a congressional atmosphere hostile to this role. But prolonged evidence of congressional weakness, plus subsequent executives with a taste for power, finally destroyed the notion that a president's legislative role is limited to a shy "please."

Presidential legislative initiatives frequently draw upon the congressional legislative hopper. [2] But unless a president incorporates them into his program, bills sponsored by individual members of the two Houses are likely to perish in the catacombs of Congress. Almost every year brings fresh evidence that Congress is unable to develop an internal leadership that can give direction and a modicum of discipline to our semi-anarchic legislature. Thus even in post-Vietnam and post-Watergate America, we confront the perennial need for a president with the vision, the courage and the skill to convert Congress into a constructive body.

Are there operational principles, confirmed by historical experience, which can be counted on to facilitate leadership of Congress? The answer would seem to be yes; there are Ten Commandments (sic) which every president can usefully ponder and profitably apply to every Congress. This is not to say that an executive who lacks the mysterious blend of character, judgment, personality, temperament, and presence which spell leadership can succeed by studying and mechanically applying a set of rules. But there appear to be principles and caveats which, when followed, fructify those leadership abilities a president does possess and which, ignored, debilitate them. Here they are.

1. The president must "know the deck."

Early in Lyndon B. Johnson's Administration, before Vietnam crippled his leadership, James Reston wrote: "President Johnson's ability to get his program

*Reo M. Christenson teaches political science at Miami University and is the author and editor of several books, including* Heresies, Right and Left; Challenge of Decision; *and* Voice of the People.

through the Congress is recognized by both political parties here, but there is still much confusion about how he does it."

"One explanation," to use Tommy Corcoran's phrase, "is that the President knows the deck. He knows the value of every card. He knows the players intimately. And he works at it night and day."

"All the popular notions of Johnson the arm twister and wheeler dealer, while partly true, debase and distort a much more intricate, delicate, and positive art."

"The problem is to know where the wires of power lie, who are the key men, what one group wants that other opposing groups can be persuaded to accept and a third group is likely to tolerate, however unwillingly." [3]

In sum, Reston reminds us that knowledge *is* power — knowledge of men, of the legislative milieu, of the contours and permutations of power. Having this knowledge does not guarantee one can *use* it wisely but an outsider like Jimmy Carter was inevitably handicapped by his unfamiliarity with the folkways, nuances and personalities of the Washington scene. One needs a *feel* for the particular political environment in which one operates and this can only come from experience.

2. A president needs a good sense of timing — to know when to lead and when to pause. Ordinarily, of course, Congress is more disposed to cooperate with a president in the first year of his term and — if the other party controls one or both Houses — is less disposed to follow his lead in election years. But Congress also reflects the national mood. It did not want ambitious or controversial programs in 1921 or 1953. The mood, instead, called for presidential emollience, and a healing of wounds. The national temper never demands presidential inaction, but it may suggest a prudent focusing on goals which can win consensus, or at least avoid major controversy. On the other hand, Congress was pleading for leadership in the early Roosevelt years. It grew restless, after Sputnik, for presidential direction which Eisenhower did not supply. In 1964, following President Kennedy's assassination, a contrite and guilt-ridden Congress was ready to give Johnson the unfulfilled portions of Kennedy's program.

Unexpected developments, usually of a tragic nature, may dramatically convert congressional resistance into congressional acquiescence — or provide a president with an opportunity to lead in areas he had ignored. The death of 76 persons from elixir of sulfanilamide in 1937 opened the door to drug reform legislation. So did the thalidomide tragedies of 1962. The mine disaster of 1968, killing 78 miners in Farmington, West Virginia, led to the Mine Safety Act of 1969. The assassination of Martin Luther King made a Fair Housing bill possible in Congress. The OPEC boycott paved the way for a comprehensive energy bill to receive serious congressional attention. Disasters or scandals enable a president to "seize the time" and obtain legislation which has become constipated by the routines and inertia of Congress.

3. A president needs to establish his priorities, in terms of both substantive importance and legislative strategy.

An activist president is always irresistibly tempted to ask for more than the most cooperative Congress will give. He needs to know, therefore, what matters most to him and to concentrate his best efforts there. Further, he needs to have thought through the order in which his proposals will be presented to and processed by Congress, so that failure of hotly controversial bills at the outset of his administration (or even their passage, under circumstances that sow undue rancor and bitterness) will not jeopardize the fate of subsequent bills. As indicated later, Franklin D. Roosevelt unwisely allowed his explosive court-packing plan to become the first order of congressional business in his second term. Predictably, it aroused passionate opposition not only among Roosevelt's enemies but also among many of his friends. The bill's smashing defeat destroyed the illusion of Rooseveltian invincibility and revitalized those forces in Congress and the nation which opposed the New Deal. The fallout from the court-packing battle vitally affected Roosevelt's Wages and Hours and Executive Reorganization bills; they faced much stiffer resistance because of the hostilities engendered by the court battle.[4]

It can be argued that controversial legislation has its best chance early in an administration and hence should receive the highest priority. True, but a president should be reasonably sure he has a better than even chance of winning. If he fails in his first major test, and Congress tastes blood, the president's ability to shape the legislative future may be considerably diminished. Congress is shrewd at taking the measure of its traditional rival in the White House and it will seize the reins if it can. Ordinarily, then, a president should strive to get off on a sure foot with Congress and build an impression of mastery which can be drawn upon when other struggles take place.

Harry Truman is the classic example of a president who seemingly lacked a sense of domestic priorities. He deluged Congress with major and divisive proposals without any clear indication of where his priorities lay.[5] He seemed more interested in going on record in favor of these bills, perhaps for personal and partisan purposes, than in getting them passed. In this respect, Truman was not unlike Richard Nixon. Partly for this reason, both men had scant success with their domestic programs.

Carter's failure to clarify his priorities in 1977 contributed to his lackluster legislative record that year. He concentrated on drawing up intelligent programs and hoped Congress would pass each of them because they were — in his judgment — so clearly rational. Alas, Congress doesn't work that way.

4. A president should consult with party leaders in Congress before launching major policy initiatives — foreign or domestic. Always! Especially when he doesn't want to.

Most presidents don't like to consult. They are willing to "brief" congressional leaders on what they plan to do but they don't want their often laboriously and painfully constructed proposals altered, prior to public unveiling, by congressional criticism. They want support, not advice. Yet there are compelling reasons for submitting proposals to party leaders *before* the president's decisions have crystallized.

If his party leaders raise considerations a president has overlooked or interpreted differently, his basis for decision is improved. If they don't, the president can move forward with increased confidence. The congressional leadership will be more cooperative and more willing to press hard for legislation if they've had their hands in the dough. And if things go badly later on, the president will be less vulnerable for having sought their advice.

Although leaders on the Hill may not always be able to make significant contributions to the discussion of a bill's substantive merits, they *can* give the president invaluable advice on the political reception which the bill will receive. Any president who doesn't want the best political intelligence he can get is not much of a politician. He may have good reasons, sometimes, to push ahead even if warned that a bill's chances are bleak, but he ought to know the odds, whatever his purposes. Ordinarily, no one can give a better reading of the congressional mood than party leaders on the Hill.

(A consistent practice of consulting with party leaders of both Houses has another signal advantage. It tends to convert the *president's* program into a *party* program. In addition to the partisan support pressures which are automatically engendered, this is the most important single step toward responsible party government which can be taken. For those who see party government as vastly preferable to the fortuities and hazards of unduly personalized executive leadership, this gives congressional consultation a significance which is hard to exaggerate.)

The case for serious congressional consultation, before Executive plans have hardened, is cogent enough on rational grounds alone. The lessons of history are even more persuasive.

One of Franklin D. Roosevelt's major defeats, on the executive reorganization bill (absurdly labeled the "dictatorship bill") was sustained largely because of failure to consult with Congress. Richard Polenberg, the principal chronicler of the bill's travails, has written that "The leaders had been shocked not only by the substance of the proposals but by the manner of presentation. Roosevelt had not consulted any Congressmen in advance; instead he had submitted a finished product that he did not want modified. . . . That this procedure aroused antagonism seems certain." [6]

Since the reorganization bill lost in the House, after narrow Senate passage, by a vote of 204-196, it can be confidently assumed that advance conferences with congressional leaders could have averted defeat.

Roosevelt also concocted his Supreme Court reorganization bill in almost complete secrecy. As Joseph Alsop and Turner Catledge observed in *The 168 Days,* prior to his reelection in 1936, Roosevelt could have been expected — on an important matter concerning the judiciary — to consult with Ben Cohen, Tom Corcoran, Felix Frankfurter, Donald Richberg, Judge Samuel Rosenman, Vice-President Garner, Majority Leader Joseph Robinson, and Speaker William

Bankhead.[7] But exuberant over his recent landslide victory, supremely confident that Congress and the country would support him on any battle line he chose to engage the Court, and relishing the prospect of evening some scores with his enemies, Roosevelt requested Attorney General Homer Cummings to quietly explore alternative methods of coping with the Court. When Cummings presented him with the option of adding an additional member to the court for each member over 70 who did not retire (up to a maximum of 15 justices), Roosevelt is reported to have exclaimed, "The answer to a maiden's prayer!" [8] Since staunch anti-New Dealer Justice McReynolds, when he was Attorney General, had proposed a similar idea (for all courts *except* the Supreme Court), this would enable Roosevelt to take sweet revenge on McReynolds. Moreover, he could count on the plan outraging his conservative opponents. Finally, it skirted the major issue — the Court's role in blocking the New Deal — by focusing on the alleged incapacity of the aging Court to meet its work load. The plan combined, said Burns ". . . his instinct for the dramatic and his instinct for the adroit and circuitous stratagem rather than the frontal assault." [9] The President reveled in the prospect of so deftly skewering his enemies.

Perhaps Roosevelt apparently feared that consultation with others might oblige him to modify or abandon a plan which he found emotionally attractive; at any rate, the President kept his secret to himself, although barely able to contain his pleasure while presiding over the banquet honoring the Supreme Court justices 36 hours before announcing his plan.[10]

When Roosevelt, in great high spirits, called the congressional leaders and the Vice-President together to unveil the plan, Burns described the scene as follows ". . . the congressional delegation sat as if stunned. Garner and Rayburn said not a word. Robinson, deep concern written on his face, gave a feeble indication of approval. Henry Ashurst, chairman of the Senate Judiciary Committee, must have thought of his heated denial during the campaign that Roosevelt would try to pack the Court but he loyally spoke out in support of the bill. Speaker Bankhead bore a poker face throughout.

"There was virtually no discussion; the President solicited no opinions from his party's leadership . . . In the Senate lobby Garner held his nose with one hand and vigorously shook his turned-down thumb." [11]

The failure to consult cost him dearly. From commanding such public acclaim and congressional support as perhaps no president has enjoyed since Washington, Roosevelt's stock plummeted dramatically. The sour taste left in Congress's and the public's mouth from such a devious and ill-conceived plan remained through the rest of his second term. Roosevelt had to fight for every inch of legislative ground from that point forward; much of the time he lost. Fortunately for his reputation, the war gave him another opportunity to demonstrate his presidential capacity.

The parallel with Lyndon B. Johnson and his plan to dispatch hundreds of thousands of servicemen to Vietnam in 1965 is instructive. In 1936 the public had been assured, through Ashurst, that Roosevelt had no intention of "packing" the Court, just as the public was assured, in 1964, that Lyndon B. Johnson was the peace candidate. After the election, Johnson stood in the same commanding position with the Congress and enjoyed vast public support. He too was "feeling his oats" after a thumping electoral victory. His plan to send masses of soldiers to Vietnam was formulated without much consultation with congressional leaders. As Reston put it, it was a policy of "stealth" on a question that vitally affected Congress's constitutional responsibilities.

Again, the failure to consult was catastrophic. Disaster came more gradually but Johnson's second term was poisoned just as surely by his Vietnam plan as Roosevelt's was by his Court-packing plan. No one can be certain that congressional leaders would not have acquiesced in the dimensions of Johnson's Vietnam expedition had they been asked for counsel but the odds are that a more cautious course would have been advised — just as congressional leaders raised the warning flag in 1954 after Dienbienphu produced Administration requests for congressional advice on our Vietnam policy.[12]

Purely from personal experience, Johnson should have been warned. He had seen Truman incur a good deal of unnecessary grief over Korea because he unilaterally ordered the troops into action, and then notified congressional leaders of his decision. Senator Robert A. Taft, Sr., whom the President could not afford to needlessly antagonize, agreed intervention was called for but did not agree the President should have acted without congressional consent.[13] When the Korean campaign bogged down, Truman's support was weakened because the initial decision had not been shared by Congress — or at least by its leaders.

As majority leader, Johnson had been among those who had counseled caution in 1954. Later, he observed Eisenhower's more consistent and successful pattern of advising with Congress on other proposed military ventures.

But with Johnson as with Roosevelt, an overweening confidence in his ability to act without congressional consultation, a confidence growing out of his hour of greatest triumph, led to disaster.[14]

Hubris, the Greek tragedians warned, inevitably exacts its price. But Richard Nixon, like his predecessors, would not be warned. Instead of consulting with party leaders, Nixon and Kissinger independently drew up their Vietnam "game plan," independently modified it to include the Cambodian venture, and grimly clung to the overall plan for over four years. Whatever one thinks of the wisdom or folly of the President's military strategy, congressional leaders were offended by Nixon's cavalier indifference to their views. Their resentment intensified by a series of major presidential challenges in 1973 (also conceived in isolation), Congress reacted furiously. Instead of the honeymoon which normally ushers in a new term, the President found himself with a congressional cold war on his hands instead.

When Gerald Ford assumed the presidency, the public was almost pathetically eager to trust him and to give him every benefit of doubt. His position vis-à-vis Congress was enormously strengthened by this support. But the pardon of

Richard Nixon caused public approval of his job performance to drop more precipitously than for any president in history. That pardon, incredible considering Ford's well-established propensity for consultation, was decided upon without the advice of congressional leaders — who would almost certainly have warned against it. Doubtless it cost him the 1976 election.

Carter's failure to consult with congressional leaders in drafting his energy program became widely recognized as a blunder — although consultation with Senate leaders was complicated by the unprecedented dispersion of political power in that body. Consultation would not have averted a bitter congressional battle but it would have helped him mobilize his potential allies more effectively.

Successful presidential leaders of Congress have nearly always worked closely with important congressional leaders. Jefferson had William Giles; Theodore Roosevelt had Boss Cannon, Wilson had John Worth Kern, F. D. Roosevelt had Alben Barkley and Lyndon Johnson usually worked with virtually anyone who could help him. . . .

In this connection, a final note. Widespread consultation will normally lead to incrementalist programs. Ordinarily this is desirable, if a president would be an effective congressional leader. But a chief executive who covets a special place in history will not always be the prudent incrementalist, insisting on measures which a characteristically myopic, middle-road Congress can be persuaded to accept. Now and then a president with vision, courage and conviction should strike out boldly, attacking an emerging or entrenched evil which may seem too powerful to challenge but which for that very reason should be challenged. The president's audacity may not bring legislative redress — at first — but the ensuing national debate may be altogether salutary.

Suppose a president demanded a federal tax system which, in fact rather than in theory, gave this nation a truly graduated personal income tax from bottom to top. No exceptions. Or suppose he were to propose a total ban on the interstate advertising of products which, as ordinarily consumed, have been found to have significantly carcinogenic effects. (Code language for cigarettes.) Or urge the spending of enough federal money to provide us with an adequate and humane prison system. The president would not get far, at first, but if he used his "bully pulpit" to best advantage, he might prepare the way for ultimate success.

Both historians and voters judge a president partly by what he tried to achieve, and not merely by what he succeeds in doing. Our economic and political system has become so resistant to major reform that only a president's trumpet notes, sounded repeatedly and insistently, can sometimes make major reforms a possibility. If not in that president's day, then in one of his successors.

But of course — not too often. A few noble lost causes may exhilarate, educate — and create a passionately loyal following. But a president can survive only a limited number of these adventures. For the most part, good politics remains the art of the possible.

5. Having consulted adequately, a president needs to follow through. Reston once said of Eisenhower, "Both in golf and politics, his back swing has always been better than his follow through." The successful leader of Congress must demonstrate that he really cares about his program, cares enough to take an active interest in its nurture at each stage of its development. If he does not follow through, or if he vacillates, he may face the embarrassment Eisenhower experienced late in January, 1958. A Budget Bureau aide testified on Capitol Hill of the importance of supporting the "program of the President" and Richard Neustadt reported that "everybody laughed." [15]

A number of historic illustrations supporting this principle could be cited. Woodrow Wilson's indefatigable efforts to achieve tariff reform set an example for future presidents to follow.[16] Wilson's example was imitated in many respects by Franklin D. Roosevelt, who usually followed the course of his bills with lively interest, kept in close touch with party leaders, and applied pressure at various points to insure their passage in a form acceptable to him. President Truman, on the other hand, had a pronounced tendency to dump batches of bills on Congress, largely ignore their disposition in Congress, and then veto bills he disliked with a scorching commentary on their specific weaknesses.[17]

Eisenhower had a limited amount of interest in what occurred on Capitol Hill, except where the military budget and foreign affairs were concerned and excepting his later struggle against inflation. When he did intervene, it was sporadically, and then usually under the prompting of his aides.

An instructive example of Lyndon B. Johnson's "follow-through" was in his foreign aid bill for fiscal 1965. Instead of padding the bill in anticipation of routine congressional slashing, the President trimmed aid to a "rock-bottom" figure of $3.5 billion and resolved to hold the appropriation at or close to that figure. Otto Passman, chairman of the House appropriations subcommittee handling foreign aid, was accustomed to mutilating foreign aid budgets and had no intention of foregoing his hobby just because Johnson was in the White House. Johnson identified three vulnerable subcommittee members and went to work on them in the inimitable Johnson manner. When Passman called the subcommittee into session to consider the aid bill, he was astonished and outraged to find himself consistently outvoted. To insure that Passman did not gain revenge on the House floor, Johnson dispatched AID director David Bell to the capitol to hold extensive briefings for members of Congress known to favor foreign aid. Later they were able to confront Passman with the information necessary to counter his normally persuasive floor performance. In a carefully orchestrated maneuver, Speaker John McCormack, majority leader Carl Albert and the White House each telephoned 53 Democrats who normally voted for foreign aid cuts. The President reputedly cut directly to the bone: "This is going to be a big year for the Democrats; are you with me or against me?" According to Elizabeth Drew, "Johnson was standing by his much-used telephone while the Aid Bill was being debated on the House floor. . . . AID officials, who sat in the galleries watching for signals from the floor, talked to the White House by phone eighteen times. . . . [A]lerted by his aides, the President would then call his floor contacts. No one was taking any chances that there would be a last minute defeat." [18]

Forty-three of the fifty-three Democrats voted with the President against a major cut in the bill, the amendment losing by 208-198. The final appropriation was only 8 percent below the President's request, the smallest reduction in the foreign aid budget in 17 years.

Probably a president "follows through" successfully only if negotiating with congressmen is something he enjoys doing. If he finds this a distasteful and onerous task, something to be endured rather than relished, he is likely to skimp the task or do it poorly. We are only good at things we like to do. Initially, Carter seemed to have little appetite for this task. On the Panama Canal treaty, however, he employed almost every pressure in the book to win the crucial votes.

On other occasions, too, he compensated for his own disinclination to stroke and cajole individual members of Congress by carefully planned political operations which utilized the persuasive skills of other members of his administration (and of supporting interest groups) to good effect. Sheer determination, combined with Stuart Eizenstat's substantive talents, gave Carter an overall legislative record that was better than his critics realized.[19]

It is important to note that presidential pressure can be overdone. At one point in the struggle over the Wages and Hours bill in 1938, Roosevelt's congressional lieutenants warned him, the congressional temper being what it was, to keep hands off the bill.[20] During the fight over the Haynsworth nomination, GOP Senate leader Hugh Scott told Bryce Harlow, congressional liaison chief, that he was "beginning to resent pressure from the White House and Justice Department. . . . If they don't stop this arm twisting, I'll announce publicly against Haynsworth." [21]

While it usually pays high dividends, active presidential involvement in the passage of important bills takes a heavy investment of time and energy. Only a president who is willing to pay the price can do the job well. If he does it well, other parts of his job will be short-changed. It is important, to repeat, for a president to have his priorities clear and to focus primary attention only on those bills which are most important to him. Fortunately, this limitation may accord with political realities. As Theodore Sorensen has written, "Only a limited number of times can key members of Congress . . . be approached with special requests." [22] The wisest of all maxims applies — "nothing too much."

6. A president needs a first-rate legislative liaison staff. While congressional leaders are indispensable political advisers, the president needs a more refined intelligence network to keep him well-informed on a day-to-day basis of the temperature of Congress and the status of legislation. For this task there is no

substitute for a competent liaison staff. The sterling work of Lawrence O'Brien for Kennedy and Johnson, and of Bryce Harlow for Eisenhower and Nixon have made this function too important to minimize.

O'Brien once quoted Kennedy as saying that in his 14 years in the House and Senate he had had no "direct or meaningful contact with a member of the White House Staff." [23] Kennedy understood, therefore, the importance of developing adequate liaison, perhaps hoping to avoid what James McGregor Burns regarded as one of Franklin D. Roosevelt's major shortcomings. Burns noted that while Roosevelt regularly consulted with party leaders and committee chairmen, he failed to "build up a position of strength with the rank and file of Congress." [24] Time does not permit any president to personally keep in touch with this rank and file but an active and skillful staff can help. Talking to a presidential aide is not like talking to the president, but if the aide is known to have the president's ear, such contacts are the next best thing. And liaison *does* provide intelligence, especially when the staff works closely with party whips.

It is rare that a president can alter the outcome of a legislative struggle in Congress unless the pending division on a bill is fairly close. It is imperative, therefore, that a president know when this situation exists. A good example of O'Brien's assistance to President Kennedy came in 1961 during the struggle to add members to a Rules committee which was expected to obstruct the President's program. O'Brien notes that "The vote was postponed twice until we felt we had sufficient troops marshalled." [25] When the vote was taken, the reformers won by a margin of only 5 votes. Contrast this with the situation in Roosevelt's reorganization battles. James Farley explained the defeat to Roosevelt by noting that 25 Democrats would have voted for the bill in a crunch but preferred not to. The administration, he said, "didn't have an accurate count of noses. It didn't know who were for and who were against. No wonder we lost when no opportunity was given those congressmen to change, whose votes the other way would have reversed the result." [26] Presidential aides who can count accurately (no mean skill!) and who can identify the undecided make possible victories that might otherwise be lost. Almost any president can win over a few votes by personal appeals.

Liaison chiefs who have demonstrated that cooperation, in a clutch, can bring tangible rewards in terms of presidential campaigning support, or a presidential boost for a cherished bill, or delivery of the more traditional loaves and fishes (if deftly done) can strengthen their personal role and enhance presidential clout.[27] On the other hand, the president has only a limited amount of concrete goodies to distribute to compliant members of Congress — and these must be doled out with the utmost discretion lest charges of vote-buying impair both the president's moral standing and his political power.

7. A president should respect Congress as a coequal institution, and respect its individual members. Obvious? Yes, but history shows presidents sometimes ignoring the obvious.

Woodrow Wilson's attitude toward members of the Senate is the prime example. Wilson once referred to senators opposing him as "contemptible . . . narrow . . . selfish . . . poor little minds. . . . If I said what I think about those fellows in Congress it would take a piece of asbestos two inches thick to hold it." [28] "Pygmy minds" was a favorite expression of his when referring to certain congressmen. Apparently Wilson did not make these remarks publicly but they seem to have accurately reflected his feelings. More important, his general demeanor toward members of the Senate was once described as that of "the schoolmaster incarnate." [29] Like Secretary of State Dean Acheson, who suffered from a similar affliction, he tried to conceal his feelings of superiority from time to time, but inevitably they cropped out in ways offensive to members of the Senate. Undoubtedly they were a factor in Wilson's defeat on the League.

After the Senate passed his Executive Reorganization bill in 1938, despite heavy lobbying pressures to the contrary, Franklin D. Roosevelt indiscreetly observed that "It proves that the Senate cannot be purchased by organized telegrams based on direct misrepresentation." This implied that those who voted against him were "purchased," an innuendo resented by many members in both House and Senate.[30] Roosevelt also made a speech in which he spoke harshly of southern congressmen who opposed his economic reforms. Vice-President Garner told James Farley that the speech had forged a solid bloc that would oppose almost anything the President might want.[31]

Again, Richard Nixon's statement, after the defeat of Harrold Carswell's nomination to the Supreme Court, gratuitously offended many members of Congress. Rather than conceding that there might be legitimate reasons for disapproving the nomination, Nixon declared, "I have reluctantly concluded — with the Senate presently constituted — I cannot successfully nominate to the Supreme Court any Federal Appellate Judge from the South who believes as I do in the strict construction of the Constitution. Judges Carswell and Haynsworth have endured with admirable dignity vicious assaults on their intelligence, their honesty and their character. They have been falsely charged with being racists. But when all the hypocrisy is stripped away, the real issue was their philosophy of strict construction of the Constitution. . . ." [32] Senators who had voted against these men for what they regarded as compelling reasons were not grateful for the President's remarks. Nixon may have felt this accusation strengthened his position in the South; it did not strengthen his position with the Senate.

There is no contradiction between firm presidential leadership and unfailing courtesy toward one's opponents. The temptation to lash out at one's Congressional foes will become intense, from time to time, but yielding to it will only produce resentments that will some day seek revenge. Today's opponents are tomorrow's potential allies — a fact no president should ever forget.

Lyndon Johnson's treatment of members of Congress was exemplary during at least the early years of his administration. Not only was he careful to show public respect for the equal dignity and status of the legislative branch of government, but he went out of his way, following the passage of important bills, to praise individual members for their support — making sure that TV camera-men were on hand to appropriately record the event. Congressmen, like all politicians, have perpetually voracious egos, and the president who gives co-operative congressmen the publicity manna they yearn for, will often find the crooked places made straight.

8. A president should seek bipartisan support for his program. This is particu-larly relevant where foreign policy is concerned, but is of no small moment in other issues as well.

The classic example is Woodrow Wilson's failure to include a Republican sen-ator among his advisers when he went to Paris after World War I.[33] President Kennedy's solicitous attitude toward Republican senators during the Test Ban Treaty struggle provides an illuminating contrast. On domestic legislation, Ken-nedy's persistent cultivation of Republican Senator Everett Dirksen won the mi-nority leader's critically important support on many occasions.[34] Eisenhower's excellent relations with Senate Majority leader Johnson and Speaker Rayburn helped produce unusually amicable relations with Congress, despite Democratic control of both Houses.

Obviously, a good deal of discretion needs to be exercised in dealing with members of the opposite party. A president's own party may resent undue so-licitude to members of the other party, especially if it seems to blunt the partisan advantage members feel their party properly merits on certain bills. Members of the opposition party may also be wary of excessive efforts to woo them in order (at bottom) to strengthen the president, and, therefore, his party, during the next election.

Nonetheless, in a political system which lacks party unity and party discipline and in which virtually all successful bills receive bipartisan support, a president is derelict if he ignores potential votes from opposition ranks. Wooing them is a delicate operation but there are various quiet and informal ways of cultivating friendly and fruitful relations with potentially cooperative members of the other party, especially if they hold common ideological attitudes (e.g., note President Ronald Reagan's ingratiating overtures to southern Democrats in con-nection with his economic programs). A president who is respectful and appre-ciative of them is sure to experience serendipity from time to time.

9. A president needs to be able to compromise — and to know when to do it. If he yields too soon, he will lose more ground than he needs to. If he waits too late, the decision may be out of his hand. If he becomes too stubborn to compro-mise at all, James David Barber will classify him as an active-negative president, doomed to disaster, with only the timetable uncertain.[35] Woodrow Wilson's in-transigence on the League of Nations and Herbert Hoover's stubborn adherence to his hobbling economic ideology are cases in point.

A prudent president must learn whom to trust, so far as timing is concerned, as well as the nature of the compromise whose time has come. It may be his con-gressional leaders, his liaison staff, a member of a congressional committee, a journalist with sure political instincts. Above all, the president should not be misled by "can do" aides who ignore convincing evidence that he is persisting in a lost cause. Or by his own ego-involvement in that cause.

10. A president needs a sound program. He needs a program which responds to the legitimate needs of the nation, one which moves, as Clinton Rossiter puts it, "with the grain of liberty and morality," and one which has been painstakingly developed.

Once again the obvious must not be slighted. No matter how scrupulously a president follows the other rules, if he presents a slapdash program or one which is politically inept, his other skills will count for little. The techniques of legislative leadership are important but the substance of legislative proposals is even more so. Congress looks to the president for its agenda and if the president prepares its poorly he can hardly lead Congress, whatever his other talents may be.

Is there any recipe for preparing a "sound program"? No infallible one, of course, even if "sound" were not subject to ideological judgments. But a president can help his chances by heeding the experience of others.

His aides can rummage through the congressional hopper for bills which look promising — and give the congressional sponsor the credit which he or she deserves. He will routinely solicit proposals from the departments and agencies; having had firsthand experience with current problems in their domain, they will have much to usefully offer. He can establish task forces to study problems in depth and appraise the various "solutions" which "experts" have to offer. Where issues of major significance are involved, he can discuss the *broad outlines* of proposed measures — including options at critical points — with his cabinet. If the cabinet agenda is circulated in advance, with key issues for debate identified and briefly analyzed, the quality of cabinet discussion can be greatly enhanced. The cabinet will not be composed of substantive experts, but many of its members have political savvy. The advice of the intelligent and experienced "outsider" (in this case, the cabinet member not directly concerned with the issue at hand) is often invaluable. If only a few cabinet members have something worthwhile to contribute, that is enough to justify bouncing ideas off this group.[36]

The same broad outlines can be profitably discussed (sometimes) with congressional committee and subcommittee chairs, and by all means with top congressional leaders. In some instances, further consultation with major interest group leaders may be in order — as Lyndon Johnson demonstrated from time to time. Will the administration virtually drown in advice, and never reach a point of decision? One can only say that the headaches which follow inadequate consultation are more to be feared than the additional weeks which "touching bases" involve. An administration isn't *really* in as much of a hurry as it thinks it is! That sense of urgency is often no more than impatient glands in disguise.

Finally, the proposed legislation should be microscopically researched and scrubbed by a domestic policy staff group[37] (headed by someone as reliable as a Theodore Sorensen, Joseph Califano, or a Stuart Eizenstat) which insures that the factual formulations are as sturdy as possible and that potential pitfalls have been identified and dealt with as judiciously as informed and intelligent minds can do.

There is no way to avoid pitched battles on truly important measures but careful planning, both on their substantive and political features, can better the odds of ultimate success. Having done all this, prayer is not inappropriate.

To repeat, no amount of fidelity to the rules can fully compensate for deficiencies in the political marrow. If a president lacks the subtle ability to command popular and congressional respect, his path is bound to be strewn with thistles. There is always an "X" factor in every successful leader which is never fully understood. But even when a president has it, someone needs to warn him when he is about to break the presidential decalogue.

SOURCE: An earlier version of this essay appeared under the title "Presidential Leadership of Congress: Ten Commandments Point the Way" in *Presidential Studies Quarterly* (Summer 1978).

## Notes

1. James M. Burns, Roosevelt: *The Lion and the Fox* (New York: Harcourt, Brace, 1956), p. 186. Rexford Tugwell agrees: "A president, as things are, succeeds or fails largely because he can or cannot persuade Congress to accept his leadership...." Tugwell and Thomas Cronin, *The Presidency Reappraised* (New York: Praeger, 1974), p. 292.
2. Thomas E. Cronin, *The State of the Presidency* (Boston: Little, Brown, 1975), pp. 88–91.
3. "Man in the White House Who Knows the Deck," *New York Times*, Oct. 7, 1964, p. 46. For examples of Johnson's skill, see Philip Meranto, *The Politics of Federal Aid to Education in 1965* (Syracuse, N.Y.: Syracuse University Press, 1967), pp. 104–109; also Eugene Eidenburg and Roy D. Morey, *An Act of Congress* (New York: W.W. Norton, 1969), pp. 32, 77–78, 92–95; William E. Leuchtenburg, "The Genesis of the Great Society," *The Reporter*, April 21, 1966, pp. 38–39; Eric F. Goldman, *The Tragedy of Lyndon Johnson* (New York: Alfred A. Knopf, 1969), pp. 299–304; Marjorie Hunter, "Issue of the Church Is Skirted in President's School Plan," *New York Times*, Jan. 2, 1965, p. 1. An excellent example of President Johnson's legislative leadership skills is also found in his management of the wheat price support bill of 1964. See Rowland Evans and Robert D. Novak, *Lyndon B. Johnson: The Exercise of Power* (New York: The New American Library, 1966), pp. 380–381.
4. Lindsey Rogers, "Reorganization: Post Mortem Notes," *Political Science Quarterly*, June 1938, pp. 161–72; Clinton Rossiter, *The American Presidency* (New York: Harcourt, Brace, rev. ed., 1960), p. 128.
5. Louis W. Koenig, *The Chief Executive* (New York: Harcourt, Brace & World, 1968, rev. ed.), p. 143. Wilfred Binkley, *President and Congress* (New York: Knopf, 1947, pp. 277–78.

6. Richard Polenberg, *Reorganizing Roosevelt's Government* (Cambridge, Mass.: Harvard University Press, 1966), p. 42. Burns, *Congress on Trial* (New York: Harper, 1949), pp. 70–73.

7. Joseph Alsop and Turner Catledge, *The 168 Days* (Garden City, N.J.: Doubleday, Doran, 1938), p. 24. Speaker of the House William Bankhead was quoted as saying, "Wouldn't you have thought that the President would have told his own party leaders what he was going to do?" Leonard Baker, *Back to Back* (New York: Macmillan, 1967), p. 21.

8. Alsop and Catledge, *ibid.,* p. 36.

9. Burns, *The Lion and the Fox,* op. cit., p. 297.

10. Burns, *The Lion and the Fox,* op. cit., p. 293.

11. *Ibid.,* p. 294.

12. Chalmers M. Roberts, "The Day We Didn't Go To War," *The Reporter,* Sept. 14, 1954, pp. 31–32.

13. Arthur Schlesinger, *The Imperial Presidency* (New York: Popular Library, 1973), pp. 135–138.

14. Interestingly, Tom Wicker warned in 1965 that Johnson might shipwreck on Vietnam just as Roosevelt did on the court. "One Year of LBJ," *The New Republic,* November 13, 1965, p. 17. Rowland Evans and Robert Novak report that Johnson was resolved, after his thumping victory in 1964, not to repeat FDR's mistake by "overplaying his hand." *LBJ: The Exercise of Power,* op. cit., p. 489.

15. Neustadt, *Presidential Power* (New York: New American Library, 1960), p. 83.

16. For a brief account of Wilson's tactics, see Binkley, op. cit., pp. 209–213. Also see Claude Bowers, *The Life of John Worth Kern* (Indianapolis, Indiana: Hollenbeck Press, 1918), Chapters 14 and 17. Arthur C. Walworth, *Woodrow Wilson and the Progressive Era, 1910–1917* (New York: Harper & Brothers, 1954), pp. 33–43.

17. Koenig, op. cit., pp. 140, 143–144. Also Elmer Davis, "Harry S. Truman and the Verdict of History," *The Reporter,* February 3, 1953, p. 20.

18. Elizabeth Brenner Drew, "Mr. Passman Meets His Match," *The Reporter,* November 19, 1964, p. 43.

19. See George Edwards, *Presidential Influences in Congress* (San Francisco: W. H. Freeman, 1980), Chapter 7.

20. *New York Times,* March 3, 1938, p. 2.

21. John L. Steele, "Haynsworth vs. the U.S. Senate," *Fortune,* March 1970, p. 158.

22. Theodore C. Sorensen, *Decision-Making in the White House* (New York: Columbia University Press, 1963), p. 28.

23. Paul Duke (Interviewer), "Larry O'Brien Discusses White House Contacts with Capitol Hill," *Congressional Quarterly,* July 23, 1965, p. 1434.

24. Burns, *The Lion and the Fox,* op. cit., p. 348. Polenberg, *op. cit.,* pp. 178–180.

25. Duke, *op. cit.,* p. 1435. The role of Rufus Poole in sounding out congressmen's attitudes toward amendments to the Wages and Hours Bill in 1938 proved to be an important factor in the final passage of the bill. See Frances Perkins, *The Roosevelt I Knew* (New York: Viking, 1946), pp. 261–262.

26. Polenberg, *op. cit.,* p. 175.

27. Also see Stephen Wayne, *The Legislative Presidency* (New York: Harper & Row, 1978), Ch. 5. The classic work is Abraham Holtzman, *Legislative Liaison: Executive Leadership in Congress* (Chicago: Rand McNally, 1970).

28. Gene Smith, *When the Cheering Stopped* (New York: William Morrow, 1964), p. 56.

29. *Ibid.,* p. 53.

30. Polenberg, *op. cit.,* p. 158–159.

31. *Ibid.,* p. 174.

32. "Nixon's Statements on Carswell Nomination Rejection," *Congressional Almanac,* 1970, Vol. XXVI, p. 44A.
33. Arthur Walworth, *Woodrow Wilson,* Book Two, p. 211. Also see Thomas A. Bailey, *Woodrow Wilson and the Lost Peace* (New York: Macmillan, 1945), p. 100.
34. Ben H. Bagdikian, "Golden Voice of the Senate," *Saturday Evening Post,* October 6, 1962, pp. 28–29. "The Ev Show," *Time,* April 20, 1962, pp. 29–30.
35. James David Barber, *The Presidential Character* (Englewood Cliffs, N.J.: Prentice-Hall, 1972).
36. Stephen Hess makes a convincing case in *Organizing the Presidency* (Washington, D.C.: Brookings, 1976), Ch. 11.
37. A useful discussion of the Domestic Council appears in John Kessel, *The Domestic Presidency* (North Scituate, Mass.: Duxbury Press, 1975), Chapter 4.

# 20. The President as Coalition Builder: Reagan's First Year

## Hedrick Smith

In his stunning first-year drive to push through Congress a radical program of budget and tax cuts, President Ronald Reagan faced a pivotal and revealing moment of decision on the warm, humid morning of June 18, 1981. Meeting with a handful of aides in the Oval Office, the President was under pressure from David Stockman, his tireless and combative budget director, to throw down the gauntlet once more to the Democratic leadership of the House of Representatives — to reject the budget cuts developed by the Democratic-dominated committees of the House and send up a second package of his own to make the House toe the line of the original budget resolution passed in early May.

"The committees have broken faith with the first budget resolution," Stockman argued. "What they have done is sadly deficient. It could jeopardize your entire economic program. We have to make a major fight to restore the provisions in your first budget."

Others cautioned the President about the perils of treading on congressional prerogatives and of kindling institutional animosities. "We just have to understand we're running a very great risk here," warned James A. Baker III, the White House Chief of Staff. "If we throw down the challenge and lose, it will sap our momentum. It will have very damaging effects on the tax program." David Gergen, the tall, lanky communications director, pointed out that this time, unlike in the first budget fight, the White House would have "precious little time" to generate broad public support.

But Stockman was insistent. He sensed that the President felt sandbagged by the Democratic leaders' pretended support of his earlier budget victory, and he played to Mr. Reagan's instinct to show them now that they could not get away with partial measures. Some of the Democratic cuts, Stockman asserted, were "phony" because they left the eligibility and entitlement rules of many big federal programs largely unchanged, which meant that these programs would grow automatically in future years.

"If you can't get those entitlement cuts," Stockman declared, "it will add to the deficits in 1983 and 1984. If you want to balance the budget in '84, you can't live with the cuts they've made."

*Hedrick Smith is the chief Washington correspondent for* The New York Times *and is the Pulitzer-prize winning author of* The Russians.

That hooked the President, who asked to look at Stockman's figures. "Well, if that's the case," he declared with irritation, "we can't accept it."

That was the call to battle. The White House swung into action. By noon, the President was going over his options at a hastily assembled luncheon of his staff, House Republican leaders, and four of the dissident conservative Southern Democrats who had broken party ranks and given him vital support for his first budget victory. These "boll weevil" Democrats now formed a crucial component of his working coalition though some of them were "a little goosey" about a new budget fight, as one White House official later recalled. But the President's legislative advisers were telling him that while Stockman's complete budget substitute would not make it, a more modest partial package could pass the House.

To prepare the way, the President put in a call the next morning to Speaker O'Neill, the shaggy Irish politician and New-Deal Democrat with whom Mr. Reagan has both kidded and clashed. Most recently they had had a public spat over Mr. O'Neill's implication that the President was insensitive to the poor. Since then the air had cleared, but, as it now turned out, their morning telephone talk again fired the President's mood for combat.

"I want a chance to send some substitute language up there on the budget and have it voted on," the President told the Speaker. "The House has worked hard and done a good job, but it hasn't gone far enough, and I. . . ."

Aides saw irritation and frustration flash across the President's face as the Speaker interrupted to remind the President that the Congressional committees had completed their work.

"Did you ever hear of the separation of powers?" Mr. O'Neill asked. "The Congress of the United States will be responsible for spending. You're not supposed to be writing legislation."

"I know the Constitution," Mr. Reagan broke in.

"Can you be specific about what you're going to send up?" The Speaker pressed on. "You always talk to me in vague generalities. I don't want to see the Republicans trying to shove something through without full consideration."

"Oh, come-on, you mean the Democrats," tweaked the President. "I was a Democrat myself, longer than I've been a Republican, and the Democrats have been known to make a few power plays."

The Speaker backed off. "O.K., we'll have a look," acceded Mr. O'Neill. "I'll get back to you." The President inserted a belated anniversary congratulations, and the Speaker closed by advising him, "Have your people talk to Jones and Bolling" (the Democratic chairmen of the Budget and Rules Committees).

Despite the genial sign-off, the President's dander was up. He became further irritated, aides said later, when O'Neill did not get back to him, though that may have been the result of a misunderstanding. (O'Neill may have thought his comment about Jones and Bolling would take care of that.) But now the die was cast, and any thought of compromise, on either budget or tax cuts, was dashed. Eager for confrontation, Mr. Reagan was ready to concentrate on his battle to beat the Democrats.

Six days later, on the eve of the crucial budget vote, the President arrived in his penthouse suite at the Century Plaza Hotel in Los Angeles after an all-day cross-country trip that had him stumping for his budget and tax proposals at the National Jaycee Convention in San Antonio. Jim Baker and others had ruled out a national television address on the second budget package because they did not want the President's prestige so totally on the line in this nip-and-tuck battle.

But the Jaycees provided a good forum. They had whooped and cheered like a political pep rally at Mr. Reagan's sallies against big spenders in "these puzzle palaces on the Potomac." It was time, the President had insisted, to "restore economic sanity" and to send a message to Congress to "finish the job."

By now, the budget battle turned on an intricate parliamentary fight over the rules, and Speaker O'Neill, sensing favorable terrain, was telling reporters he expected a Democratic victory the next day.

At his hotel suite, the President was relaxing over vodka and orange juice with his chief personal aide, Michael K. Deaver, when a call came from the White House reporting a new burst of insurrection among conservative Democrats. They were angered over the way the leadership was chopping up the Reagan package, thus reviving the President's prospects for victory. Stockman and Max Friedersdorf, the smoothly efficient chief of Congressional liaison at the White House, were urging the President to telephone some of the undecided Congressmen. But after the long trip from Washington, Mr. Reagan's voice was hoarse, and Deaver was unsure how he would take to more politicking that night.

"It's pretty close back there," Deaver reported, "and if you made a few calls, that could swing it."

"Get them on the phone," the President offered quickly.

"It may be as many as 20 calls," Deaver said, testing him.

"What time is it back there?"

"About 9 o'clock back East," Deaver said.

"Well, we'd better get going."

The President sat down in slacks and an open-necked shirt at a little desk with a lamp and note pad while the White House switchboard tracked down 16 members of the House at dinner parties, in restaurants, or at home. For two and a half hours he stalked votes.

"Gee, I know it's late back there and I'm sorry to bother you," Mr. Reagan would begin. "I hear you're still on the fence. If I could answer any questions, I'd be happy to. I know you've been under a lot of pressure. But I hope you can find your way clear to supporting us tomorrow." If someone had a specific problem, he'd make a note and say, "I'll get the fellows back to you on that one."

He caught John Breaux, an influential sixth-term Louisiana Democrat, at a downtown dinner party. "The President comes across on the phone as smooth as he does on TV," Breaux would recall later. "He's a generalist, doesn't talk details. But he knows enough of the big picture. He's easygoing, not strong-arm like Lyndon Johnson. It's a soft sell and it's very effective."

The next day, the President sweated out each vote, pestering Deaver for results or asking why there were so many procedural ballots before the House actually got to his budget package. But he won what turned out to be his toughest fight in the long economic offensive, telling reporters: "I've never felt better in these last five months than I feel in this particular moment."

Reagan the convinced conservative crusader, Reagan the strategist, Reagan the battler, Reagan the cheerleader, Reagan the political charmer, has staked the fate of his presidency on his single-minded campaign to enact a radical turn in the nation's economic policy. Using his capacity to persuade Congress to enact the largest budget and tax cuts in American history, he was able to move Congress on this one central issue, and establish his national leadership. In slightly more than six months, he achieved far more than political Washington had dreamed possible on the day of his Inauguration.

His accomplishment was striking not only because it came in spite of a Democratic majority in the House, but also because such political mastery of the legislative branch eluded the last three occupants of the White House — Carter, Ford, and Nixon. For not since Lyndon B. Johnson's Great Society surge in the mid-sixties had Washington seen a president perform so persuasively with the legislature, devising a working political coalition of Republicans and conservative southern Democrats for a program that has put the country on a new political course.

In his first six months as chief executive, Mr. Reagan had been bold and purposeful, firm about his major objectives but flexible at the margins. As a public figure, he had enjoyed an extended honeymoon and warm popularity. Sheer luck had also helped. His presidency was born in the special upsurge of national emotion that greeted the release of the American hostages from Iran. It got another boost from the successful Columbia space shuttle. Public sympathy and support rose further in response to his gallant geniality after the attempt on his life, an event that he turned to political advantage with a dramatic appearance before Congress. Fate also spared Mr. Reagan any major foreign crisis up to that point and had given him a global oversupply of oil that helped ease the fires of inflation.

To the electorate, he had come across as Mr. Nice Guy with the Eisenhower grin and the infectious optimism of the boy next door. But on Capitol Hill, legislators had discovered his political grit and competitive streak. He may have had a reputation for 8:30 to 5:30 office hours, but when the chips were down, he was willing to roll up his sleeves. As political chairman of the board, he delegated wide latitude to his lieutenants and left the details to others, but the administration's programs indisputably bore his philosophical hallmarks. Comments in Washington about his age quickly evaporated. Nor did other politicians disparage him as a former actor. Many expressed amazed respect for his deft salesmanship and his taste for political combat, both vital ingredients to his success.

"In dealing with Congress, he's closer to Lyndon Johnson than anyone else," observed Senate Majority Leader Howard H. Baker, Jr. "Johnson had a feel for the way the legislature works. He was a product of the legislature. Reagan understands it instinctively. He understands legislative politics, but he doesn't try to bull his way through the way Johnson did. Carter never understood the legislative process. Ford understood but he couldn't do anything about it. Nixon never paid enough attention to it to be successful. For give-and-take with Congress, Reagan is the best I've ever served with."

Grudgingly, experienced Democrats also tipped their hats; though they contended Mr. Reagan's success was temporary. "Reagan's six months is comparable with Johnson's first six months on the Great Society," conceded Representative Morris K. Udall, the liberal Arizona Democrat, in August 1981. "On the budget, it was a brilliant one-shot marriage. Overall, on his dealing with Congress, I'd give him a B-plus. He's been good. He still doesn't know Congress all that well. He's got some good people who do. But I don't see this as a permanent coalition for Reagan. I don't think that because he got through a budget that he can count on a new political alignment in October on some other issue. I think the disillusionment is going to set in this fall."

Whether Reagan's economic policy will eventually cure the nation's ills or will ultimately backfire economically and polarize Americans politically is a critical question for his presidency and the Republican party. But, initially, he not only prevailed politically and pulled the entire public debate in his direction, but he also altered the political chemistry in Washington. He projected genial optimism to the public and injected a sense of motion in government.

Only four times this century has a president had such effective sway with Congress, according to James Sundquist, a presidential scholar at the Brookings Institution. He cites Woodrow Wilson after his first election, Franklin D. Roosevelt at the start of the New Deal period, President Johnson in his Great Society heyday, and now Mr. Reagan.

"The system works well at only one time — right after a landslide election," Mr. Sundquist observed. "This is one of those brief periods in our history when a president comes riding a great tide of personal popularity. I think this will change when the president's popularity begins to go down. But he has it now."

From the perspective of late 1981, it is hard to step back into the dark mood of pessimism in 1980 and to recall the flow of worried essays about the breakdown of government and the weakness of the American presidency as an institution. Just after the November election, former President Gerald Ford epitomized the concern in an essay for *Time* magazine in which he wrote: "We have not an imperial Presidency but an imperiled Presidency."

Many shared his mood, Republicans and Democrats alike. Lloyd Cutler, former President Carter's White House counsel, found there was a "structural inability" to govern under the American system of separated powers. He longingly eyed the European parliamentary model and proposed several electoral remedies to the Congress closer to the Chief Executive. Former Treasury Secretary John B. Connally, Jr., prescribed a single, six-year term for the president. Former Vice-President Walter Mondale, lamenting that the presidency had become the focus of popular discontent, called it "the fire hydrant of the nation."

The common diagnosis was that any president was institutionally crippled not only because of the impossibility of managing the sprawling federal establishment but more importantly because of the unwieldy inertia of Congress. Presidential programs got lost, defeated, or simply mired down, it was said, because Congressional leaders had lost their former clout, power had become dispersed and disorganized among a labyrinth of committees; party discipline had broken down; and the main business of the legislature was snarled in the incessant crossfire of special-interest lobbying and single-issue politics. All these prevented the formation of an effective governing coalition between the White House and Capitol Hill.

How, then, does one explain the dramatic turnaround that President Reagan achieved?

*National Consensus.* In the amalgam of causes, the most fundamental is that President Reagan picked as his first priority the issue on which he found a strong consensus and a palpable conservative trend — the urge to cut back government and the sense of a pocketbook squeeze at all levels of society. He profited greatly from a pent-up sense of frustration at the Carter government, perhaps because the Vietnam War, Watergate, and Nixon's resignation had deferred the normal rhythmic swing toward conservatism and consolidation in American politics.

The November 1980 election represented a frustrated rejection of the "ins" and their old economic policies and a demand for something new. The Reganites have contended that their man won a clear mandate for his package of budget and tax cuts. In fact, from the opinion polls on election day, it seems that the message was less precise than that — less a mandate for a specific economic blueprint than an urge for change and a willingness to grant a new president greater-than-usual tolerance to experiment. And shrewdly, President Reagan and his lieutenants fed that sentiment and built their own mandate with their constant preachments against "politics as usual" to nourish public support for Mr. Reagan's radical shift in policy.

*Clear Presidential Objectives.* With an economic program fashioned during the campaign, President Reagan immediately conveyed a sense of self-confidence and direction. He not only had exploited vacillation and zig-zag policies under Mr. Carter as a campaign issue, but he also had profited from the contrast with his predecessor once he moved into the White House.

Mr. Reagan's own clarity of purpose gave unity and thrust to his administration from the outset. It also simplified his legislative agenda. For the Reagan team deliberately avoided Jimmy Carter's early mistake of inundating Congress and confusing the public with a profusion of proposals. The priority was clear.

The message was simple. Mr. Reagan concentrated his early fire on the economic package and pushed foreign policy and controversial social issues into the background. Later, in the fall, he was unable to keep the legislative agenda as sharply focused, for the battle over arms sales to Saudi Arabia helped disrupt congressional momentum on his economic program.

*A Fast Opening.* The President's political braintrust—Counselor Ed Meese 3rd, Baker, Deaver, Stockman, Gergen, and Richard Wirthlin, the pollster, understood that Mr. Reagan's opportunity to achieve radical change was perilously short. "Normally," said Gergen, "a new president has an open window for just so long and it shuts very quickly in terms of public interest and support." To capitalize on the traditional honeymoon with the Congress, the press and the public, they felt compelled to move fast with major proposals, seize the initiative, and keep momentum rolling.

With the Administration's first $50 billion budget-cut package, the Reagan team stunned the opposition and captured political momentum before congressional Democrats fully appreciated what was happening. Soon the Democratic leaders, belatedly responding to the public's conservative fiscal mood, scrambled in disarray to play catch-up, me-too politics with the President. By then, Mr. Reagan got a second lease from the public with his graceful handling of the attempt on his life. Rather than daring to oppose him outright, the Democrats resisted him at the margins. Their budget and tax proposals ultimately became variations on basic Reagan themes, an indication of how thoroughly he had dominated the political arena. For even if he lost, the President stood to get most of what he wanted.

*Assiduous Courting of Congress.* Knowing that success depended on congressional support, the President and his entourage began courting goodwill on Capitol Hill and among the Washington establishment well before taking office. On Inauguration Day, it was not lost on Capitol Hill, where courtesies and symbolic gestures are warmly appreciated, that the President's first official acts were to sign a hiring freeze and the certificates for his cabinet officers in the President's room of the Capitol, where he stayed to have his Inaugural lunch.

In the early weeks, senior House Democrats were invited to the Oval office for a presidential chat and came away murmuring that Democratic presidents had never treated them so well. In his effort to strike up acquaintances with adversaries as well as with allies, Mr. Reagan spent roughly 20 percent of his time on congressional relations.

In the week before his first House vote on the budget, he sat down personally with 60 Democrats and 12 Republicans, either in head-to-head sessions or in such small groups that each felt the flattery of his attention, and many left with a gift of presidential cuff links or seats in the presidential box at the Kennedy Center. When the going got tougher in the second budget fight, the fence-sitters got juicier sweeteners — White House backing for a sugar price support, more funds for Medicaid, Conrail, energy subsidies for the poor, or a slowdown on mandatory conversion to coal for industrial boilers in oil-producing states. The

President and his lieutenants were not skittish about the kind of horse-trading that Jimmy Carter had found so distasteful and that Lyndon Johnson had so expertly exploited.

Louisiana's John Breaux, who zig-zagged in his support of the Reagan program, was lured into the President's camp on the crucial second budget vote with a promise of higher sugar support prices, an issue of great importance to his home state. And others went along with Breaux. "I went for the best deal," Breaux admitted candidly after the vote. But he denied that his vote had been bought. "I can be rented," he quipped puckishly, and then later proved it by voting against the President in the tax-cut fight.

*The Legislative Vehicle.* At the suggestion of Senator Pete Domenici, the New Mexico Republican who heads the Senate Budget Committee, the Reagan strategists fastened on the unique vehicle of budget reconciliation to force the legislature to dance to a disciplined drum beat. The process was set up in 1974 to provide a central mechanism to force congressional committees to abide by some overall spending ceilings and central guidance. It had been used only once before, modestly in 1980, but Domenici and Stockman saw it as a vital lever for the Reagan program.

"The driving force has been the national consensus for a program that became a magnet for support in Congress," Stockman commented afterward. "Reconciliation was the action-firing mechanism that overcame the natural inertia of Congress." Some people question whether it can be used so extensively in years to come, and it works only with the budget process — not on other legislation.

*Using Presidential Popularity from the Bully Pulpit.* At the time of his success on his economic package, Reagan was winning about a 65 percent approval rating from the American people — slightly higher than Nixon and Carter but lower than Kennedy and Eisenhower in their early months. He used the leverage of his early popularity to go over the heads of Congress to sell his program with simple, evocative language. The acme was his dramatic televised reappearance before Congress on April 28 after the shooting incident. That produced what House Republican leader Robert Michel called "the kind of reception that makes a few of the waverers feel, 'Gosh, how can I buck that?' "

Dan Rostenkowski, the veteran Democratic leader in the tax battle, conceded the point. "My problem is that the President can gear up his army with just one television appearance," Rostenkowski moaned before the final showdown. "That's fighting the Army, Navy, Marines and Air Force." Among southern Democrats, the President's public following had a noticeable effect. "Reagan won 72 percent of the vote in my district and he's a lot more popular there now than he was on Election Day," remarked Kent Hance, a West Texas Democrat who cosponsored the Reagan tax program. "It's mighty tough to go against a popular president in a district like mine, especially when he's pushing the same kind of economic policies I've been talking about all along."

*A First-Rate Political Team.* Once again, President Reagan has profited by contrast with former President Carter. His legislative operation was widely regarded as well-organized, purposeful, attentive, and usually ahead of the Democrats on tactics. As a former Congressman, Dave Stockman brought to the budget maneuvering an intimate understanding of both the budget and the congressional process. As point man on the budget, he not only overwhelmed opponents with expertise but absorbed criticism, sparing the President.

Friedersdorf, who previously served as President Ford's congressional liaison, is known as one of Washington's most experienced, best-organized and quietly effective experts on Congress. Jim Baker, another experienced political strategist, has shepherded the whole operation and teamed up well with Treasury Secretary Donald T. Regan on tax legislation. On the Hill, Senator Howard Baker and Representative Michel are given high marks for keeping Republicans in line and stepping in with advice to save the Administration from legislative pitfalls. When the fall round of budget cutting began, however, Reagan's inner circle did not work so closely with the congressional leaders, and this cost the White House setbacks on intended budget-cutting plans. But, overall, the Reagan team was strong.

*Hardball Politics in the Home Districts.* One of the least visible weapons in the Reagan arsenal is the political operation masterminded by Lyn Nofziger, the puckish, rumpled California conservative. As White House political director, he carried the budget and tax battles into the home districts of wavering members of Congress, softening them up for presidential persuasion.

The theory was that pressure from home, especially from local officials or big campaign contributors has more impact on a member of Congress than any other political force.

From 15 years of criss-crossing America in the cause of conservatism, Ronald Reagan has developed the most potent network of political activists in the nation. "That's why Reagan is not a man to trifle with," asserts Lee Atwater, the South Carolina political organizer who is Nofziger's deputy. "He's got more people committed to him than anyone else. They're ready, able and willing to go into action on a moment's notice, and technically they're well organized."

Drawing on this network during the first budget fight of last April, 1981, Nofziger ran a political blitz in 54 swing congressional districts, 45 of them in the South. His operation tapped wealthy, organized groups like the Republican National Committee, the Republican Congressional Campaign Committee, the National Conservative Political Action Committee, the Moral Majority, the Fund for a Conservative Majority, business political action committees linked with the national Chamber of Commerce, National Association of Manufacturers, Business Roundtable, National Federation of Small Businessmen, National Jaycees, American Medical Association, local civic clubs, and scores of other groups interested in cutting federal spending and taxes. They were spearheaded by a team of high-level administration and congressional speakers, direct mail, and phone banks generating grass-roots support.

"The premise of the whole operation is that political reforms and the impact of media have made it so that a congressman's behavior on legislation can be affected more by pressure from within his own district than by lobbying here in Washington," explains Atwater. "The way we operate, within forty-eight hours any Congressman will know he has had a major strike in his district. All of a sudden, Vice-President Bush is in your district, Congressman Jack Kemp is in your district. Ten of your top contributors are calling you, the head of the local AMA, the head of the local realtors' group, local officials. Twenty letters come in. Within forty-eight hours, you're hit by paid media, free media, mail, phone calls, all asking you to support the President."

More potent, perhaps, is the implication that the big political action money will oppose incumbents who line up against the Reagan program. A House Republican task force under Representative Stan Parris of Virginia cross-checked people who had contributed more than $100 both to the Reagan Presidential campaign and to the local Democratic Congressman's campaign. Computerized letters went out to get these pro-Reagan contributors to pressure their Representative to go along with the President.

"The key to these Congressional victories, of course, is muscle," says Senator Paul Laxalt of Nevada, a close friend of the President. "People here feel that most of the public is with the President. One of the greatest things that was done was to go through the lists of big contributors and get them to lean on swing people. If a key contributor calls and says, go along with this, it has an effect."

The reach of the White House political operation has astonished some fence-sitters. Representative Ronnie Flippo of Alabama was reportedly turned around by a call from Governor Fob James, a pro-Reagan Democrat. Representative Dan Mica, a Democrat representing the Palm Beach area, was leaned on by his former campaign manager. "I had a call, too, from a local mayor, a Democrat very active in the party and associated with liberal causes, and he asked me to vote with the President," Mica said. "That surprised me that they would get to him."

Sometimes ardent Reaganites have been overly zealous. Mica and Bill Nelson, another swing Florida Democrat, squawked after William Wirthlin, a lobbyist for the National Taxpayers Union, told them that unless they committed themselves to the second Reagan budget package, even before it had been publicly surfaced, his group would run radio ads in their home districts. Mica was infuriated after Worthin played for him a tape asserting that Speaker O'Neill was enlisting him to "destroy" the President's program. When Nelson protested directly to the President at a White House meeting, Mr. Reagan shook his head in disbelief. "That's about the lousiest tactic I ever heard of," he said. "We don't condone it. We don't have anything to do with it." White House aides advised the National Taxpayers Union the maneuver was backfiring and it was dropped.

Reagan aides believe that one reason the President has fared so well in his first long legislative drive was his effort to understand the predicament of the "boll weevil" Democrats. At a breakfast on June 4, John Breaux of Louisiana voiced a common fear that the "boll weevils" were getting cut off from their own party and might have to face President Reagan campaigning against them in 1982. "I don't want to end up like a turkey with an eagle (the nickname of big Republican contributors) chasing me," Breaux said.

Instantly, the President gave a widely quoted response. "I could not oppose someone who supported my principles," he said. "I could not look myself in the mirror if I campaigned against you." Even though the President left himself the loophole of fund raising in their states and stopped short of offering them immunity from Republican opposition, one aide said, "You could sense a real sigh of relief around that table."

The Reagan camp does keep score among friends and foes, meting out rewards and punishment. Because of a campaign pledge and good Republican backing in Michigan last November, Mr. Reagan went along with import relief for the automobile industry and United Auto Workers Union through seeking reduction of Japanese exports. But in June he lifted import quotas on shoes from Taiwan and Korea, a move that hit the American shoe industry in Massachusetts, home territory of Speaker O'Neill and Senator Edward M. Kennedy.

*Party-Line Support.* So much attention has focused on Reagan recruitment of Democratic dissidents that an even more impressive feat has been largely overlooked — *the near perfect party-line support among 53 Republican Senators and 191 House members.* (The Democrats have 243 in the House 46 in the Senate, and there is one Senate independent.) Neither Eisenhower, Nixon, nor Ford achieved close to that kind of party loyalty and discipline. Indeed, some scholars say that the Republican party-line votes this spring have not been equaled since the hard-headed rule of "Czar" Joseph G. Cannon, the Republican Speaker, back in 1910.

The congressional leaders, Howard Baker in the Senate and Bob Michel in the House, were extremely effective in persuading Republicans that political success is affected by President Reagan's success when it comes time for reelection. One impetus is that many newly elected Republican conservatives in Congress feel special allegiance to Mr. Reagan because they rode his coattails into office in 1980. Occasionally, Michel went to House Republicans to call for a party-line vote with the admonition that there would be "retribution" against dissidents. None was meted out in the budget and tax battles because the economic issues were the best for unifying Republicans; they split more naturally over social and foreign policy questions. Beyond that, the new experience of partisan victory fostered loyalty.

Among the first- and second-term House Republicans, partisan spirit was especially strong. "The freshman and sophomore classes make up almost half of our 191 members," observes Max Friedersdorf. "They are extremely aggressive to make their mark. They want to win and they are fully aware that they have power in unity. They have an influence on the more senior Republicans who have developed a 'minority complex' over the years and have been inclined to go off on their own. They sense that they're getting close to having a majority in the House. This makes for an esprit that I've never seen before."

On the budget votes, holding two dozen northeastern and midwestern moderate and liberal republicans led by Carl Purcell of Michigan and William Green of New York was a delicate task. Like other Republicans they chafed over the attention the White House lavished on renegade southern Democrats.

Nofziger's office tried to meet their desires for political appointments. Stockman and Michel met repeatedly with their group to adjust the budget cuts to appease them. Ultimately the frost-belt Republicans won increases in funds for Amtrak, Conrail, energy subsidies to the poor, the National Endowment for Arts and the Humanities, nurses' training, and a less stringent cap on the growth of Medicaid spending. "When you're dealing with the entire budget, there are things along the margin that give way to making the overall goal," Stockman later explained. "We were willing to make adjustments at the margin."

That approach worked well through the summer, but when the White House and Stockman came back with a new round of proposed cuts in domestic social programs and the idea of deferring the annual cost-of-living increase in Social Security benefits, they touched a raw nerve. These moderate Republicans, who called themselves the "gypsy moths," rebelled. Bill Green talked of a "double-cross" by the administration. With Purcell and others, he called for $9 billion in defense cuts as a protest against the President's choice of priorities. With close to two dozen Republicans in rebellion, Michel could no longer hold the House coalition together and pressed the White House to backtrack. The constant risk for Reagan was that as he kept pressing further on his budget-cutting, he was losing his Congressional consensus. The Gypsy Moths, facing the 1982 elections in many pro-Democratic districts, had gone about as far as they could go with Reagan fiscal conservatism.

In all the maneuvering, President Reagan has left the horse-trading to others and stayed out of the details of legislative maneuvering. His generalized approach caused Speaker O'Neill to quip that Mr. Reagan does not know very much about the specifics of his own legislation. Emerging from one meeting with the President in early June, O'Neill told reporters that when the Democratic leadership would try out variations on the President's tax program, Mr. Reagan would look at Ed Meese, his counselor, for a lead on how to reply, a charge denied at the White House.

"The President's really not as well posted on the specifics and on the machinery as Johnson, Nixon, or Ford, who used to be more intimately involved in how it all worked," observed Michel, the House Republican leader. "Sometimes I'm a little apprehensive. I think, 'My Gosh, he ought to be better posted. Where are his briefing papers?' But he's chairman of board. He's not going to be hassled over details, and anyway you get the feeling that he's just so intent that he's going to get along with Congress and get as much out of Congress as he can."

Friedersdorf credited the President's early successes to his amiable manner, his willingness to listen, and his investment of time. "Congressional relations is not just a haphazard, occasional thing with the President," he said. "It's constant.

He's very willing to take advice not only from the White House staff but the Congressional leaders. Plus, he's sold on his program and he transmits that enthusiasm in his contacts."

Both cohorts and competitors have discovered, too, that Mr. Reagan's amiability is disarming; it masks a certain toughness. Governor Hugh Carey ran into the hard side of President Reagan during one session that the President held with state governors back on February 23. Carey criticized the Reagan tax plan, of ten-percent personal tax rate reductions for each of the next three years, on grounds that it would fuel inflation. He urged Mr. Reagan to reconsider the plan.

"You could hear a pin drop in that room," said Rich Williamson, the White House aide for intergovernmental relations. "It was a very forceful challenge. They all wanted to see if Reagan was for real. While Carey was talking, Reagan got red in the face. He glared at Carey, and then he burst out: 'What you've been talking about, business as usual, has given us an economic mess. Double-digit inflation. Double-digit interest rates. High unemployment. Let's try something new.' Then he cited past examples of regenerative tax cuts, and ended: 'I'd say with vehemence that I support 10-10-10.' "

Over the next four months, the President was persuaded to drop that 30 percent tax cut to 25 percent and to delay the first effective date from January 1 to October 1 to gain support from the "boll weevil" Democrats. But that was not enough; he was still under pressure from other Democrats to go lighter and later with his tax cut.

At one session with Democrats on the Senate Finance Committee Senator Fritz Hollings of South Carolina voiced renewed concern that the Reagan tax cut would add to federal deficits. Moreover, he said, public opinion polls showed that a tax cut ranked behind inflation, a balanced budget, unemployment, and American prestige abroad in the public's view. He urged the tax cut be put off until January 1, 1982.

"We've already split the difference by moving it to October," the President demurred. "I believe very strongly that all of the things they've listed will be helped by the tax cut." He then recalled that tax cuts under President Kennedy had not only stimulated the economy but generated more tax revenues. He wanted to follow the Kennedy model.

"But Jack Kennedy did it in steps," Hollings objected. "He lowered the capital gains tax first and then moved on to personal tax cuts."

"I've come to learn over the years that government doesn't get the money it needs," the President countered. "Government spends all the taxes it gets. So if we reduce the amount of taxes, we will reduce spending."

Senator Bennett Johnston, the Louisiana Democrat, suggested having the third year of the tax cut conditional — triggered only by the success of the first two years. But Mr. Reagan rejected that tactic. "We will have difficulty convincing people that it [the third year] will really happen," he said. "If you have any loophole, we will have trouble."

Charming as he can be in private sessions, the President becomes more combative in public. He enjoys the cut-and-thrust of debate. He seems to relish political hyperbole. Visiting Capitol Hill in mid-July, he taunted the Democrats, who had been accusing him of offering a "rich man's tax bill," with the charge that they were providing a more generous tax shelter than he for the intricate tax dodges of the wealthy known as commodity straddles. Their tax bill, he mocked, was "a make-believe tax cut . . . a wolf in sheep's clothing" because it was not as big as his.

Jousting with Speaker O'Neill has occasionally gotten under the President's skin, but he is quick to patch things up. As O'Neill has said, they put aside their disagreements at 6 P.M. and mix cordially. "They can disagree and still be friends," said one White House official. "I think that sets an atmosphere for cooperation and communication. It shows junior members of Congress that some of this is political posturing and there's no real animosity."

Two terms as Governor of California gave Mr. Reagan solid awareness of the need for legislative compromise, for during most of his tenure in Sacramento Democrats controlled both houses of the state legislature. He emerged with a more moderate record than his campaign rhetoric had foreshadowed. His method, Ed Meese said, was "to stand firm on principle but be flexible enough to negotiate within the framework of principle."

As President, Mr. Reagan has left it to others to do most of the active negotiating for him. "Ronald Reagan gives more latitude to subordinates than any president I ever saw but when it comes time to make a decision, he makes it," commented Senator Howard Baker. Dave Stockman improvised many of the particulars of his budget cut package, especially after the first program was put together. Jim Baker, the White House staff chief, and Treasury Secretary Regan worked out the tax compromise. They came to him with an expanded package, adopting several items worked up by the mainstream and boll weevil Democrats, as well as a proposal to cut in half the first of his own three years of ten-percent individual tax cuts.

As a decision-maker, the President has preferred to have his inner circle thrash out the alternatives and come to him with a consensus recommendation, if possible. Usually he has ratified their proposal but if they could not agree, he has prodded them to argue their cases in front of him. "I've seen members of Congress and his staff go at it hard with the President there," Senator Baker reported. "He listens. There's almost a sense of pleasure and amusement as he watches different people argue the point. He lets it go on to a certain point and he makes a decision. The implication I draw is that this man is not afraid of controversy. He doesn't feel the need to placate anybody."

Occasionally, President Reagan has been ill-served by merely ratifying the consensus brought to him by advisers and hurt by his own lack of independent Washington experience. Thus, Stockman and Friedersdorf wanted to rush through the final stage of the budget process by having the Senate merely pass the House version and bypassing the usual House-Senate conference. At their suggestion, President Reagan called Senator Baker, who disagreed and got the support of 19 Senate Republican committee chairmen. The White House had to back down.

Far more costly was the failure of the White House to anticipate the aroused Senate reaction to the administration's proposed cuts in the Social Security program. Stockman and Richard S. Schweiker, Secretary of Health and Human Services, were anxious to send a proposal to Congress on this issue before a House subcommittee began hearings. The President's political aides were not paying close attention to the controversial dynamite in this package. They acquiesced and the President gave the go-ahead. Immediately, the Senate voted down the idea 96-0. Senate Republicans were outraged at not having been consulted in advance, and the administration had to retreat and revise its plan. Again, in the fall, Stockman and the White House team were prepared to tinker with Social Security and the revenue-sharing program, and Reagan went along (only to have to back down when the Republican leaders in Congress balked).

Those episodes illustrate that in spite of the Reagan victories and in spite of the President's solicitude toward Congress, institutional differences remain strong and plenty of problems confront the White House, despite early success. Budget and tax-cutting have been the most favorable issues for the President. Once the first stages of the economic battle had been fought, the legislative agenda could never again be so tidy, so focused, or so favorable. The single-mindedness of the administration and Congress was bound to dissipate. Legislative momentum was inevitably much harder to maintain.

It is only natural that on other issues, centrifugal political forces began to wear away at the winning coalition the Reagan forces constructed on the economic issues. Liberal and conservative Republicans had already split on such emotional and controversial issues as busing and were increasingly unhappy over further efforts to cut social programs. Similar rifts arose over abortion, school prayer, voting rights, and other social issues. Out in the country, the supporting political network also faced strains. Many business conservatives were likely to part company with the Moral Majority on social issues. Boll weevil Democrats who sided with Mr. Reagan on economics, quickly acknowledged that they differed with him on social issues. Representative G. V. "Sonny" Montgomery of Mississippi, a leader of the Conservative Democratic Forum, predicted that the group's support for the President — only partial on economic issues — would not extend to social issues.

Other divisions arose on foreign policy. One harbinger of trouble, not sufficiently heeded by the White House came when majorities in both Houses signed a letter opposing the administration's planned sale of advanced electronic reconnaissance planes [AWACS] to Saudi Arabia. Much of the President's time and energy and the legislative muscle of the White House was sapped fighting a rearguard effort to save that deal. To almost everyone's surprise, President Reagan won the AWACS fight narrowly, and spared himself a costly setback. Once again he proved his pervasive power with Congress, but the price may have been lost momentum and even some lost support on subsequent economic votes. On other issues, foreign relations committees in both Houses had made further aid to El Salvador conditional on "significant progress" on human rights in that country. They resisted the President's appeal for a $350 million "contingency" fund for responding to foreign crises. These were all warning signals to the White House.

In short, the President's success in Congress on 1981 budget and tax cuts struck many observers as a one-year phenomenon, hard to transfer into other areas. If the economy performs badly in 1982 and 1983, Mr. Reagan's first-year victories on economic issues would become difficult to repeat.

"If there was any mandate, it was pretty well confined to economics," commented Thomas E. Cronin, a presidential scholar at Colorado College. "And it is on the economic issues that Reagan has swung from the heels. But once they get into the social issues like abortion, or even policy issues like the MX missile, he's going to have trouble keeping his own party together. This is the only period, this six months, that he's going to be able to have his own way. The Reagan team has kept the other issues off the agenda and that's how they've been so impressive."

The top White House expert on Congress, Max Friedersdorf, essentially agreed, even while he was reaping the harvest of support on the economy. "I think it's too early to say we have a working coalition for the President," he said. "It's potentially there. But we've only dealt with two issues — the budget and tax cuts. On dozens of other issues — foreign policy, the environment, social issues, we haven't tested the water yet."

That assessment, made at the higher-water mark of Reagan's success in early August 1981, could hardly have been more prophetic. The pressure of persistent high interest rates, the pessimism of investors of Wall Street, talk of a recession instead of a spurt of economic growth, and the wary vulnerability of northern congressional Republicans raised obstacles that forced the Reagan White House to slow its legislative pace and curb its ambitions by mid-October. The stunning confessions of doubt about the effectiveness of the Reagan program and the admission of sometimes dubious political tactics by Budget Director David Stockman in November were another jolt to the Reagan cause.

Although the President did make some headway on further budget trims, the coalition that Reagan's team had so carefully stitched together in spring and summer began to unravel. Only by being willing to backtrack and compromise as well as talk the tough tactics of presidential vetoes could the President make even modest progress with his economic program. He had to settle in the fall session in Congress for considerably less action than he proposed in his nationally televised address on September 24. His growing difficulties seemed to confirm Lyndon Johnson's judgment that if a new president wants to achieve significant results, he must accomplish them in his first year — because after that the opportunity vanishes.

SOURCE: An earlier version of this essay appeared in *The New York Times Magazine,* August 9, 1981.

# 21. Presidents and Political Parties

## Thomas E. Cronin

It is frequently said that the president is the leader of his political party. In fact, however, a president has no formal position in the party structure. In theory, the supreme authority in our parties is the national presidential convention. More directly in charge of the national party, at least on paper, is the national committee (and each national committee has a national chairperson).

In practice, successful presidents usually control their national committees and, often, their national conventions as well. Although the national committee picks the national party chairman, a president almost always lets the committee know whom he wants. Modern presidents hire and fire national party staff almost at will. Several of our recent presidents have ignored their national party committees. Some have treated them with contempt.

Political parties once were a prime source of influence for a president. It used to be said, for example, that our most effective presidents were effective in large part because they had made use of party support and took seriously their party leadership responsibilities. But as our parties have declined in organizational importance, there has been more of an incentive for presidents to "rise above" party.

Today, the presidential-party relationship is strained. National party chairpersons come and go with embarrassing regularity and regular embarrassment. Over a fifteen-year period between 1967 and 1982, for example, there were a total of nine Democratic and seven Republican national chairpersons. Few party chairpersons of the president's party have enjoyed much influence. Many were regarded at the White House as little more than clerks.

The central concern in this chapter is the awkward alliance between presidents and their parties. Both president and party need each other. Yet both often become frustrated and even annoyed with the other. What has been the role of the president as party leader? What of the presidents' use of party as an appeal to Congress for support of their programs? Why the apparent growing divorce between presidents and their parties? What are the limits on presidents as party leaders and the limits of the party as a check on presidents? Could something be done to encourage more cohesion between presidents and parties?

*Thomas E. Cronin teaches political science at Colorado College and is the author or coauthor of several books, including* The State of the Presidency, Government by the People, *and* U.S. v. Crime in the Streets.

## President as Party Leader?

Our earliest presidents vigorously opposed the development of political parties. They viewed them as factions and divisive — something to be dreaded as the greatest political evil. By 1800, however, the contest for the presidency had become a battle between political parties. The Jefferson-led Republicans took on and defeated the John Adams-led Federalists. But even Jefferson, sometimes called the founder of what later became the Democratic Party, had doubts about party contests for the presidency. He disliked the Federalist Party and their narrow, elitist constituency. He hoped the Federalist Party would shrivel and collapse, thus allowing the more representative Republicans to remain in permanent control. Jefferson's party was in fact dominant for two generations.

Parties just naturally arose. Out-of-power interests coalesced to put their own candidates in contention for the presidency. Party clashes became routine. The evolution of political parties had much to do with the successful functioning of both presidency and Constitution. They solved in part the problem of presidential recruitment. They served also as a means of checking presidents, of keeping them responsive to concerned grass-roots citizens, for to remain in office a president would have to win renomination from his political party.

As they evolved, parties helped narrow down the number of candidates, prepared platforms, and creatively mediated among the diverse interests that were pressing claims and pushing ideological views on future officeholders. Parties usually were able to find the common middle ground among more or less hostile groups so that agreement could be reached on general principles.

Moreover, the parties enabled officeholders to overcome some of the limitations of our formal constitutional arrangements. Political parties facilitated coordination among the branches. President Jackson especially used his resources to promote partisan control of government. Jackson's achievements as party leader transformed the office, so much so that he is often called the "first modern president."

> The President became both the head of the executive branch and leader of the party. The first six Presidents usually acted in a manner that accorded Congress an equality of power. However, starting with Andrew Jackson the President began more and more to assert his role not simply as head of the executive branch but as leader of the government. By the skillful use of his position as head of the party he persuaded Congress to follow his lead, thereby allowing him to assume greater control of the government and to direct and dominate public affairs.[1]

Many historians and political scientists hold that the effective presidents have been those who have, like Jackson, strengthened their position by becoming strong party leaders. Cooperation and achievement could be achieved through party alliances. "Since the office did not come equipped with the necessary powers under the Constitution, they had to be added through a historical process by the forceful action of vigorous Presidents whose position was strengthened by the rise and development of political parties." [2]

Few presidents have been able to duplicate Jackson's success. Most have found it exceedingly difficult to serve as an activist party builder and party leader while trying to serve also as chief of state and national unifier. President William Taft lamented that the longer he was president, "the less of a party man I seem to become." [3] President William Howard McKinley said he could no longer be president of a party for "I am now President of the whole people." [4] Others complain that they cannot simultaneously be faithful party leaders and serve the nation impartially.

What, at least in theory, are the obligations of a president as a party leader? These vary, of course, depending on one's conception of the presidency and the party system. The textbook model has generally held that the president should promote party platforms, reward party loyalists, punish party mavericks, run proudly with the party ticket, and heed the interests and advice of party leaders. The president — at least in theory — should be a party builder and strengthen the party ranks by communicating the party's purposes and positions. Presidents, it is believed, should be as much the product of their parties as their leader. It should be a two-way street, with parties serving to check ambition and to ensure accountable leadership. A president would be expected to consult regularly with local, state, and national party committee officials.

Presidential practice is distinctly different. Few of our recent presidents have spent much time working with party officials save as it was absolutely necessary for their renomination. Most presidents of late have mistreated their national party committees. David Broder wrote, for example, that Lyndon Johnson acted as though party obligations and partisanship were the enemy, not the servant, of responsible government.

> He [Johnson] did not see political parties as necessary vehicles for communicating the often inchoate preferences of the voters to those in power. Nor did he see the parties as instruments for disciplining the whims of the elected leaders and holding them accountable for their actions. Instead, he saw them as unwanted intruders on the process of consensus government.[5]

The Nixon presidency in many ways was the ultimate in presidential hostility toward its own party. Nixon dumped Republican Party Chairman Ray Bliss, who was widely acknowledged as a brilliant party builder. Nixon time and again sought to divorce himself from the Republican label and from supporting Republican candidates. Nixon regularly ignored Republican Party officials and set a similar tone for his White House staff. Once, when National Chairman Robert Dole had been trying for some time to see the President, a White House aide is alleged to have said to Dole in an obvious put-down: "If you still want to see the President, turn on your television set tonight at 7:00. The President will be on then." Nixon yearned to be above partisan responsibilities. He yearned to be a bipartisan foreign policy leader. Accordingly, Nixon's definition of presidential leadership was that a president is there to make global decisions that no one else can make. He also felt that party officials do not know enough to clarify foreign policy issues, not to mention to make foreign policy decisions. Thus Nixon would be the peacemaker, the statesman, the globe-trotting diplomat.

But when a president strives to be above party, critics say, what often results is that he and his aides grow dependent on more secretive and covert political operations. The campaign abuses of 1972 are the result. A president who divorces himself from his party does so at the risk of becoming a prisoner of his own whims. A partyless presidency is potentially an arbitrary one, one which may be too much in the business of self-promotion at the expense of party and public interests. Walter Mondale said it well when he wrote:

> A President out of touch with party politics is a President who feels no accountability to the men and women who are close to the realities of political life. Such a President has severed one more essential link in maintaining the sense of perspective vital for the effective functioning of the Presidential office and the achievement of restraint on arbitrary Presidential action.[6]

## Limits on Presidential Party Leadership

Once in office, presidents often bend over backward in an attempt to minimize the partisan appearance of their actions. This is so in part because the public yearns for a "statesman" in the White House, for a president who is above politics. A president is not supposed to act with his eye on the next election; he is not supposed to favor any particular group or party.

Herein lies one of the major paradoxes of the presidency.[7] On the one hand, a president is expected to be a pure and neutral public servant, avoiding political and party considerations. On the other hand, he is supposed to lead his party, help cooperative members of Congress get reelected, and work closely with party leaders. Also, he must build political coalitions and drum up support, including party support, for what he feels needs to be done.

To take the president out of partisan politics, however, is to assume incorrectly that a president will be so generally right and the leaders and rank and file of his party so generally wrong that a president must be protected from the push and shove of political pressures. But what president has always been right? Having a president constrained and informed by party platforms and party leaders is what was intended when our party system developed.[8] How often this was actually done is difficult to estimate.

If past is prologue, future presidents will more often than not shun the image of party leader. In an era of weaker party identification and rising independents, it is inevitable that presidents will strive to be impartial officeholders. This may be why so many of our recent presidents have appointed a few cabinet members from the opposition party. John Kennedy appointed Republicans Robert McNamara and Douglas Dillon to two vital cabinet posts (defense and treasury). Johnson chose John W. Gardner to head up the Department of Health, Education and Welfare, the cornerstone agency for his Great Society. Presidents of both the major parties relied on Henry Kissinger, James Schlesinger, Elliot

Richardson, and Daniel P. Moynihan. Ronald Reagan appointed Jeane Kirkpatrick, a Democrat, as United States ambassador to the United Nations — a
cabinet-level post.

Another profound influence which limits the modern president as party leader
is the fact that he must now communicate to citizens by television. Television is
the main source of information for the citizen. Television is also a major weapon
in the arsenal of presidential leadership. But it is also one that apparently forces
a president to bypass party structures. The nonpartisan direct television appeal
has replaced the party rally. As a result, the party has lost one of its main functions — namely, being a source of information and communication between citizens and their government.

Presidents know that appeals to party on television addresses are not politically
wise. Presidents are instructed by their pollsters and marketing managers to rely
on popular appeal and encourage popular leadership rather than party leadership. Party organization thereby becomes subordinate. Time and again, a personalized entrepreneurial politics emphasizing the president triumphs over a
politics emphasizing party purposes and party issues.

Television has also provided a means for third-party and extraparty interests
to communicate their views to the public and bypass traditional party structures.
George Wallace, John Lindsay, and Independent James Longley of Maine all
were beneficiaries of the availability of television time. News coverage of the
Ralph Naders has helped to promote yet other alternatives to the party process.

Another more subtle factor in lessening the role presidents play in party activities lies in the fact that for at least a generation now, ours has been a candidate-financed election system, not a party-financed system. A few states are an
exception to this pattern — states such as Wisconsin. Most of the time, most
candidates raise their own funds and organize their own staffs and campaign
committees. Generally speaking, the ablest organizers, campaigners, and media
consultants have worked for candidates — candidates for the presidency, candidates for Congress, and so on. As the parties have grown weaker and as can-
didate-based organizations have become the routine, people who have remained
as workers with party organizations are often less talented — or so at least is
the perception of many people now involved in elective politics. The most talented campaign people now are usually in the White House or in Congress,
either in office or in staff positions. So much is this the case that elected officeholders and their staffs often do not take "the party people" very seriously.

Such a view has generally been present in the White House. During the Carter
presidency, the Democratic National Committee staff was controlled by the
White House staff. They took their instructions from Hamilton Jordan and Tim
Kraft, two of the people who masterminded the Jimmy Carter primary victories
in 1976. Neither Jordan nor Kraft were party professionals or party leaders. On
the contrary, they were candidate loyalists who proved themselves and won their
reputations as candidate promoters. Similarly, top Reagan strategists went to
the White House after 1980, not to the Republican National Committee.

Not surprisingly, these candidate-oriented professionals look down on party officials and, especially, party staffers. What have they ever won? This may not be as it should be, but it is the way attitudes get formed in the world of the practitioners.

Every recent White House has had an aide — usually a senior aide — assigned the function of liaison with the national committee staff of the president's party. Such persons (Kenneth O'Donnell for Kennedy, Marvin Watson for Johnson, Tim Kraft for Carter, and Ed Meese and others for Reagan), meet with the chairperson of the national committee, arrange for an occasional presidential visit to state and national party fund-raising functions, and host visits from visiting party delegations. Sometimes, for example, a state party chairperson or even a state party committee will be invited to the White House for staff briefings and perhaps even a lunch with the president. This liaison aide will also oversee sensitive party patronage decisions and handle suggestions and complaints coming from national committee members and state chairpersons.

But the work of this White House aide has been overshadowed by the gradual development in the contemporary White House of an office of interest-group liaison. With a notable institutionalization in the Nixon White House, this staff (sometimes numbering as high as twenty-nine or more staffers) has sought an outreach to ethnic, professional, labor, business, religious, and every conceivable citizen interest organization. Aides such as William Baroody, Jr. (Nixon and Ford), Midge Costanza and Anne Wexler (Carter), and Elizabeth Dole (Reagan) have pioneered this effort of working directly with groups that once enjoyed their access to politics primarily through the political parties. These aides bring delegations of these interest-group leaders to the White House for briefings. They provide an opportunity for these interest groups to bring their views and grievances directly to top White House aides. In addition, these White House aides try to provide information and inside know-how to these group leaders, with the hope they will back the president's programs in Congress and try to get their organization to support the president. It is estimated that the Carter interest-group liaison operation worked with as many as 800 groups and organizations by 1979. Groups and officials that once may have worked through party leaders (or bosses) now are organized on a national scale and often as not have a lobbying office in Washington ready and willing to deal directly with White House aides and cabinet officials. Mayors, governors, county executives, labor leaders, ethnic group advocates, and so on — they no longer need or want to go through the party bosses to be heard. Plainly, this direct access and direct consultation operation has removed yet another function that party officials often believed was theirs.

Presidents in recent years have also believed, rightly or wrongly, that many of the toughest problems they face are policy controversies that defy party clarification or traditional party problem-solving approaches. These presidents develop the view that many of the great issues of the day require study by blue-ribbon bipartisan presidential advisory commissions or by White House task forces. In order to get a prominent elder statesman or top professional of some standing to accept the chairpersonship of such a commission, a president usually has to promise that partisanship will play no role in the selection of personnel for such commissions. Time and again, the reliance on these presidential advisory system mechanisms has further minimized the role that party organizations have played as agenda setters and problem definers, not to mention as problem solvers.[9] A similar problem faces a president when he tries to recruit significant well-known individuals to serve as cabinet officers. One of the first things such persons often ask is: "Can I have a free hand in selecting my deputies and top aides in this department?" It is as if they are saying the concerns of this department have outgrown party definition. They will often say as well that if they take the job, they will be seeking nonpartisan answers and will need nonpartisan or bipartisan support. In effect, they are also saying: Don't visit on me any party hacks or former campaign advance men or defeated party officeholders!

In sum, these are several, but by no means all, of the limits that make it difficult for a president to serve aggressively as a party leader. I have not bothered to elaborate on the well-worn observation that our parties become truly national only for the purposes of electing a president and organizing the national legislature. Although national committees and national government now enjoy greater influence in the conduct of presidential nominations, they still have little influence over our decentralized party structure between elections.[10] Hence, a president's practical influence over his party is sharply limited. His power as party leader comes to end when he needs it most. He is virtually unable to recruit party candidates for Congress or other offices and has little or no influence in the selection of state and local party officials. His once vast influence over patronage appointments is now considerably circumscribed. Presidents and cabinet members must weigh patronage claims of the party against their own need for expertise and talented assistance. Patronage has its limits. President after president is amazed at the ingratitude of those who have been on the receiving end (and, of course, for every one person who wins a position, or a lucrative contract, or some other presidential favor, there are several more who felt they should have won it instead).

## Presidents and Use of Party Appeal in Congress

Presidential control of party supporters in Congress has seldom been great. "Party indiscipline," writes Arthur Schlesinger, "far from being a novelty of our fallen times, is one of the conditions that American democracy has endured from the start."[11] Of course, the situation varies from time to time. If Ronald Reagan enjoyed surprising party unity on his 1981 economic package, he enjoyed it less on social issues and defense spending matters. President Carter assuredly experienced a lack of party discipline among the Democrats in Congress. He found members of his own party were strong-minded and independent.

Many of the Democrats who were elected in the 1972 and 1974 elections came from previously Republican districts, and they acted, not surprisingly, as if they owed their primary allegiance to their district or state constituencies rather than to party platforms or to the White House.

Carter found that appeals to party were of marginal benefit, as he increasingly found he needed Republican votes as well to secure most of his victories. Douglass Cater said it well several years ago when he noted that "a President, Democrat or Republican, finds himself measuring Congress in terms of the coalitions for him and against him on specific issues. His task of building a winning coalition provides a constant temptation to devise means of persuasion other than appeals to party loyalty.[12] This was a pre-Vietnam, pre-Watergate observation that would appear to be even more valid today.

When presidents such as the recent ones fall in the polls, their ability as party leaders in the Washington community withers. A sag in the president's popularity worries members of Congress of his party, for they fear his standing may make them more vulnerable to opposition attacks back home. A senior political aide to Carter put the matter in useful perspective:

> When the President is low in public opinion polls, the Members of Congress see little hazard in bucking him.... After all, very few Congressmen examine an issue solely on its merits; they are politicians and they think politically. I'm not saying they make only politically expedient choices. But they read the polls and from that they feel secure in turning their back on the President with political impunity. Unquestionably, the success of the President's policies bear a tremendous relationship to his popularity in the polls.[13]

Presidential attempts to unseat or purge disloyal members of Congress in his own party have not worked. Roosevelt's celebrated "purge" of nonsupportive Democrats in the congressional elections of 1938 was mainly in vain. Anti-New Deal Democrats won reelection or election for the first time in most of the places where he tried to wield his influence.

Presidential coattails, once thought to be a significant factor in helping to elect members of a president's party to Congress, have had little effect in recent years. Recent research studies indicate that there are fewer competitive congressional districts. Members usually get reelected because of the quality of their constituency services and the fact that they can take advantage of incumbency — not on whether or not they have worked cooperatively with the White House. Congressional races are not notably affected by national issues or national trends anymore. Time and again, presidents have found in midterm congressional elections that they can do little to help members of their own party who are in trouble. Ford campaigned vigorously in 1974 for dozens of members of Congress only to see most of them defeated. Carter experienced similar disappointments in 1978, especially in Senate races.

Presidents today have little retaliatory leverage to apply against uncooperative legislators. Members of Congress, as a result of various congressional reforms, have more and more resources (trips home, larger staffs, more research facilities, more home offices and office staffs in their districts, and so forth) to help themselves win reelection. With the dramatic growth of government programs and governmental regulation, members of Congress are in a good position to make themselves nearly indispensable to local officials and local businessmen, who need to have a Washington "friend" to cut through the red tape and expedite government contracts or short-circuit some federal regulation. These kinds of developments have enhanced reelection chances for most members while, at the same time, making them less dependent on the White House and less fearful of any penalty for ignoring presidential party appeals. A student of congressional elections sums up these developments as follows:

> As late as 1958, congressional votes could be characterized as overwhelmingly party-line votes. Consequently, they were broadly reflective of the general policy differences which divided the parties. As the federal role has expanded, however, and federal programs have come to touch the lives of countless citizens, the relationship of a congressman to his constituency has changed. Increasingly, congressmen are elected as individuals, not as members of a party, and increasingly they are elected as nonpartisan, nonideological providers of constituency services.[14]

Note too that many members in Congress today are the product of "movement" or "new politics" experiences. Many of them had to buck local party establishments to win election in the first place. In this age of television and direct mail campaigns, candidates for Congress have often run virtually as independents or as outsiders. Their loyalty to party is thin to begin with. Their base back home is much more tied to professional, business, new politics, consumer interest groups and political action committees than to old-line political party operatives. Moreover, they have often built their own personal organization rather than tried to infuse new life into local party organizations. Often, the local party apparatus is moribund anyway.

From the president's vantage point, it is seldom helpful to punish party mavericks. In this reformed Congress, with power more dispersed and decentralized and where nearly everyone has a piece of the action, there is just too much risk for a president to single out a few party "disloyalists" for retribution. White House congressional relations aides know all too well that it is best to abide by the motto of "no permanent allies, no permanent enemies." You may lose someone on a vote today, but his or her vote may be crucial on some other measure next week. Then, too, a president has fewer patronage plums or perquisites these days with which to persuade a wavering member of Congress. More and more patronage jobs of the past are now civil service positions or are selected on the basis of merit. More and more governmental contracts or so-called pork-barrel expenditures come under close congressional or press scrutiny or are subject to some funding formula.

In short, a president's appeal to his fellow party members in Congress is effective only some of the time. It sometimes will help, but this kind of appeal is more unpredictable today than in the past. Party caucuses may be a bit stronger in Congress, but legislators know that neither the White House nor fellow members in Congress will penalize them if they can claim that "district necessities" forced them to differ with the party on a certain vote — even a key vote. Regional differences in Congress these days are sharper than they have been in the recent past, and these, too, have increased party fragmentation. Presidents doubtless will contrive to encourage party cohesion, but just as clearly, party support will vary on the kinds of measures the president is asking them to support and on whether or not parties continue to lose importance in national political life.

## Proposals to Increase Cohesion Between President and Party

Our national parties, it is suggested, are fast becoming an endangered species. With this development have come proposals that might revitalize the parties and might help them recapture some of their historic mediating and moderating influence in U.S. political life.

Readers should be warned that most Americans could not care less. Most Americans are indifferent — at best — to the purposes of our parties. Moreover, even some informed observers say they do not know whether there is much realism in trying to resuscitate the parties. Critics of party renewal efforts sometimes contend there is too much nostalgia for a romanticized two-party system that seldom or never really existed.

Still, rethinking public policy toward the parties is much needed. In the campaign to revive and protect them, the following are the measures, at least bearing upon the presidency, one hears most often. I will examine some of their merits and defects.

Many proponents of party renewal say federal funding of presidential elections should be abolished or at least significant portions of this public financing should be channeled through the parties. They say federal funding bypasses parties too much and encourages autonomous, entrepreneurial political adventurers who are unaccountable to anyone. Campaign funds, these proponents argue, should go to the party organization. Party regulars or party establishments would then have some control and, thereby, more of a function. Candidates would have to demonstrate their loyalty and their willingness to run with the ticket and on the platform as a quid pro quo of getting adequate financial help. This would presumably tie a candidate, and perhaps later the officeholder, to a closer relationship to the national committee. Moreover, it is pointed out by veteran observers that the two national committees already have experienced accounting offices and these staffs could help reduce the staff work, start-up costs, and probable errors of a newly formed candidate organization. Campaign financing legislation encourages separate candidate committees to be set up to receive and account for public funds, at least in primary elections.[15] If candidates trusted their national committees and national committee staffs, the funds could — at least in theory — come through these party officers to the candidates (this could be done at both the primary and general election stage).

However, the abuses of our previous system of private financing to candidates had to be remedied. The system we have had for a long time has been predominantly a candidate-financed system, vividly illustrated by this description from the late U.S. Senator Hubert Humphrey:

> Campaign financing [talking about the pre-1974 system] is a curse. It's the most disgusting, demeaning, disenchanting, debilitating experience of a politician's life. It's stinky, it's lousy. I just can't tell you how much I hate it. I've had to break off in the middle of trying to make a decent, honorable campaign and go up to somebody's parlor or to a room and say, "gentlemen, and ladies, I'm desperate. You've got to help me.". . .
> And you see people there — a lot of them you don't want to see. And they look at you, and you sit there and you talk to them and tell them what you're for and you need help and, out of the twenty-five who have gathered, four will contribute. And most likely one of them is in trouble and is somebody you shouldn't have had a contribution from.[16]

In response to these kinds of situations and the Watergate revelations, Congress passed the Campaign Reform Act of 1974. This is not the place to outline that act. But it is true that it reaffirmed a primarily candidate-oriented public finance system. It substituted in effect a publicly financed candidate system for a privately financed candidate system. National party committees receive some public funds ($2 million each in 1976, about $3 billion in 1980) for running the quadrennial national conventions.

Why did this campaign finance reform ignore and bypass the parties? Most members of Congress just did not want to strengthen party committees. Members of Congress have little interest in giving party officials more power over who gets money in national elections. Congress obviously was thinking of itself as well. If public financing is extended to congressional campaigns, a possible development at some future date, the last thing a member wants is to have to submit to local and state party officials for campaign funds. As things stand now, the candidate raises his or her own funds. It is a highly individualistic arrangement, and few members of Congress will entrust so important a career lifeblood factor to party bosses. Especially is this the case with officeholders who had to buck the party to get elected merely a few years ago. Further, in its weakened state, party machinery sometimes gets taken over by extremist factions. Take the Massachusetts Republican Committee. Its officers in recent years have often been rightish issue-oriented extremists. Yet the Republican officeholders (Edward Brooke, Silvio Conte, Margaret Heckler, and so forth) have been moderates. Why would these officials support funds to be given to the party state committee? For similar reasons Senator Robert Kennedy helped lead a fight against public funds going to the national committees in 1967. He hardly wanted a Johnson-dominated Democratic National Committee to control funds for the 1968 elections.

If public funds are made available to the national committees, it will probably be done through indirect side payments of some kind or another. Thus, Congress in 1979 approved a lower postal rate for parties to use in fund-raising efforts. Another subsidy, which would make sense, is the provision of free television time to national party committees to present their views and purposes to the American people. Modest assistance of this kind may help to prop up the major parties. Too much funding of the parties, however, might cement into permanence the present parties at the expense of some future party that would be deserving of a chance to catch on.

A second general proposal to enhance cohesion between presidents and their parties calls for giving more power to party regulars. One variation calls for holding fewer direct primaries on the grounds that party conventions or party caucuses would allow party loyalists to have more of a say in the presidential nominating process. (Many people remain unconvinced, however, that a return to the smoke-filled-room technique for candidate nominations will measurably strengthen our parties.) Another variation of this proposal urges an automatic seating of state party chairpersons and more elected party officeholders — such as governors and U.S. senators — at the national convention. (The Democrats did this on a modified basis in 1980.) The reasoning here is that these kinds of persons have long-standing commitments to the preservation of the party and have a stake in the future of the party — not just in who the candidate will be this time. It is thought that these party professionals know better how to bring disparate factions together and how to compromise on explosive issues that might divide the party.

Yet another proposal calls for regular party midterm conventions. Actually, this is not all that new an idea. Both parties have experimented with policy councils and midterm conferences of one kind or another for several decades. However, these are usually favored by the out-of-office party. Issue-oriented party participants not now holding office favor these as occasions when the party can take stock of how it is doing on its old agenda of issues. It can also provide, they claim, a forum to adopt new positions and reaffirm the party platform commitments of two years earlier.

Critics of these miniconventions, as they are sometimes called, say they invite too much party divisiveness in full public view. The Democrats in recent years have held midterm conferences — in Kansas City in late 1974, in Memphis in late 1978, and in Philadelphia in June 1982. At the simplest level, these conferences strike many people as public entertainments — part sporting events and part theater. Will the liberals condemn the moderates? Will a Ted Kennedy upstage President Carter or Walter Mondale? To what extent can a president turn it into a party and personal rally? Media attention focuses, predictably, on who wins and who loses, as well as upon mavericks, who often get more attention than they probably deserve. Still, an incumbent president who comes to listen and learn as he meets for a few days with several thousand party regulars and activists is a president who avoids that great temptation for presidents to become isolated. Further, he gets a chance to see and hear the intensity of concern over contemporary issues. He must hear also about whether or not he is handling the job of president in an appropriate manner. There is much to be said for this midterm party audit — an audit of the president, as well of party policy positions. These party midterm conferences are to be encouraged. They deserve to be continued.

Be aware, however, that members of Congress (and many state legislators and statewide officeholders) often view these midterm gatherings with a luke-warm-to-opposed stance. Democratic party leaders deliberately reduced the size of their 1982 conference to make it more of a leadership conference than a mass participatory event for activists. There are two reasons for this. First, it can complicate congressional elections (especially if the conventions are held before early November) by raising issues that a legislator would rather not run on or have to take a side on. Second, the platform or policy clarification role to some extent competes with, and even threatens, the responsibilities of the congressional party caucuses. Members of Congress, moreover, believe they are in a much better position — as elected officeholders and as members of congressional committees with extensive staffs — to formulate policy positions than are party delegates to the party's midterm convention.[17]

## Prospects

One of the many reasons politicans rely on the media rather than the party organization is that the media route is easier. Keeping a party organization intact or rebuilding a political party in a community is an exacting undertaking. It is no accident that more and more groups in America are single-issue organizations. It is very difficult to hold a multi-issue group together for long, and that is what a party is. We need to have a better understanding of why this is and why there appear to be patterns of party organization and practices of local parties that apparently ensure decay. Could it be otherwise? Might different practices or different incentives help overcome the ruts and the rot?

There have been some healthy signs in the 1970s. The party caucuses and party conferences in Congress have shown more signs of life. Indeed, the Democratic Party caucus in the House of Representatives in the mid-1970s was instrumental in revitalizing that institution.[18] Party caucuses were used to help modernize and democratize the House of Representatives. The party caucus is also a place to discuss party commitments and adapt old commitments to new policy problems. Reagan benefitted from extraordinary party caucus loyalty from Republicans in both legislative chambers in 1981.

Then, too, there is a growing appreciation that parties need to be preserved: they need to be made constructive and a vital part of the political process. Those who are aware of the chaos and paralysis produced by thousands of new interest groups, each having an impact directly on the government in narrow public policy areas, long for almost any instrument that might prevent direct parochial impact and encourage intermediary processes of trade-off, mediation, and so forth. Stronger parties would obviously help here.

Party organizations may simply be no longer effective in many of those traditional functions, but parties are definitely worth saving. They help to give the electorate reasonable choices at the election booth. They can provide a forum for candidates of somewhat common perspectives to agree on broad purposes. They certainly will continue to be important in organizing the legislative branch. Perhaps, too, they sometimes will formulate strategies that can help us overcome some of our toughest economic policy questions.

Perhaps most important to the preservation of parties is a commitment to avoid further weakening of them. Direct popular election of the president (as a substitute for the Electoral College) ought not to be considered. A move to do this was defeated in the U.S. Senate in midsummer 1979. To move to the direct election plan would encourage splinter and single-issue parties and further weaken our major parties.[19] Similarly, a national primary might be a severe blow to our party system. Political scientist Austin Ranney views the national primary proposal with alarm, saying it not only would greatly weaken state parties but it would mean "a virtual end to the national parties as anything more than passive arenas for contests between entrepreneurial candidate organizations." [20]

Can parties as institutions be made to serve as a more effective check on presidents? This might be desirable, but again, the weakened condition of the parties and the history of party fragmentation and lack of discipline suggests that the prospects are not inviting. One should not overlook, however, the role party officials and party stalwarts have played in checking and balancing presidents of their party. Johnson was forced to quit his 1968 bid less by Eugene McCarthy's insurgency than when Robert Kennedy and party regulars in Wisconsin and elsewhere made it clear he was unacceptable to broad segments within the Democratic Party. So, also, Nixon was forced to resign when it was clear the stalwarts in his own party — men like Goldwater, Hugh Scott, and others — could no longer support him.

Parties need to be protected and preserved even if they are not likely to be much strengthened. Presidents in the future, as in the past, will find party leadership a necessary yet exacting task. The incentive is to ignore the party. A six-year nonrenewable presidential term would encourage that tendency and for that reason, among others, should not be approved. The four-year term with the necessity of renomination at least ensures that most presidents in the first term will recognize the importance of the party to their political survival. A political party should retain the threat of dumping a president who has turned his back on his party's pledges or has ignored the party platform. We shall have some presidents in the tradition of the Jacksons, Wilsons, and Roosevelts who will serve as party leaders — but just as likely, we will have presidents in the Eisenhower mold, who eschew party responsibilities.

We really have not had a president in recent decades who has gone the extra mile and tried to be a party leader. The incentive system may seem stacked against it, but the counterintuitive strategy might just pay some surprising dividends. Thus, former cabinet member and citizens' movement leader John W. Gardner can say:

> As a mobilizer of some experience, I can't help but wonder whether a President strong enough and imaginative enough to rebuild his party aggressively might not get an interesting payoff. Someone spoke the other day of "the fashionable wave of grassroots participation," as though it would pass rather quickly. I don't see it that way. There was a wave in the 1960s, followed by a wholly different wave in the 70s — and I anticipate others to come. The feeling for grassroots participation will be, I think, a dependable part of our future. If I were a President looking for a means of moving a nation in disarray — and wondering, as every modern President must wonder, whether it is even possible — I would not neglect the possibility of turning my party into an instrument of mobilization. I know all the realities that make it an impossible dream — but I'd sure as hell try it.[21]

That is a pretty supportive statement from a respected *nonpartisan* leader — and that is the turnaround sentiment that will have to spread as precondition for taking parties seriously. Parties will doubtless endure, but in the future as in the past, they will serve us in direct proportion to our taking them seriously and our willingness to make them work.

SOURCE: An earlier version of this essay appeared in Gerald M. Pomper, ed., *Party Renewal in America* (New York: Praeger, 1980).

## Notes

1. Robert V. Remini, "The Emergence of Political Parties and Their Effect on the Presidency" in *Power and The Presidency,* ed. Philip C. Dolce and George H. Skau (New York: Scribners, 1976), p. 32.
2. Ibid., p. 33. See also Robert Remini, *Martin Van Buren and the Democratic Party* (New York: Columbia University Press, 1959).
3. Quoted in Arthur B. Tourtellot, *The Presidents on the Presidency* (New York: Doubleday, 1964), p. 387.
4. Ibid., p. 5.
5. David Broder, *The Party's Over* (New York: Harper & Row, 1971), pp. 76–77. Related evidence of presidential manipulation and failure to engage in party-building or even party-heeding activity is found in Donald Allen Robinson, "Presidents and Party Leadership: An Analysis of Relations Between Presidents, Presidential Candidates, and Their Parties' National Committee Headquarters since 1952" (Paper delivered at the Annual Meeting of the American Political Science Association, Chicago, Illinois, September 1974). The reader may also

want to consult the now dated but historically useful study of national party committees and their functions: Cornelius P. Cotter and Bernard C. Hennessy, *Politics Without Power: The National Party Committees* (New York: Atherton Press, 1964).

6. Walter F. Mondale, "The President and the Parties: In Need of Revival," *Democratic Review* (October/November 1975), p. 93. See also Walter F. Mondale, *The Accountability of Power* (New York: McKay, 1975).

7. I have discussed the paradoxes of the presidency at length in my *The State of the Presidency,* 2d ed. (Boston: Little, Brown, 1980), p. 322.

8. See James W. Ceasar, *Presidential Selection: Theory and Practice* (Princeton, N.J.: Princeton University Press, 1979).

9. A description of the rise of presidential advisory groups is provided in Thomas E. Cronin and Sanford Greenberg, eds., *The Presidential Advisory System* (New York: Harper & Row, 1969).

10. On this nationalizing trend, see Austin Ranney, *The Federalization of Presidential Primaries* (Washington, D.C.: American Enterprise Institute, 1978).

11. Arthur Schlesinger, Jr., "Crisis of the Party System, I," *Wall Street Journal* May 10, 1979, editorial page.

12. Douglass Cater, *Power In Washington* (New York: Vintage, 1964), p. 192.

13. Quoted in Dom Bonafede, "The Strained Relationship," *National Journal* (May 19, 1979), p. 830.

14. Morris P. Fiorina, "The Incumbency Factor," in *Public Opinion* (September/October 1978), p. 42. See also Morris P. Fiorina, *Congress: Keystone of the Washington Establishment* (New Haven, Conn.: Yale University Press, 1977).

15. See Gerald Ford's response to this problem in his memoir, *A Time to Heal* (New York: Harper & Row/Reader's Digest, 1979), p. 295.

16. Quoted in "How It Was for Mr. Humphrey," New York *Times,* October 13, 1974, p. E18.

17. I want to thank political scientist John Kessel for reminding me about this reality.

18. See Norman J. Ornstein, "The Democrats Reform Power in the House of Representatives, 1969–75," in *America in the Seventies,* ed. by Allan P. Sindler (Boston: Little, Brown, 1977), pp. 1–48.

19. For a more modest reform of the electoral college that blends the best of these two plans, see Thomas E. Cronin, "Choosing a President," *The Center Magazine* xi:5 (September/October 1978), and Thomas E. Cronin, "The Direct Vote and the Case for Meshing Things Up!" *Presidential Studies Quarterly* 9:2 (Spring 1979): 144–62.

20. Austin Ranney, *The Federalization of Presidential Primaries* (Washington, D.C.: American Enterprise Institute, 1978), p. 39.

21. John W. Gardner, in personal communication to author, August 1, 1979.

# Rethinking the Presidential Advisory System

# VIII

**22. Revitalizing the Executive Office of the President**

*Don K. Price and Rocco C. Siciliano*

**23. Rethinking the Vice-Presidency**

*Thomas E. Cronin*

# 22. Revitalizing the Executive Office of the President

## Don K. Price and Rocco C. Siciliano

Proposals for change in the Executive Office must recognize that the presidency is occupied by an individual with personal preferences, needs, interests, and methods of operating. Formal designs for the Executive Office which go against the grain of this fundamental reality are useless.

However, this country can no longer afford the luxury of a de novo educational process every time a new president assumes offices. Whatever a president's personality, the Executive Office must be adjusted to the needs of constitutional government in the modern era. The internal arrangement and staff resources of the Office must be able to serve a succession of presidents and to cope with continuing national problems.

What is needed is a general framework, not a detailed blueprint for the Executive Office of the President . . .

Our recommendations are founded on the ten basic principles:

1. Presidential management is primarily a matter of working with others to achieve national purposes. Presidents and the public should recognize that the president is politically accountable not for the day-to-day, detailed management of the executive branch, but rather for leading others to sensible, concerted action on the important matters facing the nation. Each president will adopt his own approach to this management task. Some will use a chief of staff; others will prefer a different arrangement. The exact structure is less important than the concept.

2. The dominant approach by the president in dealing with others should be a collaborative one. Both the Constitution and the nature of the current crisis in public management demonstrate that ours is a government of separated and shared powers. Presidents must normally strive to work in concert with others, especially the Congress.

*Don K. Price is a former Dean of the John F. Kennedy School of Government at Harvard University and author of numerous books, including* The Scientific Estate. *Rocco C. Siciliano is chairman and chief executive officer of TICOR, a Los Angeles based financial services corporation. He is a veteran of high governmental service, including service as Under Secretary of Commerce. Price and Siciliano were co-chairmen of a panel on presidential management of the National Academy of Public Administration.*

3. To exercise effective political management, presidents need a reliable base of non-partisan, unbiased advice. The institutional staffs reporting to the president should have a highly professional ability to supply objective and factual information. This need is particularly stringent for those staffs responsible for policy development, administrative management and coordination, and budgeting.

4. The number, uncertainty, and interdependence of issues necessitate a systematic means for sorting and organizing matters coming before the president and for rejecting those which should not. Again, each president will have his own approach to this need, some preferring a regular flow of decision memoranda and others opting for a less formal arrangement of consultations. Whatever the method, a president should adopt and enforce an effective system to bring the necessary range of relevant information and conflicting opinion before him in a timely manner.

5. Because presidents manage primarily through other people, presidential appointments are of immense importance. Presidential appointments, both to the Executive Office of the President and to departments and agencies, should be made with the utmost care. A far higher level of managerial ability than has been customary will be required in the 1980s. Presidents are thus well advised to make effective use of career and non-career personnel in the new Senior Executive Service.

6. The immediate staff of the president should be small. A large staff of personal assistants will reduce the president's ability to control those persons who speak directly in his name.

7. Except in extreme national emergency, broad operating responsibilities belong in the executive departments and agencies, not in the Executive Office of the President. Generally, statutory authority rests with departmental and agency officials. It is there that detailed knowledge exists, and it is there that legal accountability resides.

8. Limiting the operational responsibilities of the presidency requires a corresponding increase in the ability of the Executive Office to intervene selectively on matters of substance and to promote a central perspective. An effective Executive Office must be equipped to initiate, prod, convene, facilitate, educate, and follow-up on the processes of collaborative policymaking and administration — not as a blanket authority, but selectively and in a responsible and supportive manner.

9. The Executive Office should not mirror special interests represented elsewhere. There is often a short-term political advantage in adding units to the Executive Office which represent special interests. Unless this temptation is avoided, the presidency will be hampered in bringing a governmentwide, na-

tional perspective to problems and will tend to second-guess or duplicate the work of departments and agencies that possess operating responsibilities.

10. The Executive Office cannot promote steady courses of action on vital national issues unless it contains important elements of continuity and planning. Without these elements of continuity and planning, personnel dealing with daily issues are unlikely to benefit from the perspectives and knowledge of those with longer term frames of reference. . . .

Taken together, [these ten basic principles] produce the conception of a presidency that speaks for national interests but that does not ride roughshod over the divided and shared powers in our pluralistic society and world.

Any reforms must be sufficiently flexible to allow for an individual president's personality and interests, but not so flexible as to subordinate the central machinery of government to personal whim. The responsibility of a president for coping with immediate crises must not outweigh his responsibility for promoting orderly, ongoing processes of government management. Staff members are needed who will help to spark creative presidential policy initiatives as well as help to carry out the Constitution's injunction to "take care" that the laws passed by Congress are faithfully executed.

Guidelines for the appropriate reforms are implied by our diagnosis of the current situation. As policy and administrative problems have become more interconnected, presidents need to be better equipped to perceive and act upon the interconnections. This need implies the support of staff with broader competence than prevails today.

If power has become greatly dispersed, the presidency should have a heightened capacity to bring disparate and powerful interests together in a way that is orderly and sensitive to governmentwide and national needs. Such a capacity implies an Executive Office that is organized to facilitate collaboration with others, not one that simply tries to impose the will of the president and his staff.

If short-term political considerations inevitably (and legitimately) crowd into the Oval Office, presidents must be assured access to individuals with continuing experience in the management of government affairs. Such assurance implies the presence of people in the Executive Office who can help presidents assess longer-term policy and administrative problems and the larger implications of day-to-day presidential decisions.

Although it is necessary to present our proposals individually, the recommendations . . . should be considered as an integrated unit. This set of proposals would reconstitute the core of the Executive Office of the President into a body of staff assistance for policy development, information coordination, and management improvement. More important than any one recommendation is the interrelationship among all.

[W]e propose three staff units, each roughly comparable in function and status, to assist the president in the development of policies for international, domestic, and economic affairs. We also propose the creation of a small staff secretariat to help coordinate the information processes for presidential decision-making, and we suggest improving the capacity of the Executive Office to provide longer-range policy studies. A small number of White House aides would serve the immediate personal needs of the president in his daily work. . . .

[T]he Executive Office of the President and, within it, the White House Office have become a melange of units and staffs located there for all manner of reasons, but principally because of the higher status that comes from closer association with the presidency. This desire for status should no longer be the guiding principle in the development of the Executive Office.

Instead, the Executive Office of the President should be reduced to encompass only those functions that are vital to the president in the performance of his government-wide duties. To that end, we believe that if our recommendations for strengthening the core of the presidency were implemented, it would become easier to analyze, one by one, other Executive Office units and to transfer many out of the Executive Office.

We are not proposing the creation of a closed bureaucratic elite in the presidency. Each staff unit would be headed by a senior White House assistant appointed solely at the discretion of the current president. Below this top level should be a combination of non-career appointees and civil servants, including the federal government's new Senior Executive Service. It would be a mistake to equate political appointees with "policy" and career public servants with "administration." Career civil servants can and do function effectively in highly sensitive policy roles. Likewise, formal political appointees often have a technical competence that transcends their political-party credentials. Our proposals would integrate both types of personnel into the service of the presidency.

The personnel performing in this Executive Office system, although they may have specialized backgrounds, must have advanced to the point that they have the government-wide objectivity to comprehend, analyze, and coordinate information flowing to the White House. Like presidents, they must be professional generalists.

We propose a new structure that would reverse the trend toward self-assertive, narrowly focused, haphazard assistance to presidents. Staffs should play a facilitating role, helping the president to work out major policies and administrative problems with the leaders in Congress and in the executive departments and agencies.

This presidential staff work cannot be a mechanical process. Those who do it must have a passion not simply for anonymity, but also for making the machinery of government work. Rather than handing down presidential decisions or fulfilling some personal policy agenda, their mission is to help the president frame and implement his national agenda in conjunction with the many other participants in our complex government system.

To play this facilitating (or "honest broker") role, staffs must be regarded both as loyal to the president and as fair and evenhanded by the major parties involved. While remaining mindful of the president's interests, they must search for compromise wherever possible. Where issues must be brought to the president for resolution, the presidential staff must ensure that all positions are fairly presented, that the president is fully informed about all relevant facets of the problem, and that any staff recommendations have been subjected to vigorous scrutiny by the interested parties.

In other words, the system of presidential staff work we propose would help to organize, scrutinize, and augment the information necessary for effective presidential leadership. Our design for the Executive Office would multiply the eyes, ears, and hands of the president as a constitutional chief executive.

## Size and Functions of White House Staff

### Recommendation 1
*The trend toward enlargement of the immediate White House staff should be reversed. Rigorous efforts should be made to keep this staff small. It should be structured to serve the immediate functional and personal needs of the president, not to reflect various special interests.*

The optimum size of a staff cannot be determined by formulas and quotas. Therefore, the dictum that Executive Office staffs be kept as small as possible is one that should be applied on a case-by-case basis. The Office of Management and Budget, for example, presently has a complement of approximately 600 people for overseeing the budget and administrative work of the entire executive branch. . . . [T]his is not sufficient to its responsibilities.

However, the pressure to keep Executive Office staffs small should be applied with special vigor to the White House. Major personnel increases in this staff can be forgone if the other, more institutional units of the Executive Office are adequately manned to do their jobs. The size of the White House staff should be limited for two reasons. First, it is here that the temptation to speak on behalf of the president and to "second guess" the line agencies is especially strong; the larger the staff, the wider the circle of persons who may yield to this temptation, and the greater the chances of building an image, if not the reality, of White House aggrandizement. Nothing more quickly destroys confidence in the "honest broker" function. Second, a vital function of elements of the White House staff is, under guidelines from the president, to filter information and preclude irrelevant material from reaching his desk. The larger the size of these staffs, the more likely they are to duplicate the expertise of executive agencies, to develop their own biases, intervene where they should not, and in short to create unnecessary work.

The desire for a trim White House staff is not intended to constrain, but rather to enhance, the president's ability to function effectively. An examination of any typical day in the White House would reveal the importance to the president of those who serve him in such vital functions as appointments, media relations, congressional relations, speech-writing, executive recruitment, and others. These staff members should have a high order of political intelligence, functioning as presidential troubleshooters and coordinators, not only in their own particular fields of interest but also to ensure that the other units of the Executive Office are working smoothly and well. It is to such vital presidential needs that the White House staff should be oriented, not to a proliferation of offices and assistants representing specialized interests in our society.

## Economic Affairs Staff

*Recommendation 2*
*An Economic Affairs Staff should be created within the Executive Office of the President, to be headed by a Director with the status of Senior Assistant to the President.*

The complexity of economic issues and their significance in both the domestic and international spheres argue for the creation of a separate Economic Affairs Staff. The current division of the policy and program coordination function in the Executive Office between "domestic" and "national security" staffs has become increasingly unwieldy. Individuals with recent experience in these areas have told us that their most significant problems occurred in attempting to integrate the economic aspects of domestic and foreign affairs.

Virtually every domestic activity of the government has important effects on the economy, either directly or indirectly. And we have come into an age when problems, trends, and events abroad have profound effects on domestic programs and the economy. In turn, the state of the economy obviously has a vital effect on foreign as well as domestic affairs. The need to integrate these domestic/foreign/economic policy considerations might suggest the desirability of a single policy coordination staff encompassing all three, rather than the tripartite structure we propose. However, we think the latter is advisable to allow for a better division of labor and to preserve distinctions which, although broad and general, are nevertheless useful in a government as enormous and complex as ours. The domestic/foreign/economic areas each comprehends a large community of executive agencies; each has a distinctive focus that should be maintained. Moreover, it would be more effective to allow the competing demands and tensions to surface among these three areas than to take the risk of submerging them.

Our recommendation for an Economic Affairs Staff is not intended to diminish the status of the Council of Economic Advisers or to duplicate the work of its staff. Rather, our recommendation preserves the status and role of the council and prevents it from being drawn increasingly into additional considerations, including microeconomic and sectoral issues and the specific economic implications of agency policies and programs.

The Council of Economic Advisers' economic reports represent one of the four principal economic instruments of the government, the others being the role of the Treasury in tax policy, of the Federal Reserve Board in monetary policy, and of the Office of Management and Budget in fiscal policy. We are not satisfied that the ebb and flow of relationships among the economic policy streams is being monitored adequately by anyone at the present, not for purposes of control but for information, coordination, and clarity. This is a staff function, an important potential one for the Economic Affairs Staff.

## Domestic Affairs Staff

*Recommendation 3*
*The Domestic Policy Staff should be reconstituted as the Domestic Affairs Staff, to be headed by a Director with the status of Senior Assistant to the President.*

The Domestic Council was created during the Nixon administration in an effort to improve the ability of the Executive Office to coordinate the vastly burgeoning federal activities primarily concerned with domestic policy. It was reconstituted by the Carter Administration as the Domestic Policy Staff.

The creation of a White House unit concerned with domestic policy caused apprehension within the Office of Management and Budget because it impinged on some of the traditional responsibilities of that agency. Many line agencies also viewed the unit with misgiving, regarding it as another bureaucratic layer impeding access to presidential decision-making and at times functioning in a high-handed manner.

Although these problems appear to have eased over the years, the present situation remains less than satisfactory. One reason is the steady growth in the size of the staff, which now numbers approximately 60 persons. This creates a tendency for staff members to become specialized and for the "honest broker" function to break down.

We believe that the creation of an Economic Affairs Staff would ease the workload of the Domestic Affairs Staff and improve the division of labor, in addition to providing a valuable focus on the economic aspects of domestic and foreign concerns.

As emphasized earlier, the Domestic Affairs Staff, like the president's other policy coordinating groups, should be staffed to include professional generalists drawn from the Senior Executive Service and elsewhere. Among such persons one could expect to find greater resistance to pressures to specialize as well as temperaments better suited to the facilitative role. Moreover, such staff members would be more likely to survive changes in administration, and this likelihood would help to serve the goals of continuity and consistency.

## International Affairs Staff

*Recommendation 4*
*The staff of the National Security Council should be replaced by an International Affairs Staff, headed by a Director with the status of Senior Assistant to*

*the President. The statutory National Security Council should remain as an interagency committee to be used as the president needs.*

The National Security Council is an interagency committee consisting of the president, vice-president, secretary of state, and secretary of defense, with the director of Central Intelligence and the Chairman of the Joint Chiefs of Staff as statutory advisers. Since its inception, it has been a valuable presidential resource in the area of foreign affairs. However, the special status built up over the years by the National Security Council staff has not been conducive to the integration of domestic and foreign policies.

The council's staff has tended to function recently as an agency unto itself, a power base for personal prominence, complete with public information officers. Yet at times in the past, the council's staff has functioned as a model staff, operating circumspectly, anonymously, and with careful attention to the distinction between objective process and advocacy. This latter method of operating is obviously much to be preferred in the best interests of presidents and of the society at large. One reason we now recommend the creation of an International Affairs Staff is to promote and reinforce this preferred style of operating in the international sphere.

Another reason for recommending the creation of the International Affairs Staff is that we believe the time has come to provide a mandate and perspective broader than the concept of "national security." The National Security Council's staff has traditionally focused on two areas of expertise — political and military affairs. These are clearly of primary importance and should remain paramount considerations of the International Affairs Staff. But we think it would be productive to place them within a larger frame of reference. Just as our society has become increasingly fragmented, so has the world. American influence has diminished, and we must now be partners as much as leaders and adversaries in world affairs. Economic, social, and cultural matters are assuming new importance on the international scene and must now be given attention equal to their importance.

## Policy Research and Analysis

*Recommendation 5*
*The Executive Office of the President needs institutionalized arrangements for longer-term policy research and analysis. One approach would be to establish a new office headed by a Director who reports to the president. Another would be to develop a more fluid system of long-term working assignments among the core staff of the Executive Office. In any case, this function should operate on a continuing basis within the presidency.*

Various recommendations have been made over the years for some type of planning agency within the Executive Office. Several attempts have been made to implement this idea, but none has survived. One reason, we believe, is that most of these proposals have been accompanied by grandiose expectations, which in turn have given rise to exaggerated fears and misunderstandings regarding what "government planning" is and can accomplish.

Partly for this reason, we eschew "planning" in favor of "policy research and analysis" in describing this function. Expectations should be kept within reasonable bounds, and it should be recognized that the products of future-oriented studies would not be "plans" in any rigid sense. They would instead be concerned with trends, developments, and alternatives that might have profound implications for U.S. policy.

We believe such an understanding of the role would dispel another major barrier to the establishment of this function — the fear of presidents and their close advisers that a "planning agency" would embarrass the president by setting goals for him, controlling his agenda, and thus involving him in matters he would wish to avoid. We clearly intend this function to have no such effects. The products would constitute only one link in a chain of contributions to the process of policy formulation, coordination, and integration.

This link is missing at present, for all practical purposes. Given the complexities of the modern world that we have discussed thus far in this report, and the relative diminution of U.S. influence and margin for error, the time has come when a staff must be available to the president that can look beyond the short term in a systematic and ongoing way.

We see no inherent reason for future-oriented studies to be restricted to a single time horizon; in fact, we believe it would be advantageous if time frames were varied. However, as noted, one purpose of this staff would be to perform ongoing studies of longer-range trends, 10 to 25 years out, in key areas.

In this regard, the recently concluded "Global 2000" study has some important lessons. This cooperative effort, involving some 15 executive agencies, was a herculean task because of the disparate nature of the forecasting, planning, and modeling capabilities of the agencies, disparities that made comparability and correlation extremely difficult. The study revealed a compelling need for a high-status function to give long-range studies a permanent mandate and framework, to set standards and requirements, and to coordinate results.

This implies what we in fact believe: that this function need not be performed by some massive agency that does all of the work itself. The participating agencies (and outside resources) should do most of the research and data processing. The role of Executive Office staff should be to stimulate, standardize, correlate, and coordinate.

The other major longer-term work of the Executive Office staff would consist of special research assignments from the president or the three policy coordinating staffs, with time horizons of 2 to 10 years. In many cases, these studies would concern analyses of the possible consequences of alternative policies and courses of action.

We also believe that, whatever the structure of this policy research activity, its staff should have the discretion to select and undertake studies on its own initiative, within guidelines established by the president. Such discretion would stimulate intellectual ferment, as well as provide a measure of independence.

The staff must also have the authority to use grants and contracts to foster outside research. This ability would help to limit the number of staff members (it is important for this staff to be no larger than any of the three policy coordination staffs we have recommended). The staff should also have a particularly close working relationship with the President's Office of Science and Technology Policy. We believe that the existence of this function in the Executive Office would help to reduce the number of ad hoc presidential commissions required in the future. Many assignments could instead be done by temporary working groups. In those cases where special commissions were needed, Executive Office staff could help to systematize their work by providing a common administrative base and technical assistance.

## White House Secretariat

### Recommendation 6

*A White House Secretariat, headed by a Senior Assistant to the President with a small staff of generalists, should be established to help ensure that materials come to the president's desk in an organized manner best-suited to his methods of operating and his needs for review and action. The secretariat would not engage in substantive decision-making, but would be entirely process-oriented. It would develop procedures for summarizing and presenting materials and ensuring that relevant parties are consulted.*

The volume and complexity of materials that now flow into the Oval Office argue persuasively for a more regularized system for organizing and presenting those materials. . . .

The function of the secretariat would be adminstrative in nature and neutral with regard to particular policies. The secretariat should *not* be another layer in substantive decision-making. Instead, the secretariat staff should be process-oriented.

We do not mean to suggest that the secretariat would constitute a paper-processing mill that could be ignored with impunity by those intent on pressing their substantive view on the president. This is one reason we stress that the secretariat should be headed by a senior assistant to the president. The overriding concern of the secretariat should be to protect the integrity of central decision-making process, making sure that incoming work consistently meets the president's standards of quality, that executive summaries are well and objectively done, that all relevant bases are touched. The secretariat chief's abilities should be such that he or she could serve as a trusted adviser to the president on matters of process, evaluating the adequacy and reliability of existing sources of information and helping to find new sources. If the secretariat's function, on both formal and informal dimensions, were performed with consummate professionalism, it would quickly come to be seen as a help by those wishing to reach the president on substantive issues. . . .

The head of the secretariat should be helped . . . by a small staff — perhaps not more than 15. This number should be rigorously maintained, if for no other reason than that, at this staffing level, the work load itself should reduce the temptation of secretariat staff to duplicate or second-guess the substantive work of others.

We stress that the secretariat should follow a general "rule of reason" approach in its work. The essence of this work would be judgmental, not mechanical. Only a staff of the highest caliber could effectively judge whether a particular matter was exposed to the right people and to a broad range of views, and balance the need for consultation against the need for urgent action. Only a staff with the utmost discretion could be counted on to maintain the confidentiality of their information and the fairness of their actions. The secretariat must not be a place for bureaucratic clerks, political opportunists, or policy advocates. Its staff members must be impartial, except in their commitment to an effective presidency. It must be self-effacing, except in defending the integrity of its processes. It must be bureaucratically adept but politically sensitive, lest its process rigidify into a paper-shuffling operation that loses sight of its larger purpose in serving the president's needs. . . .

In the final analysis, the enforcement of proper discipline to protect the integrity of the secretariat process would be the responsibility only of the president. Agency heads who abused the privilege of direct access and used it to short-circuit the secretariat could be called to account by no one other than the president.

In our recommendations we have proposed four Senior Assistants to the president: three to head the policy coordinating staffs and one to head the secretariat. We have also optionally proposed a director for long-range policy studies. These assistants, plus the director of the Office of Management and Budget, would be responsible for what we have called the core processes of policy coordination, policy advice, information flow, and management. These senior aides would constitute an informal "management committee" for the Executive Office as a whole, meeting as frequently as necessary to ensure that communcations and the division of labor are working effectively on behalf of the president. A chief of staff, if one were chosen by the president, would be the natural chairman of this committee. . . .

If the Executive Office staffs we have proposed were to fail in functioning as facilitators — if they were to act more as assistant presidents than as assistants to the president — pressures by department heads for direct access to the president would mount, thereby increasing the burdens on the president and defeating the entire coordination process. Failure to perform the Executive Office staff role properly would inevitably intensify congressional demands to levy statutory requirements on the Executive Office and to bring unduly powerful presidential aides to account before the legislature. Our hope is that an implicit trade-off might be achieved in our unwritten constitution. In return for a more collaborative approach by the president, the Congress might be persuaded to refrain from encumbering the Executive Office with additional statutory requirements unless such were sought by the president, thus allowing him the maximum degree of freedom in organizing his staff and institutional resources. . . .

## A Strengthened Office of Management and Budget

. . . A presidential agency for management improvement already exists: the Office of Management and Budget. What is needed is to strengthen this office to deal with the pressing problems of public management in the 1980s. . . .

Created in 1921, the Bureau of the Budget became a major resource to presidents for central management capabilities, particularly after it was transferred to the Executive Office in 1939, at a time when the scale and complexity of government were rapidly accelerating. Although little known outside of Washington, the bureau became of enormous importance as the agency responsible for preparing the president's annual budget, for clearing his legislative program, for acquiring administrative information, for proposing reorganizations, and for undertaking special managerial assignments.

As a result of these functions, staff members of the bureau came into intimate contact with the administrative realities of every agency of government. The neutrality and competence that were hallmarks of the agency made it the trusted and reliable center of information networks that extended throughout the executive branch and into state and local governments. It became an invaluable source of intelligence, advice, and assistance for presidents, White House assistants, legislative leaders, and state and international agencies. The bureau not only compiled dependable information on people, programs, and problems, it also generated useful solutions.

The Bureau of the Budget thus came to have a double value — for the specific functions it performed and for the informational and problem-solving capability it represented. In these ways, the agency for decades has been a reliable, professional resource for presidents and their aides in maintaining a hold on the sprawling executive branch. . . . .

In 1970, the bureau was reorganized and renamed the Office of Management and Budget. The budget remains its most potent tool, one that has been the backbone of its effectiveness. The budget is by any definition a tool of management, as are the coordination of the president's legislative program and all other functions of the Office of Management and Budget. However, at almost the same time that the agency was reorganized, both its budget and management sides were being weakened.

After the reorganization, the administrative management functions were pared to a skeletal staff. Moreover, as pressures to cut the budget intensified, the agency's normal preoccupation with the budget became ever more dominating. A measure of political layering occurred and the agency became more political in its outlook, losing some of its anonymity and becoming more visible and subject to special-interest pressures. The Office of Management and Budget's congressional relations during this period became increasingly strained.

Serious efforts have been made in recent years to overcome some of these problems, but several key OMB functions remain weakened. Clearly, the Office of Management and Budget is not an end in itself. The end to be achieved is the need for improvement of the key managerial functions and processes that presidents and their associates must rely on for information and for effective program implementation and coordination. . . .

## Strengthening the Budget Process

### Recommendation 7
*Strengthening the president's management capability requires an improved and expanded budget process. Steps should be taken to: (1) improve it as the vehicle for integrating presidential and congressional decisions about government income and the allocation of resources, (2) enhance its potential as an instrument for improving managerial discipline and the execution of federal programs, and (3) improve its accuracy as a measure of the effectiveness of governmentwide activity and expenditure.*

[T]he increasing size and complexity of government during the past several decades have contributed to a radical change in the character of most federal activity and expenditures, a fact still not fully realized by even the informed public. Although the effects of these trends in any given year may not be particularly noticeable or startling, their cumulative impact over a generation is definitely so. One of the most profound effects has been the progressive weakening of the annual budget process as a framework for decision-making, managerial discipline, and information.

Today, three-fourths of expenditures are "controllable" only over the long term and only by legislation. Most budget dollars are not expended in the purchase of goods or the delivery of services by the federal government itself. Rather, most of the federal budget comprises transfers to individuals (e.g., social security checks), payments to private contractors, grants to states and cities, and a host of other financial arrangements with the private sector and subnational governments.

At the same time, Washington has resorted extensively to federal commitments and actions not reflected in the budget, such as special tax provisions, loan guarantees, regulatory provisions, and various other techniques. Frequently, these are designed specifically to escape the discipline of the budget process or a budget ceiling imposed by the president or the Congress.

It would be a mistake to make the general judgment that all of these trends are inherently bad. Considering all of the decisions made over many years that resulted in mandated expenditures or "off-budget" programs, it probably would be difficult to find many that did not seem reasonable and persuasive. They seemed so to their proponents who, at various times and in varying combinations, have included presidents, executive agencies, congressional committees, and major interest groups. Many of those decisions represented ingenious solutions to problems which the normal budget process could not resolve. Nevertheless, the cumulative result of these decisions is undesirable, as are the degree to which these trends have come to dominate the process and the inability of the tools and resources of the Executive Office to cope with this changed situation. There has not been a sufficient countervailing force to protect the integrity of the budget process and to wage a consistent rearguard action against the trends we have noted.

A major effort should now be made to resist these trends and to begin to reverse them. Not all mandated requirements are of equal value. Not all indirect expenditures are of equal value. We recognize that an extremely difficult, long, and painstaking process would be required to incorporate the extra-budgetary expenditures into the budget process. It would require an unusual degree of mutual understanding and collaboration between the executive branch and the Congress, with leadership coming from key elements of both branches. Given such a concerted effort, the discipline of the budget process could be restored to a greater part of federal government activities.

The new congressional budget process is built around the two budget committees and the Congressional Budget Office. Far from being a threat to the presidency, this process could be influential in bringing under control the specialized interests that now undermine the discipline of the budget system.

Simultaneously, a major effort should be made to simplify the actual work involved in compiling the budget in the Executive Office of the President. Over the years, the accretion of paperwork and the detailed requirements for data, many of them levied by Congress, have made budget preparation a nightmarish process. Budget examiners are rarely able to make field visits as they once did, and as a result know less about the grass-roots operations of their assigned agencies. This lack of firsthand knowledge has introduced a certain air of unreality into the budget process and has contributed to the decrease in OMB's effectiveness. Many of the detailed requirements that have helped produce these conditions are unnecessary and could be eliminated. A concerted effort to simplify the process, undertaken by the Office of Management and Budget and Congressional Budget Office with the support of the appropriate congressional committees, could yield very positive results. . . .

## Strengthening Administrative Management

### Recommendation 8
*Appropriate measures should be taken to strengthen the Office of Management and Budget's capabilities to improve administrative management on a government-wide basis.*

The crucial importance of effective administrative management is unfortunately not widely recognized. It is largely seen as routine in contrast to the high visibility and importance of presidential decision-making. Yet the development and coordination of important government policies and programs will be undercut without consistently competent follow-through in the setting of standards, the provision of assistance, and the evaluation of results. Without such effective implementation, the creation of new government policies and programs may be futile exercises.

The mission of the Office of Management and Budget's administrative management staff should be to use its prestige and that of the president to improve organization and management throughout the federal government. Its functions should include the improvement of management and administration, information, personnel policy, productivity, program evaluation, and organization. The OMB is the only Executive Office agency in a position to perform these tasks. From its activities, OMB could derive a rich source of experience and information useful to other agencies, its own internal divisions, and to the president and his advisers. Properly conceived and given proper leadership, these functions would benefit and should be welcomed by the executive agencies.

Yet, as we have noted, the Office of Management and Budget is unable to meet the government's growing need for administrative management services. A virtual explosion of legislation now defines and regulates administrative authority, organization, processes, and procedures, as well as objectives and policies, often in inconsistent and contradictory ways. Programs have been launched without adequate planning as to how they would be administered, without using expert assistance in organizing them, and without prompt revisions based on experience. Policy developers frequently overlook the requisites of administration and often appear to assume that policies are self-implementing. Inadequate follow-through and implementation contribute to the stream of problems that eventually find their way to the president.

A major drive must in consequence be mounted to help improve manegement performance throughout the government, to protect the president from unnecessary problems, to help restore public and congressional confidence in government administration, and to make possible the proper devolution of decision-making and operational responsibilities to the line agencies. Such a revitalization of management capabilities would require a determined effort by OMB with the full support of the president, his close advisers, and the Congress. Administrative management functions should be given the proper organizational framework and status within OMB. An enlarged staff might be required; if so, emphasis should be given to recruiting the most seasoned and competent management experts that can be found.

## Strengthening Program Evaluation

*Recommendation 9*
*The Office of Management and Budget must be strengthened in its ability to improve program evaluation. A Program Evaluation Staff should therefore be*

*created within the agency to set standards, provide assistance, monitor progress reporting and productivity improvement, and evaluate effectiveness in accomplishing objectives.*

The previous recommendation included productivity improvement and program evaluation as two of the many functions that logically come under the general heading of administrative management within OMB. Regardless of the precise organizational arrangement, we believe these functions should be singled out for special attention and a new mandate.

In any rational management system, program evaluation is a vital function which provides essential "feedback" information for managerial, policy-making, legislative, and accountability purposes. Without reliable evaluation, it is impossible to know if a program is being administered effectively, if it is attaining its specified purposes, if its funds are being properly spent, and if its benefits are worth its costs.

We are well aware that program evaluation is a difficult task. It is more an art than a science, and no method or system is universally applicable. Yet advances are being made. The General Accounting Office has become competent in some aspects of evaluation, and most agencies have evaluation staffs and are making genuine efforts to advance their skill.

What is missing is a central focus for a sustained drive to improve executive branch program evaluation. This is a prime responsibility of every agency, but the agencies need help. Without objective standards, an agency's evaluation of its own programs is, fairly or unfairly, often regarded by congressional committees and others as self-serving.

In addition to assisting individual agencies, a central evaluation capability should monitor related interagency, intergovernmental, and intersectoral programs, and assess the effects of one agency's program on the program of another.

To fulfill these and other needs, a central program evaluation service of major dimensions would be needed. The Office of Management and Budget would be the obvious location of such a service. The Office of Management and Budget should establish a Program Evaluation Staff with a mandate to set standards, provide assistance, work for comparability in evaluation methods throughout the government, encourage productivity improvements, and monitor results. Properly supported and led, this group should become a clearinghouse for the state of the art within the executive branch, working in cooperation not only with the agencies but also with the General Accounting Office, congressional groups, and private-sector resources.

## Administering Intergovernmental Assistance

### Recommendation 10
*The federal government should make a firm commitment to a thorough and consistent effort to simplify, rationalize, and improve the many programs of*

*federal assistance to states and local governments. The focal point of this effort should be a new Federal Assistance Administration Staff created within OMB.*

One of the most difficult managerial problems confronting the federal government is the need to overhaul the system of federal assistance to states and local communities. This system has become overwhelmingly complicated.

Categorical grant programs to state and local governments now number over 500. More than 50 federal agencies are involved in administering assistance programs to states and local communities. There are now 59 "cross-cutting" requirements which apply national goals and values to the assistance programs of two or more agencies.

In addition to the problems generated by the sheer size of the system, a "crisis of confidence and competence" permeates federal assistance, according to a recent study by the Advisory Commission on Intergovernmental Relations. The study pointed to poor peformance and inadequate results, excessive cost and waste, and lack of adequate control and responsiveness.

A determination to improve the system has often been voiced by political leaders, but to no avail. In truth, it is hard to imagine a more difficult task. The federal assistance structure has become the new form of political patronage, and as a result there can be no hope for significant improvement in the absence of a firm commitment from the president and the Congress.

The difficult and long-term nature of the task is apparent when one realizes that change in the most critical areas would require legislative action. A serious beginning would require a focus and pressure point — a dedicated staff with sufficient authority and resources, and with the requisite leadership and functional abilities.

The Office of Management and Budget has had an intergovernmental affairs staff for some time, but this staff is at a relatively low level in the organizational hierarchy and lacks the necessary mandate and resources. The Federal Assistance Administration Staff that we propose would represent a new beginning. It would elevate the status of the present unit and expand its staff. It would work cooperatively with federal agencies, recipients, and other involved parties in an ongoing program to simplify the assistance system. It should institute more structured management processes, help to resolve conflicts and problems, and propose needed legislative change.

## Improving Regulatory Decision-Making

### Recommendation 11
*Systematic procedures should be established in the Office of Management and Budget to enable the president and his advisers to review publicly major proposals for new regulatory rules that they may (1) consider the proposed rule in relationship to other policy development activities, and (2) provide administration views to the rule-making agency.*

A drastic increase in regulatory activity has occurred in recent years in such areas as health, safety, and the environment. Moreover, congressional enactments often leave substantial discretion to the implementing agency, to the extent that some crucial issues are resolved not in the development of the legislation, but instead in the preparation of the implementing regulations.

We are aware that substantial controversy exists over whether presidents have the authority to overrule the decisions of regulatory bodies or to participate in regulatory decision-making outside of the public comment process. These are matters of deep constitutional concern that are now before the courts and about which it would be inappropriate for us to comment.

As a practical matter, a president is not in control of the independent regulatory agencies, even though he may popularly be held accountable for their actions. His main power is twofold: (1) he makes the initial nomination of a regulatory commissioner, and (2) he is able to inform the public of his views on general regulatory problems and, where appropriate, to seek corrective legislation. Presidents are well advised to limit themselves to this public comment role, for any behind-the-scenes attempt to intervene on a specific issue before a regulatory agency is understandably seen as an attempt to exert inappropriate presidential control.

The fact is, however, that presidents are at present poorly equipped to offer a coherent public response or to play a broad educational role in the regulatory process. Historically, the Executive Office and agency heads have not commented in a systematic manner on the development and issuance of government regulation. However, we believe that the increased scope and changing character of regulatory activities now require this pattern to change, and that a systematic mechanism must be established to respond to major regulatory proposals involving important policy issues. The president, as the principal integrating force in our system of government, must play an important role in this regard. . . .

To remedy this, we recommend the establishment of a systematic process, modeled on the legislative clearance process conducted by the Office of Management and Budget for many years, to assist in the formulation of administration views on major regulations involving significant policy issues. This process would be coordinated by a special staff within the Office of Management and Budget and would allow the Executive Office and interested agencies to review major proposed regulatory rules. The administration would thus be able to prepare coordinated and informed comments on the proposed rule's effect on other regulatory goals and other government policies. Although OMB would coordinate the preparation of administration views, the affected agencies would have responsibility for analyzing the proposal and preparing the comments.

It is not our intention to suggest that the Executive Office should review all proposed regulations, or that presidents should assume the rule-making authorities now vested in the agencies. Nor is it our intent to short-circuit the procedural safeguards built into the regulatory process or to encourage the injection of unwarranted considerations into regulatory decision-making. The objective of this recommendation is simply to provide a systematic, manageable structure through which presidential efforts can be made to relate regulatory decision-making to other policies. . . .

We believe there are important dividends to be gained from placing all these functions within the Office of Management and Budget, rather than creating additional independent staffs reporting to the president. The five functions we have discussed have much in common with others currently existing in OMB. All would require a high degree of managerial skill and sustained effort, and for these and other reasons could be mutually reinforcing if housed within the same agency. . . .

In such a restructuring of the Office of Management and Budget, the question of balance should be carefully considered so that the budget process does not dominate the other functions. The variety of functions within OMB and the high level at which many of them must be performed suggest a more horizontal type of structure than the present one. Major functions should be structured to have an independent identity, yet they must be related to one another so that mutual reinforcement and interchange occur. With regard to this point, it is important to note that the value of OMB as an information source does not derive from any one function, but from them all — indeed, from the interactions among them. . . .

SOURCE: Taken from Don K. Price and Rocco C. Siciliano, *A Presidency for the 1980s,* a panel report of the National Academy of Public Administration, copyright 1980; with permission. The complete report is available for $5 from the National Academy of Public Administration, 1225 Connecticut Avenue, N.W., Washington, D.C. 20036.

# 23. Rethinking the Vice-Presidency

## Thomas E. Cronin

The vice-presidency is now very much a part of the executive branch and the presidential establishment. This has not long been the case. Nor has it been a neat linear advance. During our first 150 years vice-presidents served primarily, and usually only, as president and presiding officer in the U.S. Senate. In most administrations a vice-president was at best a kind of fifth wheel and at worst a political rival who sometimes connived against the president.

Until recently Americans were more inclined to joke about the office than think about it. However, for a variety of sensible reasons, presidents have begun to take the vice-presidency more seriously and its responsibilities, while still mainly ad hoc, have expanded.

Still, the vice-presidency remains a somewhat ambiguous and paradoxical office. To the founding fathers it was pretty much an afterthought. To some scholars it is one of our most conspicuous constitutional mistakes. To some modern day presidents it still appears to be more of a headache or a threat than an asset. To vice-presidents it is often a confusing and unhappy experience. "A damned peculiar situation to be in," said Spiro T. Agnew, "to have . . . a title and responsibility with no real power to do anything." Lyndon B. Johnson said that much of the unhappiness in the office stems from knowing you are on "a perpetual death watch." "The buck doesn't stop here," said George Bush.

Paradoxes abound. A vice-president's chief importance still consists of the fact he may cease to be vice-president. We yearn for someone to fill the post who has the competence to be president yet it is a kind of an "off-the-job" training and waiting post. Perhaps the prime paradox is how we select vice-presidents. We select our presidential nominees by a process of exposure and deliberation that is long and grueling. But we continue to leave the designation of the vice-presidential running mate almost entirely to the personal judgment of the presidential nominee — a judgment that more often than not is made hastily in a few hours when the presidential nominee is overextended and exhausted.

Another paradox is that technically a vice-president is neither a part of the executive branch nor subject to the direction of the president. In practice, however, our most effective vice-presidents have taken an office in the White House and serve primarily as presidential advisers.

The main purpose of the job is to have a standby competent leader available

*Thomas E. Cronin teaches political science at Colorado College and is the author or coauthor of several books, including* The State of the Presidency, Government by the People, *and* U.S. v. Crime in the Streets.

if accident befalls the president. Frequently, however, the main criterion used in selecting a vice-presidential nominee is who might balance the ticket and help win crucial electoral college votes. These two needs, *competence* and *electoral utility,* need not be incompatible but they often are. The question also arises: How can we get vice-presidents of presidential quality if once in office they may have little to do and doubtless will be maligned before we really need them, if we need them? Some presidents only share "hatchet-man" responsibilities with their vice-presidents. Some do not share much at all, for fear of being upstaged and outshone. Others have understandably refused to delegate responsibilities because of sharp policy differences. One student of the office concludes that there really can be no deputy or alternate president, because of the "indivisibility of presidential leadership and the lack of place for tandem governance for two." [1]

Originally the person who received the second highest vote in the presidential election became vice-president. This was changed, after a bitter dispute over the election in 1800, when Aaron Burr and Thomas Jefferson both received equal votes. With the Twelfth Amendment to the Constitution (1804) the president and vice-president are elected on separate ballots. However, in recent times, more and more presidents pretty much dictate the choice of their running mates and their successors. Thus Roosevelt, Kennedy, and Nixon have picked their own successors, a notion assuredly the founding politicians did not intend. Some people believe this practice of leaving this vital choice of future national leadership to the discretion of a single individual — the presidential candidate or the president — is unacceptable in a nation that professes to be democratic.

Considerable support exists for devising better ways to pick vice-presidential nominees. The search for a better way to select and use vice-presidents is made more urgent by the fact that eight presidents have died in office — four by assassination — four by natural death, and one president (Nixon) has resigned. One-third of our presidents were once vice-presidents, including four of our last eight presidents.

The vice-presidency has been significantly affected by two post-World War II constitutional amendments. The Twenty-second imposes a two-term limit for the presidency and means vice-presidents have a somewhat better chance of moving up to the presidency. The Twenty-fifth, ratified in 1967, confirms prior practice that on the death or resignation of a president, the vice-president becomes not acting president but president. Of perhaps greater significance, this amendment provides a procedure, albeit somewhat ambiguous, to determine whether an incumbent president is unable to discharge the powers and duties of his office. Thus the amendment allows an incapacitated president to lay aside temporarily the powers and duties of the office without forfeiting them permanently — a procedure whose constitutionality had previously been in doubt. Further, the amendment creates a mechanism through which a vice-president together with a majority of the cabinet may declare the president incapacitated and thus serve as acting president until the president recovers. This procedure answers several problems but also, as shall be discussed, raises new questions.

The Twenty-fifth amendment also established procedures to fill a vacancy in the vice-presidency (a procedure used when Nixon selected Ford and Ford selected Rockefeller). In the event of a vacancy in the office of the vice-president, the president nominates a vice-president who takes office upon confirmation by a majority vote of both houses of Congress. This procedure will usually ensure the appointment of a vice-president in whom the president has confidence. If the vice-president, under these circumstances, has to take over the presidency, he or she can usually be expected to reflect most of the policies of the person the people had originally elected.

The notably positive Mondale-Carter experience (1977–1981) prompts reexamination of the vice-presidency. The way Mondale was selected and used has enhanced the position.

This essay looks first at the traditional problems of the office. Then it considers the Mondale model. Finally it treats questions of vice-presidential selection and succession.


## Traditional Problems

The office is often condemned as a superfluous nonjob. The position itself, and any serious duties or prerogatives given vice-presidents, come only at the pleasure of the president. "I am not in a leadership position," said Vice-President Nelson Rockefeller. "The President has the responsibility and the power. . . . The Vice-President has no responsibility and no power." [2]

No office has been so disdained and lampooned. Our first vice-president, John Adams, wrote to his wife in 1793 that: "My country has in its wisdom contrived for me the most insignificant office that ever the invention of man contrived or his imagination conceived." Daniel Webster remarked in 1848 when he turned down the vice-presidential nomination: "I do not propose to be buried until I am dead." John Nance Garner, FDR's first vice-president, said the job "isn't worth a pitcher of warm spit" (and many people believe that was a sanitized version of what he really meant). Gerald Ford could not get himself to accept Ronald Reagan's 1980 offer of running mate because he knew from experience that the job just did not amount to much.

Five hundred and thirty-seven elected officials are sent to Washington by American voters. Five hundred and thirty-six have a reasonably clear idea of their role and functions. The vice-president, however, is never exactly sure of whether or not the functions of that office will change from week to week. Over time, however, the jobs of the vice-president have grown. On paper, they even look somewhat impressive:

1. President of the U.S. Senate
2. Member of the National Security Council
3. Chair of several national advisory councils

4. Diplomatic representative of president and U.S. abroad
5. Senior presidential adviser
6. Liaison with Congress
7. Crisis coordinator
8. Overseer of temporary coordinating councils
9. Presider over cabinet meetings in absence of the president
10. Deputy leader of the party
11. Apprentice available to take over the job of the presidents, either on an acting or full-time basis
12. Future presidential candidate

Vice-presidents have done all of these things. Some vice-presidents have served their president and their nation well. In general, however, the obstacles — political, psychological and structural — that stand in the way of constructive use of vice-presidents are considerable. As I shall discuss later, Mondale was able to overcome many of these. However, many of these constraints may endure, Mondale and Bush to the contrary notwithstanding.

### President of the Senate

Until about 1940 most presidents and most Americans viewed the vice-presidency almost exclusively as a legislative job. Vice-presidents were to serve as president of the Senate, presiding there and casting an occasional tie-breaking vote.

Originally the Senate was comprised of a small number of elder statesmen; twenty-six men plus the vice-president. Tie votes were more frequent: Vice-President John Adams (1789–1797) cast twenty-nine tie-breaking votes, and Vice-President John C. Calhoun (1825–1832) cast twenty-eight. Nowadays however, mainly because the Senate has grown to one hundred members, tie votes occur about once every two-and-a-half years. For example, Lyndon Johnson cast none, Agnew cast two, and, in his four years, Mondale cast only one tie-breaking vote.

The Senate was designed in many ways as an ideal place for a vice-president to learn the business of government and to serve along with the nation's leading political thinkers. The Senate was intended to pass laws, shape national policy, confirm major presidential appointees, oversee treaties, and advise and counsel presidents — particularly in foreign affairs. Over time, as it grew, it delegated more and more of its powers to the president, cabinet, and even to Executive Office advisers — so much so that the Senate is now almost indistinguishable from the House of Representatives; neither a council of state nor the prime presidential counseling body.

Technically, vice-presidents could become arbitrary presiders in the Senate. In practice they have not. The job of presiding over the Senate has become a thankless one without any real power. Today, the job of presiding over the Senate offers little training for the position of chief executive. One observer concluded that "the single job conferred on a Vice-President by the Constitution — presiding over the meetings of the United States Senate — can be performed by any six-year-old. The presiding officer need do no more than sit there like an elegant dunce, and repeat aloud whatever the parliamentarian stage-whispers to him. It is about as challenging as having your hair cut. . . ." [3]

Senators nowadays view vice-presidents as semi-intruders, certainly not as providers of instruction or leadership. Members of Congress now look upon a vice-president as a member of the executive branch. Lyndon Johnson, upon election as vice-president, for example, sought to retain a certain measure of the control over Democrats he enjoyed as majority leader. He apparently talked Senator Mike Mansfield into inviting him to preside over Democratic caucus meetings, even though he was about to become vice-president.

The proposal that LBJ as vice-president serve as presiding officer of all the Senate Democrats whenever they met in a formal conference was opposed not only by several of his liberal antagonists but also by members of his own so-called "Johnson Network." The liberals wanted revenge for his having ridden roughshod over them too long. One argument they put forth was that it was an unnatural mixing of the separate branches: "We might as well ask Jack Kennedy to come back up to the Senate and take his turn at presiding," snapped Senator Albert Gore. More telling was the opposition of a long-time Johnson intimate:

> Senator Clinton Anderson specifically noted his support at Los Angeles and the debt all Democratic Senators owed Johnson for his leadership in the Senate the past eight years. But the office of the Vice-President, said Anderson, was more a creature of the executive branch than the legislative branch. Therefore, quite apart from the fact that the Senate Democrats would look ridiculous electing a non-Senator to preside over them, to do so would violate the spirit of separation of powers.
>
> The debate continued in a mood of embarrassment. Johnson was present. . . . [4]

Johnson understood the message and seldom again did he try as vice-president to influence Senate proceedings.

Vice-presidents rarely are used effectively in congressional liaison work. This is often because they are not properly prepared by their president. Harry Truman, in his brief tenure as a vice-president, wanted to become an effective link between Congress and the White House. But this depended on close contact with FDR, which was virtually nonexistent. Lyndon Johnson was similarly underused. Johnson was simultaneously rebuffed by both Congress and the White House. Caught both coming and going, he retreated into a nearly three-year sulk.

Franklin Roosevelt's troubles with John Nance Garner were legendary. Garner was an important figure in the Congress and he skillfully assisted the passage of a number of New Deal measures in FDR's first term. But he grew upset with the pace and sweeping scope of later New Deal measures and became outspoken in his opposition to several of them. He opposed Roosevelt's scheme for packing the Supreme Court. He opposed FDR's bid for a third term. By the end of his second term, Roosevelt avoided Garner as much as possible and considered him an impossible person.

The limits of vice-presidential influence in the Senate are illustrated by one of Spiro Agnew's transgressions of political convention. Early in his tenure, Agnew tried to interest himself in mastering Senate rules as well as learning the Senate's informal folkways: "But he violated protocol by lobbying on the Senate floor in behalf of the tax surcharge extension supported by the administration. 'Do we have your vote?' he asked Senator Len Jordan of Idaho, a Republican. The Senator replied, 'You did have until now.' Thus, was established Jordan's rule: When the Vice-President lobbies on the Senate floor for a bill, vote the other way." [5] Thereafter, Agnew seemed to lose interest in trying to become presidential emissary on Capitol Hill.

Vice-President Hubert Humphrey had served in the Senate for sixteen years prior to becoming vice-president. He was aware that as presiding officer he was to be seen but not heard, except for procedural matters. This was a difficult adjustment for the loquacious Humphrey. Custom, folkways, and good manners dictated his behavior as Senate president:

> You recognize the majority leader whenever he seeks recognition. You recognize the minority leader following the majority leader. You try to recognize a Democrat and then a Republican, that is on ordinary matters. When you get into a hot debate, when the issues are difficult, you recognize on the basis of who is up first — whether the Vice-President's eye catches a particular person. Now, of course, you can occasionally blink. But I think that most Vice-Presidents try to play it pretty fair, and, as we say, on the level.[6]

As matters now stand, a vice-president is a full member of neither branch. The office, because of the duties as presiding officer of the Senate, is clearly a constitutional hybrid, limiting somewhat the use a president can make of a vice-president. Thus, President Eisenhower "asserted repeatedly in his memoirs that the vice-president 'is not legally a part of the Executive Branch and is not subject to direction by the President.' In Eisenhower's view, any performance of executive functions by the vice-president was voluntary and by his request." [7]

Some say a vice-president should be relieved of traditional Senate functions and freed to participate more directly in executive branch responsibilities. The late James F. Byrnes of South Carolina, a former senator, associate justice of the Supreme Court as well as secretary of state, offered this perspective:

> If a motion (in the Senate) does not receive a majority vote, it should be considered lost. It is not wise that the Vice-President, a representative of the executive branch of government, should affect the will of the legislators by casting a decisive vote. In short, participation by the Vice-President in Senate voting, either in support of his own views or the President's, constitutes a violation of the

spirit of the fundamental provision of the Constitution that the three branches of our government shall forever be separated.[8]

Byrnes urged we adopt a constitutional amendment to effect this change.

Constitutional scholar Joseph Kallenbach also favored such a change, contending the vice-president could then become a sort of "minister without portfolio," subject to executive assignments as a president may direct. "This would not only insure he would function in a subordinate administrative capacity to the President and not be tempted to become a rival; it would also make possible assignments over a period of time would enable him to acquire a wider knowledge of the operations of government as a whole." "In this way," adds Kallenbach, "he could be given a better opportunity than at present to prepare himself for the responsibility of serving as chief executive in case fate should thrust the role upon him." [9]

This suggestion has pretty much been ignored just in the manner as most recent vice-presidents have dismissed their Senate "job" as virtually irrelevant. Vice-presidents do show up on certain ceremonial occasions — such as on opening day and when the president addresses a joint session of Congress. But otherwise they have moved down Pennsylvania Avenue.

### Vice-Presidents as "Assistant Presidents"

Corporate officials are often baffled with the way presidents underutilize their vice-presidents. The trend in top management circles in the private sector, particularly in recent years, has been to form corporate managerial teams. The chief executive officer usually relies heavily on an executive vice-president and vice-president for finance, a vice-president for marketing, and often a series of group vice-presidents heading up major divisions or subsidiary companies. Collegial leadership, although not always a success in practice, is a celebrated ideal in business communities. The talented chief executive in the private sector delegates well and delegates often. Nurturing up-and-coming executive talent is widely applauded.

Presidents do delegate some of their responsibilities — but less to vice-presidents, who are often considered outsiders, than to their own insiders, such as Harry Hopkins, Joseph Califano, H. R. Haldeman, and Ed Meese. Have presidents tried to nuture their vice-presidents, assigning them important executive apprenticeship experiences? Sometimes, but not as much as one should expect.

The cabinet is as nebulous an entity as the vice-presidency. But a brief examination of vice-presidential involvement in the cabinet helps to illustrate the changing, if still limited, vice-presidential executive portfolio.

George Washington conferred on occasion with Vice-President John Adams, but Adams only acted in his official executive capacity one time, when he attended a cabinet meeting in 1791. Washington was away and wanted his department heads to get together in his absence, and he requested Adams to join them. Jefferson declined President Adams's invitation to attend cabinet meetings.

Other vice-presidents for the next 120 years stayed away from the cabinet sessions — either by personal or presidential desire, usually both. Then in 1918 Thomas R. Marshall substituted for Woodrow Wilson when Wilson was in Europe. President Warren Harding invited his vice-president, Calvin Coolidge, to come to cabinet meetings, thus reviving the practice George Washington had begun. FDR's second vice-president, Henry Wallace, an experienced administrator who had already served two terms as Secretary of Agriculture, was the first vice-president to be assigned major administrative duties. Roosevelt made Wallace chairman, successively, of the Economic Defense Board, the Supply Priorities and Allocations Board, the War Productions Board, and the Board of Economic Warfare. In the latter post Wallace became an aggressive administrator and an outspoken advocate. "Wallace was restless with the failure of the American government to set forth in clear detail a plan for the future that would lift the spirits and galvanize the wills of men everywhere. He fretted not the least because the relative silence from the White House permitted other voices to seem louder and more persuasive than in his opinion they should have." [10]

Henry Wallace was idealistic, stubborn, and outspoken. He cherished the idea of succeeding Roosevelt as president, but he was always loyal. Roosevelt delegated considerable authority to Wallace — authority to oversee much of the domestic economy — strategic imports, exports, shipping, foreign exchange, and related matters. But his political base as vice-president and the authority delegated to him proved inadequate to his responsibilities. Wallace fast became embroiled in a massive collision with the departments of state and commerce, and with secretaries Cordell Hull and Jesse H. Jones in particular. Both men vigorously defended their departments from nearly every Wallace intrusion. Both men attacked Wallace viciously, Jones often in public.

To perform his executive assignments Wallace had to secure State's and Commerce's approval with some frequency, but his efforts were in vain. He sought Roosevelt's approval for enlarging his authority to correspond with his duties, but Roosevelt yielded only a little. For a year and a half — 1942 to June of 1943 — Wallace sought to make a go of it; but after several public skirmishes and open warfare between the vice-president and the Secretary of commerce, Roosevelt abolished Wallace's board. So ended a year-and-a-half experiment of having a vice-president serve as an administrator. By most standards it was an experiment that failed, although factors other than the office of the vice-presidency were involved. Thus, some people would claim that this failure was primarily due to Wallace's stubborn and apolitical temperament. Others might contend, perhaps correctly, that Roosevelt never gave Wallace adequate authority with which to do the job assigned him. In any event, the Wallace example stands out as almost the sole instance up to the present of serious administrative responsibilities being delegated to a vice-president.

Since 1943 vice-presidents have, however, been invited to cabinet meetings and related policy councils with some regularity. By a 1949 amendment to the National Security Act of 1947, the vice-president now sits as a regular member of the National Security Council. Since the Eisenhower presidency, the vice-president has been made the cabinet's acting chairman in the president's absence. Nixon chaired several cabinet sessions during Eisenhower's several illnesses. LBJ and Humphrey chaired several presidential-level councils and commissions, and, like Wallace and Nixon before them, they traveled widely as goodwill ambassadors as well as on some sensitive policy missions. FDR actually began the tradition of sending vice-presidents abroad: John N. Garner was FDR's representative at the installation of a Philippine president in 1935, and Henry Wallace as vice-president traveled to Latin America as well as to China and Siberia. Nixon traveled to fifty-four countries, LBJ to more than thirty. Humphrey and Agnew were often sent to visit Asia. Mondale conducted diplomatic missions to twenty-six nations during his four years as vice-president.

Nearly every vice-president in recent times has found it difficult to interfere with the work of cabinet members. The departmental secretaries preside over congressionally authorized departments; hence, a vice-president is very much an intruder unless a problem arises which is definitely interdepartmental. Even then, what is an interdepartmental matter to some may not be to others.

Reformers sometime urge that vice-presidents be assigned specific cabinet responsibilities, such as secretary of defense or attorney general. This might answer the criticism that the vice-presidency is a training ground for nothing at all. Critics of this suggestion say existing cabinet members are already tough to make responsive to the White House. As an elected department official, a vice-president who served also as a cabinet secretary/department head would be even tougher to get around or even to "fire." A vice-president as department head would also surely be compromised by the narrow clientele constituencies of a single agency. Such a precedent, if established, might also affect the kinds of people a president would pick for vice-president. Picking someone who might be a good department head might not always be best; it might unwisely subordinate breadth, political talent, or general leadership ability to managerial experience.

Finally, it is not wholly evident that a departmental secretary position provides presidential training. Under some circumstances it might; under others it clearly would not. How many recent department heads come readily to mind as especially promising presidential candidates? To be sure, Jefferson and Madison served as cabinet members prior to their presidencies, but so too did James Buchanan and Herbert Hoover.

Both Presidents Hoover and Eisenhower recommended the creation of an additional appointed vice-presidential post. Hoover advocated an administrative vice-president; Eisenhower a "first secretary of government" for foreign affairs. Neither proposal received much attention. More recently, Milton Eisenhower urged the creation of two executive vice-presidents, to be appointed by the president — one to deal with domestic policy, the other with international affairs, but both to work "in close collaboration with the President." Milton Eisenhower claims that the elected vice-president cannot hope to do what appointed vice-presidents could. First, he says, echoing his older brother, the elected vice-president is not a member of the executive branch. Second:

> Even though he normally is suggested to a convention by the presidential nominee as a running mate, there is no guarantee that he will be in agreement with the President; there is no legal bar to his openly disagreeing with the President. Vice-Presidents have often disagreed with Chief Executives. Vice-President Dawes frequently and openly advocated the passage of legislation which President Coolidge denounced and vetoed. Most important of all, the President cannot discharge the elected Vice-President. This point is critical. In any organization delegation of authority is workable only if the chief executive has absolute confidence in the individual to whom he delegates some of his own duties, and this confidence exists only if there is mutual trust, a shared philosophy, and a recognition by the subordinate that final authority always rests with the chief; should directives of the President be unacceptable to the appointed Executive Vice-President, and he felt that he could not loyally do what was expected of him, he would have to resign or be removed by the President.[11]

Eisenhower's suggestion has not been acted upon. Instead presidents rely on key cabinet members or those who serve on their staff.

More radical is Michael Novak's proposal that what we really need to do is to separate the presidency into two functions: the head of state and the chief executive. "What we can do, perhaps, is establish a head of state to greet foreign dignitaries and to visit them abroad, to officiate on occasions when a personification of the nation is required, to become the central figure even at the inauguration of the chief executives, and to live at the White House. The chief executive who would be elected every four years as at present, would live as cabinet members live." [12] Novak does not specify how his proposal could be implemented, nor does he relate his recommendation to the existing vice-presidential office. In any event, beguiling and perhaps prescient as the Novak innovation might be, it has generally been considered as naïve. Doubtless it smacks too much of importing the royalty feature from Great Britain. Because of this alone it probably will never gain popularity here.

### Psychological Problems or the "Throttlebottom Complex"
Tensions between a president and a vice-president are natural; after all, everybody else who works closely with a president can be fired by him.

Alexander Throttlebottom was a character in the successful 1930s Broadway play *Of Thee I Sing,* by George S. Kaufman and Morrie Ryskind. Throttlebottom was a stumbling, mumbling caricature of an unemployed vice-president. Neglected by his president, John P. Wintergreen, Throttlebottom is artfully drawn as an unknown, an unwanted, and an improbable national leader. Not only did he not want to be vice-president or know what was expected of him, he was even refused the right to resign. The character of Throttlebottom provided for splendid satire and comic relief, but the mocking portrait lives on and the name has become a familiar term for the real plight of contemporary vice-presidents.

The estrangement of vice-presidents from presidents began with Adams and Washington. Relations between the two were civil but scarcely friendly. During his tenure as vice-president, Thomas Jefferson refused diplomatic assignments from Adams. And Jefferson said of Aaron Burr, his first vice-president, that he was a "crooked gun whose aim or shot you could never be sure of." Time and again relations between presidents and vice-presidents are strained, abrasive, and cold to the point of open hostility. A few examples drawn from the accounts of observers underscore the unusual and mutual frustration.

Roosevelt and John Nance Garner:

> The once cordial relations between the two men had long since turned sour. They had little contact except at cabinet meetings, where Garner, red and glowering, occasionally took issue with the President in a truculent manner. Roosevelt hinted he would desert the Democratic cause before he would vote for the Texan for President (in 1940). By early 1940 even official relations between the two men had almost ceased; Roosevelt was hoping that the Vice-President would not show up for cabinet meetings. The President was gleeful about Garner's tribulations as a presidential candidate....[13]

John F. Kennedy and Lyndon B. Johnson:

> They made his stay in the Vice-Presidency the most miserable three years of his life. He wasn't the number two man in that administration; he was the lowest man on the totem pole. Though he has never said this to anyone (perhaps because his pride would never let him admit it) I know him well enough to know he felt humiliated time and time again, that he was openly snubbed by second-echelon White House staffers who snickered at him behind his back and called him "Uncle Cornpone." [14]

Richard M. Nixon and Spiro Agnew:

Nixon barely knew Agnew when he selected him in Miami Beach in 1968. Nixon himself had been humiliated in the vice-presidential job, a job he called a hollow shell — the most ill-conceived and poorly defined position in the American political system. He proceeded nonetheless to visit an even greater humiliation on Agnew. By most accounts Agnew was scorned by the White House staff and given little of importance to do.

Why does the "Throttlebottom Complex" persist? Is there something congenitally or structurally deficient in the relationship between the presidency and the vice-presidency? Does the relationship always have to be hollow, hostile, and counterproductive? "Mistrust is inherent in the relationship," writes Arthur Schlesinger. Vice-presidents are "intolerable reminders of their president's own mortality." [15] This mistrust is also not without historical foundation. Previous vice-presidents have turned against their presidents, mobilizing opposition in the Congress, proposing alternative legislative programs, and preparing to run for the presidency itself against the president they were then serving. Calhoun became so disenchanted that he simply resigned the office.

Although some progress has been made, a psychological barrier, an intangible distance, still seems to prevent a significant delegation of power to a vice-president. Doubtless vice-presidents do remind a president of their mortality. Doubtless many presidents are in constant fear of being upstaged. Presidents often consciously assign jobs that are unpresidential in character. Thus, "The very fact that a problem is turned over to the Vice-President argues that it's not very important, or that the Vice-President actually is going to play a far less critical role in solving it than announced, or that the President recognizes the impossibility of solving the problem and therefore wants to stay as far away from the whole thing as possible." [16]

Some vice-presidents refuse to accept demeaning jobs. Lyndon Johnson, for example, just went into a retreat. Others willingly become partisan "hit-men," straight-arming the press, slashing back at presidential opponents, and stumping endlessly for the reelection of friendly members of Congress. Thus, Spiro Agnew was used as a mouthpiece and as a surrogate presidential speaker at partisan events. His experience fits Arthur Schlesinger's generalization that the vice-presidency may be less a *making* than a *maiming* experience.

Often it is as if a vice-president is entirely unacceptable and unwanted unless he is willing to merge his identity completely with that of the president. The vice-president, it quickly turns out, is not his own man, no vice-president ever is. But some may be said, more than others, to have the soul of a vice-president. They become cheerleaders for their boss. They become expert at laying wreaths at remote ceremonial functions. They become, in a way, part of the furniture in another man's house.

The following passages from a televised "Conversation with Vice-President Hubert H. Humphrey" illustrate how one vice-president seemingly subordinated his own personal ambitions and vowed nearly feudal homage to his president:

> I did not become Vice-President with President Johnson to cause him trouble. I feel a deep sense of loyalty and fidelity. I believe that if you can't have that you have no right to accept the office. Because today it is so important that a President and his Vice-President be on the same wavelength. . . .
>
> I'd hate to have the President be worried about me, that I may do something that would cause him embarrassment or that would injure his Administration. . . .
>
> There are no Humphrey people, there are no Humphrey policies, there are no Humphrey programs. Whatever we have we should try to contribute, if it's wanted, to the President and his Administration. You can't have two leaders of the Executive Branch at one time. . . .[17]

In spite of this subservient bending of himself "to lean over backwards," Humphrey was never really trusted by LBJ. Humphrey frequently sought more substantive assignments, only to be refused. Johnson would simply exclude Humphrey from his téam of insiders whenever the vice-president sought independence or tried to develop his own line of thinking. This was especially true in the case of occasional policy differences he had with Johnson over the Vietnam war.

When is loyalty to a president carried too far? Vice-Presidents Humphrey, Agnew, and Ford sometimes became such apologists for their administrations that they could not help but diminish their credibility, perhaps undermining their own future capacity to provide serious leadership.

Experience suggests, however, that not only will most presidents not trust their vice-presidents, but the relationship in terms of real assignments will be a limited one. Can a vice-president — even an outstanding one — become a significant force in the presidential establishment? Or was John Nance Garner correct when he reasoned that a great person may be vice-president but can't be a great vice-president because the office in itself is unimportant. It may be next to impossible to relate a vice-president's performance to the results of an administration's policy. For instance, observers who say Mondale was an ideal vice-president are hard pressed to describe his share of the Carter-Mondale record. What were Mondale's achievements? Can Mondale be relieved of Carter's failures? Or, possibly, were Carter's failures lesser or greater because of Mondale?

"The relationship is a difficult one," said Gerald Ford, "and it's magnified by staff working relationships between" the president's and vice-president's offices. "Every President's staff thinks the President is all-important and there's just somebody sitting over there in the Executive Office Building and you shouldn't pay any attention to him. On the other hand, the Vice-President's staff sits over there and they think the President's staff is shortchanging them on office space, funding, personnel, prestige." [18]

Gerald Ford saw this happen between his own staff and Nelson Rockefeller's staff. Ford allows that he and Rockefeller got along famously. "Nelson was absolutely loyal to me, and he would do anything I asked him to do" writes Ford in his memoir.[19] But Ford, despite the fact he believed Rockefeller was eminently qualified to "step into my shoes" if tragedy struck, still went along with his own staff's campaign to dump Rockefeller. Ford was motivated almost exclusively in this instance by the political considerations. Later, he acknowledged, "I was angry with myself for showing cowardice in not saying to the ultraconservatives, 'It's going to be Ford and Rockefeller, whatever the consequences.' " [20]

Despite all these traditional problems, the office has endured, if not always prospered. Some of the traditional problems have been diminished somewhat by reducing the physical distance between president and vice-president and by providing more staff, perquisites, and even a permanent residence for the vice-president. Until 1961 vice presidents had to work out of their office in the Capitol. Lyndon Johnson was the first vice-president to be given a suite of offices in the Executive Office Building, across an alley from the west wing of the White House. Spiro Agnew was the first to be given an office in the White House, although he only stayed in it for a few months. Mondale was given his choice of White House offices (excepting only the oval office) and he stayed there on the main floor of the west wing for his whole four years. Nelson Rockefeller was the first modern vice-president to be given an official residence.

By the time Mondale became vice-president the trappings were near-imperial. He had offices in the White House, at the Capitol, in the Executive Office Building, in the U.S. Senate Office Buildings, another at the vice-president's official residence, another one back in Minnesota (for reasons that are not entirely clear), and yet another one in "Air Force Two," the jet made available for the vice-president's never-ending journeys. Not bad for a "nonjob."

### The Mondale Model

"It has its frustrations . . . ," said Walter F. Mondale. "But I went into it with my eyes wide open. I know there is only one President; there is not an assistant President. I'm his adviser." [21] Most students of the vice-presidency agree that Mondale enjoyed a closer and better relationship with his boss, President Jimmy Carter, than any previous vice-president. Much of the credit has to go to Carter. Carter not only said he would give his vice-president a lot to do, he probably made the vice-president as close as one can get to a working partner. Mondale enjoyed a standing invitation to attend and participate in any of the president's meetings. He had access to all reports and cables. Mondale also had a weekly luncheon date with Carter.

Mondale came to the job with several helpful assets. He was well-known and well-liked on Capitol Hill. He knew how Congress and Washington operated. In some respects, he had more of a national base or national following than did Carter. He was a protégé of Hubert Humphrey's, and yet he had an identity of his own.

Perhaps his greatest strength was his ability to get along with people — all kinds of people. He was a natural team-player and not a showboating, flamboyant credit-seeker. General Eisenhower had once said "There's no limit to how much influence you can have if you are only willing to let others get the credit for it." Mondale was a shrewd politician who understood this proverb.

Mondale also understood the "tender nature" of the vice-presidency. He knew that nearly everything affecting his effectiveness as vice-president depended on a basic personal relationship of confidence and trust with the president. He knew also that presidential powers are not divisible. He knew that he could not long be effective as chief lobbyist or as chief of staff at the White House — two jobs that Carter and his staff sometimes tried to give him. Mondale rejected the chief of staff post because he knew if he had taken that assignment "it would have consumed vast amounts of my time with staff work and distracted me from important work."

"I see my role," Mondale said in his second year in the vice-presidency, "as a general adviser on almost any issue, as a troubleshooter, as a representative of the President in some foreign affairs matters and as a political advocate of the Administration." [22]

Mondale and Carter overcame some of the traditional problems of the vice-presidency by treating Mondale's staff as part of the White House staff. Some of the senior members of Mondale's staff were assigned high-level White House responsibilities, often with supervisory authority over some White House aides. Mondale's staff won high marks for professionalism and competence and for their ability to work with and for Carter as well as for their boss. In doing this, Mondale and his staff were able to set a new precedent — one that may help to remove some of the tension and barriers to success so frequently witnessed in the past.

When Carter was asked about his conception of their relationship he may have overstated it somewhat:

> I probably meet with the Vice-President on a daily basis more than all the other staff members that I have combined.
> ... there is no aspect of my own daily responsibilities as President that are not shared by the Vice-President.
> ... I would say without derogating the other members of my staff that there is no one who would approach him in his importance to me, his closeness to me, and also his ability to carry out a singular assignment with my complete trust.[23]

Carter's trust in Mondale was doubtless a significant factor in their relationship. Carter was not intimidated by Mondale. Further, Carter valued Mondale's frankness and confidential discussions. Mondale became someone with whom Carter could sit down and discuss political and policy problems. "What the President needs is not more information, although that is helpful," recalls Mondale, "he needs a few people who can honestly appraise and evaluate his performance. . . . He needs to hear voices that speak from a national perspective. He has no limit to the number of people who want to talk to him, but that does not assure him of the confidentiality he needs to speak freely." [24]

Is the vice-presidency a useful understudy position, a place where one can serve a sensible apprenticeship for the presidency? Mondale insists it was for him:

> I think it may be the best training of all [for the presidency]. I don't know of any other office, outside of the presidency, that informs an officer more fully about the realities of presidential government, about the realities of federal government and the duties of the presidency that remotely compares to that of the Vice-President as it is now being used.
> I'm privy to all the same secret information as the President. I have unlimited access to the President. I'm usually with him when all the central decisions are being made. I've been through several of these crises now that a President inevitably confronts, and I see how they work. I've been through the budget process, I've been through diplomatic ventures, I've been through a host of congressional fights as seen from the presidential perspective.
> I spent 12 years in the Senate. I learned a lot there, but I learned more here about the realities of presidential responsibilities. I learned more about our country and the world the last three years than I could any other way.[25]

As vice-president, Mondale breathed life into the possibilities of the office, instead of viewing his position as an incurably frustrating hybrid, half legislative and half executive, he adopted the view that the vice-presidency is the only office of the national government that bridges the separation of powers. He successfully played a broker role in helping to gain ratification of the Panama Canal Treaty. He gladly campaigned to help elect Democrats to Congress. Said Mondale: "[T]he only campaigns that are worth anything are those in which the politician listens carefully and tries to learn and respond to the needs of the people. . . ." In efforts to extend the president's reach to the public at large, Mondale traveled about six hundred thousand miles during his vice-presidency.

He was also a weapon in Carter's campaign to fend off Edward Kennedy's bid to snatch the Democratic Party's 1980 nomination. Some critics think Mondale may have gone too far; that he was forced into and accepted an uncomfortable and unnatural role of criticizing Kennedy's record and purposes when Kennedy's voting record was nearly identical to his own Senate record. Thus James Reston of *The New York Times* wrote "even good men like Fritz Mondale are being corrupted by the political struggle in the process." And, "It is almost startling to hear what Mondale says in this struggle for votes and support. He defends policies as Vice-President which, when he was representing Minnesota as a liberal Senator, he opposed." [26] Mondale said Reston was being unfair and overly selective. Mondale claims he was justified in asking Kennedy what he would do differently, what policies he would pursue that would be significantly different. "I have never been a 'hatchet man,' " said Mondale, "and I never would be, and the President would never ask me to be." [27] The line may have become thin at times, however.

As his term drew to a close in early 1981 Mondale told his successor, George Bush, that there were some institutional lessons to be passed along. Mondale's chief recommendations were as follows:

1. Advise the president confidentially. The only reason to state publicly what you have told the president is to take credit for his success and try to escape blame for failure. Either way there is no quicker way to undermine your relationship with the president and lose your effectiveness. . . .
2. Don't wear a president down. . . . Give your advice once and give it well. You have a right to be heard, not obeyed. A president must decide when the debates must end. . . .
3. As a spokesman for the Administration, stay on the facts. A president does not want and the public does not respect a vice-president who does nothing but deliver fulsome praise of a president. . . .
4. Avoid line authority assignments. If such an assignment is important, it will then cut across the responsibilities of one or two cabinet officers or others and embroil you in a bureaucratic fight that would be disastrous. If it is meaningless or trivial, it will undermine your reputation and squander your time. . . .

5. The vice-president should remember the importance of personal compatibility. He should try to complement the president's skills and, finally in a real sense the most important of all roles, be ready to assume the presidency. . . .[28]

Will the Mondale-Carter relationship establish a precedent for succeeding administrations? Mondale thinks it will. (George Bush hopes it will and in his first year as vice-president, Bush did enjoy a White House west-wing office and the close ties to the President and his staff that Mondale enjoyed. Moreover, Bush also was given some serious assignments in the area of regulatory reform and foreign policy.)

Some analysts say Mondale succeeded so well because he was willing to hew the Carter line and he remained exceedingly loyal — even when close friends of his such as HEW cabinet secretary Joseph Califano were being fired, even when some of his cherished social programs were being cut, and even when a rescue mission was sent to Iran. One student of the vice-presidency complained that it "was damned hard to find out on just what Mondale was influential. That was, of course, his 'be discreet' strategy." One Carter White House aide said that virtually no one around the White House challenged Carter seriously, and that Mondale concurred with Carter's preference for "harmony above all other virtues." Others say Mondale's influence stemmed from Carter's dependence on him to explain how Congress worked and to keep close ties with the labor movement. In short, the verdict is that Carter needed Mondale more than most presidents need their vice-presidents. And Mondale's patient personality and relative youth meant he (a) could wait for his own chance to become president and (b) could avoid being a threat to Carter. Even Mondale would admit, and surely Bush would agree, that it helps to be seen as a trusted lieutenant but not to be heard as an exponent of too many original views. "In effect the vice-president's influence is inversely proportional to his perceived influence." [29]

## Selection and Succession

The essential enduring problem of the vice-presidency, now we have some sensible things for a vice-president to do, is the proper selection of persons to run for or fill the office. For years the vice-presidential nomination process has tempted the fates. It's a pig-in-a-poke system, critics say, that not only is often abused but also denigrates the office.

The process invariably begins with a search for someone who will strengthen the presidential ticket but not infrequently ends with a search for someone who will not weaken the ticket. The search for someone who will "balance the ticket" causes countless problems. Sometimes it means choosing some party workhorse whose only virtue is that he has antagonized nobody. Sometimes it means choosing someone mainly because he comes from a different but politically crucial region of the nation. Sometimes this practice means nominating someone from a rival political wing of the party. In short, enormous pressure builds up to subordinate considerations of leadership ability to those of vote-getting power. Ticket-balancing has allowed the Andrew Johnsons, Arthurs, Hendricks, Tompkins, Nixons, and Agnews to rise from relative political obscurity to become vice-president.

Is it right to entrust the selection of vice-presidents to the presidential nominee? How many vice-presidents have been merely an afterthought at national conventions? The Eagleton selection by George McGovern and the Spiro Agnew selection by Richard Nixon prompted various reappraisals.

In 1973 the Democratic Party created a Commission on Vice-Presidential Selection, chaired by former Vice-President Hubert Humphrey. The Commission made several suggestions, including these:

1. Extending the convention for a day permitting a forty-eight-hour interval between the nomination of the president and the nomination of vice-president.

2. To ensure even more deliberation, putting off the selection of the vice-president for three weeks or more and ratification of the nominee by the party's national committee in a mini-convention (a procedure used in 1972 when McGovern's choice, Thomas Eagleton, withdrew and Sargent Shriver was approved as the vice-presidential nominee).[30]

Other reformers in the 1970s suggested that every aspirant for the presidential nomination might pick his vice-presidential nominees about 60 days before his party's national convention. At the convention, the two would run as a ticket. This method might, its sponsors say, allow the vice-presidential choice to emerge with more stature.

Another proposal suggests that to democratize the convention selection, the presidential nominee could be required to submit several names for vice-president to the delegates.

Yet another alternative is for the runner-up in the presidential balloting to be declared the automatic winner of the vice-presidential nomination.

Still another proposal urged that national conventions nominate only the presidential nominee. Then the November election winner would announce a choice of a vice-president in December, and the new Congress, meeting in January, would consider the choice before inauguration day. If the first name was not approved, the new president would submit another. This proposal would require a constitutional amendment.

The most radical proposal would also require a constitutional amendment: abolishing the vice-presidency altogether. The idea of abolishing the office has been proposed countless times since the beginning of the Republic. This bold measure was embraced by a dozen or more writers in the mid-1970s in the wake of Watergate and two periods of vacancy in the vice-presidency. Frustrated by the abuse and misuse of the office, critics said: "Let's get rid of the office before it sinks us." If a president dies or becomes disabled or resigns, let a designated cabinet member (secretary of state or defense or treasury) take over for 100 days and meanwhile let's conduct a special election for a new democratically elected president. Arthur M. Schlesinger, Jr., perhaps the most noted proponent of this plan, concluded that the multiple problems that now depreciate the vice-presidency could simply be eliminated by eliminating the office itself:

> There is no escape . . . from the conclusion that the Vice-Presidency is not only a pointless but even a dangerous office. A politician is nominated for Vice-President for reasons unconnected with his presidential qualities and elected to the Vice-Presidency as part of a tie-in sale. Once carried to the Vice-Presidency not on his own but as a second rider on the presidential horse, where is he? If he is a first-rate man, his nerve and confidence will be shaken, his talents wasted and soured, even as his publicity urges him on toward the ultimate office for which, the longer he serves in the second place, the less ready he may be. If he is not a first-rate man he should not be in a position to inherit or claim the Presidency. Why not therefore abolish this mischievous office and work out a more sensible mode of succession? [31]

The Throttlebottom complex would be solved. We would stop elevating to the presidency individuals who have not really won election. Presidents could appoint one or more vice-presidents. "If the principle be accepted — the principle that if a President vanishes, it is better for the people to elect a new president than endure a Vice-President who was never voted for that office, who became Vice-President for reasons other than his presidential qualifications and who may very well have been badly damaged by his vice-presidential experience — the problem is one of working out the mechanics of the intermediate election. This is not easy but far from impossible." [32]

At the heart of the matter is whether we want to be a government of and by the people. It is widely acknowledged that we often choose vice-presidents for the wrong reasons. It is equally clear, however, that today the vice-presidency has become a stepping-stone either to the presidency directly or at least to presidential nomination. Nearly twenty-five percent of our presidents did not serve out the terms they were serving.

The issues at stake, especially in this proposal, are ones of democratic procedure and political legitimacy. Many say that the nation could not afford a special election after a presidential death, as in 1945 or in 1963; but many other Western nations do so regularly. Others say intermediate elections violate the tradition of quadrennial elections. But what is so compelling or virtuous about waiting until that fourth year if what is at question is the quality and character of the nation's leadership? Moreover, the special election would merely be to fill out the remainder of the departed president's term. What could be more sensible for a self-governing democracy than that the president must, except for the briefest periods, be a person elected to that office by the people?

Plainly, there are several disadvantages to the idea of abolishing the vice-presidency and conducting a special election to fill a presidential vacancy. First, it would invite instability and turmoil during the succession period. Second, it is doubtful that a sixty- or ninety-day campaign in a nation this large would allow for the clarification of competing issues. It is one thing for Canada or France to conduct a short campaign, but the U.S. is substantially larger, and it usually takes longer here for issues to get sharpened. Finally, most people, rightly or wrongly, are not displeased by the existing system. Neither are they displeased by those who in the twentieth century have become vice-presidents through the current arrangements.

In sum, the vice-presidential nomination process has had a mixed history. We now have had nine examples of what happens when a vice-president is forced by necessity to become president. Some of them have become decent presidents. What is more disturbing, however, is that an assessment of those who have mercifully not become president, from Aaron Burr to Spiro Agnew, is not in the least reassuring.

None of these reform proposals suggested in the past decade are without liabilities. Even the most casual of political science students can discern most of the trade-offs and the deficiencies. Nor has any of them captured a following. Most people are resigned to living with the existing system.

However, even if we stick with the present system for selecting vice-presidential nominees, there are several sensible modest improvements that can be made. None of these require constitutional amendments and most of them are merely the products of learning from past mistakes. In a condensed form, these are the recommendations most frequently made:

Presidential candidates should have their staffs recommend and consider several vice-presidential candidates, well in advance of the convention. Whenever possible the presidential nominee should interview these candidates well in advance.

Presidential candidates should give highest priority to the need for ideological compatibility, treating "electoral balancing" as a secondary factor. Note, however, that the "two are neither mutually exclusive nor naturally contradictory." [33]

National parties should provide for a flexible convention schedule, permitting an extra day if necessary for presidential nominees to deliberate over the vice-presidential nominee choices. Provisions should be made, in special cases, for a delay of a few weeks and the approval of the running mate at a mini-convention. Such special cases might be on such occasions as when a classic "dark-horse" or last-minute compromise candidate wins the presidential nomination and he or she had not expected to win and hence was unprepared for the vice-presidential selection responsibility.

"The candidates should make a list of serious preferences for the Vice-Presidency before the convention, in order to facilitate media and public examination; and they are encouraged to initiate direct contact and staff liaison with potential running mates." [34]

Common sense suggestions such as these will not guarantee an error-proof selection process, but they should reduce the risks.

## Succession

Despite all of the other problems associated with the vice-presidency, the office has done one thing reasonably well — solving our succession problem. Many nations have faltered or become torn apart in searing civil upheavals because they failed to provide for a prompt, orderly means of transition. Our citizens, like most people elsewhere, long for system stability and for a heightened sense of continuity.

Americans use to joke about vice-presidents who because of some emergency become "His Accidency" or president-by-chance. However, most Americans are grateful when the leadership vacuum is replaced and the new leader, endowed with legitimacy, acts with confidence and dispatch. Our vice-presidential succession process may be imperfect, but one of its virtues is the stability it brings to our governance arrangements. Trauma, chaos, and instability are avoided, as people know well in advance that there is a plan, a legitimate plan, that will be put into effect. Whatever one may think of the succession plan, the reassurance rendered is somewhat remarkable, doubtless due to the fact that plan is well-known in advance and reasonably understood by a large segment of the population.

The founding politicians provided that the vice-president should be first in the order of succession, but they left it up to Congress to establish the rest of the order of succession. Three statutes and one constitutional amendment speak to this matter. In the first presidential succession act, passed in 1792, the president *pro tempore* of the U.S. Senate (by custom the senior member of the majority party in the Senate) was named first in line behind the vice-president, followed by the speaker of the House of Representatives. If a double vacancy occurred (that is, if something happened to both the president and vice-president) this same 1792 act provided that the president *pro tempore* of the Senate would become acting president "until a president be elected." Hence an immediate special election of some kind would have been called to elect a new president, unless the vacancy occurred in the last months of the presidential term.

This first statute was superseded in 1886 when the heads of the cabinet departments beginning with the secretary of state, were named as the line of succession. This may have been done to avoid violating the principle of separation of powers. However many people have always thought an elected official should stand first in line to fill the presidency. Hence, Harry Truman, while serving out FDR's fourth term, urged a return to succession by elected congressional officials. In 1947, Congress approved this change, placing the speaker of the House first behind the vice-president, followed by the Senate's president *pro tempore,* followed by the cabinet officers in terms of the departmental seniority, secretary of state, and so on.

Questions persisted, however, about what to do in case of a vacancy in the vice-presidency. Prior to the Twenty-fifth amendment to the Constitution the vice-presidency had been vacant eighteen times for a total of about forty years. Fortunately, during these periods there had been no need to go down the line of presidential succession. Section 2 of the Twenty-fifth amendment, ratified in 1967, now provides that "Whenever there is a vacancy in the office of the vice-president, the president shall nominate a vice-president who shall take office upon confirmation by a majority vote of both Houses of Congress."

Some critics of this provision say it gives too much power to the president. Defenders of the provision counter the criticism as follows:

> In giving the President a dominant role in filling a vacancy in the Vice-Pres-idency, the proposed amendment is consistent with present practice whereby the presidential candidate selects his own running mate who must be approved by the people through their representatives. It is practical because it recognizes the fact that a Vice-President's effectiveness in our Government depends on his rapport with the President. If he is of the same party and of compatible temper-ament and views, all of which would be likely under the proposed amendment, his chances of becoming fully informed and adequately prepared to assume presidential power, if called upon, are excellent.[35]

Some analysts also say this provision is overly vague on certain points. Thus some people would amend it to add deadlines against stalling by either the White House or Congress. Some wondered what would happen if a president resigned or died while his nomination of a vice-president was still pending. Would the nominee still stand or would the speaker of the House, who had just become president, have the right to nominate his choice? "Would Congress have the right to choose between the two nominees? The fact that there are any open questions about presidential succession is, of course, dangerous, for there is nothing more threatening to a constitutional democracy than doubts about who has the legitimate right to govern." [36]

Section 3 of the Twenty-fifth amendment provides for presidents to delegate presidential powers and duties to the vice-president for a specified period. De-bates had long raged over questions of presidential inability or disability. Two presidents had had serious disabilities; Garfield for two and a half months be-fore he died, and Wilson for about a year. In each case their vice-presidents did not assume presidential duties, in part because they wished to avoid usurp-ing the powers of that office. Now a president can temporarily step aside. Sec-tion 3 reads:

> Whenever the President transmits to the President *pro tempore* of the Senate and the Speaker of the House of Representatives his written declaration that he is unable to discharge the powers and duties of his office, and until he transmits to them a written declaration to the contrary, such powers and duties shall be discharged by the Vice-President as Acting President.

But will a president invoke this section, save in extraordinary occasions? Reagan's aides chose not to do so during his operations for bullet wounds after the March 1981 attempt on his life. Reagan's aides did not feel the President would be totally incapacitated for more than a few hours — which was the case, although the first couple of days were rough. But there are political implications as well. Invoking this section of the Twenty-fifth amendment might alarm the public, might dramatize the president's vulnerability, might weaken the image of strength of the incumbent.

What if there is contention about whether the president is disabled or fit? Section 4 of the Twenty-fifth amendment speaks to this, though here again, the provisions invite ambiguous interpretation. The beginning of this section reads:

> Whenever the Vice-President and a majority of either the principal officers of the executive departments or of such other body as Congress may by law provide, transmit to the President *pro tempore* of the Senate and the Speaker of the House of Representatives their written declaration that the President is unable to discharge the powers and duties of his office, the Vice-President shall immediately assume the powers and duties of the office as Acting President.

The "principal officers of the executive departments" refers implicitly, if not explicitly, to the members of the cabinet. However, nowhere in the Constitution or anywhere else is there a formal definition of who is in the cabinet. It varies not only from president to president but from season to season, depending on whom the president wishes to include.

Another problem in this section that may raise uncertainty and even confusion in the future involves the provision of how a president may regain his powers. A president, so the amendment provides, can inform the leaders of Congress that no inability exists and ask to resume the powers, but the vice-president, together with a majority of the cabinet, can contest the president's assertion. What then? Well, says the provision, Congress has to decide very quickly whether the president is able or unable. Complications can plainly arise in the vague wording of this section. A president could conceivably keep stating he was able to continue. Meanwhile, while Congress would be debating the issue, two persons could both be attempting to exercise the powers and duties of the presidency.

Plainly, the Twenty-fifth amendment is a compromise of many different proposals, none of them truly satisfactory. Constitution-writing is always hard. To try to accommodate every possibility is unreasonable and impracticable. The Twenty-fifth amendment is assuredly an advance even though not definitive. Judgment on its effectiveness must await several tests of its various provisions.

## Conclusion

What of the future of the vice-presidency? It is an office that is here to stay, tensions and all. The office, as suggested, does solve our critical succession problem. The office can be made into a useful learning and advisory position. The office will remain attractive to aspiring politicians if only because it is one of the major paths to the presidency. The Mondale and Bush experiences have added to its prestige.

Vice-presidents will continue to have, and perhaps should have, a more or less undefined set of troubleshooting and advisory functions. Different incumbents will bring different skills and strengths to the office. Some will be better at diplomatic functions. Some will be gifted political negotiators and coalition-builders. Some will be excellent liaisons with mayors and governors. A certain flexibility is needed.

Given all its problems and all the ambiguities of the position, a case can be made to abolish it. However, this is not going to be done. Our tradition, Constitution, and political tendencies all point toward retaining the office. An effort should be directed to making it work. Plainly, an important way to enhance the vice-presidency is to enhance the quality of the vice-presidential selection process. Fortunately, both that process and the position are taken more seriously these days. No job, to be sure, can fully prepare an individual for the job of president, but recent experience suggests that the office can be refashioned to do this job as well as any other post.

SOURCE: "Rethinking the Vice-Presidency" was written for this volume.

## Notes

1. Allan P. Sindler, *Unchosen Presidents* (Berkeley, Ca.: University of California Press, 1976) p. 41.
2. *Time,* January 20, 1975, p. 23.
3. James M. Naughton, "Above the Battle," *The New York Times Magazine,* June 24, 1973, p. 49.
4. Senator Clinton Anderson, quoted in Roland Evans and Robert Novak, *Lyndon B. Johnson: The Exercise of Power* (New York: New American Library, 1966), p. 307.
5. Donald Young, *American Roulette: The History and Dilemma of the Vice Presidency* (New York: Holt, Rinehart & Winston, 1972), pp. 353–54.
6. Hubert H. Humphrey, "A Conversation with Hubert H. Humphrey," National Educational Television, April 1965.
7. Paul T. David, "The Vice-Presidency: Its Institutional Evolution and Contemporary Status," *Journal of Politics,* November 1967, p. 733.
8. James F. Byrnes, *All in One Lifetime* (New York: Harper & Brothers, 1958), p. 233.
9. Joseph E. Kallenbach, *The American Chief Executive* (New York: Harper & Row, 1966), pp. 234–35.
10. John Morton Blum, ed., *The Price of Vision: The Diary of Henry A. Wallace 1942–1946* (Boston: Houghton Mifflin, 1973), p. 25.
11. Milton Eisenhower, *The President Is Calling* (New York: Doubleday, 1974), pp. 540–41.

12. Michael Novak, *Choosing Our King* (New York: Macmillan, 1974), pp. 263–64.
13. James MacGregor Burns, *The Lion and the Fox* (New York: Harcourt, Brace, 1956), p. 414.
14. Sam Houston Johnson, *My Brother Lyndon* (New York: Cowles, 1970), p. 109.
15. Arthur M. Schlesinger, Jr., "Is the Vice-Presidency Necessary?," *Atlantic,* May 1974, p. 37.
16. Alan L. Otten, "Sorting Out a Role for the Veep," *Wall Street Journal,* 17 August 1972, p. 10.
17. Hubert H. Humphrey, "A Conversation with Hubert H. Humphrey," National Educational Television, April 1965.
18. Gerald Ford, quoted in *Newsweek* June 28, 1980, p. 25.
19. Gerald R. Ford, *A Time To Heal* (New York: Harper & Row/Reader's Digest, 1979), p. 327.
20. *Ibid.,* p. 328.
21. Walter F. Mondale, quoted in *National Journal,* December 1, 1979, p. 2016.
22. Quoted in *National Journal* March 11, 1978, p. 379.
23. President Jimmy Carter, News Conference, *The New York Times,* September 30, 1977, p. A. 18.
24. Walter F. Mondale, lecture on "The American Vice-Presidency" at The University of Minnesota, February 18, 1981, mimeo, p. 3.
25. Walter F. Mondale, interview, *National Journal,* December 1, 1979, p. 2016.
26. James Reston, "Fritz Mondale's Blitz" *The New York Times,* November 2, 1979, p. A.31.
27. See Mondale interview, *Politics Today* (March/April, 1980), p. 48.
28. Adapted and condensed from Walter F. Mondale, speech on "The American Vice-Presidency" University of Minnesota, February 18, 1981, mimeo, p. 7.
29. Dick Kirschten, "George Bush — Keeping His Profile Low So He Can Keep His Influence High" *National Journal,* June 20, 1981, p. 1096.
30. See *Official Report of the Vice Presidential Selection Commission of the Democratic Party* (December 19, 1974), mimeo. See also "Hearings of the Vice-Presidential Selection Commission of the Democratic National Committee" *Congressional Record* October 16, 1973, S19245 ff.; and Allan P. Sindler, *Unchosen Presidents* (Berkeley, Ca.: University of California Press, 1976).
31. Arthur M. Schlesinger, Jr., *The Imperial Presidency* (New York: Popular Library, 1974), p. 481.
32. *Ibid.,* p. 493.
33. Report of the Study Group on Vice-Presidential Selection, Institute of Politics, Kennedy School of Government, Harvard University, June 14, 1976, monograph, p. 7. This report contains several of the proposals summarized here.
34. *Ibid.*
35. John D. Feerick, "The Proposed Twenty-Fifth Amendment to the Constitution" *Fordham Law Review* (December, 1965), p. 197. See also Feerick's *The Twenty-Fifth Amendment* (Bronx, N.Y.: Fordham University Press, 1976).
36. J. W. Peltason, *Understanding the Constitution,* 8th edition (New York: Holt, Rinehart and Winston, 1979), pp. 232–233.

# Presidents as Policymakers

# IX

**24. Presidents as Domestic Policymakers**
*Paul C. Light*

**25. Presidents as Budget Policymakers**
*Donald H. Haider*

**26. Presidents as National Security Policymakers**
*James K. Oliver*

# 24. Presidents as Domestic Policymakers

## Paul C. Light

The president's agenda is a remarkable list. It is rarely written down. It constantly shifts and evolves. It is often in flux even for the president and his top staff. Moreover, because of its status in the policy process, the president's agenda is the subject of intense conflict. Sometimes the conflict is resolved through mutual consent or collegial bargaining; sometimes through political struggle and domination. It is not surprising that we know so little about it.

We do know that all presidents make choices. Some are major — from the selection of cabinet members to strategic decisions during crises. Some are minor — from White House tennis court scheduling to dinner invitations. All presidents face both the routine and the extraordinary. We also know that the most important decisions of any administration involve the choice of issues and alternatives for the political debate. Under intense pressure to limit the span of national attention, the White House is often forced to choose between competing items for the president's agenda; to restrict the scope of presidential concern. These are the decisions which set the tone and direction of national policy making for the term of office — and beyond.

If we are to understand these choices, we must understand how presidents come to recognize certain issues as potential agenda topics; why some issues are accepted for the president's program and others discarded or delayed; how issues are linked with alternatives; how presidents eventually rank their priorities. In presidential agenda-setting, many are called, but few are chosen. It becomes our task to discover how the few emerge.

In the following pages, we will concentrate on just three of these questions: (1) When is the president's agenda set? (2) How are the agenda issues selected? (3) How are the agenda alternatives drafted? In answering these questions, we will restrict the focus to the domestic agenda. This distinction reflects real world differences in the presidential policy process. Foreign and domestic policy staffs operate in separate environments; paper loops move through different departments and agencies; information contacts are separate, calendars are incompatible, and Congress is somewhat more willing to grant presidential discretion in foreign policy. Though the distinction between foreign and domestic policy is increasingly blurred, we will remain primarily in the domestic arena. Moreover, though presidents often prefer to spend their time in foreign

*Paul C. Light teaches political science at the University of Virginia, is the author of* The President's Agenda: Domestic Policy Choice from Kennedy to Carter, *and is completing a study of the vice-presidency.*

policy, they still commit the bulk of their political capital to domestic affairs.

The following discussion will also focus only on our five most recent presidents: Kennedy, Johnson, Nixon, Ford, and Carter, with notes on the domestic agenda under Reagan. The research covers a twenty-year time span; not long by historical standards, but lengthy for presidential studies. Most of the analysis is based on interviews with 126 staff members in the administrations from Kennedy through Carter. In selecting respondents from each of the five administrations, particular attention was given to several key groups in the Executive Office of the President: (1) the Congressional Liaison Office, (2) the domestic policy staffs, (3) the Bureau of the Budget/Office of Management and Budget, (4) the economic policy staffs, and (5) the president's personal staff — legal counsels, speech-writers, press assistants, public liaison aides, and the inner circle of top White House staff members.

## Defining the President's Agenda

Just what is the president's agenda? Technically, every legislative or administrative proposal originating in the executive branch belongs to the president. The number of items is staggering. The legislative clearance process, located in the Office of Management and Budget, is designed to review all proposals and reports leaving the executive branch en route to Congress. According to one OMB official, by 1982 an estimated 25,000 items will move through the clearance process every two years — with roughly half surviving OMB scrutiny. In 1977 alone, OMB approved 2,360 congressional requests for information, 4,242 agency reports to Congress, and 552 draft bills. Is this the president's agenda? It includes far too many items which cannot be classified as presidential.

Within the tangle of executive branch proposals, there is a second group of requests that are in accord with the president's political commitments. As OMB completes a review of a specific bill, the draft is labeled "i/a" or "in accordance" with the President's program, "c/w" or "consistent with" the program, or "n/o" or no objection to the draft. Still other items are rejected outright. Though the original purpose of the clearance system was to give Congress guidance on the mass of executive branch proposals, OMB only screens formal proposals — there is no record of presidential phone calls or informal conversations. Johnson's famous poolside meetings with congressional leaders were never recorded. Nor is there any evaluation of the countless informal requests which originate in the bureaucracy. Do the "i/a" draft bills constitute the president's agenda? Again, the list is too extensive.

Only a small percentage of the items given "i/a" status are presidential requests — most never pass through the White House; few are ever recognized as presidential priorities. The White House simply cannot catalogue all the proposals moving through the clearance process, let alone the myriad requests for administrative action. Indeed, that is precisely why the OMB clearance process was originally created. Thus, within the set of items "in accordance" with the president's program, there is a final set of items that are presidential priorities. These are the president's personal programs — the ideas that are discussed and refined in the Oval Office. This agenda contains the items that belong to the president and receive maximum White House support. This definition of the president's agenda is quite restrictive — it includes only a small number of programs. Yet it is a definition built from staff perceptions. Several aides argued that only two or three programs ever occupy the president's agenda at any single moment. A Kennedy assistant argued that "Federal Aid to Education and Medicare were so dramatic compared to Kennedy's other requests. Those two programs have to be considered separately from unemployment, agriculture, or the tax reforms. Those two programs had such long-term impact that they were considered essential to the President's place in history." A Reagan aide echoed the argument: "I'd say we have two basic programs that we want for the first two years: the budget cuts and the tax plan. Everything else is secondary. If we don't win the economic plan, the term will be pretty damn unpleasant."

For the sake of simplicity, we can define the president's agenda as all requests that are cleared "i/a" by the Office of Management and Budget *and* mentioned in at least one of the president's State of the Union messages. Though this definition places a premium on legislative priorities; it is a useful method for measuring the president's agenda across time. When coupled with the staff interviews, we may be able to discover just how the few emerge.

One final distinction must be made. Every agenda item has at least three distinct components. Each item (1) addresses an issue, (2) involves a specific alternative, and (3) has some priority in the domestic queue. Issues are the first component of any presidential agenda request and involve the definition of the problems. Here, presidents ask *which problems merit national attention*. The president and his staff recognize some political or social need which suggests a federal response. Thus, inflation, declining productivity, and overregulation were all issues on the Reagan agenda in 1981 — they reflected Reagan's perception of the most important problems. Alternatives are the second agenda component and center on the specific programs that will address the issues. Here, presidents ask *how the problems will be solved*. In the policy process, alternatives generally take the form of detailed draft bills. If inflation is an issue, then spending cuts may be one alternative; if productivity is a problem, tax cuts may be one alternative.

## Presidents and Resources

Resources have always occupied a prominent position in the presidential literature. Scholars have talked about personal resources — the sense of power, self-confidence, bargaining skills. They have talked about political resources — public approval, Washington reputation, congressional support. They have talked about institutional resources — the White House staff, legislative liaison, vantage points. However, we have often blurred the distinction between resources and the formal prerogatives of the office — resources are dynamic, ever-changing; formal prerogatives are relatively stable. As one OMB official remarked, "You ought to think of the presidency as an engine. Each president enters office facing the same model — the horsepower is generally stable and the gears are all there. What differs is the *fuel*. Different presidents enter with different fuel."

If presidential scholars agree that resources are important, they rarely agree on the basic formula for the fuel. Some believe that personality is the most important resource; others continue to confuse prerogatives with power. Neustadt (1960) argues that professional reputation and public approval are critical; Sperlich (1975) suggests that command has been underrated. Which formula is correct? According to the 126 staff members interviewed for this research, there are at least two packets of resources which shape the domestic agenda. One involves internal resources; the other external resources. The first centers on internal, problem-solving resources: time, information, expertise, and energy. Time is simply the duration of the president's term: how long does the president have to set the domestic agenda? Information involves the amount of knowledge available for choices between issues and alternatives: how much does the president know about the problems and programs under consideration? Expertise centers on the administration's political and technical skills: How effective is the president in guiding the policy process? Energy focuses on the sheer amount of physical and intellectual stamina available for the domestic agenda: How much energy can the president expend in the day-to-day conduct of business?

The second packet of resources involves external political support, what many respondents called "presidential capital." According to the staffs, the president's political capital rests on several sources: party support in Congress, public approval, electoral margin, and professional reputation. For the staffs, capital was simply a word which captured their view of the policy process. The president starts the term with a fixed amount of capital and spends it with each decision he makes.

Capital must be distinguished from the problem-solving resources of time, information, expertise, and energy. Capital reflects the president's political strength and is generally committed in Congress, while internal resources are used to reduce the president's decision-making costs. Though time, information, expertise, and energy have an impact in Congress — e.g., the president has to have a certain amount of time to make legislative compromises — they are usually expended within the White House. This is not to argue that internal resources are unimportant. Rather, according to the White House staffs, the president's legislative success on Capitol Hill is only marginally related to internal resources. As one Johnson aide remarked,

> We saw time as something we had to have to make the decisions. If we didn't have the time, we couldn't bring the staff together to make the choices. If we

didn't have the time, we couldn't get the hearings scheduled or the liaison effort on track.

We saw congressional support in an entirely different light. If we didn't have some basic support, it didn't matter how much time we had. We could have a twenty-year term and it wouldn't make a tinker's damn. Congress was the basic force in our success — time was important only in as much as it gave us the opportunity to get the compromises nailed down. Beginning takes time, but time does not give the president the power to win bargains.

Resources have retained their meaning in the Reagan administration. The Reagan staff has been quick to note the president's effort to limit his agenda to a few carefully selected issues. "We don't want to waste any of our energy on minor issues," one Reagan aide said in early February, 1981. "We won't be using the shotgun approach like Carter did. We want to conserve as much as possible for the economic program." As with administrations before it, the Reagan White House understands the value of scarce internal and external resources. It also seems to recognize the importance of allocating its resources across a small number of priorities.

The impact of resources on the domestic agenda can best be described as a function of *policy cycles*. Certain resources decline over the term, while others increase. "The more we seemed to learn about the domestic system," one Nixon aide complained, "the less we could do. We had our best shot at the start of the term, but didn't have the organization to cash in. By the time we had the organization, the opportunity was closed." Looking at both internal and external resources, two basic cycles of domestic choice emerge.

The first pattern might be called the *cycle of decreasing influence*. Presidents can expect a steady drop in their political capital, time, and energy, with a slight rebound at the end of each term. There is little doubt that presidential influence ebbs over the term. There is usually a midterm loss in congressional party seats and a month-by-month erosion in public approval, both leading to reduced influence in shaping the domestic agenda. The midterm loss has been an uninterrupted pattern since 1934, while the near-linear drop in public approval has plagued the past five presidents. Though Reagan hopes to reverse his party's fortunes in the 1982 midterm elections, his public approval has already slipped. Despite a brief surge in approval following the March, 1981, assassination attempt, Reagan's approval dropped well below its early peak. Moreover, Reagan staff members openly predicted a public backlash as deep social spending cuts angered past supporters. Reagan is not immune to the same cycle of decreasing influence that affected his presidential predecessors. As one Ford aide argued in 1979, "each decision is bound to hurt somebody; each appointment is going to cut into support. There's really no way that the president can win. If he doesn't make choices, he will be attacked for being indecisive. If he does, he will satisfy one group, but anger three others."

Time and energy also contribute to the cycle of decreasing influence. As the term winds down, the president simply does not have enough time to pursue major initiatives. Attention turns away from the domestic agenda and toward the coming election. In the first term, presidents must choose between the campaign and the agenda. In 1979, for instance, Carter became the first president to announce his reelection effort in the third year of office. As both terms come to a close, energy also touches bottom. There is less energy and creative stamina to draft new programs.

The second pattern of change in resources might be called the *cycle of increasing effectiveness*. Presidents can be expected to learn over time — the presidential information base should grow, while the president's expertise should increase. As the president and staff become more familiar with the working of the office, there will be an inevitable learning curve. Staffs will identify useful and trusted sources of information and will develop more effective decision loops. Further, prolonged contact with specific policy issues will produce both specialization and knowledge. Regardless of where each administration starts, all administrations learn; it always leaves office more qualified to govern than when it entered.

## The Timing of Domestic Choice

Timing is often taken as a critical tool of presidential leadership. The decision to announce a major program at just the right moment is believed to have a major impact on passage. Moving the most controversial legislation early in the term is sometimes viewed as the best method to take advantage of the cycle of decreasing influence. Presidents are expected to recognize the moment of greatest impact; to hold the agenda like a poker hand, revealing the cards at the exact moment of maximum effect. As Lyndon Johnson once noted,

> Congress is like a dangerous animal that you're trying to make work for you. You push a little bit and he may go just as you want but you push him too much and he may balk and turn on you. You've got to sense just how much he'll take and what kind of mood he's in every day. For if you don't have a feel for him, he's liable to turn around and go wild. And it all depends on your sense of timing (Kearns, 1976, p. 238).

The following analysis of presidential timing will concentrate on two basic questions. First, when are the agenda decisions made on a year-by-year basis? Is there substantial variation which would reflect a sense of timing? Second, when are agenda decisions made within the given years? If most activity falls in the first year of office, do presidents move early in the year or late? Again, is there evidence of a sense of timing?

According to Neustadt, there is a "certain rhythm in the modern presidency." The first year in office is a "learning time for the new president who has to learn — or unlearn — many things about his job." This "intensive learning time comes at the start and dominates the first two years." If the president is to make a mark in the first term, Neustadt tells us it must be in the third year — for in the fourth, the president must turn to reelection. If the president captures a second term, the fifth and sixth year hold the key to success (1960, pp. 198–199). Yet, for the staff members interviewed for this study, if the first two years of the term are for learning, they are also the most important years for agenda-setting. The bulk of agenda choice is made in Neustadt's learning time. Where Neustadt argues that the first year must be for learning, the White House staffs said that it must be for action. Despite the fact that information and expertise are at a general low in the first year of the first term, presidents must still select the dominant domestic themes and directions during that critical period. Those early decisions tend to haunt the president throughout the rest of the term.

The Office of Management and Budget records confirm this theme. Recall that we define the agenda as all legislative requests cleared "i/a" by OMB and mentioned in at least one State of the Union message. Table 1 summarizes the number of repeat requests from the prior year's State of the Union address. The number of repetitions indicates how much of each president's agenda remains from the earlier year.

Table 1 suggests all presidents experience a drop in agenda requests following the first year in office. The number of requests always falls in the second year, while the number of repeats steadily grows. Presidents set their domestic

*Table 1. Requests for Legislation by Year*

| Year | | Total Requests[1] | Total Repeats[2] |
|------|------|------|------|
| 1961 | | 25 | 0 |
| 1962 | Kennedy | 16 | 8 |
| 1963 | | 6 | 12 |
| 1964 | Johnson I | 6 | 11 |
| 1965 | | 34 | 4 |
| 1966 | Johnson II | 24 | 7 |
| 1967 | | 19 | 8 |
| 1968 | | 14 | 12 |
| 1969 | | 17 | 0 |
| 1970 | Nixon I | 12 | 9 |
| 1971 | | 8 | 12 |
| 1972 | | 3 | 14 |
| 1973 | Nixon II | 20 | 3 |
| 1974 | | 5 | 11 |
| 1975 | Ford | 10 | 0 |
| 1976 | | 6 | 7 |
| 1977 | | 21 | 0 |
| 1978 | | 8 | 3 |
| 1979 | Carter | 8 | 5 |
| 1980 | | 4 | 7 |

[1] OMB Legislative Reference Division clearance record, hereafter referred to as OMB data.
[2] Number of repeats from previous year's State of the Union address.

agendas early and repeat them often. Yet presidents also vary in the rate of decline in their agenda activity. Nixon had the greatest drop of the five presidents, falling from twenty requests in 1973 to six in 1974, while Johnson sustained his level of agenda activity the longest. Though most presidents' activity declines at roughly the same rate, Nixon's dramatic slip was tied to the Watergate crisis. As the crisis expanded, Nixon's agenda contracted.

Why is the first year so important for the president's agenda? The answer rests on the cycle of decreasing influence. Presidents and staffs are painfully aware that their most valuable resources dwindle over the term. They understand that capital evaporates over time. Though information and expertise are rarely at a peak in the first year, presidents and their staffs are not inclined to call themselves either inept or stupid. Capital is perceived as the essential resource and must be committed early — to wait is to squander scarce momentum. Moreover, major initiatives take more time. As a Kennedy aide remembered, "It just makes sense to move as fast as humanly possible. A major program like Medicare takes a good year just to pass through Congress. It will take at least two to implement. By that time, you'll want to make some changes — increase the funding, rewrite some regulations. That may take another two years. If you don't get going early, you'll be out of office before you get the programs set." Ultimately, first-year pressure is the result of competition for scarce agenda space. The president is only one actor among many. As Carter quickly discovered, there is considerable competition for scarce congressional agenda openings. There is also competition for media attention and public recognition. If the president is to compete for the scarce space, it is to his advantage to move early — even if the programs are not perfect. As one Reagan assistant argued in 1981, "the budget cuts had certain flaws and we knew we'd have to go back for more later. However, we felt that Congress and the public were getting restless and needed to have something quick. The budget process is not geared to fast action. The only way to get Congress to act on our proposals was to get them to work fast. Even with the problems, we felt Congress needed something as soon as possible."

*The First Months*

If presidents are encouraged to act within that first year, they are also well advised to move as early as possible within that year. January is far more valuable to the president than the following December. However, presidents vary greatly in their ability to set the agenda early. Looking at the precise dates when presidents announce their agenda requests, we can measure the relative speed of each administration. Kennedy and Johnson emerge as far more successful in moving their programs than either Nixon or Carter. Where the bulk of the Kennedy and Johnson first-year programs moved in January, February, or March, the Nixon and Carter agendas were delayed until summer. When Kennedy is compared to Nixon and Carter, the disparity is dramatic. All three presidents entered office following close elections; all three succeeded a president of the opposition party. Yet, 71 percent of the Kennedy agenda was in Congress by the end of March, 1961, while only 11 percent of Nixon's 1969 agenda was ready by the same time, with Carter at 38 percent in 1977.

Is it important that Nixon was six months later in 1969 than Johnson in 1965 — that Nixon's revenue sharing came in August instead of March? Once again, we can return to resources. Presidents can always expect at least a limited honeymoon. The honeymoon usually lasts four to six months and wears off by early summer. In Reagan's first year, for instance, House Speaker Tip O'Neill announced that the honeymoon was over on June 23. Though public approval may remain stable over the first months, it begins to drop as decisions are made. Even if the administration fails to offer a single program, capital declines. If a program is offered in January, it will be considered under the most favorable circumstances. Presidents gain no advantage by waiting. By delaying until summer, the programs will enter Congress just as the president begins to slide. Presidents and their staffs recognize that fact, but have differing success in meeting the goal. As one Carter aide remarked, "We knew we were losing time, but no matter how hard some of us pushed, it was impossible to get action. Welfare reform got gummed up in the works and even a presidential deadline couldn't get it out."

The need for speed is no less important for Reagan, particularly in dealing with the economy. According to David Stockman, Reagan's Budget Director, early action is essential in avoiding a "GOP Economic Dunkirk":

> Things could go very badly during the first year, resulting in incalculable erosion of GOP momentum, unity and public confidence. If bold policies are not swiftly, deftly and courageously implemented in the first six months, Washington will quickly become engulfed in political disorder commensurate with the surrounding economic disarray. A golden opportunity for permanent conservative policy revision and political realignment could be thoroughly dissipated before the Reagan administration is even up to speed (in *The Washington Post,* 14 December 1980, p. C5).

Stockman was eventually able to complete a budget review in record time, finishing a set of revisions that normally take a year in less than six weeks.

With recent changes in the political environment, neither Congress nor the public is willing to wait for the president's agenda. Individual members have pet projects and constituent demands. The ability of the president to influence the congressional calendar depends on his ability to move quickly. There is no shortage of competing ideas on Capitol Hill. All administrations were aware of this fact. Yet, why was Carter still so late? Why were Kennedy and Johnson so fast? Two answers arise from the interviews.

*Expertise*
One important explanation for differences in speed rests on the president's expertise. Both Kennedy and Johnson were well prepared when they entered office.

Both had considerable contact with the legislative process before assuming office; both understood the need for speed in announcing the domestic agenda. According to the two White House staffs, both Kennedy and Johnson put heavy pressure on the domestic process in the first months. Despite the usual exhaustion following a campaign, Kennedy pressed his staff to devote full time and energy to the domestic agenda during the transition. Johnson, however, faced a different situation in 1965. He did not enter his transition as a novice — he had been president for a year and already had a full legislative agenda. There was less confusion and uncertainty.

Unlike Kennedy or Johnson, Nixon and Carter were not as prepared for the rigors of the presidential transition. Though Nixon appointed a number of post-election task forces, he was not particularly interested in the domestic agenda. He preferred to concentrate his energies on foreign policy. Part of the problem in delays rested on the complexity of the domestic issues — welfare reform, for instance, was a very detailed problem and demanded considerable time. Part of the problem rested on the absence of an interested hand in the Oval Office. For Carter, despite the reputation for planning, the actual record suggests several major problems. Carter's transition was marked by intense conflict between Jack Watson, head of the transition policy team, and Hamilton Jordan, Carter's chief political adviser. During the campaign, Jordan's staff complained that energy was being diverted from the election by Watson's staff; Watson's staff replied that not enough attention was being paid to the post-election needs of a new administration. The arguments reflected a struggle for power between the two advisers. The conflict had its most damaging effect early in the transition. The Carter transition was also complicated by the relative lack of experience among the staff. Most had never worked in Washington; few understood the policy process.

*Available Alternatives*
A second, more powerful explanation for differences in speed rests on the availability of program alternatives. Though presidential programs can range from the simple to the complex, most requests involve considerable detail. The development of presidential programs simply takes time. The degree to which these programs are available upon inauguration influences the speed with which they can be presented. In Carter's case, most of the top programs involved considerable delay at the drafting stage. In Kennedy's first year, however, the agenda was ready to move quickly. Aid to Education, Area Redevelopment, the Youth Conservation Corps, Medicare, Wilderness Preservation, and the civil rights program had all been refined by the Democratic party during the Eisenhower years. Once Kennedy was elected, all that remained were minor changes. That was not the case for Nixon — he could not rely on a ready-made program. Though Nixon assumed office after eight years of Democratic control, the Republican party had not been as active in developing an agenda as the Democrats of a decade before. As the minority party in Congress, Republicans had been

more concerned with resisting the Great Society than with drafting a new agenda.

What about Carter in 1977? After all, Carter entered office following eight years of Republican control. Had Congress been less active in generating programs? One problem rested on Carter's recruitment — he did not come from the Democratic mainstream. As one aide suggested, "We just didn't know what was on the stove." Carter had not been involved in the long struggle for national health insurance, nor had he been present for the battles over Ford's frequent vetoes. Carter was an "outsider," and his inexperience with federal policy created problems in office.

### The Sense of Timing

Does the sense of timing exist? Perhaps only inasmuch as presidents respond to the pressure to move quickly. Presidents still worry about the precise timing of legislative requests — most staffs still believe in Lyndon Johnson's view of the policy process:

> A measure must be sent to the Hill at exactly the right moment and the moment depends on three things: first, on the momentum; second, on the availability of sponsors in the right place at the right time; and, third, on the opportunities for neutralizing the opposition. Timing is essential. Momentum is not a mysterious mistress. It is a controllable fact of political life that depends on nothing more exotic than preparation (Kearns 1976, pp. 236–238).

Yet even Johnson recognized the importance of the first months. Though the president could manipulate the timing of legislation in weeks and days, the first year held the secret of legislation impact. Johnson subscribed to the ideal of "maximum attention in minimum time." As Johnson also argued, "I keep hitting hard because I know this honeymoon won't last. Every day I lose a little more political capital. That's why we have to keep at it, never letting up. One day soon, I don't know when, the critics and the snipers will move in and we will be at stalemate. We have to get all we can, now, before the roof comes down." (In Valenti, 1975, p. 144) Though Johnson varied the timing of several important bills in 1965, he was keenly aware of the need to get *all* the bills to Congress before the end of the year. Johnson understood the cycle of decreasing influence and therein lay his sense of timing.

## Selecting the Issues

The president's domestic agenda is not the result of some hidden hand or invisible force. All presidential decisions are purposive. Presidents select issues on the basis of their goals. Whether because of a desire for reelection, historical achievement, or good policy, presidents select domestic issues in a purposive, goal-directed manner. Though the political environment may elevate certain issues, presidents are not controlled by a hidden hand. Though the president must present an annual State of the Union message, he is not required to propose any new legislation; though the president must present an annual budget, he is not required either to cut or expand programs. Rather, presidents choose to act; presidents concentrate on the selected issues because those issues match their personal and political goals — not because of statutory responsibilities. In an extreme sense, nothing forces a president to act on any issue if a president does not want to act.

Thus, if presidents are motivated by power, it is important to ask "power for what?" It is also essential to distinguish between the president's activities (e.g., bargaining) and the president's goals (e.g., reelection). In the following pages, we will look at three main goals which motivate the presidential search for domestic issues: (1) reelection, (2) historical achievement, and (3) good policy. As presidents choose among competing domestic issues, they allocate their resources on the basis of these three goals.

## Reelection

First-term presidents are interested in reelection, a behavior learned in the very first campaign — whether for president, governor, or mayor. According to one Ford assistant, "Some candidates will say they aren't interested in campaign politics. Don't believe it. Every candidate for office wants it. That's why they are willing to give up their freedom and their private lives." How does reelection affect the domestic agenda? Primarily because presidents and staffs believe that specific issues determine public support. Whether that view is rational or not, presidents are convinced of the impact of issues on electoral success.

The calculation of electoral benefits rests on presidential perceptions: presidents seem to subscribe to a "critical promise" theory. According to this theory, issues are essential in building and maintaining the electoral coalition. As candidates draft the campaign platform, these perceptions influence choices. As presidents draft the domestic agenda, impressions of what worked in the campaign return to influence choices again. The notion that one or two promises held the key to election is remarkably prevalent in the White House policy process.

Despite the importance of reelection in the first term, we would expect the goal to dissipate in the second four years. Theoretically, the search for electoral rewards should decline under the two-term limitation. However, presidents may continue to court the public simply because it is what they were trained to do. Since only one of the five most recent administrations survived to a second term, and since that administration fell after a year, there is little recent data to draw on. Interviews with Eisenhower aides suggest that the pressure on reelection predictably fades in the second and final term. According to one Eisenhower assistant:

> We felt a definite freedom from pressure after 1956; a freedom to take a little
> more time and a freedom to take on the high rollers. The speech on the military-

industrial complex was one example. You can do things in a second term that you could never attempt in the first. I like to think we were a bit more courageous.

## Historical Achievement

Presidents are usually interested in historical achievement. They are aware of the historical rankings of past presidents and are definitely interested in the paths to "greatness." As one Nixon aide argued, "The President spent a great deal of time wondering how his decisions would fare in twenty or thirty years. That was the original intent behind the tape system. He wanted a detailed record so he could write his memoirs with the utmost historical accuracy." Just as presidents measure potential policies against electoral reaction, they also consider the judgment of history. It is a powerful influence on their choice of issues.

History is important for several reasons. First, it is a tradition of the office. It is difficult not to be preoccupied with history when a president works behind a desk once used by Thomas Jefferson. Each corridor in the White House contains subtle reminders of a president's potential place in history; each portrait hanging in the halls suggests the impact of historical judgment. Second, the Washington community openly encourages the historical orientation. Comparisons between one president and another are common in the press. Where does Johnson stand with Kennedy? Where does Reagan stand with Carter? The Washington community often draws historical comparisons between presidents — comparisons that are not lost on the White House.

Historical achievement is easily the most abstract of the three policy goals. Unlike reelection, which is realized in actual ballots, or good policy, which is reflected in the programs themselves, historical benefits must await the passage of time. The president must be willing to wait for the eventual judgments. However, that does not seem to reduce the value of history to the president and his staff. In the heat of day-to-day politics, a sense of history can provide an attractive source of support.

## Good Policy

All presidents enter office with personal beliefs. Whether the president simply wishes to defend the status quo against further encroachment or wants to propose sweeping expansion of federal programs, all presidents have policy commitments. A president can be expected to support certain issues just because they match his personal belief system. According to an OMB careerist, "Not everything in the Executive Office can be explained by electoral pressure. There are some issues that emerge just because the president believes them to be right. Presidents are often willing to go out on a limb for those kinds of issues." A Johnson aide agreed: "There comes a time in any administration when the president must say to hell with Congress, when the president has to proceed because he is right. Even if Congress tears his program to bits, it is important to do what the president believes to be correct." Moreover, no president enters office to create bad programs; presidents generally want to succeed. Though there are inevitable errors, presidents do search for issues that fit their views of the way the world should look. In the search, presidents start with very real hopes for good policy. Unfortunately, as presidents develop the programs to match the issues, they are subject to an entirely different set of constraints. As presidents search for issues, they can afford to be idealistic; once they begin drafting specific programs, they become sensitive to the "politics of the possible."

### Goal Conflict

Thus far, we have ignored the potential for conflict among the three goals. Yet, is the goal of reelection compatible with the goals of historical achievement and good policy? Programs that benefit reelection may hinder historical achievement — presidents may be labeled as overambitious or shortsighted. Programs that answer the goal of good policy may undermine reelection — calls for national sacrifice may fall on deaf ears. All presidents face some degree of goal conflict during the term. However, there has been a basic change in the pool of potential domestic issues over the past decade, a change that has heightened goal conflict for contemporary presidents. During the 1960s, most domestic issues satisfied multiple goals — Johnson's poverty program answered his drive for reelection as well as good policy. For Kennedy and Johnson, there was potential linkage between competing goals; one program could provide more than one benefit. As we enter the 1980s, however, the bulk of the domestic issues involve at least some element of goal conflict. Energy, welfare reform, budget cuts, social security financing, hospital cost control, even deregulation are examples of the rise of what might be called "constituentless" issues: issues without natural political support. The rise of a new generation of policy problems has profound effects on the domestic policy process. Thus, at Reagan's first cabinet meeting during the transition, he told his newly appointed advisers *not* to consider the political impact of the agenda issues. Symbolic or not, Reagan's admonition indicates just how serious the goal conflict has become for the national agenda. As one Reagan aide argued, "No one would have thought to make such a statement ten years ago. Politics and policy were naturally linked. Now, the political situation is so screwed up that you either consider politics or you look at what the nation needs. That's a hell of a change from the '60s."

## Selecting the Alternatives

The search for agenda alternatives generally begins with decisions on basic directions. Presidents must set initial guidelines along political and philosophical lines. Presidents do not search for program alternatives in a "blind" process. They look for alternatives that fit their perceptions of the original issues. Ronald Reagan was no more willing to approve vast expansions of the federal role than Lyndon Johnson was to rescind the New Deal. Once alternatives are found, presidents make final choices on the basis of policy costs — whether political, economic, or technical. However, at the start of the search process, presidents must decide how the search will proceed. In this sense, alternatives are the product of what Cyert and March (1963) call "problemistic search." The search for domestic alternatives reflects the effort to solve a perceived problem and is biased by presidential goals. Moreover, as we shall see shortly, the search usually stops with the first available alternative.

Given each president's initial resources, the choice among different alternatives often involves a theory of *legislative expense.* The basic assumption here is that each presidential program has a specific "cost" and that some programs are more "expensive" than others. Legislation is more expensive than vetoes — passing a bill requires a majority vote, while sustaining a veto requires only a third plus one in either house. Large-scale programs demand more capital than small-scale programs; new programs demand more capital than simple modifications of old programs; and, with recent increases in fiscal pressure, spending programs clearly are more "expensive" than non-spending programs. The kinds of alternatives each president can afford thereby depends on available resources. Johnson could "afford" very different kinds of programs from Nixon and Ford.

Thus, as presidents search for specific alternatives to match the domestic issues, the main criteria rest on costs. The emphasis on costs may exist from the beginning of the search. In 1977, for instance, Carter asked for a welfare reform plan with zero additional cost to the federal budget. Yet, whether the discussion starts early or late, costs are the central presidential tool for choosing among policy alternatives. According to the presidential staffs interviewed for this study, there are three basic costs which act to screen policy alternatives: political, economic, and technical.

Presidents evaluate political costs at virtually every step in the policy process. They evaluate the potential for congressional enactment and the impact of public opinion. Throughout, the central question is "will the program fly?" Congress is the most important factor in the answer. Depending on the party composition in Congress, the "price" of specific alternatives can vary greatly. In Reagan's first year, for example, the price of budget cuts in the Senate was significantly lower than the price in the House.

With the increased budget pressure of the 1970s, economic costs have emerged as a powerful influence over the domestic agenda. Here, the question is simply, "How much will it cost?" For the Ford, Carter, and Reagan administrations, economic costs became the first question asked in the search for policy alternatives. Indeed, under Reagan the first question may well be, "How much can we save?" If economic costs have grown in importance over the past decade, a major explanation rests on the increased budgetary conflict. Part of the conflict stems from the White House's perception of economic reality. Ford, Carter, and Reagan each believed that inflation was a number one economic problem; each also believed that the federal budget was to blame. Though the concern for economic costs reflects real world pressure, the emphasis also involves presidential perceptions. Nixon, Ford, Carter, and Reagan all subscribed to a tight budget as one solution to the inflation problem. However, as one Carter economic adviser remarked, "There is very little difference between a budget deficit of $30 billion and $20 billion. The actual amounts have very little effect. It is the impression that seems to make the impact." A second Carter aide agreed: "Containing the deficit is an important goal, but the image is critical. If the president had introduced a massive health plan, it would have opened the floodgates of backlogged (spending) legislation."

Beyond political and economic costs, presidents have an interest in technical costs. The impact of technical costs is best expressed by the question, "Will the program work?" Unfortunately, this is often the last question asked and is sometimes ignored completely. The question of workability is generally left to the departments or lower-level White House staff. Because of limits on internal resources — time, information, expertise, and energy — presidents have little opportunity to investigate workability. Instead, the policy process often blindly assumes that the alternatives will work. Even when the resources are available, the incentives to check workability rarely exist. Program effectiveness is simply not a particularly important political variable. Moreover, even if both resources and incentives were available, could the staffs answer the original question of workability? Given the political nature of presidential priorities, it is difficult to estimate just what the program objectives are.

### The Available Alternative

The absence of technical expertise and other internal resources elevates the importance of the available alternative. Presidents have neither the incentives nor the resources to develop truly new alternatives. In general, the presidential search for alternatives stops with the first available program. There is little reward for going further. As one Carter assistant argued, "Once you begin your search, you will run into agencies that already have specific programs already drafted. They have the figures and the sample bills; they may even have sponsors in Congress. It's hard to ignore them. They can save you a lot of time."

At least in domestic policy, available alternatives have three basic advantages in the agenda process: First, the available alternatives arrive earlier than the competition. Recall that presidents react to the cycle of decreasing influence. With the pressure to move the agenda quickly, the White House often adopts a "first come, first served" approach. According to a Johnson assistant, "The first ideas have the greatest chance of adoption. Think of the domestic agenda as a grain hopper. What goes in first will come out first." Second, the available alternatives generate greater bureaucratic support — a significant advantage on Capitol Hill. Departments and agencies often develop programs that resurface over time. These programs are carefully drafted and well-documented — they may reflect years of bureaucratic compromise. Once these bills move to Congress, they have a greater chance of passage. Third, regardless of whether the available alternative is eventually accepted, it tends to frame the debate. The presidential policy process has a habit of focusing on a single alternative as the basis of discussion. The end result of reliance on available alternatives is the neglect of potential innovation. The development of innovative alternatives usually takes much more time.

## The First Question

In structuring the search for alternatives, presidents assign different weights to political, economic, and technical costs. The first questions asked of alternatives act as evaluative screens through which all potential programs must pass. When the presidential staffs were asked to describe the first questions in the domestic policy process, the increased impact of economic costs was evident. The responses from the five White House staffs are presented in Table 2.

There is no question that economic costs currently control the search for domestic alternatives. Where both Kennedy and Johnson gave passing reference to economic costs, Nixon, Ford, and Carter turned to economic costs in the vast majority of domestic decisions. The pressure has not declined for Reagan. One result of this increasing competition for scarce federal dollars has been a renewed interest in the federal budget. The Reagan demand for increased defense spending and a three-year across-the-board tax cut leaves the budget as the new battleground for domestic policy.

Much of the pressure on the budget comes from the steady drop in spending flexibility. Over the past two decades, the budget has been increasingly encumbered by "uncontrollable" spending — programs that are generally safe from political attack. Yet, as the available dollars have dropped, the number of potential claimants has risen. There is less money available, but more demand. In the first months of the Reagan administration, the budget was caught in a squeeze between expanded defense spending and supply-side tax cuts. Eventually, Reagan opted for both, leaving domestic policy as the new focus of budgetary conflict.

Perhaps the most disappointing finding in Table 2 is the lack of interest in technical costs. Regardless of administration, workability is not a frequent first concern. According to one Johnson assistant, "There have never been incentives

*Table 2. The First Question*[1]

| President[2] | Economic Costs | Political Costs | Workability |
|---|---|---|---|
| Kennedy | 22% | 68% | 10% |
| Johnson | 26 | 64 | 10 |
| Nixon | 60 | 31 | 9 |
| Ford | 84 | 11 | 5 |
| Carter | 72 | 24 | 5 |

[1] Question: "When the administration looked at potential programs, what do you remember as the first question asked about the specific alternatives? Did you ask about the economic costs? The congressional reaction? Workability?"
[2] Total number of responses equals 90.

for more planning. Congress certainly wouldn't reward us for taking the time to carefully evaluate the programs.... If anything, the community wanted as much as we could give. Johnson was never asked to prove that the programs would work, nor did Congress seem particularly interested." The emphasis is still on moving as quickly as possible. "We all believe there should be more planning," one Carter aide remarked. "The President has stressed the need for more caution. But, when we fall behind, the President will impose a deadline. It is still a political system."

### A No-Win Presidency?

The domestic presidency has changed dramatically over the past two decades. White House staffs complain of increasing constraint and decreasing success. Though the structure of domestic choice remains fairly stable, the relationship between the president and Congress has undergone a revolution. Congress has finished a decade of internal reform; the basic issues that feed the policy gristmill have changed, and there is a new atmosphere of surveillance in Washington. As one Carter aide suggested:

> This has become a "no-win" job. It involves a series of obstacles; one hurdle after another. Each problem is followed by a second, more difficult problem. We simply can't get closure on the issues.... The office of the president has not changed much over the past decade — a new Office of Management and Budget, a new Domestic Council, but not too much else. Maybe not so much in formal terms, but in the way the president interacts with the rest of Washington and the nation.... I simply think that it is more difficult to succeed now than in 1960. Lyndon Johnson would be a very frustrated president.

The growth of this no-win presidency is a 1970s phenomenon. It was kindled by a series of presidential misjudgments — most notably, the Vietnam War and Watergate — and fueled by a string of congressional reactions — most importantly the War Powers Resolution and the Congressional Budget and Impoundment Control Act. Presidents are increasingly caught in a political vise. They are cross-pressured from a number of angles with little opportunity for release. In domestic policy, this no-win presidency involves at least five separate trends. Separately, the trends have created unique problems for each president; together, they have increased the price of presidential success.

First, there has been a rise in the amount of congressional competition for scarce domestic agenda space. Part of the explanation rests on the backlog of legislation left after the Nixon and Ford years — a backlog created by legislative stalemate. An equally large part originates in changes in the congressional environment. Congress has new sources of information, more technical expertise, larger staffs, and increased incentives to draft its own agenda. The president can no longer rely on automatic access to the legislative agenda. Thus, at the height of the budget struggle in 1981, Reagan had to contend with a flood of conservative social legislation ranging from bills on human life to discussions of teenage chastity.

Second, the domestic policy process has continued to fragment, thereby increasing legislative complexity. The rise of subcommittee government in Congress has reinforced White House frustration — legislation must now pass through more stops on the road to enactment. Though there are fewer single obstacles to passage, the number of active participants has spiraled upward. The growth of complexity has limited the president's ability to influence outcomes, while increasing the problems of White House liaison. Lyndon Johnson's personal style of lobbying is not as effective when applied to a subcommittee system.

Third, presidents face a significant drop in their potential influence in Congress. The White House can no longer rely on the president's party to automatically produce the margin of support in either Congress or the electorate. The parties have been drowned out in the nominating process, while losing considerable strength in Congress. Thus, despite Carter's substantial congressional majorities in 1977 — majorities which rivaled Johnson's Great Society margins — he was unable to secure passage of his domestic program. Though Carter's problems involved far more than party politics, the lack of party discipline hampered his efforts to pass his domestic agenda. Party is falling as the "gold standard" of presidential influence.

Fourth, presidents must now operate in an environment of increasing surveillance. The mood of public distrust for the presidency has not abated in the post-Watergate era, nor has Congress relaxed its oversight of presidential decision-making. Presidents are increasingly limited by the use of the legislative veto. Indeed, Reagan faced his first major challenge in foreign policy over potential legislative veto of a sale of AWAC radar planes to Saudi Arabia.

Fifth, and perhaps most important, the domestic issues have changed. As noted earlier, the issues of the 1980s seem to violate the traditional coalitions and jurisdiction. Carter's energy plan and welfare reform failed to fit the familiar political framework. Unlike the issues of the Kennedy and Johnson years, these new issues have few active constituents and no shortage of enemies. The changes in the pool of issues reflect a more pervasive shift in the political environment. The price of domestic policy has increased, while presidential influence has not.

Together, these five trends have steadily raised the cost of presidential success. The increased competition and complexity, the declining party support, the pervasive surveillance, and changing issue pool have created new sources of presidential frustration. Presidents must be more careful about timing, as well as selecting "winnable" issues and alternatives. Presidents no longer have the resources to spend on educating the public, nor do they have the resources to search for new ideas and programs. If anything, presidents have fewer resources.

The cost of presidential policy has grown, while the president's ability to influence outcomes has declined. What remains is a remarkable no-win position with few available solutions.

## Notes
Cyert, R. M., and March, J. G. *A Behavioral Theory of the Firm* (Englewood Cliffs, N.J.: Prentice-Hall, 1963).

Kearns, D. *Lyndon Johnson and the American Dream* (New York: Harper & Row, 1976).

Neustadt, R. E. *Presidential Power: The Politics of Leadership* (New York: John Wiley and Sons, 1960).

Sperlich, P. W. "Bargaining and Overload: An Essay on *Presidential Power.*" In *Perspectives on the Presidency,* edited by A. Wildavsky (Boston: Little, Brown, 1975).

# 25. Presidents as Budget Policymakers

## Donald H. Haider

Americans expect presidents to allocate the nation's resources wisely and prudently. They expect the president's budget to maintain strong national defense, promote economic stability and growth, provide for the citizens that are least well off, and protect the economic and social gains achieved largely through government since the 1930s. The public demands that these things be done without substantially increased tax burdens and within the constraints of a balanced federal budget.

Presidents, in turn, have found these goals to be irreconcilable in any one year or single budget. To move toward these goals, presidents have had to balance single-year objectives with longer term budgetary plans. These considerations plus changes in the economy and in the budget process have compelled recent presidents to spend increasing amounts of time on budget making. Political demands on budget making, in fact, have transformed the modern presidency, while budget outcomes have increasingly affected the political fortunes of presidents.

Between 1950 and the early 1980's, the federal budget grew by over 1000 percent. Even measured by constant dollars, that increase means federal spending more than doubled. With such growth has occurred a certain budgetary momentum that is simply incompatible with current economic performance. Plainly, the very structure of the budget — purchases, transfers, grants-in-aid, and interest on debt — have substantially narrowed the margin for presidential maneuverability while sharply increasing the risks of policy choices.

A president's budget problem is tied to the nation's economic problems. The time frame for dealing with the nation's economy is long-term, while the budget process is more short-term. The budget-making process for presidents is characterized by competition and conflict, negotiation and compromise, maneuver and strategy. The process has become a year-round, consuming activity that has multi-year consequences.

What was once thought of as a major instrument of the powerful, purposeful president has often become more of a trap that frequently victimizes presidents. This is so because presidents are usually overly optimistic about economic growth and because they have underestimated the sluggish effects of stagflation. The

*Donald H. Haider teaches at the J. L. Kellogg Graduate School of Management at Northwestern University and is a former Deputy Assistant Secretary of the Treasury and a former Budget Director for Chicago. He is the author of* When Governments Come to Washington: Governors, Mayors and Intergovernmental Lobbying.

budget has become so large, so dynamic, and so tied to the complexities of economic forecasting that only rarely can a president hope to understand its full implications and consequences. It has become, in many respects, a multi-year budget. It has also become an almost mysterious array of outlays outside of the tradition annual budget — featuring costly trust funds, loans and loan guarantees (e.g., to Chrysler), tax expenditures (revenue losses due to tax loss) and procurement-construction programs.

A president's proposed budget no longer serves as a measurable test of a president's professional reputation nor is it a one-shot ritual commanding a month or two of presidential negotiations between their advisers, cabinet heads and senior congressional leaders. It is an endless process that changes as the economy changes, adjusts to congressional action or inaction, and is carried out over a multi-year time frame, interspersed with congressional and presidential elections. The modern budget is not a fine tuning device for achieving a full employment balance as some once believed. Rather it has become an unwieldy, truncated instrument, international in scope and interdependence, and responding to and shaped by an economy that is vast and complex.

That presidents face increased competition in budget-making is not simply due to resurgence of congressional influence over the budget but also to the increased participation by claimants upon a federal budget that affects nearly all aspects of American life and electoral constituencies. Indeed, the federal budget has all the earmarks of becoming *the* fundamental domestic problem that presidents will encounter in the 1980s and 1990s.

## Increased Claimants

The federal budget is a perennial battleground of American politics. Everyone joins the fray: agencies and bureaus within federal departments; departments with each other; all of the above with the budget bureau; the president and his advisers; executive with legislative; congressional leadership, committees, subcommittees, and staffs; one level of government with another; international organizations and foreign governments; parties; interest groups; and the media. It could hardly be otherwise, considering the structure of our government, the dispersion of political power, and the vital interests that are at stake.

As the federal budget has grown, so has competition for resources. Basic decisions are made in the budget regarding allocations between the public and private sector; between federal and state local governments; between national defense and income transfers; between mandated expenditures and discretionary spending; and between higher taxes and higher deficits. A dollar may be a dollar in the budget but different kinds of expenditures can have different economic impacts and different political consequences. Where and how the federal government allocates its resources has wide-ranging impact.

From an expenditure perspective, claimants upon the federal budget have increased in number, size, scope, organizational resources, and political sophistication. Representation and specialization of interests groups have grown geometrically in the nation's capital. Both the growth and shift in federal expenditures help explain the increased competition for federal funds. Between 1954 and 1979, federal outlays for domestic programs rose from 6 percent to 15 percent of the Gross National Product (GNP), while expenditures for national defense declined from 12.9 percent to 6.5 percent.

This gradual shift in national resource allocation came about through concern for the poor, the aged, the sick, and the elderly. Thus between 1960 and 1980 federal entitlement and related income security programs (e.g., social security, medicare, medicaid, food stamps, supplementary security income, aid to families of dependent children, and other programs) not only doubled as a share of the federal budget, but also federal payments to individuals increased at a rate 2.5 times faster than growth in the GNP.[1] These income transfer programs affected increasingly larger segments of the voting population and their families: 36 million retired and disabled workers, aged dependents, and survivors receiving social security; 21 million food stamp recipients; 25 million beneficiaries of school lunch and other nutrition programs; 28 million medicare and 18 million medicaid beneficiaries; and 11 million recipients of aid to families of dependent children (AFDC).[2]

In 1960, 130-odd intergovernmental fiscal transfer programs amounted to less than 2 percent of GNP and 15 percent of state and local government expenditures. By 1980, the 500-plus separate programs amounted to 3.4 percent of GNP, 25 percent of state-local outlays, and affected millions in terms of services, programs, and employment. Federal grant-in-aid programs affected all the states and the vast majority of local and county governments. Due in large part to this stimulation, state and local government grew twice as rapidly as the economy for 25 years between 1949–1974, as did employment in this sector.[3] More revealing of this growth than the figure for expenditures has been the changing manner by which the federal government decided to conduct its business, namely, the shift from direct to indirect or "third party government." Totally new instrumentalities for achieving national purposes and goals produced a variety of nonfederal implementers who exercise various degrees of discretion over spending and use of public authority: states, cities, special districts, nonprofit corporations and entities, hospitals, schools, financial institutions, private businesses and individuals. Grants-in-aid and transfer payments constitute only two of multiple devices for conducting the public's business. The others include loans and loan guarantees, subsidies, licenses, tax incentives, and contracts. Each represents expanded federal involvement into the public, private, and not-for-profit arenas of the economy.

Organized interests have come to understand the budget-making process, and also how to penetrate its inner workings effectively through networks that link executive agency personnel, congressional subcommittees and staff, and outside support groups. The obscurity, secrecy, and complexity of budget documents have diminished as special interest groups and Congress itself have become more professionally knowledgeable. Laymen, even, have learned to follow budgets, from understanding the underlying economic assumptions to keeping of rough, general scorecards on individual appropriations. Presidents now have extensive competition.

## Part-Time to Full-Time Preoccupation

From 1960 through 1966, the federal deficit averaged about $3.5 billion per year. With rising American involvement in Vietnam, deficits mounted. Economic growth slowed and inflation increased. Amid "guns vs. butter" debates, fiscal strain upon the budget set in, and spending conflicts became hard to resolve in the old incremental manner for satisfying new claims without depriving prior ones. It was clear to the president and to most in Congress that both were losing control over the federal budget. Rising uncontrollable expenditures and back-door spending provided ample evidence of gradual budget deterioration. Consequently, executive agencies and departments sought protection from the presidential budget apparatus; legislative committees and their supporters sought shelter from appropriations committees through entitlement programs, greater contract authority, loan guarantees, and other devices that bypassed not only the appropriations committees but even Congress itself. The Ways and Means Committee (which serves as the tax committee for the U.S. House of Representatives) fought with the Appropriations Committee, and both fought with authorizing committees over spending limitations, revenue generation, debt ceilings, and institutional turf. Congress became more open to demands, more decentralized as to decision making, more vulnerable to nongermane riders to bills. Moreover, numerous reforms in legislative procedures, committee leadership, and decision-making made consensus building more difficult, more costly, and more time-consuming.[4]

The Congressional Budget and Impoundment Control Act of 1974 markedly transformed the budget-making process not simply within Congress and its constituent parts, but also between the president and Congress. Sparked by President Nixon's unconstitutional impoundment of congressionally appropriated funds, Congress responded by transferring to itself more budget-making and fiscal policy control. The new act created a framework for linking previously independent legislative decisions on revenues and expenditures into a single process. Thereafter, the federal budget would become a full-time, yearly preoccupation of the domestic presidency as opposed to a rather episodic, action-forcing pressure that once deserved concentrated presidential interest from late fall through the mid-January State of the Union and later budgetary messages.

The Budget Reform Act created new budget committees in each chamber of Congress, a Congressional Budget Office (CBO) to enable Congress to view the budget in its entirety, and a rigorous timetable for action that regulates the process through the fiscal year. By extending the fiscal year from July 1 to October 1, Congress gained an additional three months to deliberate on the president's proposed budget. The new budget schedule prescribes a work schedule for completing specific tasks, and a resolutions process that reconciles differences in revenues, outlays, and debt legislation within and between the two houses of Congress.

From congressional perspective, the first stage in this process covers November 10 to April 15, beginning with the president's current services-estimates (what next year's budget would look like without any changes — if this year's budget were simply left on automatic pilot). This period includes the president's January budget as well as the information gathering, analysis, preparation, and submission of the congressional budget by the Congressional Budget Office and budget committees. The second stage falls between April 15 and May 15, when Congress debates and both houses adopt their first concurrent resolution on the overall budget, the resolution that is to guide authorization and appropriations committees by setting appropriate levels for budget authority, outlays, revenues, overall surplus, deficit, and changes in the public debt. Next, Congress proceeds to complete action on all spending bills by one week following Labor Day — a period when guidelines for expenditures within major functional categories are translated into specific appropriation bills and programmatic details. Finally, Congress moves to reconcile differences in spending, revenue, or debt legislation between September 15 and September 25. Budget committees report out a second budget resolution and, when feasible, a reconciliation process is used to bring tax and spending decisions in line with the second budget resolution. Congress is not supposed to breach the limits set by the second budget resolution unless it passes a new resolution which carries into the beginning of the new fiscal year.

The Budget Act provides Congress with a better understanding of the interrelationships between the budget and the economy. It provides a structure for congressional decisions. The process and timetable are self-enforcing and rely on consensus-building to generate agreement on meeting timetables, budget aggregates, and priorities. Congress cannot be compelled to do what it does not want to do.

Accordingly, presidents can ill-afford to be either budget spectators or simply passive actors in the new process. Instead, they must be active in all facets of the budget process, from the beginning of a legislative session to its end. The simple threat or actual use of presidential veto runs a significant risk of upsetting months of delicate negotiation and compromise within the Congress. The mutuality of presidential and congressional interests in making the new budget process work has contributed as much as anything else to continuation of this reform.

Observers differ on the degree of difference with the new process, as measured by spending totals, priorities, and new programs. President Reagan's success in achieving his initial budgetary goals has suggested the process could work to curb spending growth. By focusing public attention upon the 1982 fiscal year budget, and by building a successful coalition behind the budget reconciliation process, Reagan gained adoption of his tax program and a $37 billion budget reduction from current service-estimates (e.g., reduced the rate of federal spending increases from a 14 percent to an estimated 7 percent rate of growth). First invoked in 1980, the reconciliation process enables the entire Congress to vote on instructions to spending and taxing committees in order to bring their totals in line with amounts specified in the budget resolution.

If presidents are to influence budgetary and fiscal outcomes, they and their staffs have to understand Congress and its workings in order to carry out the lengthy negotiations with authorizing, appropriating, and budgetary tax committees and staffs. They must deal with the leadership, outside interest groups, and the media. This is also the case with monitoring, coordinating, and orchestrating administration policy within the executive branch. Presidential budget-making has become a year-round operation whose toll on the president's time, energies, and political capital has increased enormously. The consequences for the presidency of this shift in presidential resources have not been fully appreciated nor have its implications for other aspects of the presidency, including other presidential roles, been fully explored. They are significant.

### Splintered Domestic Presidency

Between 1939 and the early 1960s, the Bureau of the Budget (BOB) evolved into the most highly developed staff institution in government. It was the first and remains the largest staff unit in the Executive Office of the President (EOP). Its supporters like to say it is the agency most likely to have a neutral and objective perspective on executive-branch policies. It is also the backbone of the institutionalized presidency. The bureau has jealously guarded its mission of supplying presidents with information on program, administrative, and fiscal matters. Some of its early leaders saw in BOB the prospects for being the focal point between institutional perspectives (budget, economic, fiscal, managerial, and programmatic) and the presidents' personal perspectives (immediate advisers and political concerns). It has not turned out this way.

Events and new circumstances have changed the Bureau's monopoly as purveyor of presidential services as well as its relative institutional anonymity. New EOP units were created — sometimes for symbolic purposes, and sometimes to respond to crises or to carry out specific functions. An expanding White House staff became more involved in program development, clearance, and policy questions, blurring the distinction between institutional and presidential staffs. Endless attempts were made to separate budget from policy, budgetary policy from fiscal policy, domestic from international, and management from budget issues.[5] As a result, presidents faced increased conflict and competition within their own house. The increase in staffs, councils, and advisers has led to a more fragmented presidency.

The increased complexity and stakes involved in the federal budget stemmed not only from the relative shrinking of appropriable resources and the narrowing of viable options, but also from the fact that more and more issues either cut across departmental structures (e.g., energy, trade, inflation, unemployment, regulation, etc.) or involved multiple departmental perspectives in presidential decision-making. Distinctions blurred between domestic, international, and economic policy questions and, as this occurred, new EOP units, policy clusters, interagency committees, and task forces filled the policy-coordinating and advice-giving vacuum.

The old Bureau, and its 1970 successor, the Office of Management and Budget (OMB), would be variously criticized for being too powerful or too weak, too political or too bureaucratic, too involved in "number-crunching" or too overreaching in its activities. In fact, the institutional presidency suffered from information and reporting overload: longer legislative sessions, more detailed legislation, endless reports and bill clearances, an endless number of required impact statements, and expanded duties in procurement, management, and intergovernmental relations, to name a few of the many changes. Although the number of OMB budget examiners remained largely constant through the 1960s and 1970s, the budget expanded fourfold and the workload escalated. Greater attention to budget detail, especially after the Budget Reform Act, meant greater OMB preoccupation with numbers and increased dealings with Congress, and less time for more critical presidential services such as program analysis and evaluation, or program coordination. Presidents often turned elsewhere for help.

## Economic and Budgetary Deterioration

The condition of the U.S. economy and the federal budget are interrelated. Economic conditions have a tremendous impact upon the budget, and the budget, in turn, affects economic conditions. Budget receipts fluctuate with individual and corporate incomes and these respond both to real economic growth and to inflation. Conversely, budget expenditures for a growing number of federal programs are linked to economic conditions: transfer payments to cost-of-living adjustments are linked to inflation; automatic stabilizers are linked to levels of unemployment; and interest on the federal debt is linked to market interest rates and to the overall size of the budget surplus or deficit.

The importance of the complex interrelationships between the budget and the economy can be best illustrated by the magnitude of budgetary swings that occurred as a result of deviations from the administration's economic assumptions for the fiscal year 1981 budget. A one percent drop in the projected annual economic growth rate raised expenditures by $6 billion, reduced receipts by $13 billion, and increased the deficit by $19 billion. A one percent increase in the nation's unemployment rate reduced receipts by $13 billion, increased outlays by at least $7 billion, and raised the deficit by $20 billion. In the volatile economy of the 1970s such fluctuations and deviations from administration economic assumptions and forecasts were the rule rather than the exception. Major shifts in receipts and outlays occurred without presidential or congressional action, and these changes then had major consequences.

Federal budget rigidity is the other side of budget and economic volatility. From World War II through the second half of the 1960s, the nation's economy sustained a period of real economic growth, low inflation, and relatively high employment. Both the average rates of inflation and real productivity increases came within a 2 percent range. During this high-growth period the basic structure of the federal budget grew with a momentum that increasingly became inconsistent with the limits imposed by the poor performance of the economy during the 1970s: high inflation and unemployment, low growth, declining productivity and capital investment.

Increasingly larger segments of the federal budget became locked into its basic structure and operating base. By the late 1970s, more than 75 percent of the federal budget contained relatively uncontrollable expenditures that were mandated by the existing statutes, prior-year contracts or obligations. Roughly 50 percent of expenditures became linked to judicially enforceable entitlement payments such as social security. Some 30 percent of expenditures became fully indexed, which meant benefits would be adjusted one or more times each year for cost of living and inflation. Moreover, defense expenditures for weapon and system procurement also became linked to inflation insofar as multi-year budget authority, which allowed for production and acquisition, typically exceeded existing inflation rates. As deficits increased throughout the 1970s, together with interest rates, so did federal interest on the debt, which rose from 6 percent of outlays up to 10 to 11 percent of the budget. This momentum reflected past presidential and congressional decisions.

The growing frustration with what was rapidly becoming an uncontrollable structural deficit — one that persisted in good economic times as well as bad — was aptly captured by David Stockman in 1975 when he wrote, "For some time now, the built-in momentum of the federal budget and the exigencies of fiscal politics have produced expenditure growth rates that not only outpace current year revenues, but also absorb the 'fiscal dividend' of economic growth up to a half-decade in the future." [6] Congress gradually came around to understanding this dilemma.

Presidents have contributed to their own and their successors' budgetary problems by responding to changes in unemployment and inflation through a variety of restraining or economic stimulating actions. Given the budget's structure, cuts in spending have proven to be more difficult in the short run and do not have much impact unless sustained over the long term. On the other hand, short-run budget increases have long-term cumulative consequences by way of building a larger expenditure base. Tax cuts employed in 1969, 1971, 1975, 1978, and in 1981 have responded both to the need for economic stimulus and to mounting cries for tax relief. Inflation has pushed an increasing number of people into higher tax brackets without much real growth (in fact, actual decline) in their real disposable income. Thus, budgetary erosion has occurred both on the expenditure and revenue fronts since the late 1960s.

The basic structure of the budget — income transfers, long-term contracts or obligations, interest on the national debt, and basic defense spending (personnel, retirement, operations, and maintenance) — leaves each successive president with a diminished range of maneuverability. What relative discretion exists, lies largely in the area of federal grants-in-aid to states and local governments. This is a budgetary component that rose from 5.3 percent of total federal outlays in 1950 to 16 percent by 1980. Not surprisingly, then, more than one-third of President Reagan's 1981 fiscal year budget reductions were in this expenditure category. Further reduction of any major size, excluding interest on the debt, means that future presidents will have to deal with entitlement programs, such as social security, and national defense, that together comprise nearly 75 percent of the budget.

The economy has been the ruin of recent presidents, which is to say, they have been victimized by the budgetary trap of slow growth, high inflation, and unemployment. That trap has not been well-understood by presidential candidates, or by their advisers.

## From Powerful to Blunt Instrument

Economists of the Keynesian persuasion had unbridled faith in the prospects for fine-tuning the economy to achieve economic stabilization. Budget deficits and surpluses could be adjusted to maintain long-term growth with full utilization of resources. Full employment budgets became the order of the day. Fiscal policy had become the major underpinning of economic policy.[7]

However, theories of the 1960s clashed with the realities of the 1970s. Inflation and unemployment occurred simultaneously rather than as simple trade-offs. Full employment budgets vanished in budgetary lexicon. The distinction between budget "deficits of weakness" and "deficits of strength," and "economics without constraint" gave way to the chronic and rising deficits of the Vietnam Era. The structural defects in the U.S. economy had become more apparent. If beliefs still persisted among policymakers that discretionary monetary and fiscal policy had greatly eliminated the possibility of a severe recession, the nation's most severe post-war recession in 1973–1975 completely shattered this view. A new budgetary era had arrived.

From a period when policymakers debated the use of the post-Vietnam budget surplus and the adoption of federal revenue sharing to prevent "fiscal drag" upon the economy, the 1970s meant the beginning of a period of fiscal strain and budgetary deterioration in Washington. Conventional economic wisdom turned against deficit financing in terms of both credit markets and the money supply. With unemployment rates at a 6.5 to 9 percent level, and inflation rates at 9 to 13 percent levels, fiscal policy choices became more risk-laden. Economic time-horizons lengthened, while political time-horizons shortened. The benefits of specific actions had to be weighed against the economic consequences of higher deficits or higher tax burdens, with renewed growth solutions harder to come by.

As uncontrollable expenditures mounted, and low growth constrained real revenue increases, the budget contained less flexibility for employing fiscal policy to promote economic stabilization. Fiscal policy no longer could be turned on and off to meet changing economic conditions and, again, attempts to do so had longer-term economic and budgetary consequences. Former Budget Director George P. Shultz and Ken Dam epitomized the disillusionment with the "fine-tuning" when they observed: "In the United States fiscal policy is an unwieldy tool that can be applied to the economic machine only with the greatest clumsiness, however refined the mental processes of policymakers." [8]

No more classic example of a president victimized by economic changes and budgetary volatility can be found than President Jimmy Carter's 1981 fiscal-year budget, which began with an estimated $15.8 billion deficit in January of 1980. This goal was to mark the lowest federal deficit in seven years. As public pressures mounted for a balanced budget, Congress responded by enacting a first budget resolution in June 1980 that provided for a balanced budget with a $100 million surplus. Six months later, the same Congress approved a second budget resolution calling for a $27 billion deficit in response to a worsening economy. The final 1981 fiscal-year deficit came to roughly $54 billion. The political consequences of this turnaround from forecast to actual result was catastrophic. As President Carter's key budget architect observed, "The restrained budget of 1980, upon which Jimmy Carter had spent so much political capital, ended up a symbol of his profligacy and loss of control." [9] President Ronald Reagan may face a similar fate in his program to stimulate economic growth and to achieve budget balance through multi-year tax cuts and reduced federal expenditures.

## *Non-Budget*

Budget volatility has greatly diluted the potency of fiscal policy in overall macro-economic planning by presidents. In contrast to volatility, large aggregates of budget receipts and expenditures swing in tandem with economic changes and, hence, presidents face increased rigidity in their budgets as well. Not only has the federal budget been locked in by mandated and uncontrollable outlays, but also presidential discretion has been further circumscribed by legislative restrictions governing presidential impoundment of funds and by legislative vetoes. More than half of all legislative vetoes in existence came into being during the 1970s. Little wonder, then, that President Reagan, in late 1981, openly called for a fundamental revision of the budget process that would increase the president's power to control government spending while lessening congressional authority.[10]

Exactly what the federal budget is produces a variety of responses from experts, budgeteers, and presidents alike. We think of budgets as a public document (*The Budget, Special Analyses, The Appendix, The Budget in Brief*) containing plans for expenditures of government as a whole for a period of time. We also might think of a budget as a management tool, a plan for achieving goals, and as a method for control. It can be a political game, a mechanism for conflict resolution, a precedent, aspiration, and so forth. Indeed, the federal budget has become a gigantic, movable feast, involving hundreds of thousands of transactions and literally thousands of presidential decisions that, in a strict accounting sense, happen to end on one day of the year and begin anew on the next.

In a very real sense, the federal budget is a non-budget due to the fact that so much governmental financial activity goes on outside the budget and budget process, and because the federal budget increasingly occurs in a multi-year context. Traditionalists and accountants may howl at this description, but from the vantage of an earlier presidential era, or even as envisaged by the architects of the unified budget in 1967, ample cause exists for such characterization. The federal budget, as a document, has been bent every which way to accommodate departmental, congressional, and presidential needs.

The concept of a unified budget, as proposed by the President's Commission on Budget Concepts and implemented in 1968, was to include all budget transactions between the federal government and the public. All federal outlays to the public would be recorded — cash payments, purchases of goods and services, and direct lending — while loans guaranteed by the government (unless in default) would be excluded even though many such loans carried a subsidy and represented the use of private capital for public purposes.[11]

As appropriable resources shrank in the 1970s, government resorted to "back door" spending through a bewildering and often inconsistent maze of loans and loan guarantee programs outside the control of the budgetary process. Since guaranteed loans could substitute for on-budget direct lending or direct outlays, federal guaranteed loans more than doubled during the 1970s approaching $300 billion outstanding or nearly one-half of annual direct outlays. The escape from budgetary controls included entire agencies, beginning with the Export-Import Bank in 1971, and was further facilitated by creation of the Federal Financing Bank within the U.S. Treasury as a central facility for coordinating debt management activities of federal agency borrowers. Although the FFB functioned effectively as a fiscal intermediary, an increasing proportion of federal activities escaped budgetary scrutiny and control.[12]

The rising loan and loan guarantee activity, some on-budget and subject to control and others off-budget and largely removed from control, increased government borrowing in the credit markets. The scope of federal financial activities was understated, as was the federal deficit. Future government resources were mortgaged through direct or contingent liabilities.

Federal credit activities constituted one form of federal-sector transactions within the possible scope of the budget, while tax expenditures constituted another means by which government pursues public-policy objectives as alternatives to budget outlays. Reported in the budget, as required by the 1974 Budget Reform Act, the nearly $300 billion annual tax expenditures consist of revenue losses attributable to federal tax laws that allow exemptions, exclusions, deferred liability, special credit, or preferred tax rates for individuals, groups, corporations, and other entities. Rarely are these reviewed systematically by Congress and tax committees, and they are not fully integrated into the budget process.

Thus, the totality of federal financial activity escapes the budgetary process and presidential decision-making on the budget, while the multi-year context in which presidents make decisions is expanding, not decreasing. Multi-year budgeting began in earnest in the early 1970s, was mandated by the 1974 Budget Reform Act, and took hold with presidents, and in Congress, in the late 1970s. However, yawning gaps still exist in this process between OMB and executive departments, between both houses in Congress, and between budget and appropriations committees.

Due to the fact that such vast amounts of the federal budget are fixed, or constitute a seemingly imperturbable base, short-term budgetary adjustments (either up or down) do not have major impacts until future years. No president dedicated to reducing the rate of federal spending or to reallocating resources from one area of activity to another can afford to operate in a single year's context. So, too, an announced presidential goal of a balanced budget three-to-four years in the future means that cumulative decisions, year-by-year, lead toward or away from that goal, on the assumption that the economy responds to such forecasts.

The combination of frustration with the budget process, and the lure of applied management techniques to make the job easier, have given rise to the perennial presidential quest for using the budget to improve governmental management. Presidents Johnson, Nixon, Ford, and Carter each employed different government-wide techniques: program-planning-budgetary (PPB); management-by-objective (MBO); presidential management initiatives (PMI); and zero-base budgeting (ZBB). Each had different emphases or objectives — planning, management, control, program evaluation — and each tried with varying degrees of limited success to achieve other objectives.[13] Neither these techniques nor equally blunt instruments, such as reorganization, have relieved presidents from budgetary decisions. Whatever slack may have existed in the budget or in its timetable has become totally consumed by a yearly process that marches to a schedule and by documents inundated by complex details. The budget is an inescapable reality for presidents. Techniques do not make decisions.

## *Instant Gratification:*
## *From Chief Executive to City Councilman*

As federal programs and activities have reached all aspects of state and local governments, the tendency has been to "intergovernmentalize" every problem — large and small — from welfare reform to jellyfish control, and from pollution control to providing federal funds for bikeways. Just as mayors, governors, and other local officials turned into Washington lobbyists and claimants upon the federal budget, so, too, presidents have had to enter the intergovernmental thicket by delivering goodies to local constituents and mediating squabbles among competing local factions over control of federal largesse. As David Walker has observed, of both presidential role reversals and public expectations of political executives, "The presidency has become a weird mixture of somebody who appears to be a mayor or a neighborhood council chairman at one moment and the nation's chief executive the next." [14]

Plainly, the roles of presidents, congressmen, cabinet heads, governors, mayors, and local councilmen have changed markedly over a 20-year period. Washington has extended its reach into all facets of state and local government, from police enforcement to graffiti on billboards. Interaction among government levels has become more complex, more confusing, and more dysfunctional. Instead of dealing directly with 50 states and 25 or 30 large cities, as was the case in 1960, the federal government now deals — often in a substantial way — with 79,000 units of state and local government. Everyone has someone to blame.

With the growing ambiguity over who finances what, who administers what, and who is accountable for what, demands upon government increased throughout the political system. The overload found its way into the presidents' office as more and more local issues came to be concentrated there. As much as presidents and their advisers tried to avoid involvement in local matters and minor concerns, the political imperatives of the office compelled dealing with individual legislative concerns and the demands of mayors and governors. Political party disintegration and new presidential convention rules required that presidents pay attention to assembling bits and pieces of local coalitions.

Once the engine of state and local government spending slowed in the mid-1970s, followed in 1978 by a downturn in federal aid (constant dollars), presidents incurred the instant wrath of state and local government constituencies for the retrenchment that followed. Presidents had to deal with well-organized, politically active groups mobilized to fight budget reductions. Beginning with the alliance politics that helped stem President Nixon's widescale budget impoundments in 1972–1973, coalitions to fight budget reductions formed among service-providers and beneficiaries, as well as across program and sectoral lines.

The incrementalism of former budgeting practices gave way to a kind of non-zero-sum game. Attempts to shift allocations from domestic to defense, or even to slow governmental spending generally, produced instant retribution from defenders of the elderly, the poor, minorities, the sick, the cities, and the unemployed. For presidents, it was not simply the staying power of weathering economic cycles, rather, they had to contend with their own party's constituencies that could threaten their prospects for renomination to a second term in office. President Carter's determination to embrace rather modest restraint in his 1979 budget split the Democratic Party at its mid-term convention in Memphis, which eventually produced a challenge to his renomination in 1980 from his own party left. Simultaneously, his refusal to engage in substantial military buildup produced a challenge from his party's more conservative wing. Budgetary issues not only divided interest groups, governmental levels, and parties in government, but also divided a president's own political party.

No easy way out of the budgetary dilemma exists for presidents. Increased taxes introduce the risk of another dilemma even if they are automatically in-

duced by dint of inflation. President Reagan's proposed plan for economic recovery — multi-year tax reductions and slower governmental growth — began
as a relatively painless growth-oriented solution for dealing with unemployment
and inflation. Even if this plan were to achieve its goals, its implementation runs
smack into the president's budgetary dilemma: the public's impatient timetable
is shorter than the political-electoral timetable, and the time necessary to deal
with the nation's more durable economic problems spans more than a presidential term. Budgetary corrections are unlikely to be achieved, as some Reagan
advisers believe, simply by cutting fraud, waste, abuse, and bureaucrats. The
budgetary problem runs far deeper, and most Americans have yet to be persuaded that this is the case.

Nowhere are the front-loaded risks of budgetary reallocations greater for presidents than in national defense. Assuming current staffing levels, reasonable pay
and retirement increases, and adequate attention to operations and maintenance
of military systems, defense expenditures would have to increase in real terms
simply to keep pace with inflation. The hard presidential choices lie both in
beginning major new weapon systems and in the protection of existing nuclear
deterrent forces.

Simply stated, the lead time necessary for the design, development, acquisition,
and production of a major new system (the B1 bomber, for example) spans a
4- to 6-year period with rising and cumulative costs in successive years. The
risks and political consequences of taking such action increase dramatically from
year to year. The costs of these systems generally is underestimated, while accelerated production competes directly with the private sector for skilled labor,
application of new technology, and production facilities. Given the lead time
necessary for full production, one president takes all the political risks and heat,
and the benefits ensue to his successor in the oval office. Increasingly, presidents
have ducked this choice or announced intentions to proceed into development,
but in reality have passed along the budgetary headaches of actual production
to their successors. Once again, the budget imposes long-term dilemmas constrained by short-term consequences. Try as they may, recent presidents have
not successfully broken out of this narrowing box.

## *From Presidential Benchmark to Movable Target*

Among scholars of the presidency, the budget has emerged as one of the key
benchmarks for judging a president's professional reputation in Washington.[15]
That is, the extent to which a president understood his proposed budget, orchestrated its adoption, and defended his key stakes in the torturous, often fatal
congressional disposition of that budget, had a critical bearing upon his reputation-building. Reputation is only one, although important, aspect of presidential leadership, and is related to the larger issue of how a president protects
his power stakes in his own acts of choice. Still, nowhere is the power of persuasion more amply tested than on a president's budget.

The past four presidents have pleaded for spending moderation, and have sought credibility for their proposed budgets by invoking such phrases as "lean and austere," "prudent and responsible," "minimum and necessary." However, what presidents have proposed in January has become farther removed from what actually transpires in the fiscal year that does not end until twenty months later. Again, presidential budgets have fallen victim to the economy, and the credibility of the budget and the economic assumptions on which it is based have, as a consequence, strained presidential credibility. Presidential budgets are no longer realistic estimates, but instead have become elastic, movable targets.

Over the last twelve annual budgets, only once have a president's proposed outlays come in under estimates. In nine of the past twelve years, budget deficits have run higher than originally forecast; in five of those years, deficits have been more than double the forecast (even excluding off-budget deficits). Under the Budget Reform Act, Congress officially revises the president's budget forecasts three to four times annually, while the administration may engage in a half dozen or more revisions from early January through the twenty-month budgetary span. The swing of $20 to $50 billion between original estimates and the final budget may not seem much in a $3 trillion economy, but a three to five percent change in receipts and in outlays has a systematic effect on congressional behavior, the business and financial community, and the president's reputation. Budgetary volatility has destroyed campaign promises, undermined budget balancing goals, and shortened presidential careers.

Due to rapid or unexpected changes in economic performance, presidents have had to alter their economic policies to meet actual or anticipated consequences. Budget outcomes increasingly reflect external events, most of which are beyond the control of presidents and our political institutions. Due to constant budgetary revisions and changing economic policies, both the public and Congress are often left wondering which president's budget is being defended at any one time.

This is not to suggest that the budget has ceased to be a major instrument of presidential leadership. Surely President Reagan's 1981 successes indicated otherwise. Rather, in an uncertain economic environment, presidential knowledge and defense of budgets have become far less of a means of reputation-building than they were perhaps once thought to be. No president since Truman has had greater command of the budget, and no recent president has incurred greater economic and political setbacks than President Ford. More than skill and familiarity are needed; presidents also need a good deal of luck in timing and in favorable economic conditions.

## Concluding Observations

The budget has become the fundamental domestic problem for presidents. As the momentum underlying budgetary growth and government commitments has proved to be incompatible with desired economic performance, government has confronted limits, and presidents have encountered increasingly more difficult choices. These limits and hard choices generated institutional changes within Congress and have resulted in constantly changing advisers, processes, and institutional arrangements within the presidents' own house. The budgetary problem grew out of the late 1960s, emerged full force with inflation and recessions of the early 1970, and began consuming the domestic agenda by the late 1970s.

A president is the one figure in our political system who can effectively deal with the difficult choices the nation faces: growth, inflation, domestic needs, and defense imperatives. Economic constraints mean that budgetary belts cannot be tightened without major segments of the public giving something up that government provides or has promised. Presidents must convince the public that the risks of not giving up government services far outweigh the costs of the sacrifices involved in maintaining them. If we are to solve the problems that the budget presents, then presidents will have to convince a skeptical Congress of the necessity of choice. To lead the Congress, presidents must educate and lead the American public. To date, however, presidents have not been successful in doing this.

The 1970s constituted a period of successive shocks for the American public: Vietnam, Watergate, energy dependency, high inflation, low growth, and much economic turbulence. Distrust in government rose, general optimism concerning the future fell. Three successive presidents struggled with the economy, and a fourth came to office in 1981 with a promise to slow government growth and to balance the federal budget. President Reagan acted decisively in making the budget *the* issue. His successor will have to pick up where he left off, because the budget has become an inescapable phenomenon of the presidency. Major economic corrections are unlikely to occur in one term or under one administration.

If the presidency has been substantially transformed over the past decade by the budgetary process, as has been argued, then perhaps future presidents still have the opportunity to utilize the budget to transform the presidency. With better understanding of what the budget is — the limits and risks as well as the opportunities — the presidency can be strengthened and its leadership position reasserted. This is both a prospect and a hope.

SOURCE: "Presidents as Budget Policymakers" by Donald H. Haider was written expressly for this volume. Copyright © 1982 by Donald H. Haider.

## Notes

1. Executive Office of the President, *America's New Beginning: A Program for Economic Recovery*, February 18, 1981, p. 11.
2. *The Budget of the U.S. Government, Fiscal Year 1981*, pp. 258–273.
3. The Advisory Commission on Intergovernmental Relations, *The Federal Role in the Federal System: The Dynamics of Growth* (Washington, D.C., 1981), pp. 1–6.

4. Allen Schick, *Congress and Money: Budgeting, Spending and Taxing* (Washington, D.C.: The Urban Institute, 1980).

5. S. Hess, *Organizing the Presidency* (Washington, D.C.: The Brookings Institution, 1976): Allen Schick, "The Budget Bureau That Was," *Law and Contemporary Problems* 35 (1970), 519–539; and Richard Rose, *Managing Presidential Objectives* (New York: The Free Press, 1976).

6. David A. Stockman, "The Social Pork Barrel," *The Public Interest* 39 (Spring, 1975), 3.

7. See Walter Heller, *New Dimensions of Political Economy* (Cambridge: Harvard University Press, 1966), pp. 39–40; Richard Rose and Guy Peters, *Can Government Go Bankrupt?* (New York: Basic Books, Inc., 1978), ch. 6.

8. George P. Shultz and Kenneth W. Dam, *Economic Policy Beyond the Headlines* (New York: W. W. Norton, 1977), p. 23.

9. W. Bowman Cutter, "The Battle of the Budget," *The Atlantic Monthly* 247 (March, 1981), 63.

10. *New York Times,* October 18, 1981, p. 1.

11. See, *The Report of the President's Commission on Budget Concepts* (Washington, D.C.: GPO, 1967); *Issues '78: Perspectives on FY 1978 Budget* (Washington, D.C.; GPO, 1977), pp. 235–241; and address by Elmer B. Staats, Comptroller General of the United States, George Washington University, Washington, D.C. November 21, 1980.

12. See, "Loan Guarantees and The Federal Financing Bank." Hearings before the Subcommittee on Economic Stabilization, Committee on Banking, Finance, and Urban Affairs, 95th Cong., 1st sess., 1977. A credit control system integrated into the conventional budget system begins to emerge in 1980.

13. Donald H. Haider, "Presidential Management Initiatives," *Public Administration Review* 30 (May/June, 1979), 248–259.

14. David Walker, "The Current Condition of American Federalism," School of Public and Environmental Affairs *Review* 2 (Winter/Spring, 1981), 15.

15. Richard E. Neustadt, *Presidential Power* (New York: J. Wiley and Sons, 1960). Neustadt recounts how Eisenhower's professional reputation was affected by the degree to which he clearly and consistently defended his proposed budget — from equivocation and uncertainty in 1957–1958 to strength and full commitment by 1959.

# 26. Presidents as National Security Policymakers

## James K. Oliver

Harry Truman observed once that the president as national security policy-maker had powers that "would have made Ceaser, Genghis Khan or Napoleon bite his nails with envy." [1] Two decades later a succession of presidents complained about the hobbling limitations placed upon their power by Congress and the courts. Whereas the late 1960s and early 1970s saw great concern about a swollen and imperial presidency, the latter decade closed with worried reflections on the state of a diminished and "imperiled" presidency.[2] For Truman the powers of a presidency that took on imperial proportions were necessary for the prosecution of World War II followed by global cold war. Twenty years later, however, policies and powers framed during Truman's administration, institutionalized during Eisenhower's years, and reinvigorated and extended under Kennedy and Johnson had culminated in Vietnam and Watergate. Presidents Ford and Carter chafed under the restrictions placed on the office in reaction to a presidency and a foreign policy seen as having become too strong and activist. Yet on the threshold of the 1980s, Carter was swept from office because he and his policies, if not the office he held, were thought to be too weak. Moreover, the man who defeated him was applauded for the strong leadership he showed in pushing his economic program through Congress even as he was being criticized for his lack of an equally well-defined and forceful foreign policy.

The presidency characterized by post-World War II national security policy would seem, therefore, to be the epitome of what Thomas Cronin has called the ultimate paradox of a paradox-ridden modern presidency:

> ... [I]t is always too powerful and yet it is always inadequate. Always too powerful because it is contrary to our ideals of a "government by the people" and always too powerful, as well, because it now possesses the capacity to wage nuclear war (a capacity that unfortunately doesn't permit much in the way of checks and balances and deliberative, participatory government). Yet always inadequate because it seldom achieves our highest hopes for it, not to mention its own stated intentions.[3]

Undoubtedly much of this paradox can be explained in terms of the policy and ideological predispositions of the observer. A president is a statesman when pol-

*James K. Oliver teaches political science at the University of Delaware and is the author and coauthor of several books including* U.S. Foreign Policy and World Order *and* Foreign Policymaking and the American Political System.

icy conforms to our preferences; a dangerous threat to the constitutional balance when he acts in a manner that offends our values. Moreover, presidents themselves always seem sensitive to the limitations of their position as national security policymaker precisely because they may have to use their capacity to wage nuclear war and must, on a day-to-day basis, make and administer policies in an international environment increasingly less responsive to their perspective.

But there is more to the paradox-ridden domain of the national-security-policy-presidency than is revealed by the sometimes self-serving arguments made by observers and occupants of the office. Notwithstanding enormous institutional capability, there are real constraints acting on the presidency. First, there are constraints resulting from the constitutionally imposed relationship between the president and the Congress. Second, there are limits resulting from the structure and dynamics of the policymaking institutions that make up the modern national-security-policy-presidency itself. Third, there are domestic political constraints growing out of the relationship of the presidency and the American people. And finally, there is the external domain within which foreign and national security policy must be conducted. For no matter how real and important the domestic dimensions of foreign policy, policymakers must contend with the contemporary world political system.

## The Executive-Legislative Relationship

Of the constitutionally defined institutional relationships, the intersection of presidential and congressional powers has recently elicited the greatest concern from both observers and policymakers. The preoccupation of the framers of the Constitution with implementing the compromise of Hamilton's preference for a strong executive in matters of foreign intercourse and national security and the Madisonian system of checks and balances is nowhere more apparent than in the foreign and national-security policymaking structure. Thus the president as commander-in-chief is charged with the responsibility for the conduct of military operations by forces raised and maintained by the Congress and in conflicts entered into via a congressional declaration of war. Similarly, the president is to conduct the nation's diplomacy but share in its formulation by means of a treaty-making process that requires senatorial advice and consent.[4]

Though perhaps adequate for a nation on the geographic and political periphery of world politics, these arrangements have been the source of unease throughout the post-World War II period. When coupled with deep partisan disagreement, the constitutional structure has become a source of mischief for a presidency that sought to lead not only the United States but virtually the entire noncommunist world through decades of cold war and then tenuous detente. Especially in the wake of the fractious McCarthy years of the early 1950s, the accommodation of institutional and partisan conflict has lain in the notion of "bipartisanship." Originally conceived and advanced by the Truman administration as a means for gaining Republican support for the cold-war initiatives in the late 1940s, bipartisanship was extended during the Eisenhower administration to encompass the suppression of institutional conflict between the two ends of Pennsylvania Avenue as well. Given the perception of a dangerous and pervasive global threat and the perceived inefficiencies of the fragmented policy-making structure when combined with partisan debate, the necessity of strong presidential leadership seemed self-evident. Thus in response to crises in Europe, Asia, the Middle East, and Latin America, presidents requested from and were granted by Congress a series of resolutions, budgetary mandates, and accession to unilateral assertions of presidential power in the formulation and conduct of foreign and national security policy.

In this manner the presidency accumulated a reservoir of explicit and implicit powers that provided the means for circumventing the institutional constraints of the constitutional structure — a necessity if an involvement in world politics far beyond that counseled by the framers of the Constitution was to be pursued successfully, and a necessity jointly perceived by both executive and legislative branches. The hypothetical dangers of constitutional imbalance in this development were understood but usually dismissed,[5] until the policy which had led to this *de facto* amendment of the constitutional design began to fail in the late 1960s. Then and only then, as the policy consensus began to collapse, did the image of an imperial presidency become commonplace, bipartisanship vanish, and Congress exert itself to reform the executive-legislative relationship in foreign and national-security policymaking.

Throughout the 1970s this process centered on the extent to which Congress and the president would "codetermine" American foreign and defense policy. There is, at the onset of the 1980s, considerable evidence of an increased institutional capacity on the part of Congress to engage in some aspects of codetermination. A war powers act that seeks to limit presidential initiative in committing American military forces; a restructured congressional budget system; provisions for congressional intervention in, and veto of, presidential initiatives in programs where formerly presidential latitude was granted; and greatly augmented personal and institutional staffing have all contributed to greater capacity for programmatic participation and oversight.[6] On the other hand, it is less clear that these new powers and procedures will operate as intended or that they have provided Congress with any greater ability to participate in the initial determination of foreign policy assumptions and objectives. Here the president retains the initiative insofar as the president possesses the prerogatives and responsibilities associated with the day-to-day conduct of diplomacy and national security policy. Standing astride the numerous action streams of international intercourse, the president retains a capacity to shape domestic perceptions of international reality, a capacity that Congress cannot match. Moreover, it is expected by both the Congress and the people that the president will do so.

Nonetheless, to the extent that policy must take the form of commitments of resources through extended programs, the opportunity for congressional involvement remains large. A major treaty such as SALT II may be blocked, or, as in the case of the Panama Canal treaties, a price may be exacted for Senate approval. A congressional veto may be threatened, thereby compelling executive-legislative negotiations. Or, in the presence of popular pressure, Congress may block or deflect presidential initiative. Thus, in 1974 Congress overrode the president and cut off military assistance to Turkey in the wake of the Turkish invasion of Cyprus. Likewise, the Ford and Carter administrations were forced to modify proposed military sales in the Middle East or face the possibility of a congressional veto.

The president's national-security policymaking latitude is therefore restricted by the constitutionally mandated executive-legislative interaction. Insofar as the president is clearly responsible for the conduct of foreign and national security policy, the presidency possesses a measure of positional advantage in the relationship. But it seems clear that the reforms of the 1970s have increased congressional potentiality for interfering in the exploitation of this advantage. It remains to be seen, however, whether this balance of executive-legislative power can be sustained, especially if, after passing through a phase of post-Vietnam retrenchment, renewed American activism emerges.

In the final analysis, evaluating conflicting claims about the adequacy of presidential power cannot be undertaken outside a particular political and policy context. But it would seem that the relationship that emerged in the mid and late 1970s at least complicates the formulation and conduct of the kind of activist foreign policy of the late cold war years. In some respects the present relationship is close to the original Madisonian design, with its emphasis on mutually reinforcing constraints on the executive-legislative nexus of the policymaking process. But Madison's was a policymaking design for an isolated and minor international actor. Insofar as the United States maintains its contemporary role at the center of international relations, one can expect that the constitutional design will continue to be perceived as a constraint.

## The National Security Policymaking Establishments

A second set of institutional influences and limits on the national-security-policymaking-presidency is the policymaking establishment that has grown up around the modern presidency. Indeed, to speak of *an* establishment is an oversimplification. There are in fact *several* establishments that have developed since the onset of American global activism. In addition to the diplomatic establishment centered on the Department of State, the foreign and national security policymaking presidency extends to the Department of Defense, itself a complex of bureaucracies, and the intelligence establishment built around the linkage of the Central Intelligence Agency, National Security Agency, and the intelligence bureaucracies of the Departments of Defense and State. Moreover, as world politics has become suffused with complex social and economic forces, other agencies and departments have assumed major and sometimes overriding importance in the formulation and conduct of foreign affairs. Thus, during the 1970s, the Treasury Department and the Department of Agriculture became salient as international economic and food security issues forced their way onto the foreign and national-security policy agenda.

These bureaucratic establishments are both a source of and a constraint on the president's policymaking capabilities. They constitute significant concentrations of policy expertise essential to the conduct of the modern national-security-policy-presidency. Coordinating the capabilities represented by these agencies and departments, and bringing them to bear on the several dimensions of the national interest, can be seen as the operational essence of foreign and national-security policymaking. Access to and control of these establishments become, therefore, necessary conditions for the successful conduct of foreign and national-security policy.

Underscoring the importance to the president of the foreign and national-security establishment is also, however, to emphasize its constraining role. For over a decade observers of foreign and national-security policymaking have suggested that "policy" emerges from an elaborate and often prolonged process of intra- and interbureaucratic bargaining rather than a majestic orchestration by the chief executive.[7] In this process of "bureaucratic politics," conceptions of the national interest are colored by the institutional perspectives and needs of the several bureaucratic actors that are inevitably a part of the policy process. The policymaking process becomes, therefore, a struggle over which image of reality will prevail, whose policy prescriptions will dominate, and, therefore, which agency will command the preponderant share of budgetary resources devoted to the pursuit of the national interest.

Bureaucratic players recognize and accept the central position of the president in this process. But in practical terms this means a president becomes as much the object of the bureaucratic political process as its controller. Insofar as a president "makes" foreign and national-security policy, bureaucratic actors contend for control of the flow of information and policy options from which the president must choose. Similarly, once a decision is made, the process of carrying out policy is the subject of the same process, as agencies seek to protect their respective interests or advance their claims on the resources available for the conduct of policy.

Plainly, the management of the national-security policymaking process within the executive branch has been a major concern of presidents from the outset of the post-World War II period. Beginning with the National Security Act of 1947, presidents have sought to develop policymaking arrangements responsive to their particular perception of their policymaking needs. Perhaps the most important institutional manifestation of this quest has been the emergence of the National Security Council (NSC) as a coordinating mechanism and the increasing importance of the Special Assistant for National Security Affairs (or Security Adviser) as the president's personal adviser and, upon occasion, a foreign policymaking official of no less importance than the Secretaries of State and Defense.[8]

Originally conceived as a framework for coordinating the advice and activities of the foreign and national security departments, the NSC developed throughout the 1950s and 1960s a presidential staff function independent of these agencies. Increasingly, the NSC staff, though small relative to the foreign and national security policy departments, came to be viewed as the *president's* national security staff. Even more important, the security adviser, as the director of the staff, became the president's closest foreign and national security adviser. Among the factors contributing to the emergence of the security adviser and the NSC as the center of the national-security policymaking process was their sheer propinquity to the president. But more important was the perceived need by a succession of presidents that they required a presence in the national-security policymaking process that was more responsive to their needs and perspectives than the secretary of state or other senior officials could be. The latter officials invariably found themselves cross-pressured by the demands resulting from their position as heads of their particular departments and their allegiance to the president who appointed them. To the extent that they became advocates of their departments they became part of the very bureaucratic political process the president sought to manage. The security adviser, on the other hand, had no such department. He was responsible only to the president. Indeed, throughout most of the post-World War II period, the security adviser, as a member of the president's personal staff, was even beyond the reach of the Congress, whereas the secretaries of state or defense were inevitably occupied with the time-consuming task of representation of the administration's foreign and defense policies at the intersection of executive-legislative relations.

The specific role of the NSC and the tasks performed by the security adviser have depended on the administrative and policymaking styles of the president as well as the personalities of the security advisers themselves. In some instances in which presidents have had a strong sense of personal responsibility for policymaking (Truman) and/or very close working relationships with their secretaries of state or other members of the cabinet (as during the Truman and Eisenhower administrations), the role of the NSC has been relegated to that of an executive secretariat responsible for monitoring the flow of policy recommendations to and policy decisions from the president. In other cases, however, a combination of deep personal involvement in the formulation of foreign and national security policy by a president during periods of intense policy activism has led to dramatic expansion of the role of the security adviser.

Undoubtedly the culmination of the trend toward a strong or even dominant role for the security adviser and the NSC came during the administrations of Richard Nixon and Jimmy Carter in the 1970s. Nixon's deep suspicion and distrust of the bureaucracy was matched by the conviction of his security adviser, Henry Kissinger, that bureaucracies and the processes of bureaucratic politics were inherently incapable of producing creative foreign policy leadership. The upshot was the establishment of Kissinger and his expanded NSC staff at the center of Nixon's national-security policymaking operations. Kissinger's role expanded far beyond the strong advisory and coordinating roles played by his predecessors. Before becoming secretary of state during Nixon's abbreviated second term, Kissinger had undertaken major secret negotiations on the most important issues confronted by the Nixon administration, e.g., Vietnam, the reopening of relations with China, and as the administration's chief strategist and negotiator in the secret "back channels" of the SALT process — as well as serving as the ubiquitous "senior official" who made "authoritative" but "off-the-record" pronouncements on American foreign policy.[9]

The Carter administration, having campaigned against both the style and substance of Kissinger's foreign policy, nevertheless produced a security adviser and NSC that were if anything even more prominent than Kissinger had been. In this case a president with little background in foreign affairs, heading an administration deeply divided concerning its fundamental foreign policy orientation and objectives, became increasingly dependent on his forceful security adviser, Zbigniew Brzezinski. Brzezinski not only played the central advisory role of his strongest predecessors but also became a vocal and visible policy advocate in the often turbulent national-security policymaking processes of the Carter administration. The security adviser traveled the world as chief negotiator, regularly appeared on television, and regularly held press conferences. By the end of the administration, Brzezinski had become the loudest of the many voices claiming to speak for Carter on foreign and national security.

As the fourth president in a decade assumed office in January of 1981, close observers of the presidency were worried.[10] The closing months of the Carter administration seemed to confirm that what had been established as a means to help the president maintain control of the national-security policymaking establishment — the NSC and the security adviser — had become a major part of the problem. Surely Mr. Carter's own policy ambivalence contributed to the spectacle of the secretary of state and his chief aides engaged in often rough public debate with the security adviser and members of his NSC staff, which culminated in the secretary of state's resignation. But there was something deeper at work in the late 1970s. What was now viewed as the disruptive prominence of the security adviser had grown out of more complex and extensive conditions than the personalities of the presidents and most prominent security advisers of the 1970s.

The security adviser and the NSC came to prominence, it must be recalled, because of the perceived needs of presidents over the last thirty years. Those needs developed in part from the structure and dynamics of the very policymaking establishment that is a source of much of a president's capability as a national security policymaker. Inasmuch as those bureaucratic politics are likely to continue as the essence of the policymaking process, the president's need for someone capable of intervening in and "brokering" the bureaucratic political game will remain. What is called for, in short, is what I. M. Destler has described as a "... foreign policy facilitator with broad substantive reach but a relatively anonymous, process-oriented style." [11] If the security adviser also engages in the conduct of diplomatic negotiations and becomes a vocal and highly visible advocate of policy positions, he invariably becomes a competitor with the secretary of state and the other senior foreign and national security policy-making officials.

But if the security adviser has tended to become something more than a "low-profile White House facilitator," it bespeaks the existence of factors other than bureaucratic politics at work on the national-security-policy presidency. Domestic political pressures, public expectations, and a more complex and less responsive international environment all reinforce the presidential impulse to create responsive instruments of policymaking "control." [12] In sum, presidents predictably see their capacity for controlling an activist foreign policy as inadequate. Under these conditions, it seems equally predictable they will vest great authority in an individual or individuals perceived to be responsive to their political and policymaking needs. Understanding these constraints requires, therefore, that our analytical purview encompass the domestic and international contexts within which the national-security presidency must operate.

## *The Political Context of Presidential National-Security Policymaking*

In the 1830s the perceptive French observer, Alexis de Tocqueville, worried about the capacity of a democracy to conduct an effective and coherent foreign policy. De Tocqueville's pessimism was based in part on his concerns about the implications of the institutional fragmentation that we have examined above. But he was even more fearful of what he thought would be the pernicious effects of democratic politics on the formulation and conduct of foreign affairs.

The conventional wisdom among analysts of American public opinion has been that the American people are for the most part ignorant or at best indifferent concerning foreign affairs. Although there is some evidence that this situation has changed in the direction of greater public understanding and attentiveness in recent years, it probably remains the case that much of the time the public is prepared to grant latitude to the foreign policymaking establishment and its chief executive, the president. Thus the president stands at the center of public foreign policy expectations. However, we are once again faced with a paradox. A decade of foreign policy frustration has both increased expectations (often fed by presidential rhetoric concerning change) as well as diminished the degree of latitude, confidence, and public patience available to a president. As public opinion analyst Daniel Yankelovich put it recently, we have reached the end of "president knows best." [13]

Insofar as demands and expectations continue to be directed toward the presidency, the opportunity for presidential leadership is high. Thus, the frequently lamented ignorance and fickleness of the public are seen as remediable through the guidance of presidential vision and policy direction. But such leadership has proved to be an uncertain thing during the last few decades. Rather, as Yankelovich has noted, there has been a tendency for leadership to "blow hot and cold" as it has alternately sought to mobilize people to respond to the rigors of cold war or relax in the warmth of detente. These sometimes contradictory attempts at public mobilization have perhaps contributed to skepticism, cynicism, and ultimately indifference on the part of an angry public.[14]

Events doubtless have contributed to shifts in the direction of presidential leadership. Thus, the Carter administration was forced to deal sequentially with building support for SALT II followed by a hard turn back toward cold war in the wake of the Soviet invasion of Afghanistan. But even these two cases were related to more basic political constraints that operate in the domestic political environment. During the Carter administration, as during the first administration of any president, an electoral clock was ticking. Further, the electoral clock runs for Congress as well as for a president, thereby further constraining presidential leadership. Indeed, it is at the intersection of the electoral process and foreign policymaking that we find the crux of concern about the democratic prospect in the world arena.

The impulse to manage foreign and national security policy with an eye on the electoral calendar seems irresistible. There is pressure to accomplish something that sets one apart from one's predecessor and lays the basis for the re-election run. For example, Carter, upon assuming the presidency, found a nearly complete SALT II treaty negotiated by the man he had just defeated. Believing and proclaiming that he could do better, the president decided to renegotiate the agreement. Though he eventually achieved an agreement with the Soviets that did go beyond that negotiated by the Ford administration,[15] it cost him more than two years of additional bargaining, during which time Soviet-American relations beyond SALT deteriorated. Moreover, by the time the renegotiation of the treaty was complete, the onset of the 1980 election was at hand, which immensely complicated the politics of treaty ratification in a Senate that after the 1978 election was decisively more conservative than the one facing the president in 1977.

The onset of the electoral season may also contribute to a presidential attempt to submerge or retard foreign policy developments that might affect reelection prospects negatively. Thus President Ford apparently decided in 1975 that, notwithstanding recent breakthroughs in negotiating SALT II, the political threat to his nomination posed by Ronald Reagan was sufficient that he had to minimize all appearance of being "soft" on the Russians until after the election. Consequently the SALT negotiations were suspended and "detente" was eliminated from the lexicon of the Ford administration. Similarly, Carter sought to downplay his embarrassing inability to negotiate or force the release of American hostages in Iran during the 1980 presidential campaign — *except* in the spring of 1980, when it served his political interests to underscore his immersion in the crisis, thereby evading head-to-head confrontation with his primary rival for the Democratic nomination, Senator Edward Kennedy. Likewise, it seems hardly coincidental that Richard Nixon's negotiation of the SALT I agreement and Henry Kissinger's announcement that "peace was at hand" in Vietnam corresponded with the reelection year of 1972 or that Nixon's trips to the Soviet Union and the Middle East were made as the Watergate crisis mounted.

Authoritarian and totalitarian governments are often accused of trying to divert the attention of their populations from domestic difficulties by means of wars or fabricated international crises. It seems, however, that American presidents faced with their own domestic pressures are no less susceptible to attempting to manage the national-security policymaking process so that their personal political interests might be at least engaged in, if not married to, the national interest. Indeed, the expectation that this will occur is so great both within the U.S. and abroad, that it is commonplace for knowledgeable domestic and foreign observers and policymakers to anticipate a hiatus in the conduct of relations with the United States during these periods. Further, if an incumbent president is defeated or is constitutionally prohibited from succeeding himself, the discontinuity in American policy can last for months as the old administration serves out its term and the new administration works through its transition period.

Finally, much of a president's potential for popular leadership is a function of his position as the authoritative source of people's information about, and their image of, the world and America's interests in it. However, during the last decade serious challenges to the president's authority have emerged. Years of presidential optimism concerning Vietnam were contradicted by growing casualties and ultimately failure; Watergate became a fatal cancer on the Nixon presidency. Thus, the credibility of the presidency could not help but suffer given the events of the late 1960s and early 1970s. In addition, as American policy was frustrated in Southeast Asia and seemed to stand impotent in the face of the international financial and energy crises of the early and mid-1970s, the formerly resilient and coherent world-view of the small but influential group of people — current and former government officials, academics, journalists, and members of the business establishment who concern themselves with American foreign and national security policy on a regular basis — gave way. The great national newspapers such as *The New York Times* and *Wall Street Journal,* the weekly newsmagazines, and national television networks no longer served as generally supportive mediating agents transmitting and explaining presidential leadership on foreign and defense policy, as had been the case in the 1950s and early 1960s. Presidents were now confronted with more adversarial media that reflected and transmitted to the American people alternative and, from the president's viewpoint, often antagonistic, perspectives on international reality.

Often the disarray, skepticism, and dissent evident within the so-called policy elite and among opinion leaders attached themselves to another important manifestation of the breakdown of political consensus during the late 1960s and early 1970s — the single-issue and action-oriented interest groups. Though perhaps more in evidence with respect to domestic issues such as women's rights, abortion, civil rights, or gun control, groups formed around the several poles of the debate on foreign and defense policy as well. Thus even as Jimmy Carter embarked on his presidency with vague intimations of a desire to redirect American foreign policy away from the path of cold war, a group of conservative former officials and analysts formed something called the Committee on the Present Danger. The committee, along with other groups and sympathetic members of the foreign and national security bureaucracy, became, during the ensuing Carter years, a virtual shadow foreign and national-security-policy government on the right. It vigorously and effectively challenged the Carter administration's detente inclinations, the SALT II treaty, and attempts to reduce the defense budget. Ultimately, those who made up this challenge to the Carter foreign-and-national-security-policy presidency, comprised a personnel reservoir for Ronald Reagan when he set about creating his own foreign policy establishment.

Thus, the 1970s seemed to confirm many of the ancient fears concerning the efficacy of the American political system in dealing with the world. The potential for presidential leadership is still strong if for no other reason than the American people expect presidential leadership and initiative in foreign and national security affairs. At the same time, however, there is evidence that the American people are now less patient than in the past. This works in turn to exacerbate presidential anxiety about electoral retribution. Moreover, a president is faced with a more skeptical policy elite, segments of which have demonstrated a capacity to mobilize against and thereby constrain presidential initiative and leadership.

It should not be forgotten, however, that all these elements of the American system have come into play during and in response to a decade of foreign policy difficulty and even defeat. A reversal of fortune might well dispel much of the present concern about a hobbled foreign-policy presidency. Success could prove to be the solvent of institutional and political constraint. If so, the prospects for a relaxation of domestic pressure on the national-security-policy-presidency will depend in part on the nature of the international conditions with which the president must deal. Henry Kissinger once said that the ultimate test of American foreign policy is whether it is accepted by the American people.[16] The trial is conducted in large part, however, in the arena of world politics.

## The President, National Security Policymaking and the World

Challenges in the world arena will doubtless be no less demanding than in the past. The continuities from the past would be very nearly sufficient in themselves to preclude totally satisfactory outcomes in foreign and national-security policy. In an international system in which the continued security and survival of the United States is no longer solely a function of the policymaking processes of the United States government, but is now inextricably interdependent with those of the Soviet Union, it will be difficult for a president to deliver on simple policy prescriptions. Further, the last decade provides ample evidence that the terrifying complexities of security in the nuclear age are now compounded by new political economic forces that can be, in their own fashion, as disruptive and consequential for the human condition as war once was.

Moreover, the capacity of the United States to control events in this domain has changed through time. With the change, new problems impinge on the foreign-and-national-security-policy-presidency. Most fundamental has been the decline of the United States from a position of hegemony in the international system. Both the structure and character of power have changed in the international system. Military power still counts for a great deal, but its disposition is no longer the sole measure of national security. What constitutes power in world politics has changed as resource dependency and international economic interdependency have grown during the post-war years. Further, even as the elements and means for the exercise of power have proliferated, so too have the possessors of the instruments of power. Power in world politics remains the capacity to control the behavior of others, but the distribution of the means has become more diffuse.[17]

The United States retains its superpower military status, but it must share that position with the Soviet Union. Further, substantial military capability is now more widely dispersed throughout the world system, and significant nuclear proliferation seems an inevitability. Thus, the exercise of American superpower becomes a more difficult task. Similarly, the American economy remains the central economy of the international system, and the American dollar remains the key currency in international financial transactions. However, huge quantities of those dollars are now held outside the United States and are employed within a private international financial system largely beyond the reach of the United States government. The American economy is no longer the only large economy in the world and finds itself subject to resource and trade vulnerabilities and economic linkages undreamed of or regarded as ultimately unimportant during the cold-war years of the recent past.

In view of the central position of the presidency in the formulation of foreign and national security policy, these broad and deep changes in the character of international relations inevitably become the problems of the president. During the period of American hegemony, American policy and, hence, presidents were the beneficiaries of circumstances in which the American political economy was in large measure insulated from the immediate consequences of American activism abroad. With the exception of war, foreign and national security policy were largely "out there." However, with the emergence of economic units that could successfully challenge American economic primacy; the onset of resource dependencies that made the American economy vulnerable to supply disruptions; the penetration of the American domestic market by lower-priced but higher-quality goods in key market sectors such as automobiles, steel, or home appliances; and terrorism, foreign policy became more intimately tied to domestic affairs. Even seemingly positive developments, e.g., increased U.S. agricultural sales abroad, could have domestic consequences, e.g., rising food costs at home.

American society has become interpenetrated with other societies; the American political economy interdependent with the political economies of other nations. Thus Americans for the first time during the post-World War II period have begun to experience what most domestic societies have experienced throughout the period: the sometimes disruptive domestic effects of international relations. Predictably, as the concept of "security" assumes a more immediate and personal connotation (i.e., inflation, concern about one's job) the old problems of military security persist, and the demand for order and control increases. And in a foreign and national-security policymaking system that is presidentially centered, those demands are directed at the president.

Insofar as the president becomes the immediate object of these demands and expectations, the presidency's advantages of initiative vis-à-vis the other elements of the policymaking system are reinforced and his positional superiority enhanced. But if the president cannot relieve the pain and anxiety resulting from the international environment, the president's initial advantages will be transformed into political liabilities. For in the absence of the resolution or accommodation of the problem, the president — again, because of his central role in the policymaking process — becomes the target of frustrations. And given the electoral pressures discussed above, presidents often compound their problems by raising expectations concerning their capacity to control these developments.

In the contemporary international environment, the likelihood of rapid and definitive resolution of foreign and national-security problems is not especially high. Concerning military security, the traditional core of national-security policy, a return to the halcyon days of security defined as American superiority over its adversaries seems unlikely. In a world of superpower parity and proliferating military capability, the social and economic costs of reestablishing "superiority" are likely to be politically and economically forbidding. Thus presidents are likely to be faced with lengthy arms control negotiations and/or accelerating defense spending and sometimes frustrating and painful foreign entanglements, none of which can deliver superiority or peace.

The political economic dimensions of foreign and national security promise no more solace for presidents caught between domestic demands and expectations for order and protection and an international political economy no longer subject to American unilateral control. Trade negotiations; international financial management; the development of legal regimes for the oceans or the environment; or the control of the activities of multinational corporations are prolonged and technical, and the province of increasingly transnational bureaucracies drawn from governments, international organizations, and the private sector. In a political economy that has become interdependent, protracted multilateral negotiations in a context of difficult executive-legislative interactions, rather than dramatic presidential initiatives, may well become normal policymaking procedures. Presidents may be tempted to try the bold unilateral stroke in this domain — witness President Nixon's sundering of the dollar from gold and effective dissolution of the Bretton Woods system, the regnant international economic regime since the end of World War II. But it is not self-evident that such actions have had or will have positive long-term effects.

Of course, presidents may not seek such effects. There is considerable evidence that presidents seek to manipulate economic policy for their electoral benefit.[18] To the extent that international economic forces become more and more central to the lives of more Americans, we should not be surprised if policy decisions affecting them carry a significant political component. At the same time, we should not be surprised that, notwithstanding dramatic presidential initiatives or assertions of economic nationalism in response to domestic political pressure, the international political economic environment itself remains unchanged or even deteriorates.

In sum, the international environment of presidential foreign and national-security policymaking has become a more difficult one within which to operate. Perhaps this is because the United States now finds itself caught up in a more "normal" world politics. Obviously an international system characterized by two powers capable of destroying not only one another but the system itself, represents a departure from the past. On the other hand, the international system is no longer the simple bipolar world of the late 1940s and 1950s. In a world of cold war, the imperatives of American policy and a presidentially dominated policymaking system seemed obvious. However, in an environment in which the U.S. and the Soviet Union coexist in an uneasy state of strategic parity and other nuclear powers may be aborning, as well as the fact that the system is also characterized by political economic forces and powers that have reduced the former hegemony of the United States, the relationship of America to the world is different and in some respects more traditional. That is, the United States is no longer the world's only great power as it was in the years immediately after World War II. Thus, the United States finds itself confronted with circumstances similar to those faced by other great powers in the past in international environments comprised of many great powers. In such environments, great powers were not without the capacity to act in pursuit of their interests. Nor is the United States today. But if massive disruption of the international environment were to be avoided, the great powers had to act with an acute awareness of the interests of other great powers and sensitivity to the full context of the constraints at work. No less is demanded of the United States today.

And, of course, this means that no less is demanded of the presidential center of foreign and national-security policymaking. It may be, however, that because of the almost unparalleled position of the United States in the world of the 1950s and much of the 1960s, Americans and their presidents have come to expect too much of presidential power. For in a world of American primacy, but also of cold war, the constitutional, institutional, and political constraints on the presidency were readily made more manageable. But in a world less yielding to American power, Americans — and presidents — have become frustrated, demanding first more and then fewer limits on presidential power. The national-security-policymaking-presidency has what it always had: enormous capacity to take the initiative, to shape an image of reality, and propose means to presidentially defined ends. But American foreign and national-security policy must now be made in a more constrained domestic political arena and operate in a more textured international environment than in the past. Creative presidential leadership means therefore, as much as ever, facilitating the operation of the classical conception of diplomacy: the patient adjustment of differences.

Perhaps the most fundamental constraint on the president's ability to carry out this task, however, lies not in the institution or the individuals that occupy the presidency (though these are real), but in the domestic and international environments within which the president must operate. For unless Americans come to grips with the implications of the changed strategic and political economic position of the United States, they may well foster a domestic politics and, in response, a presidency incapable of the responsible exercise of great power in the late twentieth century.

## Notes

1. Cited by Clinton Rossiter in *The American Presidency*, 2d ed. (New York: Harcourt, Brace, Jovanovich, 1960), p. 30.
2. On the "imperial presidency" see Arthur M. Schlesinger, Jr., *The Imperial Presidency* (Houghton Mifflin, 1973) and for a view of the presidency as "imperiled" see Thomas E. Cronin, "An Imperiled Presidency?" *Society* (November-December 1978) and his *State of the Presidency*, 2d ed. (Boston: Little, Brown, 1980).
3. Cronin, *State of the Presidency*, p. 22.
4. For the statement of the elements of these positions see Hamilton's "Federalist Paper No. 24" in *The Federalist Papers* (New York: New American Library, 1961) and James Madison, *Notes of Debates in the Federal Convention of 1787* (New York: W. W. Norton, 1969), p. 214.
5. See, for example, the exchange between Senators J. William Fulbright and John Sherman Cooper during floor debate on the Tonkin Gulf Resolution, August 6, 1964. *Congressional Record*, Vol. 110, Part 14, 88th Cong., 2d Sess., August 6, 1964, pp. 18407–18410.
6. For an elaboration of these developments, see Thomas Franck and Edward Weisband, *Foreign Policy by Congress* (New York: Oxford University Press, 1979) and Cecil V. Crabb, Jr., and Pat M. Holt, *Invitation to Struggle: Congress, the President and Foreign Policy* (Washington, D.C.: Congressional Quarterly Press, 1980).
7. On the foreign and national security policymaking bureaucracy see Graham Allison, *Essence of Decision* (Boston: Little, Brown, 1971); Morton Halperin, *Bureaucratic Politics and Foreign Policy* (Washington, D.C.: The Brookings Institution, 1974); and Robert Art, "Bureaucratic Politics and American Foreign Policy: A Critique," *Policy Sciences*, Vol. 40 (1973).
8. For a more detailed review of the development of the NSC system see I. M. Destler, *Presidents, Bureaucrats, and Foreign Policy: The Politics of Organiza-*

*tional Form* (Princeton, N.J.: Princeton University Press, 1972) and Destler, "National Security Advice to U.S. Presidents: Some Lessons from Thirty Years," *World Politics,* Vol. 29 (January 1977), pp. 143–176.

9. On Kissinger's role, see his memoirs, *White House Years* (Boston: Little, Brown, 1979) and the more critical examinations of Kissinger's National Security Council in John P. Leacacos, "Kissinger's Apparat," and Destler, "Can One Man Do?" in *Foreign Policy,* No. 5 (Winter 1971–1972), pp. 3–40.

10. See, in particular, Senate Committee on Foreign Relations, Hearing, *The National Security Adviser: Role and Accountability* (Washington, D.C.: U.S. Government Printing Office, 1980), especially Philip Odeen's "National Security Policy Integration," pp. 106–128. See also Destler's, "National Security Management: What Presidents Have Wrought," *Political Science Quarterly* (Winter 1980–1981), pp. 573–588 and "A Job That Doesn't Work," *Foreign Policy,* Vol. 38 (Spring 1980), pp. 80–88.

11. Destler, "What Presidents Have Wrought," p. 587.

12. Alexis de Tocqueville, *Democracy in America,* Vol. 1 (New York: Vintage Books, 1945), p. 243.

13. "Farewell to 'President Knows Best,' " *Foreign Affairs — America and the World, 1978,* Vol. 57, No. 3 (1979), pp. 670–693.

14. Daniel Yankelovich and Larry Kagan, "Assertive America," *Foreign Affairs — America and the World, 1980,* Vol. 59, No. 3 (1981), pp. 696–713.

15. See Thomas Wolfe, *The SALT Experience* (Cambridge, Mass.: Ballinger Books, 1979) and Strobe Talbot, *Endgame* (New York: Harper & Row, 1979).

16. Henry A. Kissinger, *American Foreign Policy,* 3d ed. (New York: W. W. Norton, 1977), *passim.*

17. See Seyom Brown, *New Forces in World Politics* (Washington, D.C.: The Brookings Institution, 1974) and Robert O. Keohane and Joseph S. Nye, *Power and Interdependence* (Boston: Little, Brown, 1977); see also Joan E. Spero, *The Politics of International Economic Relations* (New York: St. Martin's Press, 1981).

18. Edward R. Tufte, *The Political Control of the Economy* (Princeton, N.J.: Princeton University Press, 1978).